Structural Equation Modeling and Natural Systems

This book presents an introduction to the methodology of structural equation modeling, illustrates its use, and goes on to argue that it has revolutionary implications for the study of natural systems. A major theme of this book is that we have, up to this point, attempted to study systems primarily using methods (such as the univariate model) that were designed only for considering individual processes. Understanding systems requires the capacity to examine simultaneous influences and responses. Structural equation modeling (SEM) has such capabilities. It also possesses many other traits that add strength to its utility as a means of making scientific progress. In light of the capabilities of SEM, it can be argued that much of ecological theory is currently locked in an immature state that impairs its relevance. It is further argued that the principles of SEM are capable of leading to the development and evaluation of multivariate theories of the sort vitally needed for the conservation of natural systems. Supplementary information can be found at the author's website, accessible via www.cambridge.org/9780521837422.

JAMES B. GRACE obtained his Bachelor of Science from Presbyterian College his Master of Science from Clemson University and his Ph.D. from Michigan State University. He served on the faculty at the University of Arkansas and later at Louisiana State University, where he reached the rank of Professor. He has, for the past several years, worked at the US Geological Survey's National Wetlands Research Center in Lafayette, Louisiana where he is a Senior Research Ecologist. He holds an Adjunct Professorship at the University of Louisiana.

Structural Equation Modeling and Natural Systems

JAMES B. GRACE

CAMBRIDGE
UNIVERSITY PRESS

CAMBRIDGE UNIVERSITY PRESS
Cambridge, New York, Melbourne, Madrid, Cape Town, Singapore, São Paulo

Cambridge University Press
The Edinburgh Building, Cambridge CB2 2RU, UK

Published in the United States of America by Cambridge University Press, New York

www.cambridge.org
Information on this title: www.cambridge.org/9780521837421

First published 2006

Printed in the United Kingdom at the University Press, Cambridge

A catalog record for this publication is available from the British Library

ISBN-13   978-0-521-83742-2 hardback
ISBN-10   0-521-83742-1 hardback

ISBN-13   978-0-521-54653-9 paperback
ISBN-10   0-521-54653-2 paperback

To my wife Peggy,
for her joyous spirit, wisdom, and laughter.

To my mother and my sister, Diane,
for a lifetime of love and support.

and

To Robert Wetzel, my Major Professor,
for his example of dedication to the pursuit of knowledge.

Contents

PART V   THE IMPLICATIONS OF STRUCTURAL EQUATION MODELING FOR THE STUDY OF NATURAL SYSTEMS

Preface

This book is about an approach to scientific research that seeks to look at the system instead of the individual processes. In this book I share with the reader my perspective on the study of complex relationships. The methodological framework I use in this enterprise is structural equation modeling. For many readers, this will be new and unfamiliar. Some of the new ideas relate to statistical methodology and some relate to research philosophy. For others already familiar with the topic, they will find contained in this volume some new examples and even some new approaches they might find useful. In my own personal experience, the approaches and methods described in this book have been very valuable to me as a scientist. It is my assessment that they have allowed me to develop deeper insights into the relationships between ecological pattern and process. Most importantly, they have given me a framework for studying ecological systems that helps me to avoid getting lost in the detail, without requiring me to ignore the very real complexities. It is my opinion, after some years of careful consideration, that potentially they represent the means to a revolutionary change in scientific inquiry; one that allows us to ask questions of interacting systems that we have not been able to ask before. These methods provide many new opportunities for science, I believe, and it is my hope that others will see their value as well.

It is important for the reader to keep in mind throughout this book the distinction between statistical procedures and the scientific enterprise. The application of structural equation modeling (SEM) to research questions embodies both elements, but the priorities of one do not necessarily match with those of the other. My approach to this book is from the perspective of a researcher, not a statistician. My treatment is not designed to satisfy the requirements of statisticians nor those interested in the mathematics. Rather, I strive to keep the focus on developing models that match the questions being addressed. Many treatments of statistical methods are prescriptive and based on protocols that have been worked out on the basis of statistical requirements. While I could simply present SEM protocols for use by the natural scientist, I am of the opinion that protocols are commonly an impediment to the best use of statistical methods for research purposes (see also Abelson 1995). For this reason, my emphasis is on fundamental issues that provide the reader with the material to make their own decisions about how to apply statistical modeling to their particular research problems.

The general arena of studying complex relationships and the specifics of SEM is one where subject matter and statistical analysis intertwine to a greater degree than is customary for researchers or statisticians. What is distinctively different about the study of complex, multivariate relationships compared with univariate hypothesis testing is the degree to which the analyst has to know both the subtleties of the methods and the particulars of the system being studied. The goal of this book is to show why it can be worth the effort to develop and evaluate multivariate models, not just for statistical reasons, but because of the added scientific insights that can be gained. Those who apply these methods to their own data may find, as I have, that it is quite enjoyable. Hopefully the reasons for excitement will be evident as the reader explores the chapters ahead.

Acknowledgments

I have a great many people to thank for helping me along the way in this major venture. I thank Alan Crowden, Dominic Lewis, Emma Pearce, and Graham Bliss of Cambridge University Press for their support with this project. If this book is at all readable, it is because of the help of a great many individuals who provided numerous comments. I especially thank Glenn Guntenspergen, who not only read the whole volume in both first and last drafts, but who provided sage advice from beginning to end. To him, I owe the greatest debt of gratitude. I also wish to express special thanks to Sam Scheiner for many insightful suggestions on both content and presentation, as well as for advising me on the best way to present an illustration of SEM practice in the Appendix. I am appreciative of the USGS National Wetlands Research Center for their history of supporting the application of SEM to natural systems. Several examples in this book came from their studies.

Two of my comrades in the quest to introduce SEM to the natural sciences, Bill Shipley and Bruce Pugesek, both provided very helpful comments. It was Bill who convinced me that the first draft of this work was far too condensed to be useful to the student. The readers owe him a great debt of gratitude for the final structure of this book, which attempts to lead one gradually through the fundamentals of SEM in the beginning, in order to establish a base from which to jump into more advanced issues later. Bruce is especially to be thanked for introducing me to SEM and for working patiently with me through the initial learning process.

I am also thankful for the training and advice I received from some of the legendary figures in the development of structural equation modeling. My biggest debt of gratitude is to Ken Bollen, who saved me from several fundamental errors in the early development of many of my ideas. Ken possesses the rare combination of being brilliant, patient, and kind, which has been enormously helpful to me as I have struggled to make the statistical methodology fulfill my research ambitions. I am also grateful to Karl Jöreskog and Dag Sörbom for their week-long workshop on SEM early in my learning and for answering my many pesky questions about all those complications about which instructors hope to avoid being asked. Bengt and Linda Muthén likewise shared lifetimes of experience with me in another week-long SEM workshop, again with tolerance for my questions about fringe methods and thorny problems. Others who helped me greatly through my involvement in their training classes include Bill Black (LSU), Adrian Tomer (Shippensburg University), Alex von Eye (Michigan State University), and most recently David Draper (University of California – Santa Cruz).

There are many other people who provided helpful comments on all or part of the book manuscript, including Jon Keeley, Diane Larson, Bruce McCune, Randy Mitchell, Craig Loehle, Dan Laughlin, Brett Gilbert, Kris Metzger, Gary Ervin, Evan Weiher, Tim Wootton, Janene Lichtenberg, Michael Johnson, Laura Gough, Wylie Barrow, Valerie Kelly, Chris Clark, Elsa Cleland, and Ed Rigdon. I apologize to any who I have left off the list, the process has gone on long enough to make it hard to keep track. To all who helped, Thank you!

Last and certainly not least are the people who have provided the encouragement and support in all those more personal ways that are essential to a great and productive life. My deepest gratitude to my loving wife Peggy, who has enhanced my quality of life in every way and who led me into a better life. To my Mother and my Sister Diane, I am unspeakably grateful for all the years of love and support. To Jeremy, Kris, Zach, Abi, Erica, Madison, Sophie, and Luke, your acceptance and love means more to me than you know. To Bob Wetzel, I am grateful for his encouragement over all these many years.

PART I

A beginning

1
Introduction

The purpose and organization of this book

Structural equation modeling (SEM) represents both a different way of analyzing data, and a different way of doing science. A major theme of this book
is that one of the factors that has limited the advance of ecological science
has been the absence of methods for developing and evaluating multivariate
theories. Understanding systems requires the capacity to examine simultaneous influences and responses. Conventional univariate analyses are typically
limited to the examination of a single or at most a few processes at a time.
Further, as will be illustrated in this book, characterizing interacting systems
using univariate methods is commonly misleading and often inadequate. As I
will argue in the final section of the book, conventional univariate hypothesis
testing propagates a reliance on "theories of pieces" where one or two interacting processes are presumed to explain major characteristics of natural systems.
Single-factor hypotheses seldom provide an adequate representation of system
behavior. Worse still, such hypotheses are unable to be placed into a broader
context or to evolve into more complex theories, regardless of the empirical
evidence. Many of the simplistic theories that have occupied ecologists for so
long seem irrelevant when we are faced with the task of predicting the responses
of natural systems to environmental change. I believe ecologists have remained
focused on univariate questions because we have lacked the scientific tools to
ask and answer more complex questions.

Structural equation modeling offers a means of developing and evaluating
ideas about complex (multivariate) relationships. It is this property that makes
SEM of interest to the practitioner of science. As we shall see in this book,
SEM has both tremendous flexibility and significant requirements for proper
use. There are also some serious issues relating to how best to use SEM for
the study of natural systems. Its mode of application in other fields, such as the

social sciences where it has gained a widespread application, may or may not suit our needs. Further, ways of connecting structural equation models with the broader scientific process are needed if we are to gain the maximum impact from our models and analyses. All these issues need to be addressed if SEM is to be applied properly and is to have utility for advancing the study of natural systems.

Before I can discuss fully the potential contributions of SEM to the study of natural systems, we must first have a fairly clear understanding of the principles and practice of SEM. What is its history? What are the underlying statistical principles? How are results from SEM applications to be interpreted? What are the choices to be made and steps to be performed? After such questions have been addressed and the nature of SEM is clear, I will consider its broader significance for the study of natural systems.

To start us on common ground, I begin this chapter with a brief discussion of material that should be familiar to the majority of readers, classic univariate null hypothesis testing. This material will provide a point of comparison for explaining SEM. In this chapter, I will present only a brief and simplistic characterization of SEM, primarily from an historic perspective, while in Chapter 2, I will present an example from an application of SEM to give the reader a tangible illustration.

In Chapter 3, I begin to present some of the fundamental principles of structural equation models, emphasizing their reliance on the fundamental principles of regression. This coverage of basic topics continues through Chapters 4 (latent variables) and 5 (estimation and model evaluation). In Chapter 6, I spend some time presenting a more advanced topic, composite variables, for the dual purposes of illustrating this important capability and also to help clarify the role of latent variables. Chapter 7 provides a very superficial overview of some of the more advanced capabilities of SEM.

Chapters 8 to 11 will emphasize examples of ecological applications to give the reader more of a sense of how the principles can be applied to natural systems. Throughout this section of material, I will contrast the kinds of results obtained from SEM with those obtained from the conventional scientific methods that have guided (and limited) the natural sciences up to this point. Experience suggests that such comparisons are often the most effective means of conveying the potential that SEM has to transform the study of natural systems. This section of chapters will include an illustration of the sustained application of SEM to an ecological problem, the understanding of patterns of plant diversity (in Chapter 10). In Chapter 11, I provide a summary of some cautions as well as a set of recommendations relating to the application of SEM so as to provide all of this practical advice in one place.

In the final section of the book (Chapters 12 and 13), it will be my purpose to give an overall view of the implications of applying SEM to the natural sciences. I will discuss from a philosophical point of view some of the things that I believe have limited the advance of ecological science, and how SEM can lead to a greater maturation of our theories and investigations. Included in this last section will be a discussion of how to integrate SEM into the broader scientific enterprise. Finally, an Appendix provides example applications that illustrate some of the mechanics and logic associated with SEM. The reader will be directed to these examples at appropriate places throughout the book.

An historic point of reference – univariate null hypothesis testing

In the latter half of the nineteenth century, the quantitative sciences began to shift from a deterministic viewpoint to one that recognized the need to address explicitly the concept of probability and error. The story is told by Salsburg (2001) that as scientists began to make more and more precise measurements, they discovered that deviations between calculations and observations became more noticeable, rather than less so. Gradually, the view of a "clockwork" universe in which outcomes are presumed to be deterministic has been replaced by one based on statistics and probabilities. As a result, for most sciences, the process of scientific inquiry has evolved to the point that explicit consideration must be given to issues of error and uncertainty.

Throughout the twentieth century, the acceptance and elaboration of statistical procedures steadily increased to the point that nowadays most scientists are taught basic and even advanced statistical methods as part of their core training. For many areas of inquiry, the very essence of the scientific method has come to require statistical design and analysis. Conclusions are only deemed acceptable if based on accepted statistical conventions (though what is deemed acceptable can vary among disciplines – and among individuals).

In the natural sciences, the fundamental statistical paradigm that is usually taught can be represented by the *generalized univariate statistical formula*

$$y_1 = \alpha_1 + \Gamma X + \zeta_1 \tag{1.1}$$

Here, y_1 refers to an observed set of responses, α_1 represents an intercept for the population, X refers to some set of independent variables, Γ represents some corresponding vector of coefficients (γs) that empirically link y_1 to the elements in X (a vector of x variables), and ζ_1 represents random errors associated with the responses. Individual values of x and their associated γ_{1i} values (γ_{1i} is the effect of x_i on y_1) can represent a suite of factors, such as experimental treatments and their interactions, restrictions on randomization due to the experimental or sampling design (e.g., blocking effects), and uncontrolled covariates that influence responses.

Of course, the scientific method does not depend solely on the estimation of parameters, such as those implied by the above equation. It also involves a variety of procedures that are used to draw inferences about the parameter estimates. Associated with the univariate model there has long been a set of conventions and principles for *null hypothesis testing* that seek to determine whether parameter values are nonzero. These ideas and procedures can in large part be traced back to a combination of procedures and ideas developed by Ronald Fisher, Jerzy Neyman, and Egon Pearson (see Salsburg 2001 for an interesting historical account). The basic approach that is taught typically includes (1) the establishment of a null hypothesis (usually of no difference between groups) which is then compared to an alternative hypothesis, (2) the selection of a significance level (usually 0.05 or 0.01), (3) data collection involving some degree of random sampling, (4) calculation of estimates of means/intercepts and variances (as well as other statistical properties of the populations), and (5) determination of comparative test results and associated probability values. The values of the test statistics obtained are usually represented to be indicative of the probability that observed differences between groups may be due to chance rather than some systematic difference between populations (this is actually an oversimplification of the true interpretation of p-values). In the conventional null hypothesis testing procedure, priority is given to the null hypothesis, which is generally accepted unless there is convincing evidence to the contrary.

Many are aware of long-standing controversies over various aspects of conventional null hypothesis testing. Ronald Fisher, the founding father of much of the early development of modern statistics, as well as the originator of parametric p-values, was himself opposed to the use of fixed cutoffs for standardized hypothesis testing. In spite of this, the codified usage of null hypothesis testing based on predetermined and fixed p-values became entrenched in standardized statistical protocols (this is sometimes referred to as the Neyman–Pearson protocol). There has been a steady drumbeat of complaint about overreliance on null hypothesis tests ever since their introduction (e.g., see Taper and Lele 2004). In most areas of science, this seems to have done little to prevent the establishment of null hypothesis testing as the dominant framework. Perhaps one of the more conspicuous exceptions to this has been in the field of SEM, where priority has been placed on a-priori theory-based models for the past 35 years. The character of this model-based approach will become more apparent as we work through the material in this book. At this point, I wish only to make the point that SEM practitioners long ago rejected the logical priority of null hypotheses, though the use of p-values continues to be one of the tools used in model evaluation.

It is perhaps useful to note that null hypothesis testing has recently been under attack from several quarters. Biologists have begun to argue more vigorously for a departure from reliance on null hypothesis testing (Anderson *et al.* 2000). The lack of utility of null hypothesis testing has led to recommendations for the use of model selection procedures as an alternative basis for developing inferences. A tenacious effort to expose ecologists to this approach (e.g., Burnham and Anderson 2002) has begun to bring familiarity with these issues to many. At present, these efforts remain focused on univariate models and have not yet tapped into the substantial experiential base of SEM practitioners.

Bayesian methods for estimating parameters and probabilities (Congdon 2001, Gelman *et al.* 2004) also suggest alternatives to null hypothesis testing. While there are a number of different variants of the Bayesian procedure, the basic concept is that from a personal standpoint, the concept of probability is one that is based on the knowledge available to the investigator. In this framework, empirical evidence is used to update prior probabilities so as to generate posterior probability estimates. This form of probability assessment is preferred by many because it corresponds more directly to the intuitive meaning of probability as a measure of confidence in a result. As will be discussed in the final chapter, Bayesian approaches are now being considered for use in estimation and the evaluation of structural equation models.

What are structural equations?

Let us begin at the beginning. Directly stated, a single univariate equation such as

$$y_1 = \alpha_1 + \gamma_{11}\chi_1 + \zeta_1 \qquad (1.2)$$

representing the effect of a single x on y, can be said to be *structural* if there exists sufficient evidence from all available sources to support the interpretation that x_1 has a causal effect on y_1. If information does exist to support a cause and effect interpretation, the parameter γ_{11} provides an estimate of that effect.

There are certain points that should be made about the seemingly straightforward definition above. One is that the sort of information required to support a causal interpretation for a structural equation is basically the same as that required for a simple regression or an analysis of variance. Thus, we can see that the family of univariate equations represented by Eq. (1.1) can be classified as structural equations.

A difficulty for some may arise from the fact that our definition of *structural* includes the word *causal*. The average person who is neither a scientist nor a philosopher may be rather surprised to find that scientists and philosophers have historically had some difficulty with the concept of causation. Because of the unease some have with discussing causality, the relationships embodied in structural equations are sometimes referred to as dependencies instead of causes (e.g., "the values of *y* depend on the values of *x*"). Thus, an alternative definition that is sometimes seen for structural equations is that they represent statistical dependencies (or statistical associations) that are subject to causal interpretation. What is ultimately most important to realize is that, while the results of structural equation analyses are meant to be reflective of causal dependencies, it is not the statistical results per se that demonstrate causation. Rather, the case for making a causal interpretation depends primarily on prior experience and substantive knowledge.

There has existed over the years an ongoing discussion on the nature of causality and its relationship to structural equations. Perhaps one of the reasons structural equation modeling has been slow to be adopted by biologists has been the priority placed by Fisher on the adage that "correlation does not imply causation". His emphasis was on manipulative experiments that sought to isolate causes and this approach remains a strong emphasis in biological research. One can see this ongoing debate as a recurring process in which from time to time some feel it wise to caution against overzealous inference of causes. These cautionary periods are typically followed by a general defense of the reasonableness of causal thinking. Fisher's emphasis was on the development of rigorous experimental protocols designed to isolate individual causes. The emphasis of those who developed structural equation modeling has not been on isolating causes, but instead, on studying simultaneous influences. Both of these scientific goals have merit and, we can think of them as representing the study of individual processes versus the study of system responses.

Some clearly articulated insights into the nature of causality and the relationship to structural equations can be found in Wright (1921) and Bollen (1989), and some of these are described below. Recently, Pearl (2000, *Causality*) has addressed the issue of causation and structural equations at the level of fundamental logic. A distillation of some of these ideas as they relate to biology can be found in Shipley (2000).

There are a number of arguments that have been made about the tendency for some scientists and philosophers to steer away from using causal language. As Pearl (2000) notes, one reason that some mathematicians have steered away from discussing causation may be the fact that the language of mathematical equations relies most commonly on the symbol "=" to describe the relationships between *y* and *x*. As a mathematical operator, the "=" symbol simply represents equality, not dependence; implying that if $A = B$ then $B = A$. It is not clear to me, that the directional neutrality of the equals sign necessarily causes confusion, because the designation of y variables as dependent and x variables as independent does enable causal directionality to be explicitly specified. Thus, the equation $y = x$ does not possess the criterion of reversibility. Nonetheless, for those who find the language of equations to be insufficiently precise with regard to causality, graphical methods are often preferred as an alternative mathematical language (as we will see below).

According to Pearl, another factor contributing to confusion about the concept of causation is that the word "cause" is not included in the language of probability theory, which is the official mathematical language of statistics. On page 138 he states, "... statisticians, the arbiters of respectability, abhor assumptions that are not directly testable [via statistical assessment]."

In this same vein, I suspect that there is a degree to which scientists somehow associate the invocation of causation with a suggestion of "proof". As Popper (1959) so persuasively stated, it is very difficult to prove anything to be true. Rather, science usually proceeds by falsifying hypotheses and accepting only those that remain.

Alternatively, for some, a statement of causal interpretation may imply "ultimate" causation. This is a reflection of mechanistic thinking that generally matches poorly with inference based on statistical relationships. Rather, such thinking reflects the Aristotelean tradition of determinism, which fails to adequately reflect probabilistic causation and the degree of uncertainty that is associated with measurement.

As we shall see, structural equation modeling does not start with a null hypothesis that is given priority. Rather, structural equation models are built upon the complete body of available knowledge. Models are only rejected if the observed data do not match expectations derived from the model. This "model-oriented" philosophy facilitates the invocation of causal interpretation because it automatically incorporates the a-priori knowledge available to the scientist. This forms the basis for cause and effect interpretations. Stated in a different way, if a researcher intends to draw interpretations about x having an effect on y using structural equations, they should be prepared to defend that supposition with something other than their statistical results.

Criteria for supporting an assumption of causal relationships in structural equations

A causal interpretation of a structural equation, such as $y_1 = \alpha_1 + \gamma_{11}x_1 + \zeta_1$ (Eq. 1.2) can be supported if it can be assumed that a sufficient manipulation of x would result in a subsequent change in the values of y, independent of influences from any other factors (Pearl 2000). This criterion might be referred to as the "intervention outcome assumption". One obvious set of conditions that would support such an assumption would be if previous manipulations had shown such a result. Thus, the assumption that plant growth would be affected by a manipulation of water supply can, under many circumstances, be supported by prior experience. How many times do we have to show through manipulations that plant growth can respond to watering before this effect comes to be expected? This is *not* to say that a response in plant growth would be expected for all possible additions of water supply. Rather, the assumption being made is that if (1) there is an observed correlation between water supply and plant growth, (2) the supply of additional water occurs prior to the growth response, (3) other independent influences on growth are not simultaneously changing, and (4) an interpretation of plant growth responding to water supply is consistent with known mechanisms, then a causal interpretation of the relationship is reasonable. Of course, when structural equations are used in conjunction with manipulative experiments, the criteria for establishing causality are automatically established if the manipulations are unambiguous.

We must recognize that absolute certainty (or even absolute confidence) is not a requirement for reporting scientific results. At times we may have a stronger or weaker case in support of a causal interpretation. A great deal will have to do with prior experience with the system under investigation. I will have more to say about this subject later as it pertains specifically to structural equation modeling. My position on this is basically consistent with Fisher's ideas about hypothesis testing, we should not expect to rely on single studies to draw general conclusions. Rather, *the process of establishing a confident interpretation comes from the process of investigation.*

For now, it must suffice for us to recognize that any claim for a causal interpretation will, as always, have to be defended. At the risk of being repetitive, the requirements for supporting causal interpretations are not fundamentally different from the ones natural scientists already use. A useful discussion of criteria that can be used to evaluate the plausibility of claims based on statistical results can be found in Abelson (1995).

What is structural equation modeling?

Structural equation modeling can be defined in its most basic sense as *the use of two or more structural equations to model multivariate relationships.* Multivariate relationships, as the phrase is used here, refers to those that involve

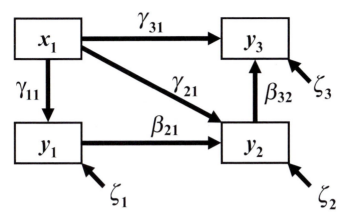

Figure 1.1. Graphical representation of a structural equation model (Eqs. (1.2)–(1.4) involving one independent (x_1) variable and three dependent (y) variables.

simultaneous influences and responses. Expressed as a series of equations, an example of a structural equation model might be

$$y_1 = \alpha_1 + \gamma_{11}x_1 + \zeta_1 \tag{1.2}$$

$$y_2 = \alpha_2 + \beta_{21}y_1 + \gamma_{21}x_1 + \zeta_2 \tag{1.3}$$

$$y_3 = \alpha_3 + \beta_{32}y_2 + \gamma_{31}x_1 + \zeta_3 \tag{1.4}$$

Using graphical representation (and omitting the intercepts), Figure 1.1 illustrates this model. A quick comparison of the equational and graphical forms of the model (Eqs. (1.2)–(1.4) versus Figure 1.1) illustrates the appeal of the graphical representation, which has been in use since structural equation modeling (in the form of path analysis) was first introduced. In this illustration, boxes represent observed variables, arrows between boxes represent the directional relationships represented by equality signs in the equations, gammas (γ) represent effects of x variables on y variables while betas (β) represent effects of ys on other ys, and the zetas (ζ) represent error terms for response variables.

The idea of combining a series of equations into a multivariate model, which should be credited to Wright (1921), has proven to be a major step forward in the advancement of the scientific method. With a series of structural equations, we can now specify models representative of systems and address many questions that cannot be answered using univariate models. In Chapter 3, we will describe the anatomy of structural equation models and illustrate in more detail the various ways structural equations can be combined and how they are interpreted. In later chapters we will include additional elements, such as unobserved (latent) and composite variables. We will also see that there are a large number of problems that can be tackled using SEM, including nonlinear modeling, reciprocal influences, and many more.

Of prime importance is that structural equation models allow us to address scientific questions about systems that cannot be addressed using univariate approaches. As we shall see, these multivariate questions are often precisely the ones of greatest importance to the scientist. An introduction to SEM brings into focus the simple fact that *up to this point, we have been studying systems primarily using a methodology (specifically the univariate model) that is not designed for examining system responses.* Rather, the univariate model, which has come to represent the scientific method over the past 50+ years, is only designed for the study of individual processes or net effects, not interacting systems. To make a crude analogy, if the development of the univariate model is akin to the development of the wheel, the advance represented by combining structural equations into complex models is akin to the attachment of four wheels to a frame to make a cart. The change is not just one of degree, it is a change of a revolutionary sort.

The history of SEM

The simple yet fundamental definitions given above for structural equations and structural equation modeling belie the complex variety of terms and emphases that exist in the literature, and the historical development of the subject. If you examine the body of papers and books relating to this subject, you will find the term SEM used in several different ways. You will also find a variety of other terms that are sometimes substituted for SEM or that seem to refer to something akin to SEM. The most general definition of structural equation modeling, which is the one espoused in this book, is "modeling hypotheses with structural equations". This definition includes both the historic predecessors of modern SEM as well as recent advances that have developed.

We can trace the modern formulation of SEM back to its roots in the analysis of path relations by Wright (1918, 1920, 1921). In these early papers, Wright clearly established a broad intent for understanding multiple causes and multiple responses, presenting both criteria for causal inference and guidelines for model building and interpretation. Wright (1932, 1934, 1960, 1968, 1984), along with others, continued to develop and refine his method of path coefficients over a substantial number of years. This method came to be known as *path analysis*. It is clear in these publications that a new generation of questions was being addressed through the flexible application of path coefficients, including both the decomposition of relationships and the estimation of underlying influences.

Reviews of the development of SEM (Hägglund 2001, Tomer 2003) emphasize that modern structural equation modeling has been influenced by a number of traditions, particularly biometrics, econometrics, psychometrics, and sociometrics (these are essentially the quantitative subdisciplines in biology, economics, psychology, and sociology). Modern SEM can primarily be attributed to the remarkable synthesis of path analysis and factor analysis accomplished by Karl Jöreskog beginning in the early 1970s (Jöreskog 1973). A close association developed initially between SEM and the particular formulation he introduced, which is the *LISREL model*. More will be said about this in a later chapter, but for now, I simply wish to introduce some of the variety of terms often associated with SEM. To add one more level of complication, LISREL refers to both the underlying notational model developed by Jöreskog and others, and to the computer software he developed (the *LISREL program*).

Various other terms can be found in the SEM literature; the meaning and importance of these will become clear later in the book. To a large degree, the different terms tend to coincide with either methodological distinctions, emphases of importance, or methodological advances. For example, the meaning of the term "path analysis" has changed from its original meaning. The techniques originally used by Wright are sometimes called *Wrightian path analysis*. This is done to distinguish the fact that *modern path analysis* is now based on the LISREL model and incorporates maximum likelihood methods and tests of overall model fit. As will become clear later, LISREL-based SEM is sometimes subdivided into path analysis (modern type), factor analysis, and combined factor–path models, which are referred to in some books as structural equation models (I suppose this usage could be referred to as "SEM *sensu stricto*").

An illustration of the use of names that represent emphases of importance is the term *causal modeling*. This term was popular when the contribution of SEM to understanding causal relations was being emphasized. Yet another term that appeared early on and that I will refer to in this book is *covariance methods* (sometimes *covariance structure analysis*). The LISREL model and program are distinctive because of the fact that they do not deal with the responses of individuals (at least they did not traditionally). Rather, they are based on the properties and analyses of covariance (or correlation) matrices. This characteristic is closely associated with LISREL and, for many, with SEM in general. As will be discussed later, there are other ways of analyzing structural equations rather than those that rely on covariances, and the synonymy between SEM and covariance analysis is becoming a thing of the past.

Another term strongly associated with modern SEM is *latent variable modeling*. The flexibility of using structural equations to represent relationships creates the ability to estimate the influences of unmeasured, underlying causes or *latent variables*. The concept of the latent variable has been traced back to Plato, although its meaning in a statistical context seems to begin with Sir Francis Galton in the late 1800s. The classic example of a latent property is the concept of human IQ (the intelligence quotient). It is presumed that the latent property of general intelligence (G) exists, but there is no direct way of observing it. Rather, it can only be evaluated indirectly by estimating its effects. Presenting a simplistic view of this complex topic, if a large number of individuals are given a battery of ability tests, those individuals who performed well across the whole range of tasks would be estimated to have a high score for G, while those who performed poorly would be estimated to have a low score for G. In addition to the presence of a general intelligence factor, it can be presumed that there may be more specific intelligence factors, such as mathematical and verbal ability, and analytical reasoning. Thus, one's capacity for answering some subsets of questions on a test might be influenced by several different abilities simultaneously. Problems of the same sort that involve the estimation of general and specific genetic factors in plants and animals were also addressed by Wright using his method of path coefficients.

The ability to construct models of latent factors and to estimate their value from a variety of correlated measures (so-called *factor analysis*) was first developed by Charles Spearman. More about the history of the development of factor analysis and its incorporation into SEM can be found in Hägglund (2001). Factor analyses can either be exploratory, in that theory is not used to guide the analysis, or confirmatory, where theory is used to structure the model. *Confirmatory factor analysis* has been an integral component of SEM since the LISREL synthesis, which combined path analysis and factor analysis into a single procedure.

Of further relevance to this issue of terminology is the fact that there are new methods related to the LISREL model, as well as to the general enterprise of SEM, that are of a different sort. For example, there has emerged a suite of techniques that analyze data at different levels (e.g., within populations and between populations). These models are variously called *multi-level* or *hierarchical models* and are natural evolutionary developments of SEM. They fit clearly within the broad definition of SEM used in this book. However, they are not all based on the covariance procedures of the LISREL model (nevertheless, they are now being incorporated into the LISREL software program).

It is hoped that this presentation of various terms and their historical associations will not distract the reader from the fundamental and unified importance of structural equation modeling. Regardless of exactly how structural equation models are analyzed and what capabilities are emphasized, the act of using

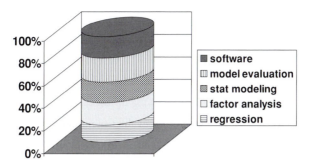

Figure 1.2. Representation of the elements of modern SEM. Stat modeling refers to statistical modeling.

combinations of equations to specify interconnected causal relationships creates a capacity for studying hypotheses about systems. As we will examine in the next section, modern SEM has come to embody many capabilities through its evolution. This evolution is continuing as more refined and varied capabilities are added to the software packages that implement solutions to structural equation models.

The elements of modern structural equation modeling

Figure 1.2 provides us with another way of looking at the elements of modern SEM. This figure is intended to illustrate the various topics that need to be considered to understand and apply SEM. As indicated in this figure, SEM can be seen as a combination of regression, factor analysis, statistical modeling, model evaluation/selection, and software. To clarify, by statistical modeling I mean the construction of models so as to match the particulars of a situation, or to allow a particular type of contrast to be evaluated.

Wright's original formulation of path analysis was an elaboration of regression, with elements of statistical modeling used to distinguish direct and indirect effects. In Chapter 3, we will examine some of the regression aspects of SEM in detail, as an understanding of the role of regression statistics in SEM is vital for understanding results and interpretations. Factor analysis, another major element of the modern method, deals with the incorporation of latent or unobserved variables in a model and is itself an extension of regression techniques, although with particular considerations of its own (to be covered in Chapter 4).

The synthesis created by the formulation of the LISREL model (Jöreskog 1973) brought together all the elements shown in Figure 1.3. One of the pivotal things associated with the LISREL synthesis is the utilization of maximum

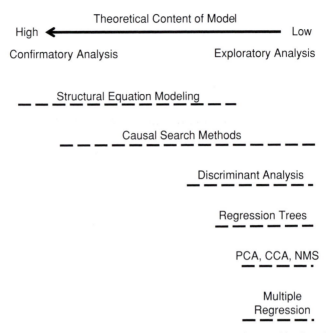

Figure 1.3. Classification of some methods used to analyze multivariate data. PCA refers to principal components analysis, CCA to canonical correspondence analysis, and NMS to nonmetric multidimensional scaling. Multiple regression, while not a true multivariate method (i.e., it is based on univariate model with single response variable), is included because it is often used to analyze data that are multivariate.

likelihood methods for estimation. It was this advance that permitted (1) a generalized solution procedure for factor and path models, (2) a proper approach to nonrecursive models, and (3) an assessment of discrepancies between observed and expected which permits hypothesis evaluation at the level of the overall model. Simultaneous to the development of the LISREL model, Jöreskog developed computer software (largely because of the iterative requirements of maximum likelihood methods), and since that time, SEM has come to be defined in part by the capabilities of the software packages used to implement analyses.

Over the years, numerous capabilities have been added to SEM, both through theoretical advances and through additions to the various software packages that have been developed. Such things as multigroup analyses, the inclusion of means modeling, numerous indices of model fit, modification indices, capabilities for handling categorical variables, and most recently, procedures for hierarchical models have been added. All of these have expanded the elements that make up SEM.

At present, a number of new developments are taking place which have the potential to strongly influence the future growth and capabilities of SEM. Novel approaches to the analysis of network relationships are emerging from fields as diverse as robotics and philosophy. Their goals range from pattern recognition to data mining, from computer learning to decision support. Some of these developments are fairly unrelated to the enterprise of structural equation modeling because of their descriptive nature. However, others have substantial relevance for the estimation and evaluation of structural equation models and are already starting to be incorporated into the SEM literature. Collectively, these new methods, along with SEM itself, fall under the umbrella concept of graphical models (Pearl 2000, Borgelt and Kruse 2002). Of particular importance are those graphical models that incorporate Bayesian methods, such as Bayesian networks (e.g., Neapolitan 2004), which permit what is now being called Bayesian structural equation modeling (Scheines *et al.* 1999, Congdon 2003).

Comparing SEM to other multivariate methods

It is legitimate to question how SEM differs from other multivariate methods that are more familiar to ecologists, such as principal components analysis, cluster analysis, discriminant analysis, canonical correlation, canonical correspondence analysis, and MANOVA (descriptions of these and other multivariate methods used for ecological analysis can be found in McCune and Grace 2002). Fornell (1982) has referred to these methods as "first generation" multivariate methods, in contrast to the "second generation" methodology of SEM. One essential distinction between so-called first and second generation methods is that the first are largely descriptive and more appropriate for exploratory studies or the development of predictive equations, while the second are capable of confirmatory tests and are thus more suitable for evaluation of multivariate hypotheses. A second key difference is that conventional multivariate methods seek to estimate generic fixed models (e.g., canonical correlation), and lack the flexibility required to represent the model that best matches a particular situation. Thirdly, SEM seeks to examine networks of causal relationships, while first generation multivariate methods are focused on net effects. Below, I elaborate on the first two of these points.

Confirmatory versus exploratory analyses

First and second generation multivariate methods differ substantially in their theoretical content. While methods used typically for exploratory analyses do sometimes provide tests for the significance of coefficients, their capacity to represent complex causal relationships is often very limited; stated in another way, their capability for specification of theoretical content is quite limited. In contrast, methods such as SEM are capable of possessing a great deal of theoretical content, although they can be used to fit and test simple models as well. As we shall see in subsequent chapters, SEM is a very generalized methodology and many familiar multivariate and univariate procedures can be seen as special cases of a structural equation model.

Aside from their potential for incorporating a large amount of theoretical content, first and second generation multivariate methods also differ in the degree to which they provide feedback from data. This feedback comes in a variety of forms, ranging from model failure to the detection of deviations between model and data. Essentially, methods that subject models to "failure tests" allow for tests of model structure, while those that only estimate parameters do not allow tests of the model, only tests of individual coefficients.

Figure 1.3 provides a classification of some common multivariate methods in terms of their capacity for including theoretical content. Those methods capable of containing high theoretical content are considered to be the most rigorous for evaluation of complex a-priori hypotheses. Note that some methods have a broad range of uses. For the purposes of this discussion, low theory methods are those that initially possess a small theoretical content and then allow a statistical routine to estimate parameter values that satisfy a set of criteria. In contrast, highly theoretical models specify relationships based on a detailed theoretical model and seek to determine if the data collected are consistent with the expectations of the model. Such analyses also provide estimates of the relative strengths of relationships in the model in a way that is more suitable for substantive interpretation; this is a major motivation of SEM that will be discussed in Chapter 3.

Since methods differ in their characteristics (Table 1.1), they also differ in the type of application to which they are best suited. For example, SEM techniques can be applied to problems that range from strictly confirmatory to highly exploratory. Other methods, such as principal components analysis (PCA), do not have procedures for directly evaluating a-priori ideas about the precise nature of underlying factors that explain a set of correlations. At present, many of the techniques shown in Figure 1.3 are used by ecologists primarily in a descriptive or exploratory way, even though they can be and sometimes are used in a confirmatory way.

It is important to keep in mind that exploratory methods can be useful or even essential in the initial stages of developing multivariate models. Results from a multiple regression may suggest a multivariate model that can be evaluated later using SEM. Principal components analysis can suggest the existence of latent

Table 1.1. *Attributes of multivariate methods related to multivariate hypothesis formulation and evaluation. SEM is structural equation modeling, DA is discriminant analysis, RT is regression trees, PCA is principal components analysis, and MR is multiple regression*

	SEM	DA	RT	PCA	MR
Include measures of absolute model fit	✓				
User can specify majority of relationships	✓				
Capable of including latent variables	✓			✓	
Able to address measurement error	✓				
Allows evaluation of alternative models	✓				✓
Examines networks of relationships	✓				
Can be used for model building	✓	✓	✓	✓	✓

variables which can be evaluated using factor analysis. It is not appropriate to use SEM in all situations and for all purposes, thus, the other multivariate methods referenced in this section will continue to play an important role in the characterization of ecological data.

Philosophy of presentation

As stated previously, the first goal of this book is to introduce the reader to structural equation modeling. There are many different ways in which this can be approached. One is to emphasize the fundamental mathematical and statistical reasoning upon which modern SEM is based. An excellent example of this approach can be found in Bollen (1989). Another approach is to emphasize the basic concepts and procedures associated with SEM. A fair number of textbooks offer this kind of introduction to the subject (e.g., Hair *et al.* 1995, Schumacker & Lomax 1996, Loehlin 1998, Maruyama 1998, Raykov & Marcoulides 2000, Kline 2005). The presentations in these works are meant to apply to any scientific discipline that chooses to use SEM; in other words, they are descriptions of the SEM toolbox, along with general instructions. A third kind of presentation which is especially popular for those who have a background in the basics is one that emphasizes how individual software packages can be used to apply SEM (Hayduk 1987, Byrne 1994, Jöreskog and Sörbom 1996, Byrne 1998, Kelloway 1998, Byrne 2001).

One other approach to the material would be to examine how modern SEM, which has been largely developed in other fields, might be applied to the study of natural systems. This is a focus of the first part of this book. Shipley (2000) was the first to devote an entire book to present methods associated with modern SEM specifically to biologists (although classic methods were presented in Wright 1934 and Li 1975). In this effort, he covered a number of basic and more advanced topics, with an emphasis on the issue of inferring causation from correlation. More recently, Pugesek *et al.* (2003) have presented an overview of the conventions of modern SEM practice, along with a selection of example applications to ecological and evolutionary problems. A brief introduction to the application of SEM to the analysis of ecological communities can also be found in McCune and Grace (2002, chapter 30).

The need for a presentation of SEM that specifically relates to natural systems is justified by the way in which disciplinary particulars influence application. The flexible capabilities of SEM offer a very wide array of possible applications to research problems. It is clear that the characteristics of the problems them-selves (e.g., nature of the data, nature of the questions, whether manipulations are involved, sample size, etc.) have a major influence on the way the SEM tools are applied. Because many nuances of SEM application depend on the characteristics of the problem being studied, its application is not so well suited to a standardized prescription. This is why various presentations of SEM often differ significantly in their emphasis. For example, researchers in the social sciences where SEM has been most intensively used thus far, often apply it to survey data, which tends to have large sample sizes, suites of related items, and a major concern with measurement (e.g., how do we estimate a person's ver-bal aptitude?). When these same methods are applied to experimental studies where a small number of subjects, for example, forest tracts or elephants, can be studied intensively, the issues that are most important shift.

I have found that natural systems scientists often find it difficult to grasp immediately the meaning and value of certain aspects of SEM. If this were not the case, the books that already exist would be sufficient and biologists would be applying these methods routinely to their full potential. While there have been a significant number of applications of SEM to natural systems, it is safe to say that the capability and appropriate use of these procedures has not been approached. A decade of effort in applying SEM to ecological problems (as of this writing) has convinced me that there are substantial challenges associated with the translation and adaptation of these methods.

In conversations with biologists and ecologists I have consistently heard requests for examples. Those in the natural sciences often do not see the kinds of analyses obtained through structural equation modeling in the social sciences as important or relevant to their problems. Very commonly, biologists still see the univariate procedures that are applied to their data as sufficient. Why, they ask, should one go to all the trouble of learning and applying SEM? For these reasons, my approach in this book will be one of illustration and comparison. The four primary things I hope to convey are:

(1) the basic principles and procedures of structural equation modeling
(2) how the capabilities of structural equation methods can be related to ecological research problems
(3) how the results from these analyses differ from those that would be achieved if just a univariate approach had been used
(4) how the process of confronting ecological data with structural equation models can transform the study of natural systems and contribute to the maturation of our science.

The approach I will use to present the material will be oriented towards examples. Often, basic issues will not be discussed until after a relevant example has been introduced. This is intended to make concepts tangible. This order will not be followed in all cases, however, for purely practical reasons, nevertheless, illustration through example will be applied wherever possible. In order to accommodate this approach, concepts and procedures will be introduced gradually. I will generally build from material that is more readily understood to the more unfamiliar or advanced topics. In the first section of chapters I will illustrate an SEM application to make the subject more tangible. In the second section, the basic principles of SEM will be introduced. A brief introduction to more advanced topics will be the subject of the third section, while example applications will occupy the fourth section. In the final section, I will discuss the implications of multivariate model evaluation for the advancement of science and consider where this endeavor may take us. With luck, this approach will provide the natural scientist with a working knowledge of the basics of structural equation modeling, how it can be applied, and what they stand to gain in their understanding of natural systems.

2

An example model with observed variables

In this chapter I present a simple illustration of a structural equation model. My purpose is to provide a concrete example of structural equation modeling (SEM) for the reader and to facilitate subsequent discussion. In this chapter, the emphasis is on illustrating SEM results and comparing those to the results achieved from univariate analyses. In subsequent chapters I will introduce the principles and procedures of structural equation models, which will shed further light on both the origin and interpretation of SEM results.

Background and univariate results

The plant leafy spurge, *Euphorbia esula* (Figure 2.1), is one of the most troublesome exotic species in North America. This species was accidentally introduced through multiple shipments of contaminated crop seed and has spread throughout the northern and central latitudes, causing substantial economic and ecological damage. Considerable effort has been spent testing and then releasing a number of biocontrol insect species, particularly in the genus *Aphthona* (the flea beetles).

The site that this example comes from is the Theodore Roosevelt National Park, which is a grassland preserve located in North Dakota, USA. From an initial infestation of 13 hectares in 1970, spurge populations have spread rapidly in the park. An aggressive biocontrol program was initiated in the 1980s. Since then, there have been more than 1800 releases and redistributions of populations of two flea beetle species, *A. nigriscutis* and *A. lacertosa*, as control agents for leafy spurge. During the period 1999–2001, 162 vegetation plots were monitored throughout the park to census vegetation as well as to estimate population densities of the two flea beetles.

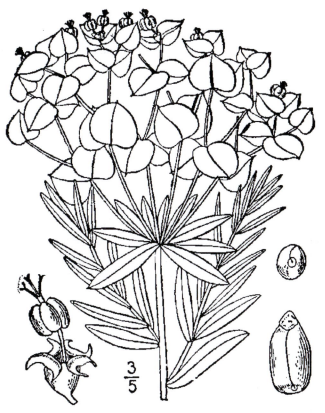

Figure 2.1. *Euphorbia esula* L. From USDA, NRCS. 2005. The PLANTS database, version 3.5. (http://plants.usda.gov).

Univariate analyses and results

There are a number of questions that can be addressed using the data collected in this simple survey; some rather obvious and others less so. What is of greatest interest is the question of whether the biocontrol program is working. In this section I will present some basic univariate results aimed at shedding light on this main question. In the next section, which presents the SEM results, we will revisit that main question and also consider a number of related issues.

Repeated measures analysis of variance was used to examine changes over time in both the proportion of leafy spurge plants that flowered, and the density of stems per plot. Examination of leafy spurge populations during the study (Figure 2.2) showed that average stem density declined from 2000 to 2001, while the percentage of stems flowering decreased throughout the study. These results would thus seem to be consistent with the premise that leafy spurge

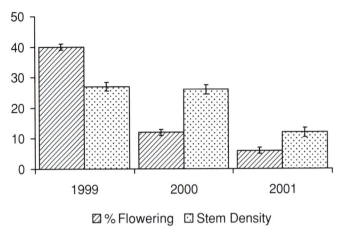

Figure 2.2. Changes in leafy spurge over time at Theodore Roosevelt National Park (means ± standard errors). Changes over time for both parameters were judged to be statistically significant using univariate procedures.

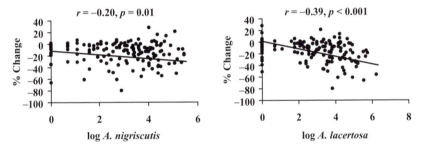

Figure 2.3. Regression of change in spurge between 2000 and 2001 against the log of the density of *Aphthona nigriscutis* and *Aphthona lacertosa*.

populations are stressed (indicated by the declining incidence of flowering) and declining in the face of the biocontrol effort.

An additional univariate analysis relevant to the main premise being examined is to see if there are any correlations between the local density of flea beetles in a plot and the rate of change of spurge in that plot. To determine this, the relationship between the change in spurge density from year to year was regressed against the density of each flea beetle to determine whether there was evidence for an effect of flea beetles on spurge. For this latter determination, linear regression analysis was used, with the log of the beetle density as the *x* variable and the percent change in spurge as the *y* variable. Changes in spurge density were found to be negatively correlated with flea beetle populations in both the 1999–2000 and 2000–2001 time intervals. An illustration of the relationship for the period 2000 to 2001 is shown in Figure 2.3. As can be seen, there

Table 2.1. *Correlations and standard deviations for leafy spurge density, change in density between years, and the population densities of two flea beetles that are biocontrol agents for spurge in 2000 and 2001. Correlations in bold are statistically significant at the $p < 0.05$ level*

$n = 162$	Spurge density 2000	Spurge density change 2000–01	A. nigris. density 2000	A. nigris. density 2001	A. lacertosa density 2000	A. lacertosa density 2001
	stems00	change	nig00	nig01	lac00	lac01
stems00	1.00					
change	**−0.63**	1.00				
nig00	**0.51**	**−0.28**	1.00			
nig01	**0.52**	**−0.20**	**0.75**	1.00		
lac00	0.15	**−0.24**	−0.12	−0.18	1.00	
lac01	**0.31**	**−0.39**	0.03	0.03	**0.70**	1.00
std dev	1.1276	18.031	1.7045	1.6647	1.9756	1.8714

was a negative relationship between change in spurge density and flea beetle density for both species. These univariate results would seem to further support the interpretation that the biocontrol agents are contributing to the observed decline in spurge.

Finally, examination of the bivariate correlations among variables (Table 2.1) provides additional insights into some of the apparent relationships among the species. For the sake of simplicity, I will lump bivariate results (i.e., correlations) with regression coefficients under the general heading of "univariate" results. Only the correlations for the period 2000 to 2001 are presented here. A more complete exposition can be found in Larson and Grace (2004). As can be seen in Table 2.1, 10 of the 15 bivariate correlations are statistically significant at the $p < 0.05$ level. Several points are worth noting about these individual correlations:

(1) The change in spurge density between years is not only negatively correlated with *A. nigriscutis* and *A. lacertosa* in 2001 (as shown in Figure 2.3), but also with their densities in 2000.
(2) The change in spurge density is additionally correlated (negatively) with spurge density in 2000.
(3) The spurge density in 2000 correlates with *A. nigriscutis* density in both 2000 and 2001, while it only correlates with *A. lacertosa* in 2001.
(4) Species *A. nigriscutis* and *A. lacertosa* only correlate with themselves across times; there are no correlations among species that are apparent.

These results indicate that the full story may be more complicated than described thus far, primarily because the change in spurge was not only related to flea beetle densities, but also strongly related to initial spurge density.

Structural equation modeling and results

Description and justification of initial model

Structural equation modeling typically begins with an initial model or selection of competing models which are formulated based on a-priori information. The initial model in this case concerns the changes in insects and spurge across years, and is shown in Figure 2.4. The structure of this model was chosen so as to disentangle the reciprocal interactions between species, which can sometimes be difficult to do. Here, the overall reciprocal interaction is addressed by parsing out the components of interaction (a positive effect of plants on insects and a negative effect of insects on plants) over time. An extra complication in this case is the potential for self regulation in spurge. Because of the potential for

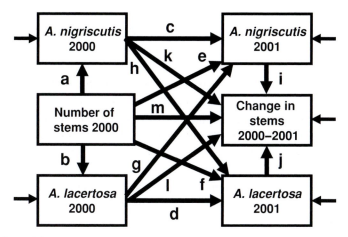

Figure 2.4. Initially hypothesized model used to evaluate factors affecting leafy spurge changes in density over time (from Larson and Grace 2004, by permission of Elsevier Publishers).

self regulation, change in spurge over time might relate both to flea beetles and to initial spurge density. These issues were dealt with by (1) separating changes in stem density over time from instantaneous values of stem density, and (2) by modeling the interaction with flea beetles over time.

The structure of the initial model (Figure 2.4) was based on a number of premises, which were derived from general knowledge about these species and similar systems. These premises are as follows:

(1) In any given year (denoted by year a), the densities of flea beetles can be expected to covary with the density of spurge because these insects depend on this species for food. These *Aphthona* species are presumed to be obligate feeders on *Euphorbia esula*, so it would be reasonable to expect that spatial variations in spurge densities will cause spatial variations in flea beetle densities (paths a and b).
(2) The densities of insects in a plot would be expected to be related over time. This premise is based on a number of biological features of the system relating to dispersal and food requirements. However, it is known that in some cases high population densities one year can lead to lower ones the next (e.g., because of interactions with a parasite), so it would not be a surprise if correlation over time were weak or variable. Thus, here we are assessing site fidelity for the insects (paths c and d).
(3) There may be time-lag effects in the dependencies of flea beetles on spurge density. This premise is supported by the fact that the flea beetles feed on

the plants for some period as larvae before emerging to feed as adults (paths e and f).

(4) An important question is whether the species of *Aphthona* may interfere with one another or otherwise be negatively associated. No a-priori information was available upon which to base an expectation, therefore, we included the pathways (paths g and h) to evaluate this possibility.

(5) The fundamental premise of the biocontrol program is that the flea beetles will have a negative effect on the change in spurge over time (paths i and j). Again, because feeding by the insects on plants begins in their larval stage (note that larvae were not directly observed in this study), it is reasonable to expect that some of the variation in spurge density changes will be related to the density of insects in the previous year (paths k and l).

(6) The change in spurge density may be expected to correlate with initial density due to density dependence. Most likely this would be manifested as a negative influence of initial density due to autofeedback (a reduced increase in stems at high densities) or even self thinning (a greater rate of decline at high densities).

The procedures by which we determine whether the data support our initial model will be presented later in this book. What the reader needs to know at this time is that there are processes whereby expectations about the data are derived from model structure, and the actual data are then compared to these expectations. This process not only provides estimates for all the parameters (including the numbered paths, the variances of the variables, and the disturbances or error terms), but also provides an assessment of overall model fit. When the relationships in the data are found to inadequately correspond to the initial model, the combination of a-priori knowledge and initial results is often used to develop a revised model, which is then used to obtain final parameter estimates. The results from revised models are not viewed with as much confidence as results from an initial model that fits well. Rather, they are seen as in need of further study if confidence is to be improved. That said, it is generally more appropriate to interpret parameters from a revised model that fits well than from an initial model that does not.

Assessment of initial structural equation model

Structural equation modeling analyses indicated that the data did not fit the initial model adequately. This determination was made based primarily on indices of overall model fit, such as chi-square tests and other measures. The reader should be aware that these measures of model fit are used in a fundamentally different way for structural equation models than for null hypotheses. In null hypothesis testing, priority is given to the hypothesis of no relationship. This is the case no matter what our a-priori knowledge is about the processes involved. In contrast, when evaluating overall fit of data to a structural equation model, priority is given to the model, and test results are used to indicate whether there are important deviations between model and data. Thus, in SEM, the a-priori information used to develop the initial model is used as a basis for interpretation. Stated in other terms, we presume that our other knowledge (aside from the data at hand) is important and that our data are meant to improve our knowledge.

Based on modification indices (which are provided by some SEM software programs to indicate more specifically where lack of fit occurs), a relationship not initially anticipated needed to be added before an adequate match between model and data could be obtained. This missing relationship indicated by the data was a negative correlation between *A. nigriscutis* and *A. lacertosa* in 2000 (the meaning of which is discussed below).

Now, the procedures in SEM are not completely devoid of null hypothesis tests. Associated with the estimation of model parameters is the calculation of standard errors for all path coefficients, and these can be used to estimate associated p-values. Unlike usual null hypothesis testing procedures, though, these paths are not always removed from the model simply because we fail to reject the null hypothesis. Rather, the decision to remove a path is based on the consequences for overall model fit, the individual p-values, and our substantive knowledge. In our example, the paths from flea beetles in 2000 to change in stem counts in year 2001 (paths k and l) were found to be indistinguishable from zero based on t-tests. Because we were initially uncertain about whether these paths should be in the model, they were removed. Also, the probability associated with path h, which represented an effect of *A. nigriscutis* on *A. lacertosa*, suggested little chance that such an effect occurred in this case. Therefore, this path was also removed. Model chi-square changed little with the removal of these paths, confirming that these relationships did not represent characteristics of the data.

The path from spurge density to *A. lacertosa* in 2000 was also found to be weak and the probability that it differs from zero unlikely. However, this path was retained in the model because of the potential that such an effect does occur some of the time. In fact, other data have revealed that the relationship between spurge density and *A. lacertosa* density does sometimes show a nonzero value. One final change to the model was deemed necessary. Results indicated that path i was nonsignificant (the effect of *A. nigriscutis* in 2001 on change in spurge stems). When this path was removed, it was found that there is actually a residual positive correlation between *A. nigriscutis* in 2001 and change in spurge stems. This relationship was represented in the revised model as a correlated error

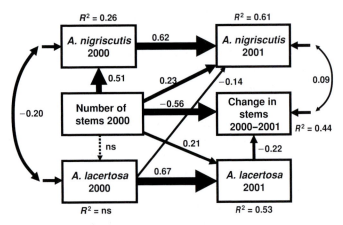

Figure 2.5. Results for revised model. Path coefficients shown are all standardized values (from Larson and Grace 2004, by permission of Elsevier Publishers).

term, which represents the effects of a joint, unmeasured causal factor (this topic is explored in more detail in Chapter 3). Following these modifications of the initial model, a reanalysis was performed.

Results for accepted structural equation model

Upon reanalysis, the data were found to correspond very closely to the revised model. As mentioned elsewhere, some aspects of this model (particularly the pathway that was added) run the risk of capitalizing on chance characteristics of the data because they are based on a revised model. However, subsequent analyses from the other years and from another area of the park were also found to be consistent with this revised model (Larson, unpublished data), which provides us with some additional confidence in our interpretations.

The results from our accepted model, which are summarized in Figure 2.5, provide a wealth of information about this system. Not only are there 11 path coefficients shown in the model, but the paths that are omitted provide important information as well. The main findings are as follows:

(1) *A. nigriscutis* density appears to track the density of spurge plants to a substantial degree (path value of 0.51) while *A. lacertosa*'s association with spurge is much weaker.
(2) *A. nigriscutis* and *A. lacertosa* in 2000 were found to be negatively correlated. There are three possible explanations for this. One is that the two species have different habitat preferences, leading to a partial separation in space. Another is that the two species were initially released in different

areas and have not fully dispersed yet. The third is that there is a negative interaction between the two species. There is currently insufficient information to resolve between these possible causes.

(3) The densities of both *A. nigriscutis* and *A. lacertosa* show a fair degree of consistency over time (path coefficients of 0.62 and 0.67).

(4) Both species of flea beetle in 2001 showed a lag relationship to spurge density in 2000 (path coefficients of 0.23 and 0.21).

(5) There is evidence for a modest negative effect of *A. lacertosa* in 2000 on *A. nigriscutis* in 2001 (path of −0.14). There is no indication that *A. nigriscutis* has a similar effect on *A. lacertosa*.

(6) Changes in spurge stem densities from 2000 to 2001 were found to be negatively related to *A. lacertosa* (path coefficient of −0.22). The most reasonable interpretation for this relationship is that it represents the effects of feeding by the insect on the plant. It does not appear that *A. nigriscutis* is having a negative effect on spurge, however. Thus, it would seem that the two biocontrol agents are not equally effective in reducing spurge.

(7) The biggest factor affecting changes in spurge density is negative density dependence.

A comparison of univariate and SEM results

The results of the analysis revealed a number of findings and implications that were not apparent from an examination of the univariate results (Figure 2.3, Table 2.1). Here I make the presumption (supported by a substantial body of theoretical statistics, as well as experience) that path coefficients are more accurate indicators of true relationships than are univariate regression results and bivariate correlations. If the reader will accept this presumption for the time being, a comparison between the univariate and multivariate results can be made. Here I summarize the SEM findings and some of the key similarities and differences that were found.

(1) *A. nigriscutis* tracks spurge strongly while *A. lacertosa* does not – *this was also found in the bivariate correlations.*

(2) *A. nigriscutis* and *A. lacertosa* had an initial negative association – *this was not found from examination of bivariate correlations.*

(3) Densities of *A. nigriscutis* and *A. lacertosa* were fairly consistent over time – *this was found from examination of correlations; however, bivariate results overestimate the fidelity by a fair bit.*

(4) *A. nigriscutis* and *A. lacertosa* both show a lag relationship to spurge density in 2000 – *this relationship could not be examined using univariate analyses.*

(5) There is evidence for a negative effect of *A. lacertosa* in 2000 on *A. nigriscutis* in 2001 – *there was no evidence for this in the univariate results.*

(6) Only *A. lacertosa* was found to have a significant effect on spurge density – *univariate results suggested that both species had effects on spurge; further, univariate results substantially overestimate the effects of flea beetles on spurge.*

(7) The biggest factor affecting changes in spurge density is self thinning – *this is consistent with the bivariate correlations; however, the correlations cannot be used to derive accurate estimates of the relative importances of factors without the use of a multivariate model.*

Conclusions

It is apparent, I hope, that a structural equation model provides a framework for interpreting relationships that is substantially superior to the piecemeal inspection of univariate results. When we look at Table 2.1, we see many correlations that are significant and some that are not. When we look at Figure 2.4, we see a whole system of interactions with complete accounting of direct and indirect interactions and the relative strengths of pathways (in the next chapter we will discuss the unstandardized path coefficients, which give the absolute strengths of pathways). Without a substantive model to guide our interpretation, it would be unclear what relationships are specified by the various correlations in Table 2.1. As it turns out, some bivariate correlations correspond to path coefficients and others do not. The reasons for this will also be presented in the next chapter.

It has also been shown that path coefficients can differ quite a bit from correlation coefficients. The most conspicuous example of that is the apparent negative relationship between *A. nigriscutis* and changes in spurge density (Figure 2.2), which turns out to be a spurious correlation. It comes about because both of these variables are influenced by a common factor, spurge density in 2000. The density of *A. nigriscutis* in 2001 is positively affected by spurge density in 2000 while the change in stems is negatively affected. This structure automatically creates a negative correlation between *A. nigriscutis* and the change in spurge density. It is through the use of our structural equation model that we are able to ascertain that the correlation is completely spurious.

Finally, the reader should be made aware that obtaining a correct interpretation depends on having the correct model. We have gone to some effort to ensure a match between model and data. The fact that they do match is no guarantee that the model (and our interpretations) are correct. We will have quite a bit more to say about this issue in later chapters. For now, let us simply say that SEM, when properly applied, has the potential to provide much greater insight into interacting systems than do traditional univariate models.

Summary

The results from this example are both ecologically interesting and also very instructive as to the value of partitioning relationships in a multivariate model. Bivariate correlations suggest that both flea beetles are contributing to the observed decline in spurge density over time (Figure 2.3). However, it appears that in actuality, during the time interval of this study, the biggest impact on changes in spurge density was from self thinning, with *A. lacertosa* having a modest effect on spurge and *A. nigriscutis* having no impact at all. This illustrates how careful one must be in interpreting bivariate correlations between variables under common influence (in this case, by initial stem densities). Stem densities appear to be a major driver in this system, both in terms of regulating flea beetle populations and in terms of self regulation of spurge densities. It also appears that there may be some negative associations between the two flea beetles, which could have important implications for biocontrol efforts. Further work, including carefully targeted experimental manipulations, can help us to continue to refine our knowledge and our models about this system through an accumulation of knowledge. I believe that this process of confronting systems using structural equation models will enhance both our understanding of the system and our ability to predict its behavior.

PART II

Basic principles of structural equation modeling

3

The anatomy of models I: observed variable models

Overview of more complex models

The versatility of structural equation modeling is reflected in the wide variety of models that can be developed using this methodology. To make the material easier to understand, we will start with the simplest types of model, those that only involve the use of observed variables. In later chapters we will introduce abstract variables into our models. The inclusion of these other types of variable greatly expands the variety of problems that can be addressed. As a preview of things to come later, here I present an example of a more complex type of model (Figure 3.1).

The model in Figure 3.1 includes four types of variables. *Observed variables* (represented by boxes) represent things that have been directly measured. Examples of observed variables include the recorded sex of animals in a sample, or the estimated plant biomass in a plot. Observed variables can also be used to represent experimental treatments (e.g., predators excluded, yes or no?), spatial locations (e.g., different sample sites), or interactions among other variables. *Latent variables* (represented by circles) represent unmeasured variables, which are often used to represent underlying causes. In the earliest example of a latent variable path model, Wright (1918) hypothesized that the relationships amongst bone dimensions in rabbits could be explained by a number of latent growth factors. While these latent factors could not be directly measured, their effects on bone dimensions could be inferred from the pattern of correlations amongst observed variables. The ability to model latent variables has come to be an integral capability of SEM. As we shall see later, latent variables can be used for a variety of purposes, and they do not always represent abstract concepts. A third variable type also occurs in Figure 3.1, the *composite variable* (represented by a latent variable with no indicators and zero error). A composite variable is one that represents the collective effect of a group of variables. While composite

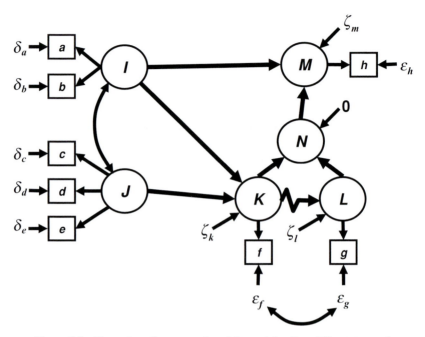

Figure 3.1. Illustration of a structural model containing four different types of variables. Boxes represent observed variables *a–h*, circles represent latent (unobserved) variables *I–M*, and the circle with a zero disturbance (*N*) represents a composite variable. The ζ term refer to variables that represent unspecified effects on dependent latent variables (disturbance effects), while δ and ε are variables that represent unspecified effects on observed variables. The zigzag arrow represents that *L* was derived arithmetically from *K*.

variables have been mentioned in the SEM literature for quite some time, it is only recently that they have begun to be considered more seriously for routine inclusion in structural equation models. Finally, *error variables* (which are unenclosed, but nevertheless true variables), represent unknown or unspecified effects on observed variables and latent response variables. Error variables are usually presumed to represent a collection of effects, including both random measurement error and unspecified causal influences (i.e., variables that were not measured). Often, error variables are treated more like summary measures of the other parameters (e.g., the sum of unexplained variance) than like variables themselves.

It is not my intention that the model represented in Figure 3.1 will be completely understood by the reader at this time. Rather, my objective here is simply to hint at the great versatility embodied in modeling with structural equations and to point to some of the things that will come later. In the rest of this chapter we will focus on models that only include observed variables. All of the principles we discuss related to observed variable models will also apply to the more complex models that are considered later, when latent and composite variables are introduced more fully.

Terminology associated with observed variable models

Models that include only observed variables (e.g., Figure 2.5) go by a variety of names. We could ignore this fact and choose just a single terminology for use in this book. Such an approach would not be helpful to the reader when trying to connect the material presented here with the writings of other authors. Therefore, its seems wise to mention the various terms that have been associated with these models. This kind of model is variously known as a (1) *structural equation model with observed variables*, (2) *manifest variable model*, or (3) *path model*. Analysis of a model that only contains observed variables is frequently referred to as *path analysis*. In the context of our historical discussion in Chapter 1, this would be *modern* path analysis. I may variously use all of these terms to refer to this type of model, depending on context.

Historic path analysis versus modern path analysis

While the topic was touched on in Chapter 1, it may be valuable to address here a question I commonly encounter, Isn't structural equation modeling with observed variables the same as the path analysis commonly used by biologists? This is a bit of a tricky question. The reason it is tricky is because the capabilities and accepted procedures for analyzing path models have evolved over the decades. Often these evolutionary advancements are omitted from the presentations of path analysis in the natural sciences. We will have opportunities to explain in more detail some of these advances in later sections of the book. However, for the time being I will mention four things that may help to distinguish "historic path analysis" from "modern path analysis".

In historic path analysis, the raw materials for analyses were correlations. In modern path analysis, the raw materials are covariances. It is now understood that the analysis of correlations limits the kinds of inferences and comparisons that can be made. This may seem like a minor point, but it is actually rather fundamental. Standardized coefficients, such as correlations, are quite valuable for extracting certain kinds of information. However, they tell somewhat less than half the story. Comparisons to other data sets depend, in part, on the use of unstandardized coefficients. The same can be said for the extrapolation of findings to other situations or predictive applications. Furthermore, comparisons among groups (say male and female members of an animal or plant population) may require the use of unstandardized coefficients. Finally, modern path analysis permits the analysis of differences in means as well as covariance relations. All these capabilities are lost when only correlations are analyzed.

Another important difference is that in historic path analysis, path coefficients were only estimated using standard least squares methods of the same sort as used in multiple regression. In modern path analysis, a number of solution procedures are available, but maximum likelihood estimation is often the preferred method. For path models in which all pathways are estimated, the results derived using standard regression methods are nearly the same as those obtained using maximum likelihood (when sample sizes are large). However, if a path model includes reciprocal effects (A affects B and B affects A), regression gives incorrect estimates. Further, if latent variables are included in a model, regression no longer suffices as a proper method for estimation. The topic of estimation methods will be discussed in Chapter 5.

Related to the issue of the accuracy of path coefficients, is the evaluation of overall model fit. In historic path analysis, fit of the data to the overall model was not assessed. However, maximum likelihood methods as well as other modern solution procedures provide for an additional assessment, that of whether the data are consistent with the specified model overall (typically through a chi-square or related test of goodness of fit). The inclusion of tests of overall model fit is a major advance associated with modern path analysis.

In historic path analysis, particularly in the natural sciences, analyses have often proceeded without regard for the distinction between exploratory versus confirmatory analyses. There is certainly a place for exploratory path analysis. This is particularly the case when a new problem is being tackled and there is insufficient experience and/or theory to provide a solid starting point for developing a-priori path models. However, within modern path analysis it is recognized that the strength of inference possible is related to the degree to which analysis proceeds in a confirmatory fashion. Thus, to the degree possible, path analysis should be based on an evaluation of a-priori models and not through a process of looking at all possible models, and then simply picking the one the author likes best.

This brief discussion greatly oversimplifies the evolution of the meaning of "path analysis" over time. A much more detailed and accurate portrayal of the history of modern path analysis can be found in Tomer (2003). The main point to be made here is that when path analysis is performed using the modern approach, it proceeds with an awareness of the capabilities of SEM. Thus, I tell those who ask, if one wants to perform a path analysis, they should

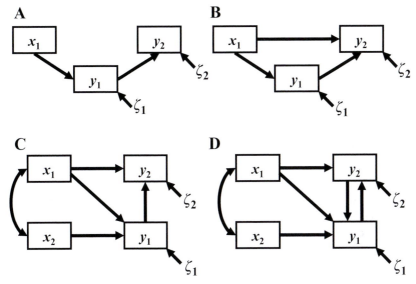

Figure 3.2. Examples of observed variable models. The observed variables are included in boxes and may be connected by various types of arrows. The unenclosed symbol ζ represents residual error variables.

read appropriate sections in a contemporary book on SEM (instead of a brief treatment of the topic in a general statistics book). When approached in this way, "path analysis" is synonymous with "SEM using observed variables".

The anatomy of observed variable models

Graphical representation of models is a fundamental part of SEM. This is not to say that the set of simultaneous equations associated with a model is unimportant. Rather, we should recognize that the visual representation of a model in graphical form is such a powerful device for expressing structural equation models that graphical models are nearly always developed by the researcher. For observed variable models, the elements of graphical representation include, (1) observed variables (in boxes), (2) double-headed curved arrows (representing unresolved correlations), (3) single-headed arrows (representing directed relationships, and (4) residual variances. Typically the symbols representing residual variances (error terms) are not enclosed by squares (see Figure 3.2).

There are several basic kinds of path model, depending on their structure and interconnections. Figure 3.2 presents four examples to illustrate some of the anatomical types. In the terminology of SEM, the independent (x) variables are referred to as *exogenous*, while the dependent (y) variables are called *endogenous*. Endogenous variables can, in turn, have influences on other endogenous variables. Commonly, causal order will flow from left to right across a model, although this will not always be the case.

The ways in which variables in a model are connected are important. Model A in Figure 3.2 is a simple example where x_1 and y_2 are only related indirectly. In other words, the relationship between x_1 and y_2 can be explained by their relationships to y_1. Thus, we would say that x_1 has an *indirect effect* on y_2 (within the context of the model). In contrast, model B contains both indirect and direct paths between x_1 and y_2. Direct paths are interpreted as relationships that cannot be explained through any other relationships in the model. In the case of model B, the correlation between x_1 and y_2 is such that it can only be explained by a direct effect of x_1 on y_2, in addition to the indirect effect mediated through y_1.

A further property of model B that should be noted is that it is *saturated*, which means that all the possible interconnections are specified. Model A is *unsaturated*, which means that some variables are not directly connected (i.e., some paths are omitted). Model C contains two exogenous variables, x_1 and x_2, which are correlated in this case. Such a correlation is generally presumed to be caused by some common influence that was not measured or is not considered in this model. Model C also has the property of being unsaturated (the path between x_2 and y_2 is omitted). Finally, model D contains reciprocal interactions between y_1 and y_2. Models with reciprocal interactions of this sort are called *nonrecursive*. Thus, models without reciprocal interactions (e.g., model C) are described as being *recursive* (the term recursive refers to the mathematical property that each item in a series is directly determined by the preceding item). In this chapter we will consider models of the first three types, A–C. Models possessing reciprocal interactions require special care to interpret and will not be addressed here.

One final property that an observed variable model may possess, and that is not shown in Figure 3.2, is a *correlated error*. Such a condition would be represented by having a two-headed arrow between ζ_1 and ζ_2, the two error terms, in any of the models. Correlated errors typically represent some unspecified cause for association. We will illustrate and discuss the meaning of correlated errors later in this chapter.

Path coefficients

The *path coefficients* specify values for the parameters associated with pathways between variables. In essence, the path coefficients represent much of the quantitative meaning of the model (although, as we shall see, there are many other parameters of importance as well). There are a number of things we will need to understand in order to properly interpret path coefficients. Some of the basic concepts will be introduced first. Later we will relate this information to our example in Chapter 2.

The building blocks of path coefficients: variances, covariances, correlations, and regression coefficients

Structural equation modeling can include a variety of statistical procedures. However, for most applications covered in this book, the procedures used are based on the analysis of variance–covariance matrices. In addition to variances and covariances, an understanding of correlation coefficients is critical because of their involvement in the interpretation of standardized path coefficients. The material covered is likely to be familiar to most readers. However, these basic statistical issues are so critical to understanding SEM that there is value in reviewing them at this time. Most importantly, this material in presented so as to alert the reader to the connection between the seemingly sophisticated procedures of SEM, and these most basic elements of statistics.

We start with a review of the concepts of variance and covariance. The formula for the best estimate of the population variance for x is

$$\text{VAR}_x = \frac{\sum (x_i - \bar{x})^2}{n - 1} \tag{3.1}$$

where x_i refers to individual sample values, $\bar{x}$ is the sample mean, and n is the sample size. The sample size refers to the total number of observations in the data set. The variance of y is given by the formula

$$\text{VAR}_y = \frac{\sum (y_i - \bar{y})^2}{n - 1} \tag{3.2}$$

The covariance between x and y is related to their joint deviations or cross products divided by $n - 1$, or

$$\text{COV}_{xy} = \frac{\sum (x_i - \bar{x})(y_i - \bar{y})}{n - 1} \tag{3.3}$$

When x and y are in some raw metric, say density of plant stems/m^2 for x and density of insects/m^2 for y, the magnitude of the covariance is related to the scale used to express the raw values. This can be illustrated using the data presented in Table 3.1.

Table 3.1. *Illustration of calculations for sums of squares and sums of cross products*

i	x	y	$x_i - \bar{x}$	$(x_i - \bar{x})^2$	$y_i - \bar{y}$	$(y_i - \bar{y})^2$	$(x_i - \bar{x})(y_i - \bar{y})$
1	2	70	−12.6	158.76	−77.3	5 975.3	973.98
2	6	55	−8.6	73.96	−92.3	8 519.3	793.78
3	9	50	−5.6	31.36	−97.3	9 467.3	544.88
4	12	156	−2.6	6.76	8.7	75.7	−22.62
5	15	115	0.4	0.16	−32.3	1 043.3	−12.92
6	15	200	0.4	0.16	52.7	2 777.3	21.08
7	19	155	4.4	19.36	7.7	59.3	33.88
8	20	202	5.4	29.16	54.7	2 992.1	295.38
9	22	295	7.4	54.76	147.7	21 815.3	1 092.98
10	26	175	11.4	129.96	27.7	767.3	315.78
$\sum$	146	1473		504.40		53 492.2	4 036.20

Note: means for x and y are 14.6 and 147.3 respectively.

For this example, the variances of x and y, plus the covariance between x and y can be calculated using Equations 3.1–3.3 as follows:

$$VAR_x = \frac{504.40}{9} = 56.04$$

$$VAR_y = \frac{53\,492.2}{9} = 5\,943.58$$

$$COV_{xy} = \frac{4\,036.20}{9} = 448.47$$

This yields the following variance–covariance matrix

	x	y
x	56.04	
y	448.47	5943.58

Here, we can see that the variance of y is larger than that of x. The mean of y (147.3) is also larger than the mean of x (14.6). Because the scales for x and y are so different, it is difficult to draw intuitive meaning from the covariance between x and y. In order to put things in terms where we can easily assess the degree of covariation between x and y, we might like to put x and y on a common scale. Typically the z *transformation* is used to adjust the means of variables to zero and their variances to 1.0. The formula for calculating z scores for variable x is

$$z_i = \frac{x_i - \bar{x}}{SD_x} \tag{3.4}$$

Table 3.2. *Illustration of derivation of z scores and standardized cross products using data from Table 3.1.* $SD_x = 7.49$ *and* $SD_y = 77.09$

	x	y	z_x	z_y	$z_x * z_y$
1	2	70	−1.68	−1.00	1.68
2	6	55	−1.15	−1.20	1.38
3	9	50	−0.75	−1.22	0.94
4	12	156	−0.35	0.11	−0.04
5	15	115	0.05	−0.42	−0.02
6	15	200	0.05	0.68	0.03
7	19	155	0.59	0.10	0.06
8	20	202	0.72	0.71	0.51
9	22	295	0.99	1.92	1.90
10	26	175	1.52	0.36	0.55
$\sum$	146	1473	−0.01	0.00	6.99

SD_x, the standard deviation of x, is obtained by taking the square root of VAR_x. The end result is that the z scores are expressed in terms of the standard deviation for that variable.

Using the information in Table 3.2, we can calculate the *Pearson product moment correlation coefficient*, r_{xy}, using the formula

$$r_{xy} = \frac{\sum (z_x \times z_y)}{n - 1} \qquad (3.5)$$

In this case, the formula yields

$$r_{xy} = \frac{6.99}{9} = 0.7767$$

Given that we have the calculated variances and covariance for the data in Table 3.1, we can also calculate the Pearson coefficient directly from the covariance and standard deviations using the formula

$$r_{xy} = \frac{COV_{xy}}{SD_x \times SD_y} \qquad (3.6)$$

which gives the same result,

$$r_{xy} = \frac{448.47}{7.49 \times 77.09} = 0.7767$$

As illustrated by this example, data can be standardized either through the use of z scores, or simply by dividing the covariances by the product of the standard deviations.

Finally, there is an important distinction between a correlation coefficient (r) and a regression coefficient (b). In regression, one variable is considered to be the response variable (y), and the other variable is considered to be the predictor (x). The association between the two variables is used to generate a predictor ($\hat{y}$) based on the formula

$$\hat{y} = bx + a \tag{3.7}$$

where b is the regression coefficient and a is the intercept. The relationship between the regression coefficient relating x and y, b_{yx}, and the correlation between x and y, r_{xy}, can be represented by the formula

$$b_{yx} = r_{xy}(SD_y/SD_x) \tag{3.8}$$

It is a simple matter to see from Eq. (3.8) that when variables have been z-transformed, $SD_y = SD_x = 1$, and $b_{yx} = r_{xy}$. Thus, the distinction between correlation and regression is only noticeable for the unstandardized coefficients. When dealing with unstandardized coefficients, the relationship between COV_{xy}, which measures association, and b_{yx} is given by

$$b_{yx} = \frac{COV_{xy}}{VAR_x} \tag{3.9}$$

It can be seen from Eq. (3.9) that in regression the covariance is standardized against the variance of the predictor (x), rather than the cross product of SD_x and SD_y as in Eq. (3.6).

The rules of path coefficients

If we return to considering path models, as presented in Figure 3.2, we can recognize two types of path, undirected and directed. Undirected paths, such as those represented by curved two-headed arrows in models C and D, can be described as unanalyzed relationships. This leads us to our *first rule of path coefficients* – the path coefficient for an unanalyzed relationship (i.e., correlation) between exogenous variables is simply the bivariate correlation (standardized form) or covariance (unstandardized form) between the two variables. No calculation is required, therefore, to find the coefficient, it can simply be taken directly from the correlation/covariance table.

Our *second rule of path coefficients* states that when two variables are connected by a single causal path, the coefficient for a directed path connecting the variables is the (standardized or unstandardized) regression coefficient. Let us illustrate this with a three-variable model of the form shown in Figure 3.3. An associated matrix of correlations is presented to facilitate the illustration.

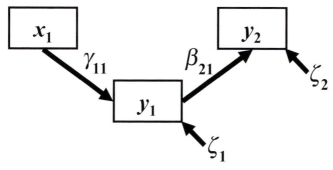

	x_1	y_1	y_2
x_1	1.0		
y_1	0.50	1.0	
y_2	0.30	0.60	1.0

Figure 3.3. Simple directed path model.

Also, for simplicity the discussion of path relations here will be based on standardized values (correlations). Following the second rule of path coefficients, the coefficient for the path from x_1 to y_1 can be represented by the correlation between x_1 and y_1 (0.50). Likewise, the coefficient for the path from y_1 to y_2 can also be represented by the correlation between y_1 and y_2 (0.60). As with the first rule of path coefficients, when the second rule of path coefficients applies and we are only concerned with standardized coefficients, we can simply pick the coefficient directly out of the table of correlations.

Continuing with our example from Figure 3.3, we can ask, What is the relationship between x_1 and y_2? This leads us to our *third rule of path coefficients*, which states that the mathematical product of path coefficients along a compound path (one that includes multiple links) yields the strength of that compound path. So, in our example, the compound path from x_1 to y_2 is 0.50 times 0.60, which equals 0.30.

We can see from the table in Figure 3.3 that in this case, the observed correlation between x_1 and y_2 is equal to 0.30, the strength of the compound path from x_1 to y_2. We can illustrate another major principle related to path coefficients by asking what would it mean if the bivariate correlation between x_1 and y_2 was not equal to the product of the paths from x_1 to y_1 and y_1 to y_2? An

Table 3.3. *Variance/covariance matrix*

	x_1	x_2	y
x_1	52 900		
x_2	21.16	0.0529	
y	3 967.5	2.645	529

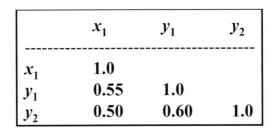

	x_1	y_1	y_2
x_1	1.0		
y_1	0.55	1.0	
y_2	0.50	0.60	1.0

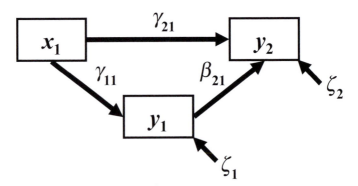

Figure 3.4. Model including dual pathways between x_1 and y_2.

example of such a case is presented in Figure 3.4. Here we see that the indirect path between x_1 and y_2 again equals 0.50 times 0.60, or 0.30. However, the observed correlation between x_1 and y_2 is 0.50. This means that the bivariate correlation between x_1 and y_2 cannot be explained by the indirect path through y_1. Rather, a second connection between x_1 and y_2 (a direct path from x_1 to y_2) is required to explain their overall bivariate correlation.

By having a direct path between x_1 and y_2, as shown in Figure 3.4, we now have a new situation, one where y_1 and y_2 are connected by two pathways, one direct from y_1 to y_2 and another that is indirect through the joint effects of x_1 on y_1 and y_2. This leads to the *fourth rule of path coefficients*, which states that when two variables are connected by more than one causal pathway, the calculation of *partial regression coefficients* becomes involved. We must be clear here what is meant by a "causal pathway". Certainly a directed path from one variable to another, such as from y_1 to y_2, is an obvious causal path. How can it be that y_1 and y_2 are connected by two causal pathways? The answer is that y_1 and y_2 are also connected through a joint causal influence exerted by x_1. This indirect pathway, which can be traced from y_1 to x_1 and then to y_2 (or, alternatively, from y_2 to x_1 and then to y_1) represents a second causal pathway, one of *association by joint causation*. Thus, it is important that we should be able to recognize when two variables are connected by more than one causal pathway, being aware that some connections (discussed further below) will be deemed noncausal. To understand this important issue further, we now need to discuss partial regression coefficients.

Partial regression and its relation to path coefficients

Understanding the related concepts of partial regression and partial correlation is necessary in order to understand path coefficients. Simply put, a *partial regression* or *partial correlation* between two variables is one that accounts for the influences of additional variables that affect or correlate with those variables. As was just stated, partial regression or correlation coefficients become involved when two variables are connected through more than one causal pathway. Let us first begin with partial regression, using the data and model in Figure 3.4 for illustration.

As we know from the second rule of path coefficients, the path coefficient between x_1 and y_1 in Figure 3.4 is the same as the bivariate regression coefficient between these two variables. This is true because x_1 and y_1 are only connected through a single causal pathway. Since we are dealing in this example with z-transformed variables (correlations), the regression coefficient is the same as the correlation. Thus, without doing any calculations we already know that the path coefficient between x_1 and y_1 has a value of 0.55.

It can also be seen in Figure 3.4 that the variables x_1 and y_2 are connected by two pathways in this model, one is a *simple* (single link), direct pathway and the second is a *compound* (multi-linkage), indirect pathway through y_1. As we have said, both of these pathways represent causal connections whereby x_1 affects y_2. The coefficient for the direct path from x_1 to y_2 is designated as γ_{21}. The value of γ_{21} can be obtained from the partial regression of y_2 on x_1, which controls for the fact that y_2 is also affected by y_1.

Note that I use the customary SEM symbology in this book. According to this symbology, which will be presented in the context of the LISREL system later (Chapter 6, Appendix 6.1), γ represents the effects of exogenous variables on endogenous variables, and β represents the effects of endogenous variables on other endogenous variables. Subscripts refer to appropriate elements. Thus, γ_{11} represents the effect on y_1 by x_1 and β_{21} represents the effect on y_2 by y_1. The value of the coefficient γ_{21} (effect on y_2 by x_1) can be obtained from the formula for a partial regression coefficient.

$$\gamma_{21} = \frac{r_{x_1 y_2} - (r_{x_1 y_1} \times r_{y_1 y_2})}{1 - r_{x_1 y_1}^2} \tag{3.10}$$

Because Eq. (3.10) is so important to our understanding of path relations, it may be worth pointing out some of its features. The numerator represents the total correlation between x_1 and y_2 minus their indirect connection. This makes intuitive sense because the total correlation between two variables equals the sum of all pathways connecting them. The denominator in Eq. (3.10) can be intuitively understood as a standardization term. In this case, the path coefficient from x_1 to y_2 is standardized by the degree to which variance is shared between x_1 and y_1. When variance is not shared between x_1 and y_1 (i.e., x_1 and y_1 are uncorrelated), the effect of x_1 on y_2 is independent of any effect from y_1 on y_2. However, when variance is shared between x_1 and y_1 (i.e., they are correlated), that shared variance is removed from our calculation of the partial regression coefficient by subtracting it from 1. What is most important about Eq. (3.10) is that it has the property of being able to yield path coefficients which have the property that they allow the sum of all paths between two variables (e.g., x_1 and y_2) to equal the bivariate correlation between x_1 and y_2. It is from this property that Eq. (3.10) is derived (see Appendix 3.1 for the derivation).

In our example from Figure 3.4, we can calculate the partial regression coefficient for the effect of x_1 on y_2 as

$$\gamma_{21} = \frac{0.50 - (0.55 \times 0.60)}{1 - 0.55^2} = \frac{0.17}{0.6975} = 0.24$$

We can now say that the standardized effect of x_1 on y_2 when the effects of y_1 on y_2 are held constant is 0.24. This means that for every standard deviation of change in x_1, y_2 changes by 0.24 standard deviations. It is worth noting that we have just obtained *statistical control* of the relationships. This is in contrast to *experimental control* where y_1 would be physically held constant and not allowed to vary. While experimental control is used to force predictors to be orthogonal, allowing for an evaluation of their separate influences, statistical control permits us to evaluate the effects while permitting predictors to inter-correlate. I will have much more to say about the relative merits of statistical and experimental control in one of the later chapters, as this is a very important concept in our consideration of multivariate hypotheses.

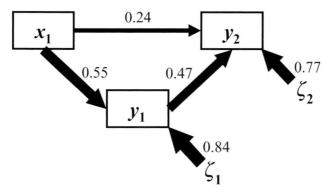

Figure 3.5. Model from Figure 3.4 showing path coefficients.

Now, there is another pair of variables to consider in Figure 3.4, y_1 and y_2. In order to determine the type of path coefficient (simple or partial) that will represent this path, we again have to ask the question, are these two variables connected by more than one causal pathway? One causal connection is obvious, the direct arrow from y_1 to y_2. You should now recognize that they are also causally connected by the fact that x_1 affects both of them. Because y_1 and y_2 are both affected by a common cause, the effect of x_1, they are causally connected through a second path, one that spans between them through x_1.

Because the connections between y_1 and y_2 match the conditions for the fourth rule of path coefficients, we can calculate the coefficient for the path from y_1 to y_2 using the proper modification of Eq. (3.10)

$$\beta_{21} = \frac{r_{y_1 y_2} - (r_{x_1 y_1} \times r_{x_1 y_2})}{1 - r_{x_1 y_1}^2} \tag{3.11}$$

which gives us

$$\beta_{21} = \frac{0.60 - (0.55 \times 0.50)}{1 - 0.55^2} = \frac{0.325}{0.6975} = 0.47$$

Using the path coefficients derived from the correlations in Figure 3.4, we can now represent the quantitative characteristics of the model as shown in Figure 3.5. It is sometimes the convention that the width of the arrows is made proportional to the magnitude of the coefficients to make the representation of overall relationships more apparent. We should always keep in mind, however, that the interpretation of the magnitude of a path coefficient requires care, as will be made clear later in this chapter. As the reader will note, we have two additional paths in Figure 3.5 that have not been discussed; those from the error variables to y_1 and y_2. More needs to be stated about these.

Error variables and their path coefficients

In observed variable path models, such as the ones we have been discussing, typically we ignore the existence of error terms for the observed exogenous variables. Actually, we are making the claim that there is no error associated with exogenous (predictor) variables and these variables are measured perfectly. We will discuss the consequences of this assumption in the next chapter. For now, we should consider what error terms are, why we describe them as error variables, and what the path coefficients representing error effects mean.

Stated in simple terms, the coefficients representing the errors are simple regression coefficients representing the unexplained (residual) variance. If $R^2_{y_1}$ refers to the variance in y_1 explained by x_1, then the path coefficient for the effect of ζ_1 is

$$\zeta_1 = \sqrt{1 - R^2_{y_1}} \tag{3.12}$$

For our example in Figure 3.5, the value of ζ_1 equals 0.84. Sometimes the path coefficients for the error terms are confusing for those first encountering them. Since the value for $R^2_{y_1} = 0.55^2 = 0.30$, we might think the path coefficient would be the unexplained variance, which is 0.70. However, the path coefficient from ζ_1 is typically expressed in the same form as for other path coefficients, the non-squared form (the square root of $0.70 = 0.84$).

In a similar fashion, $R^2_{y_2}$ refers to the variance in y_2 explained by the combined effects of y_1 and x_1, which in this case is 0.40 (the means of calculating this by hand is presented below in Eq. (3.16). Given the explained variance of 0.40, we can calculate the path coefficient as

$$\zeta_{y_2} = \sqrt{1 - R^2_{y_2}} \tag{3.13}$$

which equals 0.77. Equations (3.12) and (3.13) represent the *fifth rule of path coefficients*, that the coefficients associated with paths from error variables are correlations or covariances relating the effects of error variables. In this case, the ζ values represent the errors of prediction, though without specifying the exact causes for that error.

Alternative ways to represent effects of error variables

While the above means of representing the effects of error variables using path coefficients for error paths is often presented in textbooks, there are alternative methods that may be preferred by some. Typically we think of error associated with response variables in terms of variance explained and the related concept of the R^2. Standardized path coefficients for error effects of the sort shown in

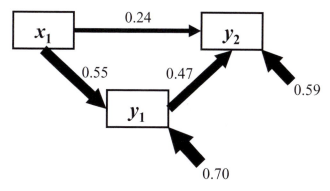

Figure 3.6. Alternative representation of effects of error variables (compare to Figure 3.5).

Figure 3.5, while logical, still require some mental arithmetic to transform the information into variance explained. Instead of presenting the path coefficients for error variables, it is possible to present the standardized values of the error itself, as shown in Figure 3.6. Here, we can directly obtain R^2 as 1 minus the standardized error. Note that in Figure 3.6, the numeric value is located at the origin end of the arrow, rather than alongside the arrow (the convention for path coefficients, compare to Figure 3.5). Also, for some audiences, simply presenting the R^2 directly may be preferred over the representation of error variables.

Partial correlation and its relation to path coefficients

There is one more type of path coefficient I would like to discuss and that is the partial correlation. Figure 3.7 illustrates a model that contains a partial correlation (between ζ_1 and ζ_2). As we have already stated, according to the first rule of path coefficients, the coefficients for unanalyzed relationships between two exogenous variables are simply the correlations or covariances (e.g., x_1 and x_2). So, what about the situation where there are two response variables, in this case y_1 and y_2, that are correlated due to some unspecified reason(s)? Our *sixth rule of path coefficients* states that unanalyzed correlations between endogenous variables represent partial correlations or partial covariances.

    The formula for a partial correlation between y_1 and y_2 in the presence of x_1 in Figure 3.7 is

$$r_{y_1 y_2 \bullet x_1} = \frac{r_{y_1 y_2} - (r_{x_1 y_1} \times r_{x_1 y_2})}{\sqrt{\left(1 - r_{x_1 y_1}^2\right)\left(1 - r_{x_1 y_2}^2\right)}} \tag{3.14}$$

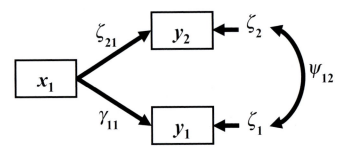

Figure 3.7. Model illustrating correlations between endogenous variables (y_1 and y_2 in this case), which are manifested as correlations between the errors.

where $r_{y_1 y_2 \bullet x_1}$ refers to the partial correlation between y_1 and y_2 taking into account their correlations with x_1. The reader should note that technically, a model with correlated errors between endogenous variables is *nonrecursive*, in that there is something akin to a reciprocal interaction between endogenous variables. In LISREL terminology the correlated error is referred to as ψ_{12} (psi one–two).

Now, for a model such as the one in Figure 3.7, but with no partial correlation between y_1 and y_2, the intercorrelation between the two response variables would simply be the product of the correlation between x_1 and y_1 and the correlation between x_1 and y_2. This would be represented by the formula

$$r_{y_1 y_2} = r_{x_1 y_1} \times r_{x_1 y_2} \tag{3.15}$$

If Eq. (3.15) were substituted into Eq. (3.14) the numerator of Eq. (3.14) will be zero. Therefore, it is a general rule that under the conditions where Eq. (3.15) holds, the partial correlation between y_1 and y_2 will be zero, and y_1 and y_2 are said to be *conditionally independent*. If the relationship in Eq. (3.15) fails to hold, there will then exist a direct path between y_1 and y_2, and its path coefficient will be the value of the partial correlation given by Eq. (3.14).

Let us consider again the example data in Figure 3.4. If y_1 and y_2 were conditionally independent, according to Eq. (3.15), their bivariate correlation should be $0.55 \times 0.50 = 0.275$. However, their observed correlation is actually 0.60; this seems to be a rather large difference. According to Eq. (3.14), we can calculate the partial correlation between y_1 and y_2 in the presence of x_1 as

$$r_{y_1 y_2 \bullet x_1} = \frac{0.60 - (0.55 \times 0.50)}{\sqrt{(1 - 0.55^2)(1 - 0.50^2)}} = 0.45$$

which represents the value for ψ_{12}. So, we can see that there is a rather large correlation between y_1 and y_2 that is not explained by their joint dependence on x_1. As we stated earlier, this correlation between dependent variables suggests

	x_1	x_2	y_1	y_2
x_1	1.0			
x_2	0.80	1.0		
y_1	0.55	0.40	1.0	
y_2	0.30	0.23	0.35	1.0

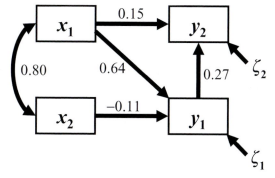

Figure 3.8. Model and correlations illustrating concepts of total effect and total correlation. The matrix represents the bivariate correlations among variables, while the numbers on the diagram are the path coefficients.

the influence of some other factors that have not been explicitly included in the model.

Total effects and total correlations

Once we have values for individual paths, we can consider how the different paths between variables add up. The *seventh rule of path coefficients* states that the *total effect* one variable has on another equals the sum of its direct and indirect effects. In this case, the total effect of x_1 on $y_2 = 0.24 + (0.55 \times 0.47) = 0.50$, which in this case, is the bivariate correlation between x_1 and y_2. Related to the seventh rule is the *eighth rule of path coefficients*, which states that the sum of all pathways connecting two variables, including both causal and noncausal paths, adds up to the value of the bivariate or *total correlation* between those two variables. To illustrate this rule, we need to involve a slightly more complex model, for example of the form of model C in Figure 3.2. Figure 3.8 provides correlations and path coefficients for such a model.

Figure 3.8 offers us a slightly more complex example. Here, we have an undirected relationship between two exogenous variables (x_1 and x_2), as well as multiple directed paths to and among endogenous variables (y_1 and y_2). The first thing we should notice when comparing the path coefficients to the bivariate correlations is that all directed paths in this case involve partial regression coefficients. Only the coefficient for the undirected path between x_1 and x_2 can be found in the table of correlations. The reader should be able to calculate all of the other path coefficients shown using Eq. (3.10).

As for *total effects*, these can be obtained from the path coefficients. Our seventh rule of path coefficients allows us to determine that the total effect of x_1 on y_1 is simply 0.64. This means that if we were to increase the value of x_1 by one standard deviation while holding the value for x_2 constant at its mean value, the value of y_1 would increase by 0.64 times its standard deviation. As we can see, there is only one directed path connecting x_1 with y_1. However, the case for the total effect of x_1 on y_2 is different. Here, there are two directed pathways, one simple path from x_1 to y_2 and one compound path through y_1. Therefore, the total effect of x_1 on y_2 is $0.15 + (0.64 \times 0.27)$, or 0.32. Again, if we were to increase x_1 one standard deviation while holding x_2 constant, y_2 would increase by 0.32 times its standard deviation. In this case, however, y_1 would covary in the process because the total effect of x_1 on y_2 would involve both paths from x_1 to y_2. Finally, the total effect of x_2 on y_2 can be seen to be $-0.11 \times 0.27 = -0.03$.

For more complex models, the business of determining which of the paths connecting two variables are causal can be slightly more tedious than in the simple example given here. Wright (1960) proposed several simple tracing rules that can help to identify causal paths. These rules are as follows:

(1) A path can go backwards as many times as necessary before going forward.
(2) Once a path goes forward, it cannot go backwards.
(3) A path cannot go through a variable twice.
(4) A path can include a curved arrow, but only one curved arrow per path.

Reflecting on these tracing rules should reveal that they are perfectly compatible with our discussion of what constitutes a causal connection. Perhaps the least transparent of these rules is number 4. To understand rule 4, we should keep in mind that a curved arrow represents an unresolved shared cause. Thus, a curved arrow between x_1 and x_2 actually represents an undescribed variable with arrows pointing at x_1 and x_2. So, when a path proceeds backwards (upstream) through a curved arrow, it should be viewed as going upstream to the undescribed variable and then forward (downstream) to the variable on the other end of the curved arrow. If we were to consider a path that included two curved arrows, we would be violating rule number 2.

As for the *total correlations*, the calculation of these involves the eighth rule of path coefficients. Thus, total correlations involve both the total effects plus the undirected relations between variables. In our example in Figure 3.8, the total correlation between x_1 and y_1 is the sum of the directed and undirected pathways linking them. In this case, that is $0.64 + (0.80 \times -0.11) = 0.55$. Note that this reconstitutes the bivariate correlation between x_1 and y_1 as seen in Figure 3.8. Likewise, the total correlation between x_2 and y_2 can be seen to be $(-0.11 \times 0.27) + (0.80 \times 0.15) + (0.80 \times 0.64 \times 0.27) = 0.23$.

As a final point of discussion relating to Figure 3.8, the reader may be surprised to find that the correlation between x_2 and y_1, which is 0.40, is substantially different from the path coefficient between these two variables, which is -0.11. When such a case is observed, it is often referred to as *suppression*. Suppression refers to the fact that the strong intercorrelation between x_1 and x_2, in combination with the relatively strong effect of x_1 on y_1, causes the effect of x_2 on y_1 to be fairly unrelated to their net intercorrelation. Keep in mind that the path coefficient of -0.11 does actually reflect the causal effect that x_2 has on y_1. However, this effect is rather weak, and as a result, the correlation between x_2 and y_1 is dominated by the influence of x_1.

The interpretational differences between unstandardized and standardized path coefficients

The analysis of unstandardized versus standardized data

As is the case with covariances versus correlations, path coefficients and other model parameter estimates can be expressed in either unstandardized or standardized form. There are two very important things to mention at the outset. First, many of the commercial software programs available for conducting SEM do not provide proper solutions for analyses based on correlation matrices. Structural equation modeling based on covariance procedures is based on the presumption that the unstandardized relationships (variances and covariances) are being analyzed. At the time of writing, only some of the available software packages (e.g., SEPATH, Mplus) provide the necessary adjustments to provide correct solutions for correlation matrices. Secondly, when covariance matrices are analyzed, significance testing of parameters is based on the standard errors of the unstandardized coefficients. Thus, any standardized path coefficients that may be presented (for example, by requesting standardized output) have not been directly tested for significance. Usually, standardized coefficients are interpreted based on the test results for unstandardized parameters. However, care must be taken when critical results are marginal and inferences are based on statements of significance about standardized results.

A basic issue to consider is the different ways in which these two types of variable are interpreted and the kind of questions each addresses. Typically, researchers are fond of standardized parameters because the scale is the same (standard deviation units) for different relationships. Thus, the primary function of standardized variables is to allow direct comparisons between relationships that are measured on different scales. For example, the unstandardized parameter relating an animal's fat deposits to its caloric intake might be measured as percent body fat per kilocalories. Meanwhile the unstandardized parameter relating body fat to activity level (e.g., kilometers traveled during migration) would be on a different scale. In this case, standardized coefficients allow for a common basis of comparison. As we shall see, however, it is easy to rely too heavily on standardized path coefficients and an appreciation for unstandardized coefficients needs to be developed by the user of SEM.

The process of partitioning path coefficients was originally developed using Pearson product moment correlations, which are standardized parameters. Further, many authors choose to introduce the basic concepts about path coefficients using standardized variables (as I have done above). Sewell Wright, in his initial work on path analysis, relied exclusively on standardized data and standardized coefficients to partition direct and indirect relationships among variables. However, he later came to calculate and report "concrete" (unstandardized) coefficients also, and discussed their use in interpreting path models (Wright 1984). Often, applications of path analysis in the natural sciences have relied strictly on the analysis of correlations instead of covariances. In modern path analysis, as well as in most other forms of structural equation modeling, we typically perform analyses based on covariances rather than correlations. Analysis of covariances permits calculation of both unstandardized and standardized results. It also permits analysis of differences between means as well. *For this reason, it is recommended that SEM be performed using unstandardized data (covariances).* It is then possible to calculate both unstandardized and standardized parameter estimates, and both can be used in drawing interpretations.

Differences between unstandardized and standardized coefficients

Here I wish to illustrate more explicitly using hypothetical examples why a complete interpretation of a structural equation model requires the researcher to examine both unstandardized and standardized coefficients. Later in the chapter we will compare standardized and unstandardized coefficients for results from a real example, our study of plants and insects presented in Chapter 2. The

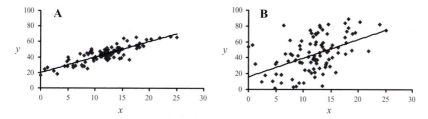

Figure 3.9. Illustration of two regressions having the same intercept and slope, but different degrees of scatter around the line. While unstandardized parameters (intercept and slope) did not differ significantly between the two data sets, the degree of correlation did, with correlation coefficients of 0.861 in A and 0.495 in B.

reason I emphasize this point rather strongly is because an inappropriate choice of which coefficients to use can lead to incorrect interpretations (see Grace and Pugesek (1998) for discussion of a specific ecological example). Here I illustrate the general issue and use a simple regression example to show what is gained by having both standardized and unstandardized coefficients (Figure 3.9). At the end of the discussion, I present some cautionary points about standardized parameters, and suggest a possible solution that involves an alternative method of standardization.

The data presented in Figure 3.9 were generated using the equation $y = a + \gamma x + \zeta$, with only the value of ζ, the error term, differing between the two cases, A and B. A random selection of x values were obtained from a normal distribution and ζ was independent from the other parameters, had a mean of zero, and a specified standard deviation. Slight, nonsignificant differences between the unstandardized parameters in A and B are the result of random sampling (sample size = 100). However, the standardized coefficients (correlations) differ strongly between cases, being 0.861 for case A and 0.495 for case B.

As this example demonstrates, unstandardized coefficients represent the effect of x on y in absolute terms. Since the slope here is 2.0 for the population, we can state that for a change in 10 units in x, there should be a corresponding 20 units change in y on average. This statement holds true for both cases, A and B.

Now, if we took the data shown in Figure 3.9 A and B and z-transformed the values, the resulting graphs would look virtually identical to each other, except that the scales for the x and y variables would have mean zero and be measured in units of the standard deviations of x and y. If we perform a regression on these z-transformed variables, we now find that standardized and unstandardized coefficients are the same and they match the correlation coefficients given in Figure 3.9. Thus, we have lost any knowledge of the absolute slope of the relationships using standardized data. The same can be said when we rely exclusively on standardized coefficients. Thus, a knowledge of the absolute slope of the relationship is of critical importance in drawing certain kinds of inferences, such as predictions, comparisons across samples, and generalizations at large.

The interpretation of standardized coefficients

In the face of the above warnings, we must still recognize that standardized coefficients are often valuable to us. However, they are frequently misinterpreted. The biggest cause of misinterpretation may come from a spill over from our training in analysis of variance; the concept of variance partitioning. When exogenous variables are uncorrelated with each other, such as is typically the case in controlled experiments, variance in the response variable can be apportioned amongst the causal factors. However, when exogenous variables are intercorrelated, variance partitioning becomes a limiting concept (as we shall see in a moment). For this reason, *standardized path coefficients are best thought of as the expected change in* y *as a function of the change in* x, *in standard deviation units.*

Now, researchers often use standardized coefficients in an attempt to address a different kind of question. Instead of discussing the expected change in y, they may try to make statements about how much of the variation in y in a sample can be associated with the variation in x in that sample. What, they may ask, causes the variations seen among my sample points in the number of bird species observed? Are factors x_1 and x_2 equally important explanations for those observed variations? The reader should note that this kind of question is primarily about the data in hand rather than about the phenomenon at large. The reason for this being about the data in hand is that the question is about observed variations in the sample. In a different sample, the span of values may be more or less, and the standardized relationships would not be constant. Furthermore, this question can only be answered unambiguously in certain types of path models, those devoid of correlated exogenous variables.

Why are we so readily misled about the interpretation of standardized coefficients? The usual culprit is that we make an analogy with simple regression, where there are no correlated predictors. For example, in the case of simple regression, we know that the square of the correlation (which is the same as the standardized regression coefficient) provides a measure of the variance in y that is explained by x. For the examples in Figure 3.9, even though the unstandardized effect of x on y is the same in both A and B, the variance in y explained by

Table 3.4. *Unstandardized path coefficients*

	x_1	x_2	y
x_1	——		
x_2	21.16	——	
y	0.065	23.81	——

x differs between the two cases. In A, x is able to explain 74% of the variation in y in the sample. In B, x is able to explain only 25% of the variation in y.

In multiple regression or a path model, relating the variance explained to different predictors is more complicated. To consider how multiple predictors relate to variance explanation in y, we need the formula for calculating total variance explained in a multiple regression. When there are two correlated predictors, x_1 and x_2, influencing y, the total variance explained in y, R_y^2 can be calculated as

$$R_y^2 = \gamma_{11}(r_{x_1y}) + \gamma_{12}(r_{x_2y}) \tag{3.16}$$

In this context, γ_{11} refers to the standardized effect of x_1 on y and γ_{12} refers to the standardized effect of x_2 on y. Both standardized path coefficients are partial regression coefficients in this case. Equation (3.16) gives the impression that we can apportion cleanly variance explanation in y among the xs. This is not the case.

Another hypothetical case can be used to illustrate the application of Eq. (3.16). Imagine a situation where y is influenced by two correlated predictors, x_1 and x_2, and the scale of y is in terms of percent change and ranges from 1 to 100. In this example, the scale of x_1 is in raw units and ranges from 1 to 1000, while the scale of x_2 is as a proportion and ranges from 0 to 1.0. For simplicity we let the standard deviation of each be a constant proportion of the range for each variable. In this example, the covariance matrix has the values given in Table 3.3.

If we analyze this variance/covariance matrix and present unstandardized path coefficients, we get the values represented in Table 3.4.

Thus, our equation is

$$y = 0.065x_1 + 23.81x_2 + \zeta$$

It is unclear from this equation what the relative importance of x_1 and x_2 might be as explanations for the observed variation in y. Now, if we look at the data in standardized form (Table 3.5),

Table 3.5. *Correlations, standard deviations*

	x_1	x_2	y
x_1	1.00		
x_2	0.40	1.00	
y	0.75	0.50	1.00
STD	230	0.23	23

we see the correlations among variables, along with the standard deviations (note, Table 3.3 can be exactly reconstructed from Table 3.5). Looking at the standardized path coefficients (Table 3.6),

Table 3.6. *Standardized path coefficients*

	x_1	x_2	y
x_1	——		
x_2	0.4	——	
y	0.655	0.238	——

the equational form or representation would be

$$y = 0.655x_1 + 0.238x_2 + \zeta$$

We can now use Eq. (3.16) to calculate the total R^2 for y.

$$R^2 = (0.655)(0.75) + (0.238)(0.5)$$

Solving this in stages, we see that

$$R^2 = (0.49) + (0.12) = 0.61$$

Thus, the total proportion of variance in y explained by both predictors is 0.61.

As stated earlier, this calculation of the total variance explained by both predictors might suggest to the reader that we can cleanly assign variance explanation to each of the two predictors in this case. However, we must recognize that the explained variance is of three types, (1) variance in y that is only associated with x_1 (x_1's unique variance explanation), (2) variance in y that is only associated with x_2 (x_2's unique variance explanation), and (3) variance in

y that is explained by both x_1 and x_2. The magnitude of the shared variance is proportional to the magnitude of correlation between x_1 and x_2.

It is possible to calculate these three components of the explained variance using the formula for a *semipartial correlation*. The semipartial correlation between x_1 and y in the presence of x_2 can be found by the equation

$$r_{yx_1(x_2)} = \frac{r_{yx_1} - (r_{x_1x_2} \times r_{yx_2})}{\sqrt{1 - r_{x_1x_2}^2}} \tag{3.17}$$

The square of the semipartial correlation in Eq. (3.17) gives a measure of the proportion of the variance in y that is uniquely explained by x_1. The meaning of a semipartial correlation or regression can be understood to be the additional variance explanation gained by adding x_1 to the collection of predictors (akin to a stepwise process). Using Eq. (3.17) and the data from Table 3.5, we can calculate for our example that

$$r_{yx_1(x_2)} = \frac{0.75 - (0.40 \times 0.50)}{\sqrt{1 - 0.40^2}} = \frac{0.55}{0.92} = 0.60$$

Thus, the proportion of variance in y uniquely explained by $x_1 = 0.60^2 = 0.36$. Because the maximum variance in y that could be explained by x_1 if it was the only predictor is the square of the bivariate correlation, $0.75^2 = 0.56$, and the variance in y uniquely explained by x_1 is 0.36, the shared variance explanation must be $0.56 - 0.36 = 0.20$.

We can further determine using the same procedure (an equation of the same sort as Eq. (3.17)) that the proportion of variance in y uniquely explained by $x_2 = 0.22^2 = 0.05$. As before, the maximum variance in y that could be explained by x_2 if it were the only predictor is $0.50^2 = 0.25$. Since x_2's unique explanatory power is 0.05, we once again arrive at a shared variance explanation of 0.20. These results are summarized in Table 3.7.

Having gone through the process of showing how variance explanation can be partitioned, I must again emphasize that this is only relevant when we are interested in associations in our sample. If we wish to extrapolate to another situation or compare groups, standardized coefficients will not serve us well unless the variances are comparable across samples. The reason is very simple. The standardized coefficients are standardized by the ratios of the standard deviations, and thus, sensitive to the sample variances. Reference back to Eq. (3.8) reminds us that the standardized effect of x on y can easily be calculated as the unstandardized effect multiplied by the ratio of the standard deviations (when this is done, the units cancel out, leaving the coefficients unitless, though we interpret them as being in standard deviation units). Since we know that further

Table 3.7. *Summary of explained variance components*

Source of variance explanation	Proportion of variance in y explained
Unique influence of x_1	0.36
Unique influence of x_2	0.05
Shared influences of x_1 and x_2	0.20
Total variance explained	0.61

samples may not always have the same variances, the standardized coefficients will not automatically extrapolate. To generalize beyond our sample, therefore, we should rely on unstandardized coefficients. Pedhazur (1997, page 319) describes the situation this way, "The size of a [standardized coefficient] reflects not only the presumed effect of the variable with which it is associated but also the variances and the covariances of the variables in the model (including the dependent variable), as well as the variances of the variables not in the model and subsumed under the error term. In contrast, [the unstandardized coefficient] remains fairly stable despite differences in the variances and the covariances of the variables in different settings or populations." Pedhazur goes on to recommend that authors present both unstandardized and standardized coefficients, and to be particularly careful to respect the assumptions involved in standardized coefficients.

Guidelines

As a generalization, there are *four kinds of conditions in which unstandardized coefficients are likely to be essential to drawing proper inferences*: (1) when the units of x and y are meaningful and there is interest in describing the absolute effect of x on y, (2) when separate path models for different groups are being compared (so-called multigroup analysis) and those groups have different variances, (3) in repeated measures situations where items are followed over time, and population variances differ substantially between times, and (4) when results are compared among datasets or used for prediction and we are interested in average changes. While some authors will state that under such circumstances only the unstandardized coefficients can be used, I think that this is not strictly true. The focus of the research question is what determines when and how the coefficients should be interpreted. *The most general rule of all about standardized and unstandardized coefficients is that researchers should use the coefficient type that is appropriate to the inferences they make.*

Summary of the rules of path coefficients

Because I have scattered these important rules through the chapter, I recapitulate them here for the reader. As we will discuss other types of variables in later chapters (e.g., latent and composite variables), we will introduce some additional rules that apply to models that include those variable types.

The rules of path coefficients (note, these are all stated in terms of standardized coefficients, though they also apply to unstandardized coefficients)

(1) The path coefficients for unanalyzed relationships between exogenous variables are the bivariate correlations.

(2) When two variables are only connected through a single directed path, the coefficient for that path corresponds to the bivariate regression coefficient.

(3) The strength of a compound path (one that involves multiple arrows) is the product of the coefficients along that path.

(4) When two variables are connected by more than one causal pathway, the calculation of partial regression coefficients is required.

(5) Coefficients associated with paths from error variables are correlations representing unexplained effects.

(6) Unanalyzed correlations between endogenous variables are represented by partial correlations.

(7) The total effect one variable has on another equals the sum of its direct and indirect effects through directed (causal) pathways.

(8) The sum of all pathways connecting two variables, including both causal and noncausal paths, adds up to the value of the bivariate or total correlation between those two variables.

Interpreting the path coefficients of the leafy spurge–flea beetle example

We now return to the results from our example in Chapter 2 dealing with the interactions between the plant leafy spurge and the two flea beetles that feed on it. The diagram (Figure 3.10) now shows both the standardized coefficients,

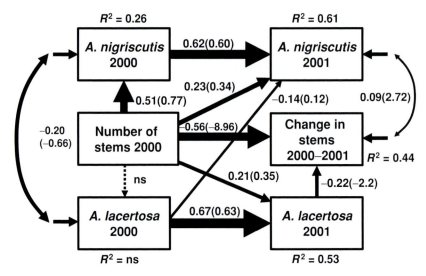

Figure 3.10. Results for leafy spurge–flea beetle model showing both standard-ized coefficients (not enclosed by parentheses) and unstandardized coefficients (enclosed by parentheses).

which were given in Figure 2.5, and the unstandardized path coefficients (in parentheses). First, we will re-examine the standardized coefficients in this model while reviewing the rules of path coefficients. Secondly, we will consider the interpretation of the unstandardized coefficients.

Application of the rules of path coefficients to our example

After considering the rules of path coefficients in this chapter, the reader should be better able to understand the meaning and origin of the various path coeffi-cients in Figure 3.10. To help with the process, I reproduce the correlations from Table 2.1 in Table 3.8. Here are some of the main points that can be illustrated from Table 3.8 and Figure 3.10 relating to standardized coefficients.

(1) According to the first rule of path coefficients, the path coefficient for an unspecified relationship (two-head arrow) between exogenous variables will take on the value of their bivariate correlation. In this case, there is only one exogenous variable, the number of stems in 2000. Therefore this rule does not apply to any of the coefficients in Figure 3.10.

(2) According to the second rule of path coefficients, when two variables are only connected through a single causal pathway, the value of the path coefficient between them will be the bivariate regression coefficient. For

Table 3.8. *Simple bivariate correlations among variables in Figure 3.10*

	stems00	change	nig00	nig01	lac00	lac01
stems00	1.00					
change	−0.63	1.00				
nig00	0.51	−0.28	1.00			
nig01	0.52	−0.20	0.75	1.00		
lac00	0.15	−0.24	−0.12	−0.18	1.00	
lac01	0.31	−0.39	0.03	0.03	0.70	1.00

standardized variables, this will be the same as the correlation coefficient. In Figure 3.10, there is one path that fits the requirements of the second rule, the path from number of stems in 2000 to *A. nigriscutis* (0.51). Reference to Table 3.8 illustrates that the path coefficient for that path does indeed match the bivariate coefficient.

(3) According to the third rule of path coefficients, the product of path coefficients along a complex path represents the strength of that complex path. This rule applies throughout our model. For example, the effect of the number of spurge stems in 2000 on *A. nigriscutis* in 2001 (in standardized terms) is $0.51 \times 0.62 = 0.32$.

(4) The fourth rule of path coefficients indicates that there are many cases where partial regression coefficients are involved; basically anywhere two variables are connected by two or more causal pathways. The number of spurge stems in 2000 has three causal pathways to the change in stems from 2000 to 2001. The number of stems also has three causal paths to the density of *A. nigriscutis* in 2001, while it has two causal paths to *A. lacertosa* in 2001.

(5) In this case, I have not presented the path coefficients for the error variable effects. The fifth rule of path coefficients can be used to determine those values. Since the path coefficients for error terms are directly related to the explained variance for endogenous variables, we can determine the path coefficients for the error variables using Eq. (3.12) if we wish to know them.

(6) According to the sixth rule of path coefficients, correlations between endogenous variable errors are partial correlation coefficients. There are two of these in this model, one involves *A. nigriscutis* in 2000 and *A. lacertosa* in 2000. The other partial correlation is between the errors of *A. nigriscutis* in 2001 and the change in stems from 2000 to 2001.

Table 3.9. *Standardized total effects of predictors (column headings) on response variables (row headings) for data in Figure 3.10*

	stems00	nig00	lac00	nig01	lac01
nig00	0.51	———	———	———	———
lac00	ns	———	———	———	———
nig01	0.52	0.62	−0.14	———	———
lac01	0.31	0.00	0.67	———	———
change	−0.63	0.00	−0.15	0.00	−0.22

(7) The seventh rule of path coefficients allows us to calculate total effects. In this case, there are several and they are illustrated in Table 3.9. The reader should be able to calculate these total effects from the information in Figure 3.10.

(8) In this situation, the eighth rule of path coefficients simply allows us to see the relationships between bivariate correlations and path coefficients. One of the more interesting cases is that for *A. nigriscutis* in 2000 and *A. lacertosa* in 2000. The two paths connecting these two variables include the shared causal effect of stems in 2000 (0.51×0.15) plus their direct correlation (-0.20). Together, these constitute the bivariate correlation, which is -0.12.

Interpretation of unstandardized coefficients for our example

As we discussed earlier in the chapter, the standardized coefficients only give part of the picture. These relate primarily to questions about shared variation in our sample. In other words, the standardized path coefficients reflect the degree to which observed variation in one variable relates to observed variation in another. So, looking at Figure 3.10, we can see that the variation we observe among plots in the change in stems between years is strongly related to variations among plots of numbers of stems, independent of the effects of other variables. The exact nature of this direct effect of stems in 2000 on change in stems, however, is represented by the unstandardized coefficient -8.96. Taking the units of both variables into account, we would interpret the unstandardized coefficient as follows: "as the number of stems in a plot goes up by 1 stem, the change in stems goes down by 8.77 percent". Therefore we would predict that if the stems in a plot increased by 10, stems would decline by 87.7%.

Some of the paths in Figure 3.10 do not show a big difference between the standardized and unstandardized values, in particular, the paths from *A*.

nigriscutis in 2000 to *A. nigriscutis* in 2001 and *A. lacertosa* in 2000 to *A. lacertosa* in 2001. This occurs because the units are the same for both variables involved with each of these paths, their variances are very similar, and variances are not too far from 1.0.

Finally, we need to be aware that the data for *A. nigriscutis* and *A. lacertosa* densities are the logarithms of the raw scale. Thus, we have to translate unstandardized coefficients if we wish to say, for example, how much *A. nigriscutis* would increase in density if we were to increase the number of stems. Basically, the answer would be 0.51 times the logarithm of the insect density.

While it is difficult to give advice on the use of standardized and unstandardized coefficients that is universally correct, we could say that when you are interested in inferences about the data in your sample, standardized coefficients are often what you should use. However, when your goal is to generalize to other samples or make predictions, the unstandardized coefficients can be required for proper interpretation.

A possible alternative standardization procedure

In spite of the criticisms of standardization, researchers would generally prefer a means of expressing coefficients in a way that would permit direct comparisons across paths. The debate over this issue goes back to Wright (1921) who originally developed path analysis using standardized variables. It was Tukey (1954) and Turner and Stevens (1959) who first criticized the interpretability of standardized values in regression and path models, and many others have since joined in that criticism. However, Wright (1960) argued in defense of standardized coefficients saying that they provide an alternative method of interpretation that can yield a deeper understanding of the phenomena studied. Later, Hargens (1976) argued that when the theoretical basis for evaluating variables relates to their relative degrees of variation, standardized coefficients are appropriate bases for inference. Therefore, we must admit that a form of standardization would seem desirable from a researcher's perspective. As Pedhazur's recent assessment of this problem concludes, ". . . the ultimate solution lies in the development of measures that have meaningful units so that the unstandardized coefficients . . . can be meaningfully interpreted."

So, how might we standardize using measures that have meaningful units? We must start by considering what it means to say that if *x* is varied by one standard deviation, *y* will respond by some fraction of a standard deviation. For normally distributed variables, there is a proportionality between the standard deviation and the range such that six standard deviations are expected to include

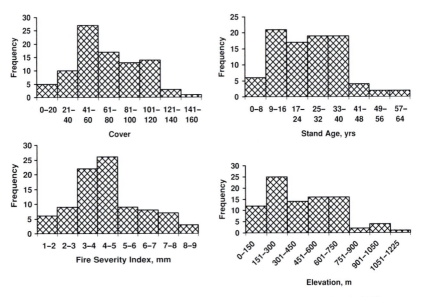

Figure 3.11. Frequency distributions for four variables from a study of wildfire effects on plant recovery, used to discuss the concept of relevant ranges.

99% of the range of values. As discussed earlier, this may seem reasonable if (1) we have a large enough sample to estimate a consistent sample variance, (2) our variables are normally distributed, and (3) variances are equal across any samples we wish to compare. The reason why many metricians oppose standardized coefficients is because generally these three necessary conditions are not likely to hold. Of equal importance, rarely are these requirements explicitly considered in research publications, so we usually don't know how great the violations of these requirements might be.

Figure 3.11 presents frequency distributions for four variables from an SEM study by Grace and Keeley (2006). In the absence of further sampling, the repeatability of the sample variance estimate is unknown. This contributes to some uncertainty about the interpretability of coefficients standardized on the standard deviations. As for approximating a normal distribution, three of the four variables are truncated at the lower end of values. Cover can never be less than 0%, elevation likewise has a lower limit of expression relevant to terrestrial communities in this landscape, and stand age is also limited to a minimum value of between 0 and 1 year. None of these deviations is substantial enough to cause major problems with distributional assumptions (i.e., these variables are not wildly nonnormal), however, the deviations from idealized normality may very well impact the relationships between standard deviations, and ranges.

The observed range for cover was from 5% to 153%, while 6 times the standard deviation yields an estimated range of 190%. The observed range for elevation was from 60 to 1225 m, while 6 times the standard deviation equals 1550. Stand age ranged from 3 to 60 years old, with 6 times the standard deviation equaling 75 years. Finally, fire severity index values ranged from 1.2 to 8.2 mm, while 6 times the standard deviation equals 9.9. Thus, observed ranges are consistently less than would be estimated based on standard deviations, and the degree to which this is the case is slightly inconsistent (ratios of observed to predicted ranges for cover, elevation, age, and severity equal 0.78, 0.75, 0.76, 0.71).

It is possible that in some cases information about the range of values likely to be encountered or of conceptual interest can provide a more meaningful basis for standardizing coefficients than can the sample standard deviations. We can refer to such a range as the *relevant range* (Grace and Bollen 2005). For example, if we have a variable whose values are constrained to fall between 0 and 100, it would not seem reasonable for the relevant range chosen by the researcher to exceed this value, regardless of what 6 times the standard deviation equals. On the other hand, it may be that the researcher has no basis other than the observed data for selecting a relevant range. Even in such a case, we can choose to standardize samples that we wish to compare by some common range so as to clarify meaning across those samples. Whatever the basis for standardization, researchers should report both the unstandardized coefficients and the metrics used for standardization.

In this case, we might choose to specify the relevant range for cover to be from 0 to 270%. Obviously values cannot fall below 0%, but why choose an upper limit of 270%? Examination of cover values for all plots across the five years of the study show that values this high were observed in years 2 and 4 of the study. By using a relevant range of from 0 to 270, we permit comparisons across years standardized on a common basis. Of course, this implies that the slopes measured will extrapolate to that full range, which is an assumption that should be evaluated closely. For elevation, we might choose the relevant range to be the observed range, from 60 to 1225 m. This span of 1165 m might be chosen because we do not wish to extrapolate to lower or higher elevations, in case relationships to other variables are not robust at those elevations. For stand age, we could specify the relevant range to be 60 years for basically the same reason. Finally, the fire index range chosen might also be the observed range, which was 7.0 mm. It is clear that values could be obtained beyond this range in another fire. It is not known, however, whether the relationship between remaining twig diameter and herbaceous cover would remain linear outside the observed range.

Based on these determinations, we can generate path coefficients standardized on the relevant ranges for an example model involving these variables.

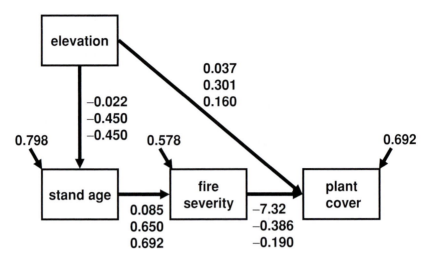

Figure 3.12. Example model comparing the unstandardized path coefficients (upper), coefficients standardized based on their standard deviations (middle), and coefficients standardized based on their relevant ranges (lower).

Figure 3.12 shows the three types of standardized coefficient. The biggest numeric differences between values is that when standardized by the relevant ranges, the values of the coefficients leading to cover are lower because of the large relevant range selected for this variable. The coefficient for the effect of age on severity is slightly higher, while that for the effect of elevation on age is unchanged. Using these coefficients now allows us to describe the importance of variables using their relevant ranges as the explicit context. These interpretations are only valid for relative comparisons within the parameter space defined by the relevant ranges. So, we can say that as fire severity increases across its relevant range, cover would be expected to decline by 19% of its relevant range. As elevation increases across its relevant range, the total change in cover from both direct and indirect causes would be an increase of 21.9% (the total effect). We now conclude from this analysis that the sensitivity of cover to fire severity and elevation (19% versus 21.9%) are roughly equivalent in this study, though of opposing sign. It is possible to test whether these two estimates are reliable differences, which in this case, they are not.

Conclusions

The sophisticated procedures of modern structural equation modeling start with the basic principles of regression and the rules of path coefficients. When these rules and principles are combined with an understanding of model structure, the anatomy and interpretation of structural equation models should become clear for a wide variety of model types. For those who wish to understand SEM, fundamental distinctions between standardized and unstandardized variables are important. Understanding these issues is especially important for those in the natural sciences where there has been much use of path analysis based on correlations. In the next chapter we will continue to build on our knowledge of the capability of SEM by considering latent variables and issues related to their use and interpretation.

Appendix 3.1 Derivation of the formula for the partial regression coefficient

From a mathematical standpoint, the formula for calculating a partial regression coefficient is quite simple. However, properly interpreting partial path coefficients is one of the basic elements of mastering SEM. The material in Chapter 3 presents the concepts associated with partial regression using one approach. Here, I approach the problem from a different direction by deriving the formula for partial regression, in case this alternative approach is more useful for some in developing their understanding. For the benefit of the reader, I show all the steps in the derivation.

There is a fundamental requirement that the correlation between two variables in a path model must equal the sum of the direct and indirect paths connecting them. This is given in Chapter 3 as our eighth rule of path coefficients. So, for a simple model of multiple regression (Figure 3.1.1), it holds that

$$r_{x_1 y_1} = \gamma_{11} + (r_{x_1 x_2} \times \gamma_{12}) \tag{3.1.1}$$

and

$$r_{x_2 y_1} = \gamma_{12} + (r_{x_1 x_2} \times \gamma_{11}) \tag{3.1.2}$$

In this case, our goal is to express the partial path coefficients (which are our unknown parameters) in terms of the known parameters (the correlations). So, we must rearrange our equations, yielding

$$\gamma_{11} = r_{x_1 y_1} - (r_{x_1 x_2} \times \gamma_{12}) \tag{3.1.3}$$

and

$$\gamma_{12} = r_{x_2 y_1} - (r_{x_1 x_2} \times \gamma_{11}) \tag{3.1.4}$$

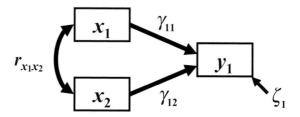

Figure 3.1.1. Simple multiple regression model.

Substitution of Eq. (3.1.4) into Eq. (3.1.3) allows us to derive the equation for γ_{11} as follows:

$$\gamma_{11} = r_{x_1y_1} - r_{x_1x_2} \times (r_{x_2y_1} - r_{x_1x_2} \times \gamma_{11}) \tag{3.1.5}$$

$$\gamma_{11} = r_{x_1y_1} - r_{x_1x_2} \times r_{x_2y_1} + r_{x_1x_2}^2 \times \gamma_{11} \tag{3.1.6}$$

$$\gamma_{11} - r_{x_1x_2}^2 \times \gamma_{11} = r_{x_1y_1} - r_{x_1x_2} \times r_{x_2y_1} \tag{3.1.7}$$

$$\gamma_{11} \left(1 - r_{x_1x_2}^2\right) = r_{x_1y_1} - r_{x_1x_2} \times r_{x_2y_1} \tag{3.1.8}$$

$$\gamma_{11} = \frac{r_{x_1y_1} - r_{x_1x_2} \times r_{x_2y_1}}{1 - r_{x_1x_2}^2} \tag{3.1.9}$$

Through similar means we can arrive at our equation for γ_{12},

$$\gamma_{12} = \frac{r_{x_2y_1} - r_{x_1x_2} \times r_{x_1y_1}}{1 - r_{x_1x_2}^2}. \tag{3.1.10}$$

While we have illustrated the formulae for partial regression coefficients using a multiple regression model (Figure 3.1.1), it is important to realize how this extends to a fully directed path model of the form shown in Figure 3.1.2 (similar to Figure 3.4). Let us see why this is the case.

In Figure 3.1.1, the first rule of path coefficients tells us that the relationship between x_1 and x_2 can be represented by their bivariate correlation coefficient. While the model shown in Figure 3.1.2 may be interpreted differently, it is similar to the previous model in that the standardized path coefficient from x_1 to y_1 is also represented by their bivariate correlation coefficient, though this is based on the second rule of path coefficients (which applies to variables connected by only one causal path).

Table 3.1.1. *Correlations associated with example analyses represented in Figure 3.1.3*

	variable 1	variable 2	variable 3
variable 1	1.0		
variable 2	0.40	1.0	
variable 3	0.50	0.60	1.0

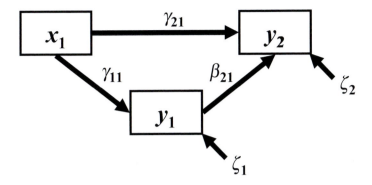

Figure 3.1.2. Directed path model.

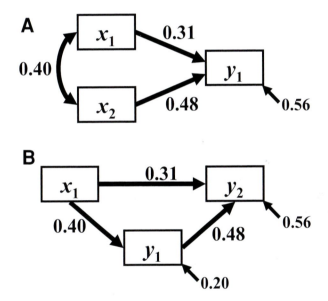

Figure 3.1.3. Illustration of similarity of path coefficients for multiple regression model (model A) and directed path model (model B).

To illustrate the similarity between the models in Figure 3.1.1 and 3.1.2, let us consider data for three variables with the correlations given in Table 3.1.1. Imagine that in the first case, we use these data to evaluate a multiple regression model like the one in Figure 3.1.1 and let variable 1 be x_1, variable 2 be x_2, and variable 3 be y_1. The reader should be able to use the rules of path coefficients and Eqs. (3.1.9) and (3.1.10) to find the standardized path coefficients for that model (Figure 3.3).

Let us now consider applying our data to a different model. Perhaps we decide that variable 2 actually depends on variable 1 and that variable 3 depends on both 1 and 2. Such a decision would have to be based on theoretical reasoning, as there is nothing about the data that will tell us the causal structure of the model. This decision would lead us to formulate our model as in Figure 3.1.3. So, now variable 1 is x_1, variable 2 is y_1, and variable 3 is y_2. We can again use our rules and equations to arrive at the standardized path coefficients. We now find that the coefficients are the same for both models. The fundamental reason for this is that in both cases, variables 1 and 3 are connected by two causal pathways, thus, the equations for partial regression are invoked in both cases. However, interpretations of the models are somewhat different. In particular, in model B y_1 is interpreted as being influenced by x_1 and has an attending error variable, while the relationship between x_1 and x_2 in model A is considered to be the result of an unanalyzed joint cause (a correlation). Also, the other difference between the two models is that the total effects of x_1 and x_2 on y_1 in model A are simply 0.31 and 0.48. However, in model B, the total effect of x_1 on y_2 is 0.31 plus 0.40 times 0.48, which equals 0.50.

4

The anatomy of models II:
latent variables

Concepts associated with latent variables

What is a latent variable?

As indicated in our overview of structural equation models at the beginning of Chapter 3, in addition to observed variables in structural equation models, another type of variable, referred to as a latent variable, is commonly included. There are a variety of ways latent variables can be defined. Strictly speaking, a *latent variable* is one that is hypothesized to exist, but that has not been measured directly. Bollen (2002) states that we can simply think of a latent variable as one that is unobserved. In spite of this simple definition, latent variables are typically used to represent concepts. However, there are many types of concept and not all of them correspond to latent variables. Further, the algorithms used to calculate latent variables define their quantitative properties, although how they are interpreted is a matter of theoretical consideration. Finally, latent variables are starting to be used in structural equation models for a wider variety of purposes, such as to represent parameters in latent growth modeling. Because latent variables are often used to represent abstractions, their meaning is not always immediately obvious. For this reason, I believe it will be best to rely on a variety of examples and a discussion of their properties to illustrate the roles latent variables can play in SEM.

An illustration of a latent variable ξ with a single indicator variable x is shown in Figure 4.1. There are several things to notice about this representation and these help to clarify some of the attributes of latent variables. First, a latent variable is typically (though not always) associated with one or more observed indicator variables. We use the term *indicator* to refer to the fact that the observed variable is not a perfect measure of the concept of interest. Rather, the observed variable serves to provide us with information about the latent

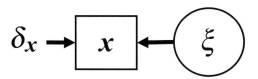

Figure 4.1. Symbolic representation of a latent variable, ξ, a single observed indicator variable, x, and the error variable δ_x associated with x.

variable. Most importantly, we presume that the values of the indicator variable are reasonably well correlated with the true latent variable values. Through this correlation, our ability to measure x provides us with information about ξ.

A second thing to observe about Figure 4.1 is that the direction of causality is represented by an arrow from the latent variable to the indicator. Initially this can be confusing since the values of the observed variables are used to estimate the values of the latent variable. However, it is important to realize that conceptually, the latent variable is the "true" variable of interest, and the indicator is a manifestation of the effects of that true entity. A classic example of latent variables is the components of human intelligence. It is presumed that people have abilities that cannot be directly measured. Rather, performance on tests of various sorts can be used to provide indirect measures of those abilities. In a similar fashion, we can presume that many concepts represent properties that we cannot measure directly but that cause observed manifestations. This is true even when the concepts are not highly abstract.

A third thing to notice about Figure 4.1 is that there exists an error associated with the observed indicator. In terms of equations, we can represent this situation with the formula

$$x = \lambda\xi + \delta_x \tag{4.1}$$

This equation makes it clear that we are stating that the values of x are the result of the influence of the latent variable ξ, proportional to λ, its effect on x, plus error, δ_x.

A tangible example of a latent variable and its indicator is represented in Figure 4.2. Here we declare that what is of interest is a concept referred to as body size and that we have a single indicator, the mass of individual animals measured at a single point in time. It is presumed in Figure 4.2 that there is some measurement error associated with the values of animal mass. By *measurement error*, we refer to the degree to which our indicator variable does not correlate perfectly with our latent variable. We may or may not know something about the magnitude of that measurement error, but making a distinction between latent

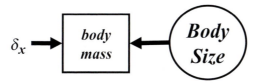

Figure 4.2. Example of a latent variable, Body Size, with a single indicator, animal mass. The term δ_x represents the error associated with our values of animal mass.

and observed variables implies that we believe some degree of measurement error does exist. The quantification of measurement error will be described below.

Reason 1 to use latent variables: distinguishing concepts from observations

Now that a simple example of a latent variable has been presented, we can start to address the question of why we might include latent variables in structural equation models. Throughout this chapter we will emphasize a number of different reasons; here we start with one of the most basic.

One reason an investigator might wish to include latent variables in a model is to make a distinction between the concepts of interest and the observations in hand. By including conceptual variables in structural equation models, we begin to consider more explicitly the theoretical content of variables. Theories are concerned with concepts and how they interrelate. A major part of the reason that latent variable models are considered to be more sophisticated than observed variable models is because of their more theoretical nature. This does not mean that latent variable models are always superior to observed variable models, only that latent variable models have the potential to embody a greater content of information by separating concept from measurement.

It should be said that from a researcher's standpoint, observed variables may clearly be embodied with theoretical content. So, I am not advocating that all SEM models utilize latent variables. However, by including the observed variables along with latent variables in structural equation models, we make explicit how we are relating observation to theory. It is often the case with observed variable models that no discussion of how observations relate to concepts is given, leaving the reader in the dark on this. This issue has significant implications for the advancement of science and I will have much more to say about this subject in the last section of the book. For now, we should recognize certain immediate consequences of including both observed and latent variables in a model. *It allows the model to have explicitly linked theoretical and empirical content.* In the natural sciences, we have traditionally related our theories to the empirical results without an explicit consideration. We theorize about the effects of body size on survival and then proceed to use some individual and specific measures of body size and survival to evaluate these theories. We may spend some time wrestling with the fact that we can measure several aspects of body size, and they do not all have exactly the same degree of relationship with our measure(s) of survival. In the end, we are most likely to pick the one measure of body size, that correlates most highly with our measure of survival in our data set. The resulting statistical model is often one that feels very specific because we have picked one predictor from several candidates, and also less like a proper evaluation of a hypothesis than we would like, because we did not have an initial theory about how our measurements would relate to our concepts. Latent variable modeling seeks to improve upon this situation. It not only makes explicit the concepts of interest and how we have estimated them, it also leads to theories that are empirically meaningful. Ecologists have a long history of theories with vague and nonoperational concepts. Explicitly linking theory and observation in the same model has the consequence of promoting theory with greater empirical validity. Thus, making a distinction between observed and latent variables would seem to have the potential to lead to better science.

Construct validity and reliability

For a model such as the one in Figure 4.2, the *validity* of the indicator refers to the degree to which the observed variable accurately reflects the concept embodied by the latent variable. Validity defined in this way is a measure of accuracy. When our model only includes a single indicator variable, as in our example in Figure 4.2, support for the validity of the indicator must be based on persuasive argument. In other words, the accuracy of the statement, "body mass is an accurate indicator of body size" is one of convention. Perhaps many scientists will be willing to accept this equivalence, but our data provide no support for this claim. In general, the more conceptually abstract a latent variable is, the more indicators are required and the more explicit the discussion needed for the latent variable to be understood.

In contrast to validity is the concept of reliability. *Reliability* refers to the degree to which our indicator relates to our underlying true parameter (which is represented by the latent variable). In mathematical terms, *reliability is usually expressed as the square of the correlation (also called loading) between indicator and latent variables. Reliability can also be defined as the proportion of observed variance in common with the true underlying parameter.* In turn,

Table 4.1. *Illustration of the type of data obtained from repeated measurements of an indicator variable, x (i.e., x – trial 1 refers to measurements of x in the first of three trials) over n cases. The average correlation among values from separate trials provides an estimate of the reliability of our indicator*

Animal	x – trial 1	x – trial 2	x – trial 3
1	1.272	1.206	1.281
2	1.604	1.577	1.671
3	2.177	2.192	2.104
4	1.983	2.080	1.999
n	2.460	2.266	2.418

the proportion of variance of an indicator that is not in common with the true underlying parameter is called the *proportional error variance* (which is 1.0 minus the reliability). As with all other parameters, reliability and error variance can be expressed either in standardized or unstandardized metric.

Returning to our example in Figure 4.2, assuming we are willing to accept body mass as a valid single indicator of body size, the reliability of our indicator is determined by its repeatability. If repeated sets of measurements of body mass are highly correlated with each other, we are said to have a reliable measure. From a computational perspective, the reliability of our indicator is equal to the average correlation between repeated measurements of body mass. Thus, imagine that we obtain the data represented in Table 4.1. Relevant to our example, we might imagine a calibration process where at the beginning of our study we took repeated measurements of body mass to determine the reliability of our measurement process. Data such as those in Table 4.1 can be used to calculate the correlations between trials, and then we can also determine the average correlation. Say, for our example, that the average correlation between measurement trials is 0.75; we would find that the reliability of our measurement of body mass is 0.75.

Once we have an estimate of reliability for our indicator, there are several things we can do with that information. If we have multiple measurements of x for all dates in our study we may simply prefer to average across the multiple measurements and use those average values. On the other hand, if we have multiple measures for only the first time period, but single measurements of body mass were taken for several additional time intervals, we may wish to use our estimated reliability to specify the relationship between indicator and

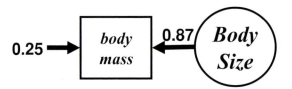

Figure 4.3. Example construct showing standardized path coefficients when the reliability of the indicator is 0.75 (see text for discussion).

latent variable throughout our model. In general terms, the advantage of such an approach is that our knowledge about indicator reliability is incorporated into our model. For single indicator latent variables, the path coefficient between latent and indicator is defined by the *ninth rule of path coefficients*. This rule states that the standardized path coefficient between a latent variable and its indicator is the square root of the specified reliability of the indicator. The specification of that reliability takes place outside the model, either through the default assumption of a perfect correlation (in which case the coefficient has a value of 1.0), or through the inclusion of some estimated reliability of our indicator (which is some value less than 1.0).

Now, as stated earlier, there is a direct relationship between reliability and measurement error. While reliability represents the proportion of variance in common between indicator and latent variables, the measurement error represents the quantity of variance in the indicator that is estimated to be error. Absolute error variance in x can be related to its reliability using the formula:

$$\delta_x = \left(1 - \lambda_x^2\right) \times \text{VAR}_x \tag{4.2}$$

where δ_x is the unstandardized error variance in x, λ_x refers to the loading between latent and indicator variables (λ_x^2 *is the reliability*), and VAR_x is the variance of x. So, if in our example, the variance of x is 0.22 and the reliability is 0.75, the error variance in absolute units is 0.055. If we were to express the results using standardized variables, where the $\text{VAR}_x = 1.0$, then the standardized error variance would simply be 1.0 minus the reliability (which would be 0.25 in this case). When programming a structural equation model, specifying the error variance (and, therefore the reliability of an indicator) is readily accomplished with a simple command statement. In Figure 4.3, our example involving body mass as an indicator of body size is illustrated assuming the reliability of body mass is 0.75. *The standardized path coefficient (also known as loading) linking indicator to latent variables is the square root of the reliability*, 0.87; and the standardized error variance is 1.0 minus the reliability, which equals 0.25.

Types of application involving latent variables

So far, I have illustrated a latent variable construct as an isolated entity, involving only one latent variable and one indicator. A more complete understanding of the use of latent variables comes from studying more complex cases, where there can be multiple latent variables and multiple indicators for individual latent variables. It may help somewhat in our consideration of latent variables to introduce certain distinctions. First, I will distinguish between parts of a latent variable model. Following that, I introduce distinctions about types of application involving latent variables and their role in regression models. Once these distinctions are introduced, I will then proceed with models having more than one latent variable and more than single indicators associated with each.

While already mentioned earlier in the book, here I reintroduce the distinction between the *measurement model* and the *structural model*. The measurement model is the portion of a structural equation model that relates latent variables to indicators. The structural model, in contrast to the measurement model, is the part that relates latent variables to one another. The name for this portion of the model is selected because it is the part that makes explicit how the latent variables are being measured. In the observed variable models presented in Chapter 3, the measurement model is missing. In models that have single indicators, the measurement model is simplistic. Later in this chapter we will present models where the measurement model comprises the entire model, as there are no directed relationships among latent variables.

The other distinction I wish to make has less to do with the anatomy of the model and more to do with its purpose. *Path-focused applications* are distinguished by the fact that we are primarily interested in the regression relationships among concepts (i.e., the structural model). In contrast, in *factor-focused applications* (named for the association with factor analysis), we are concerned primarily with understanding relationships among a set of correlated response variables and, in particular, with evaluating ideas about the number and nature of underlying factors that cause observed variables to correlate. These two types of analysis evolved from the separate traditions of path analysis and factor analysis. The synthesis of modern SEM represents a generalized procedure in which elements from both traditions can be used in a single application. Thus, we now have path-focused models with latent variables and factor-focused models with directional effects among factors. It is important to note that there is a third type of application, the *hybrid* model, in which both path and factor relationships are of strong theoretical interest. What I would like to emphasize here is that in analyses that are primarily concerned with path relations versus those primarily concerned with factor relations, we may have some subtle but important

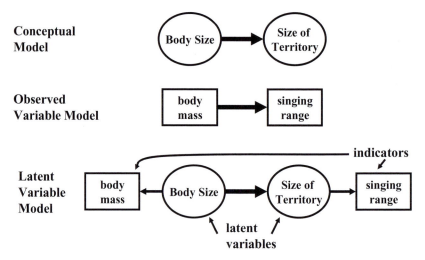

Figure 4.4. Illustration of three types of model. The upper figure illustrates a simple conceptual model, the middle figure illustrates a related model involving observed variables, while the lower figure illustrates a latent variable model combining the conceptual and observed variables.

differences in priorities. In the rest of this chapter, I will first elaborate on path-focused applications and then discuss factor-focused applications. I will end by extending a factor-focused application into a hybrid model analysis.

Path-focused applications

A survey of the published applications of SEM (including historic path analysis) in the natural sciences demonstrates that the great majority have been focused on path relationships. This holds true for models containing latent variables as well as for the widespread use of observed variable models, which by design are exclusively path-focused. Only a handful of SEM applications with a strong emphasis on understanding factors have been published in the natural sciences, although this may be expected to change as more researchers become familiar with the technique.

We continue our discussion of latent variables by considering how they can contribute to path-focused applications. Let us now imagine the situation where our interest in animal body size is with reference to its role in influencing an animal's territory size (Figure 4.4). Our conceptual model of the system at hand, whether explicitly stated or not, defines the context of our model by representing the question being addressed. In this case, the question is, how does the size of

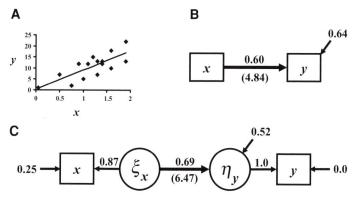

Figure 4.5. Figures used to illustrate important points about measurement error. Path coefficients in parentheses are unstandardized values. Other values are standardized. A. Representation of a raw regression of y on x. B. Representation of the regression in A in diagrammatic form, showing the standardized and unstandardized slopes as well as the standardized error of prediction in y, which is 0.64. C. Latent variable regression model in which 25% of the variance in x is assumed to be measurement error.

an individual animal's territory relate to the size of its body? Also in Figure 4.4, is the observed variable model which might represent this question if we simply used our available observed variables, and made no explicit statement about the concepts they represent. Comparing our observed variable model to our conceptual model helps to make the points that (1) observed variable models are typically more specific and less theoretical than conceptual models, and (2) there is often an unstated presumption that the observed variables used represent the concepts of interest, although this presumption is not addressed explicitly in this simple case. In latent variable modeling, we combine the conceptual and observable into a model that includes both. As a result, our latent variable model represents a more sophisticated model than either our conceptual or observed variable models by themselves.

The impact of measurement error on model parameter estimates in simple regression models

A fundamental justification for the use of latent variables comes from the impact of measurement error on model parameters. This impact applies to all types of statistical model, including traditional univariate and bivariate procedures. Figure 4.5 is presented to help illustrate in a very simple example how measurement error affects regression relationships, and thus, path-focused applications.

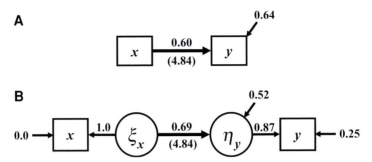

Figure 4.6. Illustration of the effects of measurement error in *y* on regression between *x* and *y*. Path coefficients in parentheses are unstandardized values. Other values are standardized.

Imagine the case where two variables, *x* and *y*, are measured with random sampling and we believe that *x* has a causal influence on *y*. Let us further imagine that there is some error in the measurement of *x*, referred to as δ_x, such that values of *x* obtained are not exactly the same as the true values of *x*. Such a situation would seem to be very common in the natural sciences, and thus may be viewed as a rather normal occurrence. Figure 4.5A illustrates our usual visualization of the raw relationship between *x* and *y*. Simple linear regression reveals a standardized path coefficient between *x* and *y* of 0.60 using least squares, which is shown diagrammatically as an observed variable model in Figure 4.5B. Now, let us further imagine that the reliability of our measure of *x* is equal to 0.75 (as in the example in Figure 4.3). One implication of measurement error in *x* is that some of the error of prediction of *y*, represented as the residual error variance, is actually not prediction error, but instead, measurement error. In other words, measurement error in *x* gets lumped in with the prediction error of *y*, leading to an underestimation of the strength of the true relationship between *x* and *y* and a downward bias of the path coefficient.

Given that we are aware of a less than perfect reliability for *x*, we can represent our regression model using latent variables (Figure 4.5C). Here, for simplicity, we assume no measurement error for *y*. In the latent variable model, ξ_x represents the true values of *x*, which are assumed to be error free by definition, while η_y represents the true values of *y*. The path from ξ_x to *x* is specified by the square root of the reliability, 0.87, and the path from η_y to *y* is set to 1.0. In this fashion, the path from ξ_x to η_y represents the true effect of *x* on *y*. Since we specify a reliability for *x* of 0.75, the error variance for *x* can be calculated using Eq. (4.2), yielding a value of 0.055 (given $VAR_x = 0.22$). In Figure 4.5, the standardized error variance is shown, which is 0.25 (1 − reliability). What difference does all this make to our estimation of the relationship between x and y? The change in the estimated effect of x on y in standardized terms can be anticipated by the formula

$$b = \gamma \times \lambda \qquad (4.3)$$

Where b is the standardized regression coefficient when measurement error is ignored, γ is the true regression coefficient in standardized units, and λ^2 is the reliability. Since in our example $\lambda = 0.87$ and $b = 0.60$, then $\gamma = 0.69$. Our estimate of unexplained variance has also changed, from 0.64 to 0.52 (comparing B to C in Figure 4.5), thus, the respective R^2s are 0.36 and 0.48 (note that $R^2 = 1$ minus the unexplained standardized variance). In this case, unexplained variance is reduced (and explained variance increased) because we have assigned part of the variance in x to error. The estimate for the unstandardized path coefficient is also increased when measurement error is accounted for, from 4.84 to 6.47. This example demonstrates an important point about measurement error – *measurement error in predictor variables results in downward bias in both the unstandardized and standardized coefficients, as well as the estimate of variance explained.*

We can explore the effects of measurement error further by looking at another simple example, in this case, one where the y variable contains measurement error but the x variable does not. Imagine that it is our y variable that is influenced by measurement error, with a reliability of 0.75, while our x variable is measured with enough precision to justify an estimated reliability of 1.0. Comparing A and B in Figure 4.6, we can see that in this case, ignoring measurement error (as is done in A) leads to an underestimate of the standardized effect of ξ_x on η_y, and also an underestimate of the variance explained (or, conversely, an overestimate of the unexplained variance in η_y). However, the unstandardized effect of ξ_x on η_y is not influenced by measurement error in y. This demonstrates another important point about measurement error – *measurement error in response variables does not bias the unstandardized path coefficients, only the standardized coefficients and our estimate of variance explained.* We can add this to the reasons given in Chapter 3 for evaluating the unstandardized coefficients when extrapolating from our results.

Reason 2 to use latent variables: adjusting for the effects of measurement error

The results given above demonstrate that failing to account for measurement error can lead to biased parameter estimates. The simple examples presented involving a single predictor and a single response variable belie the complex effects that measurement error can have on structural equation models (or other kinds of statistical model for that matter). In more complex models, a wide variety of outcomes is possible when measurement error is substantial. The varieties of consequences are such that no single example can provide a representative illustration of the kinds of effects that can be seen. Certain generalizations do apply, however. First, when there is measurement error in exogenous variables, there is generally a downward bias in path coefficients from exogenous to endogenous variables. Exceptions to this pattern can be found in models with multiple, correlated endogenous variables. Here, the effects of measurement error are quite unpredictable, with a wide variety of consequences being documented. Secondly, when endogenous variables contain measurement error, the explanatory power of the model is underestimated and standardized coefficients are biased. Thirdly, when both exogenous and endogenous variables possess measurement error, a wide variety of effects are possible.

Aside from the general consequences of measurement error on model parameters, there can be important effects on model fit and the significance of paths. For a given data set, ignoring or addressing measurement error can shift inference from one model to another. The greater the amount of measurement error, the greater the differences between models. Bollen (1989, chapter 5) provides a detailed consideration of some of the effects measurement error can have in structural equation models. There can be little doubt that measurement error has important consequences for all statistical models. Structural equation modeling and the use of latent variables provide a means of correcting for measurement error, at least in a fashion and to a degree. *This capability provides our second reason for using latent variables, to account for measurement error so as to reduce its influence on parameter estimates.*

Some realities concerning the specification of measurement error

Specifying measurement error can lead to some discomfort as we begin to realize how much it influences model parameters and model stability. Do we have a correct estimate of the true measurement error? Should we ignore measurement error and settle for the less ambitious goal of data description? If our adjusted model is different from our unadjusted model, do we really believe that the results from the adjusted model are closer to the true model? Based on my own limited experience, I would have to recommend that researchers take the issue of measurement error seriously and, when possible, use multiple measurements, multiple indicators, or estimates of reliability to correct for measurement error. Of course, this will not always be possible or feasible. In the next section, I will elaborate on the use of multiple indicators in latent variable models for cases where this is possible and feasible.

I offer three pieces of advice for those specifying reliability and measurement error for single indicators. First, we must keep in mind that reliability is a sample-specific property. In other words, since reliability is estimated as a correlation between replicate samples, the value of that correlation will be strongly related to the range of conditions over which calibration has taken place. If, for example, we are interested in the reliability of body mass values, the range of animals included in the calibration sample should match the range that applies to the data being modeled. Taking a limited or nonrepresentative calibration sample will not provide an appropriate estimate of reliability for our model. Secondly, there will certainly be plenty of cases in the biological sciences where we are working with reliable indicators. When the researcher is reasonably confident that repeated measurements would yield an extremely high correlation between trials, they are fully justified in specifying perfect reliability or ignoring the need to specify measurement error. Thirdly, we should not be complacent about specifying high levels of measurement error in our models. The reality is that when we provide a single indicator and specify that it is not very reliable, we will often find that stable solutions for model parameters are difficult to achieve (for reasons that will be discussed in more detail in Chapter 5). To suggest some more specific guidance on this matter, Kline (2005, page 59) offers the following: ". . . reliability coefficients around 0.90 are considered 'excellent', values around 0.80 are 'very good', and values around 0.70 are 'adequate'." Those below 0.50 indicate that at least one-half of the observed variance may be due to random error, and such unreliable measures should be avoided.

When reliabilities are low, it would be far better for us to use that information to try and improve the reliability of our estimate rather than to take the easy route of "solving" the problem through error specification. Despite the cautions offered here, we cannot deny that ignoring measurement error is difficult to justify. Single-indicator latent variable models allow one to explicitly address the problem of measurement error in path-focused applications.

The use of multiple indicators in path-focused analyses

Rationale

As defined, when the analysis is path-focused, the investigator is principally concerned with estimating the effect of conceptual variables on one another. Why then might they wish to complicate things by including latent variables with multiple indicators? Make no mistake that incorporating multiple-indicator latent variables does make the analysis more complex. Given this cost and the fact that the interest is primarily path-focused, why not simply use an observed variable path model?

There are two primary and interrelated motivations for using multiple indicators in path-focused analyses. One follows naturally from the above discussion of measurement error. Using multiple indicators allows for an estimation of reliability and the apportioning of measurement error, leading to more accurate parameter estimates. When multiple indicators are included in the model (as opposed to using specified reliabilities and single indicators), we are assured that the span of the sample for multiple measures matches the data being modeled. This is for the obvious reason that our multiple measures are part of the data set being analyzed, rather than taken from some other sample. This leads us to our third *reason for using latent variables – to provide for greater generality in our models.* If we are claiming that body size affects territory size, that implies that many different indicators of body size will have similar relationships with territory size. In observed variable models, we typically pick or measure a single indicator and then claim (or hope) that the result is general. In multi-indicator latent variable models, we have an explicit test of a general effect of body size, rather than a specific effect from one facet of body size.

Illustration

To further build our understanding of latent variables, let us imagine that we have in our possession two indicators of body size for individuals of a bird species, body mass and wing length. What happens if we decide to use these two measures as multiple indicators of the latent factor, body size? Figure 4.7 represents this situation.

We can represent Figure 4.7 using two equations

$$x_1 = \lambda_1 \xi + \delta_{x_1} \qquad (4.4)$$

$$x_2 = \lambda_2 \xi + \delta_{x_2} \qquad (4.5)$$

Now, it is one thing to formulate a set of structural equations, but it is another to be able to solve them for values of the unknown parameters. Our challenge in the case of a latent variable with only two indicators is that the only empirical information we have is the values of x_1 and x_2 and only one known parameter, the correlation/covariance between them. To estimate values for ξ in Eqs. (4.4) and (4.5), we must arrive at values for $\lambda_1, \lambda_2, \delta_{x_1}$ and δ_{x_2}. Since $\delta_{x_i} = 1 - \lambda_1^2$, we

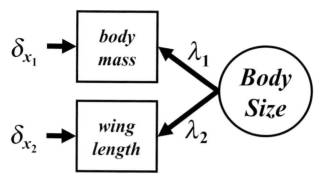

Figure 4.7. Representation of a two-indicator model of Body Size.

only have to estimate the λs. We must still make a simplifying assumption to accomplish this. Resorting to standardized variables for ease of discussion once again, we have the situation where we have one known piece of information, r_{12}, the correlation between x_1 and x_2, and two unknowns, λ_1, λ_2. Given that we have only two indicators for our latent variable, we generally have no reason to suspect that one indicator is better than the other in the sense that it correlates more closely with the latent than does the other indicator. Thus, it is logical to set the standardized values of λ_1 and λ_2 to be equal. Now, we have reduced the estimation problem to one known, r_{12}, and one unknown, λ. All that is left is to derive λ from r_{12}.

In Chapter 3 we encountered the statistical principles that relate to two non-interacting variables under joint causal control. Here we have that same situation, the only difference being that the causal control is being exerted by a variable that we have not been able to measure directly, ξ. The model represented by Eqs. (4.4) and (4.5) (and exemplified in Figure 4.7) is one in which x_1 and x_2 are correlated solely because of the joint influences of ξ. In this model there is an explicit assumption that x_1 and x_2 do not interact directly. Therefore, we should be able to calculate the loadings that would result in a correlation between x_1 and x_2 of r_{12}. As we may recall from Chapter 3, the correlation between two variables is equal to the sum of all paths connecting them, including both causal and noncausal paths (this is our eighth rule of path coefficients). In this case, the only path connecting x_1 and x_2 is the indirect one through ξ. The strength of that path is the product of the two segments, λ^2, which helps us to understand why the correlation between multiple indicators equals the reliability. Since r_{12} equals λ^2, it holds that

$$\lambda = \sqrt{r_{12}} \tag{4.6}$$

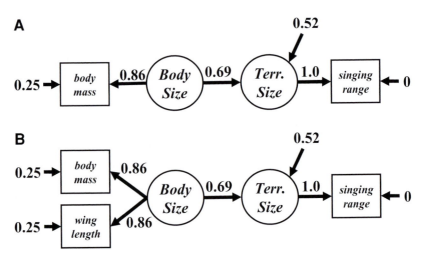

Figure 4.8. A. Illustration of model having a single indicator of body size with a reliability of 0.75. B. Model containing two indicators of body size with reliabilities of 0.75. These models represent two equivalent means of representing measurement error, either by specification or by the use of multiple indicators. Terr. Size refers to the latent variable territory size and singing range is its single indicator.

where $\lambda_i = \lambda_1 = \lambda_2$ and refers to the coefficients (loadings) linking indicators and latent variables.

We can illustrate the application of Eq. (4.6) to our example of multiple indicators of body size. Imagine that the correlation between x_1 and x_2, r_{12}, is 0.75. We would again equate this to the reliability of these two indicators. The value of λ would be 0.87. Figure 4.8 allows us to compare the situation where we have a single indicator of body mass with a reliability of 0.75, to the case where we have two indicators of body mass, each with a reliability of 0.75. The results obtained for loadings, path coefficients, and error variances are identical. What is different in this case is that our definition of body size is more general, representing the variance in common between two indicators.

I would be remiss if I did not digress here to mention that in the analysis of multi-indicator latent variable models, there always exists the need to provide some definition of the variance of the latent factor. Since the latent factor is unmeasured, we must give it some sort of scale by either (1) specifying the variance of the latent variable to be 1.0, or (2) setting the scale of the latent variable equal to that of one of the indicators. This latter approach is accomplished by specifying that the unstandardized loading for one of the variables is 1.0.

When there are three or more indicators for a latent variable

Let us now take our example of body size and territory size one step further, by considering indicators of body size more generally. We can theorize that among a set of individuals (e.g., male red-winged blackbirds, which are highly territorial during the breeding season) there is a general size factor such that larger individual birds are simultaneously heavier, have longer bodies, greater wing spans, larger beaks, and larger dimensions for other morphological characteristics. At the same time, possession of these traits might be expected to correlate with more impressive displays, louder calls, and a greater capacity to intimidate potential opponents. If our hypothesis about a general effect of body size is correct and our several indicators are valid ones, we should expect that different subsets of the several indicators should form constructs with similar relationships to territory size.

Reliabilities can also be specified for multi-indicator latent variables. Take, for example, a case where several indicators exist for a single latent variable. Factor analysis (also known as common factor analysis) can be used to estimate the loadings and errors for the indicators, as we shall discuss in the next major section of this chapter. We may then use those estimates to determine *construct reliability* using the formula

$$\rho_{x_i x_i} = \frac{\left(\sum \lambda_j\right)^2}{\left(\sum \lambda_j\right)^2 + \sum \varepsilon_j} \tag{4.7}$$

where $\rho_{x_i x_i}$ is the construct reliability, λ_j refers to the standardized loadings for the j indicators and ε_j refers to their errors. For the multi-indicator case, construct reliability can again be used to correct path coefficients using the formula in Eq. (4.3).

It is important to point out at this juncture, that the solution of multi-indicator latent variable models moves us into a realm where ordinary least squares solutions, which can be used in recursive observed variable models, are not adequate. Rather, iterative methods such as maximum likelihood estimation are needed for factor models, because of the challenges of estimating unknown parameters from our known values. These challenges come from the fact that we have no direct measures of our latent variables, thus, our formulae for calculating partial regression coefficients do not apply. Because of this, methods such as maximum likelihood are used to try different parameter values until adequate ones are found. This subject will be discussed in Chapter 5, where parameter estimation will be discussed in more detail. Nonetheless, it is still possible for us to relate the estimated parameters in models containing latent variables to

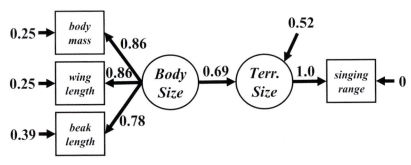

Figure 4.9. Illustration of model of body size influences on territory size having three indicators of body size.

our simple tracing rules from Chapter 3. Here I illustrate this process using a model having three indicators.

Illustration of the relationship between path coefficients and bivariate correlations in multi-indicator models

Figure 4.9 shows hypothetical results for our model of body size with a third indicator included, beak length. In this case, the example has been constructed such that beak length does not have the same loading on body size as the other two indicators; but the relationship between body size and territory size is unchanged. One way we can understand these results is to relate the standardized path coefficients to the bivariate correlations among variables, as we did in Chapter 3. To do this we need to once again rely on the eighth rule of path coefficients, which says that the bivariate correlation between any two variables is the sum of all the pathways connecting them. Thus, as discussed above, the correlation between x_1 and x_2 can be derived from the single compound path by which they are linked, which goes from x_1 to body size and from body size to x_2. In this case, the correlation between x_1 and x_2 is 0.75. Using this approach, we can determine what all the correlations between variables should be (assuming the data are consistent with the model), and these are presented in Table 4.2. Notice that this rule applies to the correlations between our body size indicators and our indicator for singing range as well (e.g., the correlation between beak length and singing range would be expected to be $0.78 \times 0.69 \times 1.0$, or 0.54).

Additional types of multi-indicator latent variables

Multiple indicators can be used in different ways to generalize a latent variable. So far, we have emphasized the case where different indicators represent

Table 4.2. *Bivariate correlations expected, based on path coefficients in Figure 4.9*

	Body mass	Wing length	Beak length	Singing range
Body mass	1.0			
Wing length	0.75	1.0		
Beak length	0.67	0.67	1.0	
Singing range	0.60	0.60	0.54	1.0

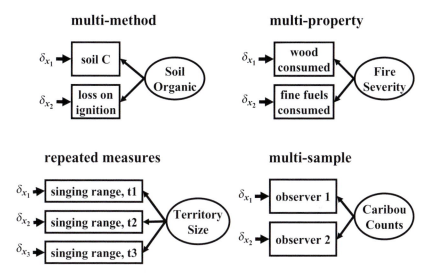

Figure 4.10. Examples illustrating different ways generality can be enhanced using multi-indicator latent variables.

different attributes. It may be worth pointing out a few other ways multiple indicators can be combined. Figure 4.10 shows four different examples. For simplicity, I only show two or three indicators for each. As described below, when feasible, more indicators are preferred. As for the examples, all these represent ways in which the generality of our latent variable is enhanced. We often select a particular method or technique of measurement, whether it is for soil analysis, water chemistry, or vegetation assessment, for economy and simplicity. When we use a single method, however, our results are method dependent. A solution to this problem is to employ more than one method to measure the attribute. Here I show two different procedures for measuring soil organic content, soil carbon determination (e.g., with a CHN analyzer), and loss on ignition.

We have already considered one example of a multi-property (or multi-attribute) model when dealing with body size. Multi-property (also known as multi-trait) models are often of interest when we wish to test general theories. The key question we have to address is whether our traits represent a unidimensional or multidimensional concept. Simply put, if they correlate consistently and strongly, then they behave as two indicators of a single trait.

Frequently, we wish to generalize over time. When we take a single measurement in time, we are often hoping, or presuming, that it generalizes over time or correlates with conditions at the critical time in which consequences ensued. Our earlier discussion of territory size implied that it is a static thing. It is reasonable to assume that for many animals, territory size is rather dynamic. One way to capture this is simply to average the values found in censuses, another is to use the repeated samplings as multiple indicators (note, sometimes repeated measures data require the inclusion of correlated error variables because historical conditions cause errors to be nonindependent). The main advantage of a multi-indicator approach compared to simply averaging the values, is that it affords us the ability to generalize to other studies using individual census survey data. If we were to use an average of, say three censuses, our results would only generalize to other cases where we again average three censuses.

One other example of the use for multi-indicator latent variables is for multi-sample data that is not explicitly repeated measures, but instead, designed to permit generalization of a different sort. Perhaps we have the case where two observer planes fly different survey lines searching for herds of caribou. Aside from the differences in areas sampled, there are different teams of observers as well. Because there are different teams of observers, we may not want to simply add the numbers together, but rather, we can use the data as multiple indicators. Many variations of such approaches can be used when employing latent variables with multiple indicators in path-focused models.

Some recommendations and cautions about the use of multi-indicator latent variables in path-focused models

There are some very good reasons for including multi-indicator latent variables in path-focused models. As I will argue in the last section of the book, one of the most important implications of SEM for the study of natural systems is its ability to allow for the evaluation of multivariate hypotheses. A latent variable with multiple indicators is, by itself, a multivariate hypothesis. While we have referred to the indicators of exogenous constructs with "*xs*", we cannot lose sight of the fact that the observed variables are response variables and only the latent variables represent true causes. Ecologists and other natural scientists frequently propose general hypotheses, such as "body size influences territory size". Rarely do we subject these to rigorous evaluation. Latent variable models hold the promise of permitting such evaluations of general ideas.

Along with the promise held by latent variable models is the need for a healthy dose of caution, as well as a fairly good fundamental understanding of the underlying theory and calculations. We have walked through some of the most basic concepts and will move to another perspective in the next section. Before moving on to a more explicit consideration of latent variables, there are a few recommendations and cautions that apply in the context of path-focused models. The reason I include these thoughts about latent variable models here rather than later is because, at the moment, the great majority of ecological applications are path-focused.

Recommendations

It is recommended that when possible, three or more indicators should be used to represent a latent variable. There are a few reasons why this piece of advice is frequently given in the SEM literature. First, there are sometimes problems with achieving unique parameter estimates when latent variables have only two indicators. This topic was addressed superficially earlier in the chapter, and will be addressed more thoroughly in Chapter 5. For now, let us just say that there are some difficulties that can arise when solving models, and having three indicators provides more information with which to work. I should also add, however, that when such problems arise, there are simplifications, such as specifying equal loadings for two-indicator latent variables, which can make model identification possible. One additional point that can be valuable is to make sure that when you have two indicators of a latent variable they are scaled so as to be positively correlated, otherwise it is not possible to set the loadings as equal.

A second reason to include three or more indicators is to determine more objectively the degree to which the indicators exhibit commonality. When only two indicators are used, as long as the correlation between them is decent (greater than 0.7), they are likely to fit and they will probably contribute equally to the latent variable. When there are three or more indicators, we can assess not only the degree of correlation among indicators, but the equality of correlations. When two of three indicators are highly correlated with each other, but much less well correlated with the third, that is a warning sign that they may not form a stable latent variable. The consideration of a number of indicators affords the researcher a broader view of the quantitative generality that applies to a concept.

We should not take the recommendation of using several indicators too far, however. In the natural sciences there may often be a single or a short list of measures best suited to measure the property of interest. Because of the nature of our data, the use of single- or few-indicator latent variables can be expected to be more common than in the social sciences, where survey data allows for measurement instruments based on many indicators to estimate highly abstract constructs.

Cautions

Individual latent variables are said to behave as single causes. From a philosophical standpoint, we must recognize that all single causes can be broken down into parts, ultimately to the quantum level. For this reason, we should understand that a latent variable is, to a certain degree, a convenience. Concepts (and latent variables) emphasize the common attributes of a particular set of items, while de-emphasizing their unique attributes. Ultimately, the value of this convenience is judged by its utility. Perhaps it is Bollen (1989, page 180) who summed it up best: "Do concepts really exist? Concepts have the same reality or lack of reality as other ideas. They are created by people who believe that some phenomena have something in common. The concept identifies that thing or things held in common. Latent variables are frequently used to represent unmeasured concepts of interest in measurement models."

Figure 4.11 attempts to further clarify the unidimensional nature of a latent variable and how this influences its role in path relations. Simply put, ξ only represents the information in common among x_1–x_3, it does not represent their unique information. Stated in another way, the model in Figure 4.11 does not represent the effects of x_1–x_3 on y. It represents the effects of the unmeasured factor that makes x_1–x_3 correlated with y. Furthermore, even if ξ is the unmeasured cause of joint correlation in x_1–x_3, if x_1–x_3 are not well correlated (i.e., unless ξ exerts strong influence on the values of x_1–x_3), ξ will not behave as a single latent cause, and we may obtain complex model relationships of the sort discussed later (Figure 4.19). Generally, correlations among a set of indicators need to exceed about 0.7 and be roughly equal, for them to adequately estimate a latent variable using covariance procedures.

One additional caution to consider when dealing with latent variables has to do with the names selected. The *naming fallacy* refers to the fact that putting a name on a latent variable does not necessarily guarantee that we have measured the concept embodied by the name. If we claim we are studying effects of body

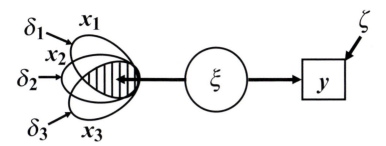

Figure 4.11. Venn diagrammatic representation of shared variance among indicators. Each indicator, x_1–x_3, shares some variance with the others (represented by vertical hatching), and the degree of overlap between them represents their correlations. Only the variance shared by all three variables is linked to the unmeasured latent variable. Error variances for each variable can be thought of as that part of the variance not in the hatched portion. This unshared variance includes both the true error and the unique information contained in the indicator.

size, but we only have a single measure, we have done little to bolster our claim. The solution to this potential problem is a dedicated effort to demonstrate the generality of the factor being estimated, which can be accomplished by studying the relationships among a large set of related indicators. So, if we show that a latent variable composed of numerous indicators reasonably related to size does indeed evidence unidimensionality, we have greatly strengthened our case. It is also worthwhile to be aware that in path-focused models, the predictive context can subtly influence the meaning of a latent variable. When we have a model that relates body size to territory size, such as in Figure 4.9, there are two different ways we can describe what that model is about. First, we might interpret this model as addressing the question, what is the effect of "body size" on "territory size"? This is literally what the model states. This statement also implies that the concept "body size" is independent of the other latent variables in the model. However, there is a tendency for the researcher to select particular indicators of body size that most strongly correlate with indicators of territory size. When we do this, our latent variable "body size" is better described as "the attributes of body size that influence territory size". Since a single word or phrase is always a shorthand statement for a more complex idea, it behooves us to describe carefully the meaning of our latent variable and the context in which it is to be interpreted. This is not a problem unique to SEM applications. Rather, the unique thing about SEM is that we give an explicit and operational statement of the meaning of our latent variable by the indicators we use to represent it. As stated earlier, this is one of the many strengths of SEM.

When we dig into it, we find that there is much to be learned from a dedicated study of correlated indicators. This aspect of quantitative science has been somewhat ignored in the natural sciences. There is much to be gained by an explicit consideration of latent factors and their relationships to indicators. This is where the topic of factor-focused analyses comes in, and is the subject of our next major section.

Factor-focused applications

Some concepts related to factor-focused applications

Factor-focused applications have as their background a considerable literature dealing with factor analysis. In factor analysis there is interest in identifying some smaller set of forces (unmeasured factors) that can explain the correlations among a set of observed indicators. Through history there have been a number of approaches proposed for studying factors, including both empirical methods (e.g., principal components analysis, also known as component factor analysis), and exploratory methods (such as exploratory factor analysis). In SEM we consider factor-focused applications that fall within the tradition of a confirmatory (i.e., theory-driven), common-factor approach.

Our presentation skips over quite a bit of background that may be of interest to the beginning practitioner of SEM. For those who wish to test hypotheses involving models with multiple indicators, a working knowledge of exploratory factor analysis (as well as principal components analysis) is valuable, though beyond the scope of our presentation. A good reference providing a relevant and comprehensive treatment of this subject for those working in the natural sciences is Reyment and Jöreskog (1996).

Figure 4.12 provides us with an overall comparison of principal components analysis (PCA), exploratory factor analysis (EFA), and confirmatory factor analysis (CFA) (as is incorporated in SEM). I need to point out that historically there has been some confusion over the term "factor analysis", which in the past included both principal components analysis (also known as component factor analysis), and what I am referring to here as exploratory factor analysis (also known as common factor analysis).

The reader is perhaps already familiar with PCA, since it is commonly used in the natural sciences. In PCA it is assumed that all observed variables are measured without error. Thus, in our representation of a PCA model, no errors are shown for the xs. The goal of PCA is to create predictors that represent the correlations among measured variables, using a reduced set of variables. This

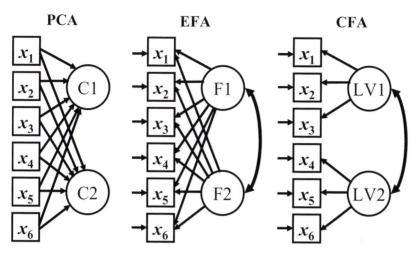

Figure 4.12. Graphical comparison of principal components analysis (PCA), exploratory factor analysis (EFA), and confirmatory factor analysis (CFA).

is accomplished using a rotation procedure that maximizes the variance of the predictors, while minimizing the deviations. In Figure 4.12, I have shown the arrows pointing from the observed variables to the components to represent the fact that components are linear composites of observed variables. Note, however, that what is usually reported for a PCA are correlations between observed variables and predictors, rather than the weightings used to create the predictors. Typically, principal components are derived so as to be orthogonal to one another (i.e., uncorrelated), though oblique (correlated) solutions are possible.

In EFA, it is assumed that some of the variance associated with the observed variables is error, and factors are estimated so as to explain the common variance among variables. As stated above, because of the emphasis on common variance, factor analysis is sometimes referred to as "common factor analysis". Because EFA places a higher priority on identifying causes (rather than predictors) than does PCA, it is more common for an oblique rotation to be used, whereby the factors may be correlated. Certainly there is no reason why causes should be uncorrelated in nature. In both PCA and EFA, all factors or components are allowed to load on all observed variables.

Confirmatory factor analysis differs in important ways from PCA and EFA. First and foremost, our factors (which are latent variables) and their linkages to indicators are posited based on theoretical grounds. Again, as with EFA, it is assumed that the factors are error free while the indicators possess error.

However, the data are not subjected to an automatic process designed to maximize common variance among all indicators. Also, rotation is not used to form factors so as to satisfy some predetermined criterion. Rather, in CFA we seek to test whether the patterns of relationships in the data are consistent with those expected from the model. In CFA, the factors are allowed to correlate or not, without a requirement for either oblique or orthogonal solutions. In CFA, as in EFA, ordinary least squares estimation is not capable of deriving parameter estimates for analyses involving factors; rather, maximum likelihood or some other iterative method must be used to arrive at weightings that satisfy the model. What is most distinctive about CFA, though, is that it permits the evaluation of theory-based expectations. Both EFA and PCA are, in contrast, simply empirical descriptions of the data. The latent variable scores estimated in CFA are computed so as to best represent underlying unmeasured causes, consistent with the objectives of SEM.

Figure 4.13 presents in more detail the structure and notation of a multi-factor model. One way we can recognize a confirmatory factor model (in contrast to exploratory models) is that the arrows from both factors do not connect to all indicators. As has been stated, it is a hallmark condition of confirmatory factor models that loadings and crossloadings are based on theoretical grounds. Also, it is the constraint of not specifying all cross loadings that permits models to be identifiable and for unique solutions to be obtained (in EFA, unique solutions are not achieved and many different combinations of factor scores can satisfy the model – a condition called indeterminacy). Structural equation modeling is about working with confirmatory models, and to put it in the simplest terms, we evaluate a CFA by determining whether the data match the expectations imposed by the model. In spite of the limitations, EFA can still be valuable when pre-existing theory is insufficient to provide adequate guidance and we are getting started towards a CFA. In contrast, PCA is generally an unreliable method for leading to interpretable factors.

Now, there is another distinction of importance to mention. The relationships in the model in Figure 4.13 can be represented by the equation

$$x_i = \lambda_{ij}\xi_j + \delta_i \tag{4.8}$$

where λ_{ij} represents the loadings and δ_i the errors. We should be aware that the error term δ_i is actually composed of two parts. This can be illustrated by decomposing the variance of x_i as follows:

$$\sigma_x^2 = \sigma_c^2 + \sigma_\delta^2 = \sigma_c^2 + \sigma_s^2 + \sigma_e^2 \tag{4.9}$$

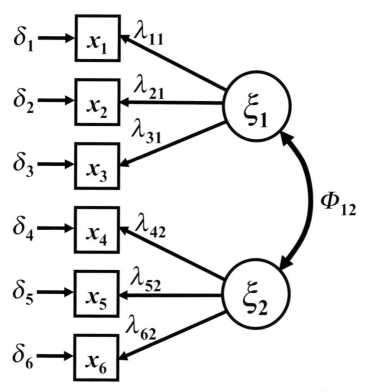

Figure 4.13. Diagrammatic representation of a factor analysis model. The term δ_i represents error for the indicator variables (x_i), λ_{ij}, represents the loading of factors ε_j on indicators, and Φ represents the covariance between factors.

where

σ_c^2 is the common variance or communality, which is the variance shared among indicators of a factor ξ,

σ_δ^2 is the residual variance or uniqueness, which is the variance of x unaccounted for by the factor,

σ_s^2 is the specific variance or specificity, which represents the variance specific to a variable that is not true error, and

σ_e^2 is the true error variance, which is solely due to measurement error and which can be estimated using repeated trials.

In practice, specific variance and true error variance are not distinguished and these two components are combined in the error variance variables, δ_i.

Illustration of the relationship between path coefficients and bivariate correlations in multi-factor models

It was instructive in a previous section to relate path coefficients to bivariate correlations. Here I extend that illustration one step further by considering models containing multiple factors of the sort shown in Figure 4.13. Once again, the eighth rule of path coefficients allows us to determine the expectations, although we have to trace the connections among variables back a little further, through the correlation between ξ_1 and ξ_2. So, the expected correlation between x_1 and x_4 can be seen to be $\lambda_{11} \times \Phi_{12} \times \lambda_{42}$.

Types of validity in multi-factor models

We considered a basic definition of the concept of validity earlier. Here we revisit that concept as it relates to multi-factor measurement models, such as shown in Figure 4.13. There is actually a rather long list of types of validity that have been considered in structural equation models. A modern discussion can be found in Kline (2005). To simplify the discussion somewhat, we can distinguish between assessments of validity that involve external versus internal comparisons. When we compare our factor to some externally established criteria, we may speak about *criterion validity*. For example, does our factor correlate strongly with some key indicator? Two key types of internal validity are convergent validity and discriminant validity, which evaluate the patterns of loadings. *Convergent validity* refers to the necessity for indicators of a latent variable to intercorrelate to a moderate degree. In contrast, *discriminant validity* refers to the necessity that indicators of different latent variables do not intercorrelate too strongly. In other words, for a model such as the one in Figure 4.13, it is generally necessary that the correlations within the two groups of indicators, $x_1 – x_3$ and $x_4 – x_6$, should be stronger than the correlations between these groups. Otherwise, the data will not show consistency with a two-factor model.

Examples of factor-focused analyses

There are only a few published examples of ecological applications where strong emphasis has been placed on discovering the underlying factors causing a suite of indicators to be correlated. A classic factor-focused biological example of this was from Wright (1968) who analyzed the skeletal characteristics of leghorn hens. Aside from the original paper, treatments of this example can be found in Reyment and Jöreskog (1996) and Shipley (2000). A second example is the reanalysis of morphological traits of house sparrows by Pugesek and Tomer (1996). This example is also presented in Shipley (2000) as part of a discussion on latent variables. Here I use data sets dealing with intercorrelated soil properties to demonstrate how correlations can be understood in terms of latent soil properties. I should emphasize that the results presented in these analyses do not represent a thorough treatment of the subject, but serve as an example.

Intercorrelations among soil properties

A Louisiana coastal grassland

Grace *et al.* (2000) measured a suite of soil properties as part of a study of spatial variations in plant community structure. The measurement of various soil properties is common in ecological studies, although it is rare for ecologists to have evaluated hypotheses about the factors causing soil properties to be intercorrelated. In McCune and Grace (2002, chapter 31) and Grace (2003b) these data were subjected to a variety of exploratory analyses as well as confirmatory factor analysis. The measurement model that resulted from these analyses is shown in Figure 4.14. Insight into the procedural steps involved in conducting a factor-focused analysis will be left for a later chapter. Here, I continue with a focus on the anatomy and interpretation of our model.

According to the results of this analysis, the observed correlations among soil properties can be explained by two general factors (latent variables) and three processes that result in correlated errors. Note that it is just as necessary to provide a justification for correlated errors as for other parameters in the model. This is an important point to make, because it is usually possible to make a factor model fit if enough correlated errors are included.

An understanding of the theory behind the model in Figure 4.14 comes, in part, from the physical setting of this study, and what is known about soil formation in the grassland being studied. The study area was a coastal post-pleistocene wet prairie, strongly and conspicuously influenced by the inclusion of hundreds of small natural mounds per hectare. These mounds generally possess a coarser soil texture and their presence creates a topology of micro-elevational variation. In the low areas, hydric soil conditions are evident by the presence of hydrophilic plants. Sampling was conducted along transects that passed through both mound and intermound areas, capturing the full span of variation in this system.

Because of the physical setting and soil formation processes operating at this site, it was expected that soil properties would be correlated with microelevation. It was also expected that mineral elements would be related to spatial variations in soil composition, while soil carbon content, soil nitrogen, and soil pH

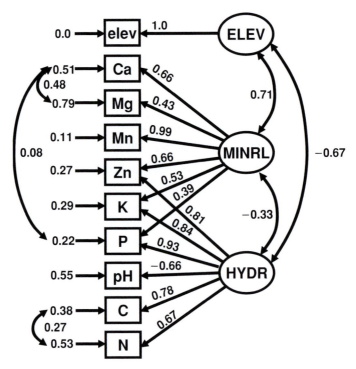

Figure 4.14. Measurement model relating prairie soil variables to latent factors (modified from McCune and Grace 2002). ELEV refers to elevational influences, MINRL to soil mineral influences, and HYDR to hydric influences. All coefficients presented are standardized values.

would be influenced by hydric soil effects. Soil chemical processes were expected to result in a number of complications to the correlational structure. Soil minerals, such as calcium phosphate and magnesium phosphate, are common and expected to contribute to correlations among elements. Finally, in this study, both carbon and nitrogen content were measured simultaneously using a CHN analyzer. This could be expected to result in correlated errors based on methodological effects.

There is sufficient complexity in the correlations among soil parameters to make the picture a little cloudier than one might like. The model in Figure 4.14 may or may not be definitive for this system. It is likely that other processes and historical influences not considered in this model are important to explain some of the discrepancies between data and model. Nevertheless, at least a major portion of the correlational structure among parameters is consistent with hydric and mineral influences. Relating these two soil properties to the

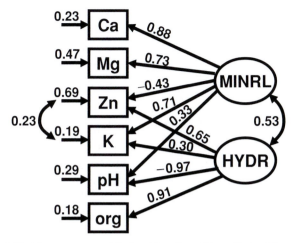

Figure 4.15. Measurement model of prairie soil conditions (derived from Weiher *et al.* 2004). MINRL refers to mineral influences while HYDR refers to hydric influences.

results of a community ordination (Grace *et al.* 2000) was quite satisfying as an explanation for the variations in plant composition across the site.

A Mississippi grassland example

Weiher *et al.* (2004) conducted a study in a tallgrass prairie in Mississippi which was designed to examine the factors controlling plant species richness. Also included in this study was the measurement of a variety of soil parameters. The parameters measured included calcium, magnesium, zinc, potassium, pH, and soil organic matter. The relationships among soil factors were examined for these data, using the model shown in Figure 4.14 as our initial theory, with missing variables (elevation, manganese, phosphorus, and nitrogen) deleted. Since the earlier study by Grace and Pugesek (1997) showed that soil carbon and soil organic content are highly correlated, the substitution of soil organic for soil carbon was considered to be acceptable. Another difference was that the pH data used in the model in Figure 4.14 were determined using a base-saturation method, while those in Weiher *et al.* (2004) were readings of aqueous extracts. Analysis of the initial model indicated (1) that the errors of calcium and magnesium were not correlated, (2) that there was a correlation between the errors for potassium and zinc, and (3) that pH cross-loaded with both the MINRL and HYDR factors. The resulting model had a good fit to the data and is presented in Figure 4.15.

Table 4.3. *Correlations and standard deviations for prairie soil characteristics
(from Grace et al. 2000). N = 105. Correlations shown in bold are significant
at the 0.05 level*

	Ca	Mg	Zn	K	pH	C	Biomass
Ca	1.0						
Mg	**0.790**	1.0					
Zn	**0.468**	**0.450**	1.0				
K	**0.400**	**0.350**	**0.687**	1.0			
pH	**0.284**	**0.309**	−0.054	−0.224	1.0		
C	0.039	0.145	**0.491**	**0.550**	**−0.410**	1.0	
Biomass	**0.288**	0.137	**0.279**	0.163	−0.127	0.120	1.0
Std. dev.	1.58	0.447	0.746	1.437	0.271	2.162	1.350

A return to the Louisiana data

Because the two models presented above are not based on the same suite of
indicators, here I return to the data from Grace *et al.* (2000), and use a subset
of the data that is more equivalent to that in Weiher *et al.* (2004). To make
the data sets equivalent, pH values based on aqueous extracts (which were
collected but not used in the original analysis) are now used. Of interest in this
more comparable analysis is the question of whether the two grasslands (which
possess quite different soil types) both show a similar factor structure. The data
for this analysis are presented in Table 4.3. Now we will look into the results a
little more deeply.

It is conspicuous when we examine data such as the correlation matrix in
Table 4.3 that most soil characteristics are intercorrelated. Of the 21 possible
correlations, 14 are significant with only a sample size of 107. Only a couple
of correlations (calcium with carbon, zinc with pH) approach 0. Clearly, the
relationships among variables are potentially complex.

It is encouraging to find that when comparable data are used, the factor
loadings and cross loading are qualitatively the same for the Louisiana and
Mississippi data (Figure 4.16). These results tend to support the interpretation
that there are similar soil formation processes at the two sites, even though the
Mississippi site does not have mounds or recent coastal influence. However,
some coefficients clearly suggest additional complications (e.g., MINRL to Zn).
I should point out that, in general, comparisons among data sets should rely
on the unstandardized parameters, rather than the standardized ones as here
(see Chapter 3). Ideally, a multigroup model (Grace 2003a), a common model
type in SEM, would allow us to evaluate directly two samples in an integrative
framework. Such a direct comparison is not possible in this case, however,

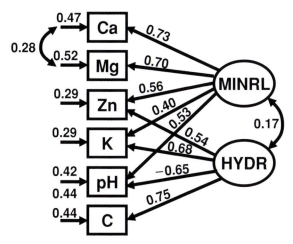

Figure 4.16. Measurement model of coastal prairie soil from analysis of data in Table 4.3. All values are standardized coefficients.

because several of the variables were not expressed on a common basis, or were not measured using the same technique, making unstandardized coefficients incomparable and a rigorous evaluation not possible. Thus, our comparison between Figures 4.15 and 4.16 can only be rather crude in this case, because of differences in the data between the studies.

Several of the specifics differ between models (Figure 4.15 versus 4.16). Based on a superficial examination, (1) the correlation between factors is weaker in the Mississippi data, (2) the correlated errors differ between models, and (3) some of the path coefficients are rather different. One's satisfaction with the similarities between the two sets of results could easily vary depending on the objectives of the investigator and the state of their knowledge. This is the first such comparative analysis of soil intercorrelations that I have seen, and the similarity between the two sets of results was substantially greater than expected given the differences between the two ecosystems and the differences in sampling. The general similarity in results is encouraging for those wishing to compare the effects of soil conditions on plant communities across systems. Substantially further work will be required, however, if we are to determine whether general factor models exist for a range of soils.

Hybrid models

Modern SEM practice and most treatments of the subject are based on the premise that analyses are fully focused – as much about the measurement model as about the path relations. This is partly due to the fact that in the social sciences, where the dedication to SEM has been the strongest, it has long been recognized that there is a compelling case for latent variables. In addition, there is also an abundance of data, such as survey data, that are well suited to factor-focused investigation. Another reason that the tradition in SEM is for fully focused analyses using hybrid models is that (1) experience has taught us that latent variables are valuable, and (2) a thorough understanding of latent variables requires factor analytic studies.

The situation in the natural sciences is different. The application of SEM to natural systems is in its infancy. The work has not yet been done that results in a fundamental merger of path and factor traditions. This is one reason that the presentation of ideas in this chapter is structured as it is. Most textbooks on SEM first discuss factor analysis and only then bring latent variables into path models. Here I have built from strongly path-focused models, starting with single-indicator latents, to models containing multiple indicators.

The ultimate goal of SEM is to work with models that match both the particular and general features of the situation. In this section, I will transition from the results from our example of a soil factor model to a model that seeks to integrate both path and factor foci. I will then follow that up with a more general discussion of the complexities that may arise in hybrid models.

Relating soil properties to plant growth

In the study by Grace *et al.* (2000), the authors possessed data that included a suite of soil parameters as well as several response variables relating to the plant community. The original analysis examined how the full suite of environmental factors related to community structure (McCune and Grace 2002, chapter 31). Here, I illustrate a hybrid model by asking how the latent factors in Figure 4.16 relate to community biomass, a question that was not considered in previous analyses. The proposed model is shown in Figure 4.17.

Note that in the model in Figure 4.17 we are asking how the common variance among soil indicators relates to biomass. Specific effects of individual soil variables on biomass are not included in this model. This is a traditional hybrid model, and our interest in latent variable effects on biomass is justified by our previous finding that mineral and hydric influences (along with an unnamed factor causing calcium and magnesium to correlate) provide an adequate explanation for our correlated set of soil variables.

The results from fitting the model in Figure 4.17 to our data in Table 4.3 are not encouraging. Evaluations of model fit (discussed in the next chapter)

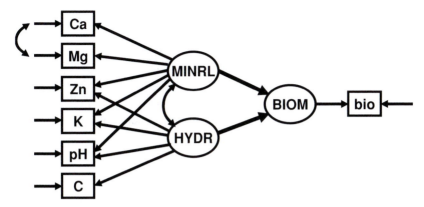

Figure 4.17. Hypothesized hybrid model relating soil latent factors to plant community biomass.

indicate that the model has gone from adequate to inadequate when the response variable biomass is included. Thus, our data do not match the expectations that can be derived from the model and we must conclude that the model is not the correct one for the situation. How can this be when the measurement model has been shown to be adequate in separate analyses and all possible paths among latent variables are included?

The answer to our dilemma can be found by looking for specific effects of individual indicators on biomass. Such specific effects are often overlooked, in part because most SEM software packages are not configured to alert the researcher to specific effects. In fact, for most software packages (excluding Mplus) we must specify a different kind of model to even include specific effects from observed indicators on biomass. In this case, when our model is appropriately configured, we are able to determine that there is a specific effect of soil calcium on biomass that is in addition to the general effects of our latent soil variables. With this reformulated model, we can approximate a satisfactory solution, which is shown in Figure 4.18.

What is conspicuous from the results of this analysis is that calcium, by itself, provides an adequate explanation for mineral influences on community biomass. Thus, while we were successful in estimating latent variables that explain the correlation structure among indicators, these latent variables do not necessarily represent the effects of soil conditions on community biomass. I cannot overemphasize the importance of this result to those wishing to employ latent variables to understand path relationships. *Just because there is evidence for latent factors causing a suite of variables to correlate, that does not*

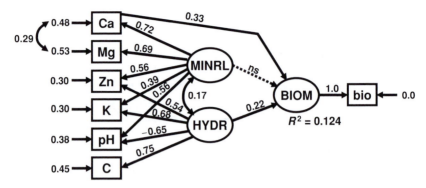

Figure 4.18. Model satisfactorily relating soil properties to community biomass, including both the general effects of latent soil properties and the specific effect of soil calcium on biomass.

necessarily mean that these latent factors are the causal agents affecting other variables in the model.

General cautions about the use of hybrid models

A very considerable amount of the effort I have spent in learning about SEM has been challenged by the need to make certain translations for a clear communication of its capabilities for use in the natural sciences. Some of the greatest difficulties have had to do with limitations inherent in the software and its usual applications. Part of this has been my own learning curve, rather than limitations of SEM software or literature. I expect that others will also face the minefields through which I have tiptoed as they apply SEM methods to their research problems. I do my very best to point out to others in the natural sciences where some of the mines reside. Some of the most important of these relate to the issue just addressed about specific versus latent effects in path-focused studies. The software and most presentations of SEM presume that hybrid models of the sort shown in Figure 4.17 are the appropriate ones to examine. I will argue that it is just as likely that models such as the one in Figure 4.19 may apply. There is no inherent reason to expect that latent factors will capture the variance that correlates with the other variables. For those engaged in analyses, with an interest in path relations, both general and specific effects are of interest. When properly applied, structural equation models incorporating multi-indicator latent variables can examine both general and specific effects, leading to a much greater understanding of natural systems.

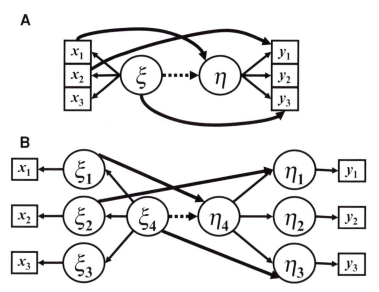

Figure 4.19. Models demonstrating a complex mixture of general and specific effects. In A, specific indicators, such as x_1, have effects on latent variables, such as η, and latent factors such as ξ can have effects on a specific indicator, y_3. In B, I have reformulated the model by specifying specific effects as single-indicator latents, and by using secondary latent variables to represent our general factors.

Conclusions

Addressing measurement issues can be valuable, both for increasing the accuracy of our analyses of relationships among concepts, and in the discovery or validation of general factors that explain correlated effects. Structural equation modeling provides us with an opportunity to correct for sampling and other forms of nonreliability in our measurements. Specification of reliabilities is generally easy to accomplish and valuable, even if our models only have single indicators for estimation of our concepts. The use of multiple indicators to specify general latent variables helps to add generality to our models. At the same time, detailed factor-focused analyses enhance our ability to deepen our understanding of multi-indicator latent variables. Often ecologists have appropriate data for the development of latent variable models, but have lacked an understanding of measurement theory and the characteristics of latent variables. When we say that an animal's size influences the size of its territory, what do we mean? Most of us have assumed all along that general concepts must be quantified with specific attributes, unaware that a general concept with robust statistical properties and theoretical components might be estimated and made tangible.

For those of us in the biological and ecological sciences, there is a need to consider carefully the value and procedures involved with using latent variables. Typically our theoretical knowledge is concentrated in the inner model and largely absent from our measurement model. Thus, the adoption of latent variables in our models requires that we become familiar with the implications of relating latent concepts to one another. Ultimately latent variables represent a potentially evolutionary step in the maturation of our theories. For this reason, latent variables inspire us to seek more general models that match general theories.

5

Principles of estimation and model assessment

Introduction

In previous chapters, I have presented structural equation model parameters, such as path coefficients, and we have considered their interpretation. Regression equations have been presented to help the reader understand the meaning of parameters and how they are commonly expressed. However, we have not yet considered the important question of how parameter values are estimated. Since we are dealing with the solution of complex multi equational systems, this is not a minor matter.

Historically, path models were solved primarily by the use of the familiar technique of least squares regression (also referred to as ordinary least squares, OLS). Today, most applications of SEM rely on model fitting programs that offer a variety of options for estimation methods, as well as many other supporting features. In this chapter our emphasis will be on maximum likelihood estimation, both because of its central role in the synthetic development of modern SEM, and because it provides a means of solving nonrecursive and latent variable models.

Another important issue that is related to the topic of estimation has to do with the assessment of model fit. One of the most powerful features of SEM is that techniques exist for comparing the observed relations in data to those expected based on the structure of the model and the estimated parameters. The degree to which the data match the model-derived expectations provides us with the capability of evaluating the overall suitability of a model. This means we have the capacity to reject models as inadequate and to compare models in direct tests of alternative hypotheses. While not always a simple matter, model evaluation is fundamental to the process of SEM and integral to arriving at suitable parameter estimates. In this chapter I will consider basic principles associated with estimation and model evaluation. In Chapter 8, illustrations of model evaluation will be given, along with additional information on some of the indices of model fit. However, before we can consider the topics of estimation method and assessment of model fit, we must first contend with a basic issue that underlies the estimation process, identification.

Identification

We say that a model is *identified* if it is possible to derive a unique estimate of each of its parameters. Similarly, we may ask whether an individual parameter is identifiable in a model, as this specific attribute relates to the overall question of model identification. The problem in practice is that for some types of models or for certain data sets, it is not possible to achieve this property of identification and, as a result, the model cannot be solved for its parameters. Before going too far into the complexities of this topic, let us begin with what should be a familiar example, the solution of multi equation systems using algebra.

Consider that we have two algebraic relations,

$$a + b = 8$$
$$2a + b = 14$$

In this case, we can readily find the solution by solving the top equation for b, ($b = 8 - a$), and substituting that expression into the bottom equation, which leads us to the conclusion that $a = 6$. Substituting the solution for a from the second equation back into the top equation allows us to derive a solution of $b = 2$.

By extension, it should be clear that when we only know one of the pieces of information, say $a + b = 8$, we have a problem with one known value (8) and two unknowns (a and b). There are any number of solutions that will satisfy this single equation, such as $1 + 7$, or $2 + 6$, or $3 + 5$, etc. Thus, we cannot achieve unique solutions and our multi equational system is not identified. This case is formally described as an *underidentified* model.

The t-rule

From this example we are able to recognize the most basic requirement for solving structural equation models, which is also known as the *t-rule*, where t, the number of parameters to be estimated, must be less than or equal to the number of known values. When considering the analysis of covariance structures, as we are in SEM, we can visualize our known information as the matrix of variances and covariances. For example, if we have observed data

Table 5.1. *Illustration of variances and covariances of observed variables, which represent the known information that can be involved in the estimation of values for unknown parameters*

	x_1	x_2	y_1	y_2
x_1	3.14			
x_2	0.72	0.26		
y_1	3.45	0.72	12.55	
y_2	1.65	0.36	3.85	9.67

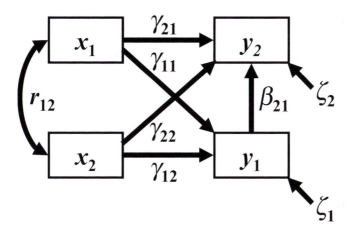

Figure 5.1. Example of saturated model involving four observed variables.

for four variables, x_1, x_2, y_1, and y_2, we might obtain data such as shown in Table 5.1. Here, we can count by hand the number of known values, which equals the number of variances and covariances in the matrix, 10. We can also arrive at this number using a simple formula $n(n + 1)/2$, where n is the number of observed variables (in this case, 4). To illustrate the problem further, we can visualize the number of unknowns for a saturated example model involving x_1, x_2, y_1, and y_2 shown in Figure 5.1. Here, the model parameters to be estimated include the variances of the four variables, plus the six structural path coefficients (r_{12}, γ_{11}, γ_{12}, γ_{21}, γ_{22}, β_{21}). Note that the two disturbance terms, ζ_1 and ζ_2, can be derived from the other parameters using the principles given in Chapter 3, thus, they do not have to be estimated independently. So, there are a total of 10 parameters to be estimated and 10 known

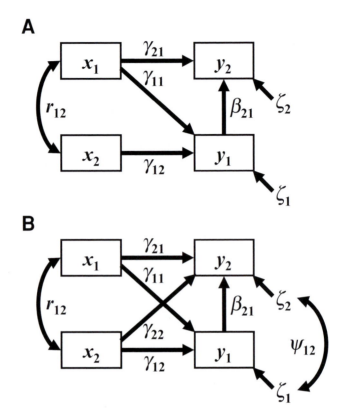

Figure 5.2. Illustration of two alternative models involving four observed variables. In model A, the model is unsaturated and only involves the estimation of 9 parameters; thus, this model is *overidentified* since our variance/covariance matrix contains 10 known values. Model B includes a correlation between the errors for y_1 and y_2. In this model there are 11 parameters to be estimated. As a result, the model is *underidentified*.

parameters. To clarify, some of the estimation process in this case, specifically the estimation of variances and the correlation between x_1 and x_2, requires only that we obtain the values directly from the variance/covariance matrix in Table 5.1.

We can extend our discussion of model identification by recognizing other kinds of models involving four variables (Figure 5.2). In Figure 5.2A our model is unsaturated, since there is no direct path from x_2 to y_2. This means there is one less parameter to be estimated for this model (compared to the saturated model in Figure 5.1). Since the number of known values remains at 10, our model can be said to be *overidentified*, which means we have more knowns than unknowns. As we shall see later, when a model is overidentified it enables us to use the surplus information to provide tests of overall model fit (see section below on assessing model fit).

Other identification requirements

To elaborate on the t-rule, the case in practice is that as a minimum, we must have as many *unique* known pieces of information as we have parameters to estimate. So, the question is, when would known values not represent unique pieces of information? The short answer to that question is, when elements of the variance/covariance matrix can be directly derived from one another, the values are not all unique. Let us illustrate with a simple example. Consider that we have two equations as follows:

$$a + b = 8$$
$$3a + 3b = 24$$

When we rearrange the top expression ($b = 8 - a$) and substitute into the bottom one, we arrive at $24 = 24$. While this is a true statement, it is not helpful. The reason that a drops out of the picture when we rearrange the equations is because the bottom equation is simply 3 times the top equation. Thus, the second equation is redundant since it contains no unique information about the relationship between a and b. So, while we have two equations, they do not represent two unique pieces of information, but only one. The same thing can happen in solving certain types of structural equation models. The most common case is when two predictors (say x_1 and x_2) are very highly correlated (e.g., $r_{12} = 0.999$). In this case, the two predictors actually represent only one unique piece of information, because they are completely interchangeable. In the estimation process, it is highly likely (though not guaranteed) that unique solutions will not be obtained for the parameters. Most SEM programs (as well as other statistical programs) will report that the matrix is *nonpositive definite*, which indicates that there is an apparent mathematical dependency among elements of the variance/covariance matrix. In cases where it is the characteristics of the data, rather than the structure of the model, that prevent the determination of unique estimates, this is referred to as *empirical underidentification*.

Identification in latent variable models

There are certain special identification issues associated with latent variable models. As we have already mentioned in Chapter 4, when latent variables

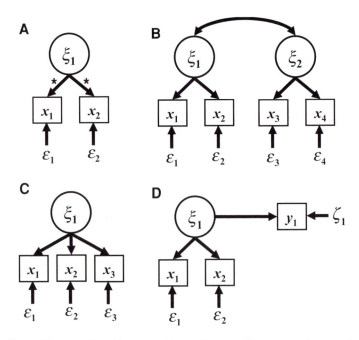

Figure 5.3. Examples of latent variable models used to illustrate certain principles of model identification.

are introduced into structural equation models, they bring with them additional parameters to consider, such as their variances. They can also act to increase or decrease the number of paths in a model. As a practical matter, evaluating the identification of a structural equation model that includes both latent variables and directed paths among the latent variables (so-called hybrid models) can be addressed by separate evaluations of the measurement and structural models. If the measurement model is identified and the structural model is identified, then the full model will be identified. While these conditions are sufficient (except in the case of empirical underidentification), they are not always necessary. Also, it is important for the potential practitioner to note that there are a variety of model parameter constraints that can be used to achieve identification, even when the original model is not identified. Let us look at a few examples to illustrate some of the possibilities (keeping in mind that a complete treatment of this topic is beyond our scope).

Our first example in Figure 5.3 (model A) revisits an issue considered in Chapter 4. Here we see the case of a latent variable associated with two observed indicators. Since our data matrix only has one covariance (between the two indicators), we lack sufficient information with which to estimate the two loadings from the latent to each indicator. The way to solve this problem in practice is usually to specify that the two loadings are equal, thereby reducing the number of parameters to estimate. Note that for an equality specification to be reasonable, the variances of the two indicators should be made equal as well (through variable coding).

Model B in Figure 5.3 represents a case where, unlike model A, we are able to satisfy the t-rule. Since there are four observed variables, we have $(4 \times 5)/2 = 10$ knowns. Including the variances of the xs, we have 9 parameters to estimate. Therefore, our model is structurally overidentified. However, there can be a problem associated with empirical underidentification for this model. If the correlation between the latent variables is indistinguishable from zero, that implies that the two constructs are independent, 2-indicator models. In this case, we have the situation where we cannot identify both indicator loadings for the latent variables, even though we satisfy the t-rule. The solution is the same as for model A, equality constraints for loadings on each latent variable will be required in order to arrive at unique solutions. Model C in Figure 5.3 represents a case where, assuming we specify the scale for our latent variable, we satisfy the t-rule and otherwise should have an identified model.

Finally, model D in Figure 5.3 represents the case where a two-indicator latent variable model is identified. Since there are three observed variables, we have six knowns with which to estimate the six unknowns (3 variances and 3 path coefficients). Therefore, involving a two-indicator latent in regression is another way in which we can estimate models containing latent variables with less than three indicators.

Solving structural equation models – the parameter estimation process

In the late 1960s and early 1970s, the search was on for a synthetic approach to solving the broad range of models related to structural equations. From an historical vantage point, it can clearly be seen that there were a variety of approaches being suggested as means to the end of a unified solution to multiequation models. This is most clearly illustrated in the collection of papers contained in the volume edited by Goldberger and Duncan (1973). Standing out from the many heroic efforts contained in that volume is a paper by Karl Jöreskog entitled, "A general method for estimating a linear structural equation system." Presented in this paper in comprehensive, authoritative form is a method for analyzing covariance structures that has come to be known as the LISREL model. The LISREL model and its attendant philosophy and procedures have had a revolutionary effect on statistical modeling. There have been many refinements,

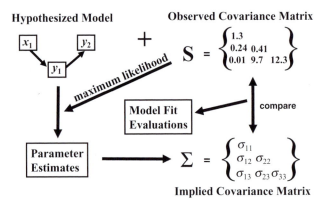

Figure 5.4. Simplified overview of the processes associated with parameter estimation and model fit assessment.

and the body of methodology continues to grow and evolve. While we can (and do) consider the many separate elements that constitute modern SEM, it is really the synthetic system that evolved from this paper and the influence of the associated LISREL software (developed with Dag Sörbom) that has become the core of modern practice. A detailed historic perspective on this can be found in Cudeck *et al.* (2001) "Structural Equation Modeling: Present and Future – A Festschrift in honor of Karl Jöreskog".

A simplistic representation of the overall process of parameter estimation and assessment of model fit is presented in Figure 5.4. The elements of the process represented in this figure are that (1) the hypothesized model implies general expectations for the observed covariance matrix, (2) when the observed matrix is combined with the model structure, we can obtain parameter estimates, (3) the parameter estimates in combination with the hypothesized model yield a model-implied (predicted) covariance matrix, and (4) comparison of the implied and observed matrices allows for assessments of overall fit of data to model.

There are several features that characterize modern SEM as represented in Figure 5.4. First, SEM is based on the analysis of covariances instead of individual observations. This is a strong departure from traditional statistical analyses. At present, the continued evolution of SEM is incorporating both covariances and raw observations, although this development is beyond the scope of the present discussion. Another aspect of modern SEM is the reliance on a comparison between observed and model-implied covariances. While methods other than maximum likelihood can be used to perform such comparisons, this approach is inspired by the maximum likelihood methodology, where the emphasis is on simultaneous solutions (in contrast to the earlier path model method of ordinary least squares regression), and on the differences between observed and model-predicted covariances. These basic features of modern SEM have profound implications, not just for the statistical procedures, but also for some of the scientific attributes of multivariate hypothesis evaluation.

Bollen (1989) has proposed the following general equation to represent the fundamental consequences of modeling covariances using simultaneous procedures, such as maximum likelihood:

$$\Sigma = \Sigma\,(\Theta) \tag{5.1}$$

Here, Σ is the population covariance matrix of observed variables and $\Sigma\,(\Theta)$ is the model-predicted covariance matrix expressed in terms of Θ, the matrix of estimated model parameters. In other words, *this equation describes the fundamental premise of SEM, that the population covariance matrix can be understood in terms of a statistical model and its parameters.* In practice, this means that we are comparing the observed covariance matrix with the covariance matrix implied by the statistical model. This comparison process involves an overall test of model fit that plays a major role in multivariate hypothesis evaluation.

Maximum likelihood estimation

Many of the fundamental properties of modern SEM are derived from the simultaneous estimation process associated with maximum likelihood estimation. Before proceeding further, however, we must recognize that we do not, of course, know the population covariance matrix Σ, only the observed covariance matrix S, which serves as our best estimate. The estimation process, thus, involves comparing the observed covariance matrix S with the covariance matrix implied by the statistical model, $\hat{\Sigma}$, and the task is to choose values for the structural coefficients in Θ such that S is as close to $\hat{\Sigma}$ as possible.

The process of maximum likelihood estimation is one that iteratively searches through progressively refined estimates of parameter values until a set is found that maximizes the likelihood that differences between S and $\hat{\Sigma}$ are only those resulting from normal sampling error. Accomplishing this involves a model-fitting procedure that minimizes deviations between S and $\hat{\Sigma}$. The most commonly used fitting function in maximum likelihood estimation of structural equation models is based on the log likelihood ratio, which compares the likelihood for a given model to the likelihood of a model with perfect fit. This fitting function is commonly expressed as

$$F_{ML} = \log \left| \hat{\Sigma} \right| + \text{tr}(S\hat{\Sigma}^{-1}) - \log |S| - (p + q) \tag{5.2}$$

where there are p indicators of endogenous latent variables and q indicators of exogenous latent variables (tr refers to the trace of a matrix). Some of the most basic properties of Eq. (5.2) can be understood by recognizing that when the sample matrix and implied matrix are identical, the first and third terms cancel each other out, as do the second and fourth terms. Thus, our expected value for F_{ML} is 0 when model and data match perfectly.

A number of assumptions are associated with Eq. (5.2) (Bollen 1989, chapter 4). We must assume that the $\hat{\Sigma}$ and S matrices are positive definite (i.e., that they do not have a singular determinant such as might arise from a negative variance estimate, an implied correlation greater than 1.0, or from one row of a matrix being a linear function of another), data follow a multinormal distribution, and the observed covariance matrix follows from a Wishart distribution (which defines the probability expected when sampling from a multivariate normal population). Maximum likelihood estimators, such as F_{ML}, also possess properties such that they are asymptotically unbiased (i.e., they are unbiased in large samples), they are scale invariant, and they lead to best estimators of structural coefficients. Collectively, the many characteristics of maximum likelihood estimation have led to its central role in the structural equation process.

Other estimation methods

There are other methods that exist for performing SEM. Some are simultaneous "full information" analyses, such as described for the maximum likelihood method. The characteristic of most importance about such methods is that they, again, do not involve individual observations, but instead, analyze covariances. One useful example of such an alternative estimation method is generalized least squares (GLS). The GLS fitting function can be represented as

$$F_{GLS} = \frac{1}{2}\text{tr}(I - S^{-1}\Sigma)^2 \tag{5.3}$$

where I is the identity matrix. This fitting function can be seen to be based on squared deviations, thus, it is in the family of least squares methods. The method is referred to as generalized because the data are weighted so as to standardize against unequal variances, achieving the property of being scale-free. The GLS method shares many of the same attributes and assumptions as

ML estimation. A more complete discussion of the various fitting functions, including a number of alternatives that are of considerable value in particular situations, can be found in Bollen (1989, pages 104–123).

Evaluating parameter significance and consideration of the violation of distributional assumptions

While SEM is indeed a model-oriented approach to hypothesis evaluation, individual parameter values still possess uncertainty, and can be evaluated using p-values derived from the attending standard errors. The principles of the Neyman–Pearson protocol, such as a critical cutoff value for "p" of 0.05, and the desirability of limiting the number of comparisons, are still widely practiced. As we shall see below, reliance on individual p-values for parameters is generally superseded by evaluations of overall model fit, which are not only of priority importance, but also favor the hypothesized model over a null hypothesis (in sharp contrast to the Neyman–Pearson protocol). Nevertheless, evaluating the significance of individual parameters is an important element in SEM. As with other applications of individual p-values, there are concerns about the influence of data distributions on the accuracy of standard errors and the accompanying p-values.

There are several points worth noting in this overview of the topic of parameter evaluation. First, an important distinction needs to be made in SEM practice between data that contain dichotomous response variables, and those that are strictly continuous. The analysis of categorical response variables is an advanced topic that will not be considered in any detail in this introductory book. Nevertheless, if the reader is familiar with logistic or probit regression, they will understand the nature of the problem of analyzing dichotomous responses. Several approaches are possible and much recent work has been done to permit a thorough inclusion of dichotomous and nominal response variables in structural equation models (Muthén 1984). Several issues are involved, only some of which relate to violations of parametric assumptions concerning normality.

A second point to be made here is that, as in other methods for the analysis of parametric data, there is no requirement that predictor variables meet parametric assumptions, such as normality. In any regression, parametric assumptions relate to the deviations from the prediction line, and therefore only involve the distributional characteristics of the response variables. This means, among other things, that predictors can be dichotomous or of any other nonnormal form (except unordered nominal) without impacting the assumptions of the analysis process.

A third point to make is that issues of data distribution (as long as data are continuous) do not generally impact the parameter estimates themselves, only their standard errors and our inferences about the probabilities associated with those parameters. Thus, while we may be concerned with sample-related problems such as outliers and influential points, we will find that the absolute values of our parameter estimates are uninfluenced by methods designed to compensate for data nonnormality.

A fourth point is that in recent years there have evolved a number of methods for evaluating and compensating for certain deviations from normality that are widely available in modern SEM software packages. Among these, one that should generally be avoided (but which still remains because of the historic role it has played) is the asymptotic distribution-free (ADF) approach. While the "distribution-free" part sounds appealing, the problem with the use of ADF methods is the "asymptotic" part, which alludes to the very large sample size requirements for the validity of such methods. Use of the ADF method has largely ceased with the development of so-called "robust" methods (Satorra and Bentler 1988, 1994). In a nutshell, such methods estimate the kurtosis in the data for the response variables, and provide specific and appropriate adjustments to the standard errors. Practitioners will find robust methods highly useful for analyses. Further information on the subject can be found in Kaplan (2000, chapter 5).

A fifth point is that resampling methods, such as Monte Carlo bootstrapping, provide another means of dealing with nonparametric data distributions. In bootstrapping, data are randomly sampled with replacement in order to arrive at estimates of standard errors that are empirically associated with the distribution of the data in the sample. The main advantage of this approach is that probability assessments are not based on an assumption that the data match a particular theoretical distribution.

Evaluating models by assessing model fit

I have stated earlier in the book that SEM philosophy is fundamentally differ-ent from the tenets of conventional null hypothesis testing. In SEM, we do not give priority to null hypotheses. Rather, because SEM takes an approach that is theory-based, a-priori, theoretically justified models represent the starting point for model selection. Also, while we are frequently interested in evaluating alternative scientific hypotheses, there is a recognition that statistical hypothesis testing is more of a means to an end, than the essence of the scientific endeavor. To quote an unpublished manuscript by Hayduk, Pazderka-Robinson, and Zed,

"Researchers using structural equation modeling aspire to learn about the world by seeking models whose causal specification match the causal forces extant in the world." Evaluating models by assessing the fit between expectations and data, or the comparative fit between alternative models represents the method of "seeking models". Characteristic of a theory-based approach, when evaluating structural equation models we consider substantive information when deciding the adequacy of a model or when choosing a "best" model. While p-values are used in evaluating both measures of model fit and individual parameters, a strict reliance on arbitrary cutoffs such as 0.05 is not adhered to. Ultimately, the goal is to estimate absolute and relative effect sizes, and to draw inferences about the processes operating in a system, rather than to reject null hypotheses. Structural equation modeling philosophy is, thus, fairly compatible with recent criticisms of null hypothesis testing by biologists (Anderson *et al.* 2000), although our approach to model evaluation and selection is somewhat different. In this section, I describe some of the elements of model evaluation, with an emphasis on model fit assessment.

The model-implied covariance matrix and the concept of residuals

As we have already seen, the estimation process uses model-implied covariance matrices in the minimization function used to derive best estimators. This iterative process arrives at a final "predicted" covariance matrix that is also used in deriving measures of overall model fit. In addition to being involved in calculations of model fit, individual predicted covariance matrix elements are also useful. One of their uses arises from the calculation of residuals that represent the distance between observed and predicted variances and covariances. A related use is the derivation of so-called *modification indices*, which are often used to help determine if better fitting models exist.

An extremely simple example of the related concepts of model-implied covariance and residual covariance is illustrated in Figure 5.5. Here standardized data are shown to simplify the presentation. Given the model shown and the data, we know from the second rule of path coefficients (Chapter 3) that our best estimate for the parameter value for the path from x_1 to y_1 is 0.40. Likewise, our best estimate for the path coefficient from y_1 to y_2 is 0.50. Based on these results, the model-implied (also known as "fitted" or "predicted") correlation between x_1 and y_2 is 0.20, the product of the two paths. We can see from the data matrix that the observed correlation between x_1 and y_2 is 0.35, thus, there is a residual (unexplained correlation difference) of 0.15.

We, of course, have the question of whether the residual that is observed is simply the result of sampling error, or whether it represents a significant

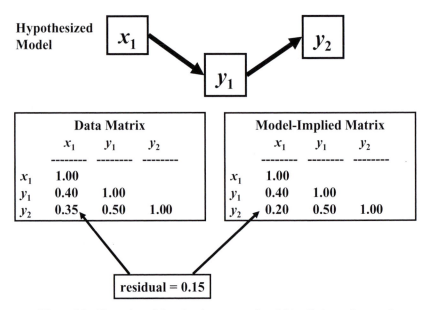

Figure 5.5. Illustration of the related concepts of model-implied covariance and residual covariance. For simplicity, covariances are standardized in this example, although the principles generalize to unstandardized (true) covariances.

discrepancy between theory (our model) and the real world (the population being sampled). This issue will be dealt with in the section that follows. For now, it is important to realize that the very simple example shown in Figure 5.5 generalizes to the universe of structural equation models, including those with latent variables. Appendix 5.1 provides a more technical and comprehensive presentation of how structural equation models can be rewritten in terms of the expected variances and covariances, and how these are represented in the LISREL system.

Evaluating overall model fit – chi-square tests

It is important to recognize that even incorrect models can be estimated using maximum likelihood or other simultaneous solution procedures. Under such circumstances, the estimated structural coefficients may be the best achievable given the model specified and yet fail to create a $\hat{\Sigma}$ that approximates S. This problem is addressed by tests of the overall fit between $\hat{\Sigma}$ and S, which determine if there is a reason to believe that the proposed model might be an adequate representation of the data. One of the most commonly used approaches to performing such tests (the model χ^2 test) benefits from the fact that the maximum likelihood fitting function F_{ML} follows a χ^2 (chi-square) distribution such that

$$\chi^2 = (n-1)F_{ML} \qquad (5.4)$$

Here, n refers to the sample size. In a model that includes paths between all pairs of variables, no degrees of freedom are available for tests of overall model fit. Rather, we say that the model is saturated and has perfect fit. However, for models that have degrees of freedom, the χ^2 test is the most unambiguous measure of overall model fit. Further, when comparing two models that differ in a single constraint, it is possible to apply single-degree-of-freedom χ^2 tests to assess the consequences of making or relaxing a constraint. Based on parametric probability theory, a change in model χ^2 that is found to be greater than 3.84 indicates a significant difference between models.

When evaluating a model, the overall χ^2 should always be examined as a first order of business. The χ^2 is of primary interest because of its fundamental relationship to the fitting function used in the estimation process (described above). When χ^2 values have associated p-values greater than 0.05, authors often deem a model to be acceptable. In my experience, in most situations when the χ^2 p-value is larger than 0.05, there are no pathways that can be added that will have significant path coefficients based on individual t-tests.[1] This condition is not true 100% of the time, however, so it is still worthwhile examining the individual residuals to see if any of them are pronounced (note that the χ^2 evaluation is based on the sum of all deviations, therefore, many small deviations may yield a χ^2 equal to that where there is one moderately large deviation). In addition, models with p-values indicating adequate fit can frequently contain paths with coefficients that are not significantly different from zero. In other words, the model χ^2 test is not symmetric in its sensitivity to missing paths versus surplus paths. Normally missing paths will be detected; surplus paths will not. For this reason, the p-values for individual path coefficients are typically examined as well. As will be discussed below, paths with p-values greater than 0.05 are not always eliminated from the model, despite the fact that a p-value of greater than 0.05 for an individual path indicates that the path may be uncalled for. Again, the philosophy of SEM is not to be a slave to arbitrary p-value cutoffs, but instead, to consider both data and theory when evaluating the adequacy of models.

As with the estimation of standard errors for parameters, deviations from multivariate normality can influence the estimated probabilities associated with

---

[1] Note that when parameter estimates are based on maximum likelihood, the ratio of a parameter to its standard error is actually a z-value instead of a t-value. T-values and z-values are virtually identical except when sample sizes are very small.

the χ^2. When data appear to have failed to meet the assumption of multivariate normality by a wide margin, robust standard errors (Satorra and Bentler 1988, 1994) provide an alternative that seems to hold up well to substantial distributional deviations. Resampling (e.g., bootstrapping) methods can be used as well, in this case it is also possible to correct the evaluation of the overall model χ^2 for distributional violations (Bollen and Stine 1992).

As just described, a nonsignificant χ^2 value (with probability >0.05) is generally taken to mean that there is reasonable fit between the model and the data. However, in practice the p-value associated with the model χ^2 test is not always a workable gauge of model fit. One reason for problems is that the p-values associated with a particular χ^2 are affected by the sample size. Models with large samples sizes will show statistically significant deviations even when the absolute deviations are small. This unfortunate property of the χ^2 test in SEM has led to substantial efforts to develop measures of model fit that are independent of sample size. Probably no other aspect of SEM has received as much attention as the consideration and development of measures of overall model fit. At present, two things are generally agreed to: (1) if the model χ^2 has an associated p-value that is nonsignificant, the model can be accepted (assuming the model is theoretically justifiable in the first place, and the data meet distributional assumptions), and (2) if the χ^2 has an associated p-value that is significant (usually, less than 0.05) and the sample size is large (say, greater than 150), other fit measures may indicate that the model is nevertheless acceptable. It should be made clear that regardless of sample size, a significant chi-square indicates deviations between model and data and this should never be ignored, although one may decide that the deviations detected are not of sufficient magnitude to reject the model entirely. The reader should be aware that the issue of adequacy of fit continues to be debated among SEM specialists.

Other measures of overall model fit

The dozens of measures of model fit that have been proposed can generally be classified into measures of absolute fit versus those that assess comparative fit. Measures can also be cross classified as uncorrected versus parsimonious, where parsimonious measures attempt to adjust for the number of degrees of freedom. A third category of classification is whether indices are only suitable for hierarchical (nested) comparisons (i.e., comparisons between models with the same number and causal order of variables, differing only in the number of pathways between variables), or can be used for non-nested models (models that differ in the number of variables or order of pathways). The topic of model fit indices has probably received more attention than any other aspect of SEM.

The literature on this subject is deep and not all of it leads to useful advice. Therefore, I will not take the time here to discuss in detail the great variety of alternative measures of model adequacy. The interested reader can consult Bollen and Long (1993), Marsh *et al.* (1996), Kelloway (1998), or Schermelleh-Engel *et al.* (2003). Consensus opinion at the moment suggests that multiple measures should be considered when evaluating model fit, particularly when sample size is large (Marsh *et al.* 1996, Kelloway 1998).

A substantial number of size-corrected indices have been developed as alternatives to χ^2. One such index is the *root mean square error of approximation* (RMSEA) proposed by Steiger (1990). This index is certainly not infallible and there is some degree of controversy about its suitability. Nevertheless, it does have certain desirable properties including (1) it is one of the few alternative measures of fit that presents associated 95% confidence intervals and probability values, (2) it is adjusted for sample size, and (3) it strikes a balance in sensitivity with deviations in the structural model versus the measurement model. Other indices include measures of goodness of model fit (GFI and AGFI), and other summations of deviations between observed and predicted covariances (e.g., the root mean residual, RMR). For measures other than χ^2 and RMSEA, only rules of thumb are available, and no associated probabilities or error can be calculated. In Chapter 8, the use of these and other measures of model fit, including information-theoretic methods (such as the Akaike information criterion described below), will be illustrated.

Non-hierarchical model comparisons

Comparing models of differing structure requires an alternative type of fit index. Chi-square differences and related indices such as those already discussed can only be evaluated for significance when comparing hierarchically related models. Assessments of model fit for non-hierarchical models can, of course, be compared in the sense that if one model has inadequate fit and the other has adequate fit (for a common data set), we may interpret one model as being a superior representation compared with the other; one of the examples presented in Chapter 8 illustrates such an application. This approach will however often not be suitable for the comparisons of interest.

In 1974, Hirotugu Akaike (Akaike 1974) employed information theory to arrive at an index that has become increasingly used to compare alternative models (either hierarchical or non-hierarchical). The resulting index, the *Akaike information criterion* (AIC), can be viewed to be a modification of the log-likelihood ratio criterion commonly used to evaluate model fit in SEM. The modification to the maximum likelihood fitting function introduced by Akaike was to correct for the fact that model fit is generally improved by including additional parameters. To counter this problem and create an index that could be applied to models of different structure (e.g., with different numbers of variables included), Akaike sought to take model parsimony as well as model fit into account. One expression of Akaike's index is

$$\text{AIC} = c - 2d$$

where c is the model chi-square and d is the model degrees of freedom. Recall from the presentation earlier in this chapter that the parameter c is one that satisfies the criterion

$$c = sF[\text{S}, \Sigma(\Theta)]$$

where s is the number of samples minus one and the function F is one that minimizes differences between the observed covariance matrix S, and the expected covariance matrix based on the model $\Sigma(\Theta)$. The reader should be aware that there are actually two different formulae for AIC in the literature, although they produce equivalent results (see Kline 2005, page 142 for a brief discussion).

Bozdogan (1987) extended the work of Akaike by further correcting for the effects of sample size on c (which are well documented), arriving at the following

$$\text{CAIC} = c - (1 + \ln S)d$$

where CAIC refers to the *consistent AIC* and S is the total number of samples.

Brown and Cudeck (1989), following a somewhat different line of reasoning, arrived at another alternative model comparison index, the *expected cross validation index*

$$\text{ECVI} = (c/n) + 2(t/n)$$

where c is $S - 1$ and t equals the number of estimated parameters. The ECVI was proposed as a way of assessing for a single sample the likelihood that the selected model will apply across replicate samples of the same size from a common population. While devised from a different starting point, the ECVI shares with the other indices a capacity to compare models of similar or differing structure.

Finally, indices of *Bayesian information criteria* (BIC) have been developed to aid in model selection among structural equation models (Raftery 1993). Such indices ask the questions which model predicts the data better, or alternatively, under which model are the data more likely to be true? More will be said about Bayesian approaches in the final chapter. For now, we can understand BIC to be another information theoretic index, similar in principle to AIC but based on Bayes factors.

The AIC, CAIC, ECVI, BIC, and sample size adjusted BIC are all employed in the same general fashion to compare alternative models. It is common practice to select the model with the lowest index value as the "best" model. For AIC, the model thus selected is the one with the combined lowest chi-square and highest degrees of freedom. For the CAIC and ECVI, there is an additional weighting of models to account for differences in sample size. A further discussion of the principles of model selection based on AIC and CAIC can be found in Burnham and Anderson (2002).

Model modification and its interpretation

It is to be expected that users of SEM will commonly find indications of the inadequacy of their models. This will be especially true in the initial stages of the study of a problem. In addition to indications from the various indices of overall model fit, residuals representing the specific discrepancies between S and $\hat{\Sigma}$ are used by the LISREL computer program to generate modification indices. Consideration of such modification indices can indicate the reduction in χ^2 that would result from including a relationship in the model that is currently absent. It is important for us to understand when modification of a model is appropriate, and how such changes are to be interpreted.

When a model is found to have an inadequate fit to a set of data, we must recognize that our statistical model has failed and also that our estimates of structural coefficients are deemed invalid. At this point, we may either simply reject the hypothesized model or, as is typically the case, we may seek to discover a model that is consistent with the data. *It is important to be aware that any subsequent models developed or results achieved are exploratory until an independent data set is obtained to evaluate the adequacy of the revised model.* This fundamental tenet arises from the fact that structural equation model evaluation is a *confirmatory process*. By this we mean that the χ^2 test is designed to confirm or reject our proposed model, not to inform us of what model might fit the data if we had been clever enough to guess it in the first place. When one explores a data set using SEM in order to generate a hypothesis, one violates certain assumptions of the method. For this reason, model modification and the interpretation of results from modified models must be handled carefully.

While the fitting of structural equation models is a confirmatory evaluation, the use of SEM in studying hypotheses can range from exploratory to comparative to strictly confirmatory. Jöreskog and Sörbom (1996) provide a good overview of this issue in the following quote:

We distinguish among the following three situations:

SC – *Strictly confirmatory*. In this case the researcher has formulated one single model and has obtained empirical data to evaluate it. The model [and its parameter estimates] should be accepted or rejected.

AM – *Alternative models*. Here, the researcher has specified several models and on the basis of an analysis of a single set of empirical data, one of the models should be selected.

MG – *Model generating*. Here, the researcher has specified a tentative initial model. If the initial model does not fit the given data, the model should be modified and tested again using the same data. Several models may be tested in this process. The goal may be to find a model that not only fits the data well from a statistical point of view, but also has the property that every parameter of the model can be given a substantively meaningful interpretation. The re-specification of each model may be theory-driven or data-driven. Although a model may be evaluated in each round, the whole approach has more to do with generating than evaluating models.

In spite of the fact that SEM can be used in an exploratory mode, results thus obtained must be considered tentative. It is particularly important that substantive interpretations be given to any model modifications. Likewise, it is not generally recommended that paths judged to be nonsignificant using an arbitrary p-value of 0.05 not be set to zero and the model re-estimated, unless one is willing to propose that the deleted path represents a process that one has now decided is not expected to be important. It is also desirable when making modifications that only the required minimum changes should be made, in order to avoid *overfitting* (defined as "the ill-advised act of changing a model based on results that are actually due to chance relationships in the data at hand, rather than based on a revised mechanistic assumption").

A second element required before the results from a modified model are considered definitive is subsequent evaluation with a new data set. This requirement has been ignored by many. Yet, the requirement for further evaluation of a modified model in SEM practice is the basis for the philosophy of viewing repeatability as a primary criterion for theory acceptance. Hopefully, in future applications there will be an increased awareness of the value of independent confirmation of SEM model results.

Summary

In this chapter I have discussed the topics of parameter identification, parameter estimation, and at least to a limited extent, some of the associated assumptions and alternative procedures. The simplistic consideration of parameter identification covered in this chapter belies the potential complexity of this topic.

As will be discussed in Chapter 6, up to the present time, model identification problems have prevented researchers from having the ability to solve a wide range of models, particularly those that include composite variables. A further discussion of these problems and some potential solutions is offered in the next section. Bayesian approaches to SEM (also discussed in the next section) can also help in some cases to eliminate problems associated with parameter identification.

A major emphasis in this chapter has been the issue of model fit assessment. A key feature of SEM is the ability to allow for the evaluation of models by comparing observed and predicted covariances. While this kind of evaluation does not demonstrate that a particular model is true, it can be very helpful in leading the researcher to reject models that are inconsistent with the data. For models that are consistent with the data, we still need to be careful to consider equivalent models, and issues associated with interpretative validity remain. Finally, Chapter 8 serves as an important companion to the present chapter, as it provides real-world examples of model evaluation that help to provide a tangible perspective on the practice of SEM.

Appendix 5.1. Technical presentation of the concept of model-implied covariances and how they relate to the LISREL model

In Chapter 5 an elementary treatment of the concept of model-implied covariance is presented. In this appendix, I present a more comprehensive representation of the matter, and tie it into the mathematical framework of the LISREL system. The first subsection dealing with model-implied covariances may provide some insight into the mathematical underpinnings of modeling covariances. Of more immediate use for the reader is the material in the second subsection of this appendix dealing with the LISREL language. In particular, the names of the various submatrices that are described have practical significance, both for reading the SEM literature and for reading the output associated with most of the leading software programs.

Model-implied covariances

As stated in Chapter 5, the following equation summarizes the formal problem of expressing the relationship between data and model:

$$\Sigma = \Sigma(\Theta) \tag{5.1.1}$$

Σ is the population covariance matrix of observed variables and $\Sigma(\Theta)$ is the model-implied covariance matrix expressed in terms of Θ, the matrix of estimated model parameters. The term $\Sigma(\Theta)$ is sometimes expressed as $\hat{\Sigma}$.

To illustrate, take for example a simple regression model

$$y = \gamma x + \zeta \tag{5.1.2}$$

where y is a dependent variable, x an independent variable, γ is the regression coefficient, and ζ is the disturbance or error term. In structural equation terms, both γ and ζ are understood to be structural coefficients, and in this case will be the two elements of the theta vector in Eq. (5.1.1). Both the variance of y and its covariance with x can be written in terms of the variances of x and ζ, as well as the structural coefficients, as shown in Eqs. (5.1.3) and (5.1.4).

$$\text{VAR}(y) = \gamma^2 \text{VAR}(x) + \text{VAR}(\zeta) \tag{5.1.3}$$

$$\text{COV}(x, y) = \gamma \text{VAR}(x) \tag{5.1.4}$$

Through these equivalencies, a relationship is established between the statistical model and its implied covariance matrix in terms of Eq. (5.1.1).

We now have an equation (5.1.5) that establishes expected values for the variance of y and the covariance of y with x, based on the form of the equation in (5.1.2) and the estimated structural coefficients. These expected values can then be compared with the observed values to see how well the statistical model fits the data.

$$\begin{bmatrix} \text{VAR}(y) & \\ \text{COV}(x, y) & \text{VAR}(x) \end{bmatrix} = \begin{bmatrix} \gamma^2 \text{VAR}(x) + \text{VAR}(\zeta) & \\ \gamma \text{VAR}(x) & \text{VAR}(x) \end{bmatrix} \tag{5.1.5}$$

To better appreciate the flexibility implied by Eq. (5.1.1), we can consider a different type of example, a simple latent variable model. In this case, the values of two measured variables, x_1 and x_2, are hypothesized to be caused by a single unmeasured latent variable ξ (x_i) as expressed by the equations (5.1.6) and (5.1.7).

$$x_1 = \xi + \delta_1 \tag{5.1.6}$$

$$x_2 = \xi + \delta_2 \tag{5.1.7}$$

Each equation includes a term for a random disturbance variable δ. We recognize that the latent variable ξ has both a mean and variance, with the variance designated by ϕ, thus

$$\text{VAR}(x_1) = \text{VAR}(\xi) + \text{VAR}(\delta_1) = \phi + \text{VAR}(\delta_1) \tag{5.1.8}$$

$$\text{VAR}(x_2) = \text{VAR}(\xi) + \text{VAR}(\delta_2) = \phi + \text{VAR}(\delta_2) \tag{5.1.9}$$

and the covariance between x_1 and x_2 is defined by the variance of the common latent factor ϕ. Now, Eq. (5.1.1) becomes

$$\begin{bmatrix} \text{VAR}(x_1) & \\ \text{COV}(x_1, x_2) & \text{VAR}(x_2) \end{bmatrix} = \begin{bmatrix} \phi + \text{VAR}(\delta_1) & \\ \phi & \phi + \text{VAR}(\delta_2) \end{bmatrix} \quad (5.1.10)$$

As will be shown in the next section, it is possible to express implied covariance matrices for a wide variety of structural equation models using the language of LISREL.

The LISREL language

Keesling (1972), Jöreskog (1973), and Wiley (1973) almost simultaneously developed the LISREL (linear structural relationships) model and its notation, which has become the standard for expressing structural equation models. Jöreskog and Sörbom went on to develop the LISREL computer software for performing SEM, which has played a central role in the application of these methods, although there are now many other software packages available.

The LISREL model is based on three matrix equations. The first is the equation describing the relationships among latent conceptual variables, sometimes also referred to as the *latent variable model* or *structural model*,

$$\eta = \mathbf{B}\eta + \mathbf{\Gamma}\xi + \zeta \quad (5.1.11)$$

This equation is composed of (1) three vectors of variables, (2) two matrices of coefficients, and (3) two matrices of covariances. The three vectors of variables are

η, an $m \times 1$ vector of latent endogenous variables,
ξ, an $n \times 1$ vector of latent exogenous variables, and
ζ, an $m \times 1$ vector of latent errors for the latent endogenous variables,

where m is the number of latent endogenous variables and n is the number of latent exogenous variables. Note that endogenous variables are dependent latent variables (i.e., those with an arrow pointing towards them from another latent variable. Exogenous variables are independent latent variables.

The two matrices of coefficients in Eq. (5.1.11) are

$\mathbf{B}$, an $m \times m$ matrix of structural coefficients describing the relationships among endogenous latent variables, and

$\mathbf{\Gamma}$, an $m \times n$ matrix of structural coefficients describing the effects of exogenous latent variables on endogenous ones.

The matrices of covariances are

Φ, an $n \times n$ matrix of covariances among latent exogenous variables, and
Ψ, an $m \times m$ matrix of covariances among the errors of latent variables.

The other two equations that compose the LISREL model represent the *measurement model*, the relationships between latent and observed variables. (Note that observed variables are also referred to as indicators, manifest variables, and measured variables, and that I switch between these terms regularly.) These two equations separately describe how the exogenous and endogenous latent variables are measured.

$$x = \Lambda_x \xi + \delta \qquad (5.1.12)$$

$$y = \Lambda_y \eta + \varepsilon \qquad (5.1.13)$$

These equations include four vectors of variables

x, a $q \times 1$ vector of observed indicators of the exogenous latent variables contained in ξ,

y, a $p \times 1$ vector of observed indicators of the endogenous latent variables contained in η,

δ, a $q \times 1$ vector of measurement error terms for the indicators of the latent exogenous variables in x, and

ε, a $p \times 1$ vector of measurement error terms for the indicators of the latent endogenous variables in y,

as well as two matrices of coefficients

Λ_x, a $q \times n$ matrix of coefficients relating xs to ξ, the vector of exogenous latent variables, and

Λ_y, a $p \times m$ matrix of coefficients relating ys to η, the vector of endogenous latent variables.

While not shown in Eqs. (5.1.12) and (5.1.13), there are two additional matrices associated with the measurement model,

Θ_δ, a $q \times q$ matrix of covariances among the measurement errors for indicators of the latent exogenous variables in δ, and

Θ_ϵ, a $p \times p$ matrix of covariances among the measurement errors for indicators of the latent endogenous variables in ϵ.

Now that we have equations and notation describing the main parts of the LISREL model, it is possible to use them to express the complete set of expectations for a full structural equation model. Equation (5.1.1) now takes the form

$$
\Sigma = \begin{vmatrix} \text{covariances} & \text{covariances} & \\ \text{among } \mathbf{y}\text{s} & \text{between } \mathbf{y}\text{s and } \mathbf{x}\text{s} & \\ \hline \text{covariances} & \text{covariances} & \\ \text{between } \mathbf{x}\text{s and } \mathbf{y}\text{s} & \text{among } \mathbf{x}\text{s} & \end{vmatrix}. \qquad (5.1.14)
$$

There is insufficient space in this short chapter to give the derivations of the four submatrix elements. The interested reader is referred to Hayduk (1987, chapter 4, section 4) for a lucid account of the process. It is helpful, nonetheless, to present the equations for the four submatrices individually. First, the equation for the lower right submatrix is

$$
\text{covariances among } \mathbf{x}\text{s} = \Lambda_x \Phi \Lambda'_x + \Theta_\delta \qquad (5.1.15)
$$

This is essentially Φ, the matrix of covariances among latent exogenous variables (ξ), premultiplied by Λ_x, the coefficients relating x to ξ, plus Θ_δ, the covariances among indicator errors. Secondly, the equation in the upper left submatrix describing the covariances among latent response variables is necessarily more complex. Here I describe it in two stages, with the first giving part of the equation in symbols and part in words, as

$$
\text{covariances among } \mathbf{y}\text{s} = \Lambda_y [\text{covariances among } \eta\text{s}] \Lambda'_y + \Theta_\varepsilon \qquad (5.1.16)
$$

Now, we fill in the words in Eq. (5.1.16) with

$$
\text{covariances among } \eta\text{s} = \mathbf{A}(\Gamma \Phi \Gamma' + \Psi)\mathbf{A}' \qquad (5.1.17)
$$

where $\mathbf{A} = (\mathbf{I} - \mathbf{B})^{-1}$, the inverse of the beta matrix subtracted from the identity matrix and $\mathbf{A}'$ is the transpose of $\mathbf{A}$. The third submatrix equation to define (lower left quadrant) is

$$
\text{covariances between } \mathbf{x}\text{s and } \mathbf{y}\text{s} = \Lambda_x \Phi \Gamma' \, \mathbf{A}' \Lambda'_y \qquad (5.1.18)
$$

which gives the expected cross-products between xs and ys in terms of their measurement models (Eqs. (5.1.12) and (5.1.13)). Finally, the upper right quadrant of our general equation (5.1.14) contains the transpose of the equation in the lower left (5.1.18)

$$
[\text{covariances between } \mathbf{x}\text{s and } \mathbf{y}\text{s}]' = \Lambda_y \mathbf{A} \Gamma \Phi \Lambda'_x \qquad (5.1.19)
$$

Plugging Eqs. (5.1.15) through (5.1.19) into (5.1.14) gives the LISREL equivalent of Eq. (5.1.1) in the form given by Jöreskog

$$
\Sigma = \begin{vmatrix} \mathbf{\Lambda}_y \mathbf{A} (\mathbf{\Gamma}\mathbf{\Phi}\mathbf{\Gamma}' + \mathbf{\Psi}) \mathbf{A}' \mathbf{\Lambda}' y + \mathbf{\Theta}_\varepsilon & \mathbf{\Lambda}_y \mathbf{A}\mathbf{\Gamma}\mathbf{\Phi}\mathbf{\Lambda}'_x \\ \mathbf{\Lambda}_x \mathbf{\Phi}\mathbf{\Gamma}'\mathbf{A}'\mathbf{\Lambda}'_y & \mathbf{\Lambda}_x \mathbf{\Phi}\mathbf{\Lambda}'_x + \mathbf{\Theta}_\delta \end{vmatrix}
\tag{5.1.20}
$$

This is not an equation that the reader needs to memorize. Rather, it is an expression of the LISREL notation that describes how matrices can be used to express, in a rather comprehensive way, the covariance expectations from a full structural equation model that includes both latent variables and measurement models.

PART III

Advanced topics

6

Composite variables and their uses

Introduction

It would seem that structural equation modeling holds the promise of providing scientists the capacity to evaluate a wide range of complex questions about systems. The incorporation of both conceptual and observed variables can be particularly advantageous by allowing data to interface directly with theory. Up to this present time, the emphasis in SEM has been on latent variables as the means of conveying theoretical concepts. It is my view that this is quite limiting. As we saw in the final section of Chapter 4, causal relationships in a model may deviate quite a lot from the stereotypic "hybrid" model. In the current chapter, I discuss the use of an additional variable type, the composite, in structural equation models. In simple terms, composite variables represent the influences of collections of other variables. As such, they can be helpful for (1) representing complex, multifaceted concepts, (2) managing model complexity, and (3) facilitating our ability to generalize. In my experience, these are all highly desirable capabilities when representing ecological systems and, as a result, I frequently find myself including composites in models.

While long recognized as a potentially important element of SEM, composite variables have received very limited use, in part because of a lack of theoretical consideration, but also because of difficulties that arise in parameter estimation when using conventional solution procedures. In this chapter I tackle both the theoretical and practical issues associated with composites. To accomplish this, it will be necessary to introduce additional terms, as well as a framework for deciding when a composite is appropriate to include in a model.

The question of what is appropriate in a structural equation model must be judged relative to the theoretical concepts, as well as the variables measured, and the nature of the data. In this chapter I introduce the idea of the "construct model", which is the theoretical precursor to the development of a structural equation model. I will consider the various possibilities for how observed variables relate to constructs and the resulting model architectures. This transition from theory to model represents a phase of SEM that is largely absent from other general treatments. I believe it is the "missing link" in most modeling exercises, and should be studied carefully by those interested in developing their own structural equation models.

History

As early as 1964, Blalock pointed out the need to represent some constructs using composites. In particular, when the indicator variables associated with a construct are viewed as causes of that construct, rather than effects, a composite variable can be used in a model to represent that association. Heise (1972) extended the discussion by providing explicit demonstrations of several examples where composites would be appropriate. In addition, Heise discussed some of the problems with estimating models containing composites, and provided a limited set of solutions within a least squares framework. Periodically, practitioners of SEM have continued to raise the need for careful consideration of the best way to represent constructs given the available data. Bollen (1984) cautioned that a set of indicators for a latent variable should possess "internal consistency" (i.e., they should represent a single entity and, therefore, would be expected to be highly intercorrelated and joint responsive). He went on to point out that we should differentiate between the case where the concept of interest is the cause of some set of observed responses (i.e., is a latent factor), and the opposing case where the observed variables have causal influences on the concept (i.e., composites). A number of authors have continued to discuss the issue (Bollen and Lennox 1991, MacCallum and Browne 1993), with an increased interest in the subject emerging in recent years (Bollen and Ting 2000, Diamantopoulous and Winklhofer 2001, Edwards 2001, Jarvis *et al.* 2003, Williams *et al.* 2003). This literature has provided a number of useful insights, diagnostic procedures, and approaches to the question of how to treat concepts with only causal indicators. Overall, however, a clear, comprehensive, and satisfying framework for considering composites has only recently begun to emerge (Grace and Bollen, unpublished). This chapter presents an overview of that framework, along with examples, diagnostics, and procedures.

Terminology

A consideration of the subject of composites requires that we have sufficient terminology to express clearly the relevant relationships. To begin with, I

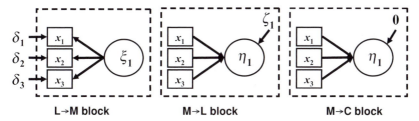

Figure 6.1. Representation of blocks specifying relationships between manifest (observed) indicators (in boxes) and latent or composite variables (in circles). L refers to a latent variable or unmeasured cause, M refers to manifest variables, and C refers to a composite, which is a direct product of some set of causes without error. It is characteristic of my presentation of composites that they have zero error variance.

distinguish between the underlying theoretical *constructs* of interest, and the conceptual variables used to represent how the data relate to the constructs. I define for this discussion two types of conceptual variable, latent variables, which are unmeasured causes, and *composites*, which are variables that represent collections of causes. Composites can reflect the joint effects of sets of either manifest or latent variables. A composite can thus be referred to as either a *composite of manifest variables* or a *composite of latent variables*. I also stress that the issue of how to represent a construct deals with the interrelations between a latent or composite variable and the associated variables that give it meaning. A *block* is the basic unit to consider and several types of block are illustrated in Figures 6.1 and 6.2. The reader should be aware that in this chapter I will use the terms "observed" and "manifest" interchangeably to refer to the directly measured variables. The term "indicator" refers to an observed or manifest variable that is associated with a conceptual variable.

In Figure 6.1 we see that, given a set of three manifest variables, $x_1 - x_3$, there are various ways they can be related to conceptual variables, depending on how the data relate to the theoretical construct. The most common representation is the L→M block, where paths go from latent to manifest variables. In this block type, the latent variable is used to represent an unmeasured cause or factor that leads to correlations among manifest variables. A great deal has been written about the properties of L→M blocks, and they form the backbone of latent variable modeling (Bollen 1989); this is the subject of Chapter 4. Some of the expected properties of blocks of this type will be considered below in Example 1, along with diagnostics that help us to evaluate whether either theory or empirical relations are consistent with this representation of a construct. An alternative terminology that has been used for this case refers to a "latent variable with effect indicators". There is a long history of the use of the alternative terms "effect indicators" (as in the L→M block in Figure 6.1 and "causal indicators" (as in the M→L block in Figure 6.1), and I also use these terms occasionally.

The M→L block shown in Figure 6.1 represents the situation where manifest variables have causal influences on a latent variable that possesses no effect indicators (no outward path to a manifest variable). By referring to the conceptual variable as a latent variable in this case, we infer that a latent factor does indeed exist, independent from our data despite the fact that we do not have effect indicators by which it can be measured. Graphically, this property of independent existence for the latent variable is represented by the presence of an error variance ζ_1, which implies that while the xs have causal effects on η_1, they do not completely define it.

In contrast to the M→L block is the M→C block, in which the conceptual variable represented is a composite. Since the error variance is specified to be 0 for a composite, this signifies that it is completely defined by its causes. There actually exist two kinds of composite – one is the *fixed composite*. In this type, the loadings from causes are specified *a priori* to have particular values by way of definition. An ecologically relevant example would be the importance value, which is defined as the sum of the relative density, relative abundance, and relative frequency (usually for a species within a community). A second type of composite is the *statistical composite*, which is the type considered in this discussion. A statistical composite represents the collective effects of a set of causes on some response variable(s). Such a composite does not exist separately from the associated response variables. In simplistic terms, the statistical composite is akin to a multiple regression predictor, some weighted combination of causal influences that maximizes variance explanation in one or more response variables. This predictor can have theoretical meaning, and can be quite useful in developing structural equation models that involve multifaceted concepts.

Composites can represent collections of influences from both latent and manifest variables. Figure 6.2 presents examples of blocks where relationships between conceptual variables are considered. The L→L block represents effects of latent causes on a latent response, where all latent variables have effect indicators. This is the standard block type found in the hybrid model discussed in most introductory SEM treatments. What is represented by this block structure is that mechanisms of causal interaction are actually among latent factors, and we can understand the covariances among a set of x and y variables based on that mechanism. Also implied is that the effect indicators associated with each latent variable serve as multiple measures of the latent factors. Because the flow of causation is from the latent factors to the indicators, error terms are used to represent how well the indicators are predicted by the model; while the latent factors are presumed to be free from measurement error.

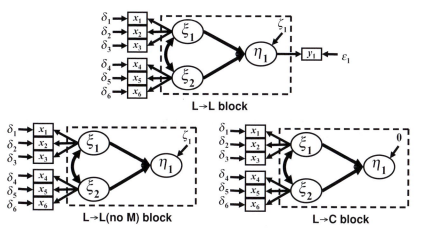

Figure 6.2. Representation of blocks specifying relationships between latent causes and latent or composite conceptual variables. Block terminology is described in the caption for Figure 6.1.

The L→L(no M) block in Figure 6.2 represents causal influence from latent variables that have effect indicators, to a latent variable for which there is no effect indicator. This block type resembles the M→L block in Figure 6.1, except for the fact that latent causes replace the manifest ones. Similarly, the L→C block in Figure 6.2 is analogous to the M→C block in Figure 6.1. The relevant situations for these representations will be illustrated in the example applications below.

Examples

Rather than continuing to elaborate on constructs, blocks, and composites in the abstract, the remaining development of ideas, as well as the development of formal notation, will be conducted in the context of specific examples. The reader should keep in mind that while not representing an exhaustive treatment of the subject, the examples chosen and procedures discussed in conjunction with those examples are broadly applicable to the general issues associated with incorporating conceptual variables into structural equation models.

Example 1: colonization of forest patches by understory herbs

Background

In a recent paper, Verheyen *et al.* (2003) addressed the influences of a variety of factors on the ability of herbaceous plant species to recolonize forest stands in a fragmented landscape. Their work can be viewed as an effort to evaluate a dichotomy of pre-existing theories. On the one hand, island biogeographic theory suggests that successful colonization will be limited by factors such as the age of an island (in this case, a forest stand is equivalent to an island), and the distance to a source population. On the other hand, the local conditions in a forest stand (such as soil conditions and the abundance of competitors) are frequently invoked as the ultimate limiting factors for successful colonization. The relative importance of effects is what is of interest in this case.

In this example, the authors examined colonization success and related it to forest stand attributes in a nature reserve in Belgium that has had a long history of agricultural use and forest fragmentation. In this landscape, much of the original forest cover was gradually removed, and in places, discrete stands of trees were replanted, creating a mosaic of ancient and contemporary stands. Land use history of the 360-ha preserve was reconstructed using maps dating back into the 1700s, and aerial photographs dating back to the 1940s. Using the historical records, the age of each forest stand in the landscape was determined. Extensive surveys of forest herb species throughout the entire preserve were conducted in 1999, along with characterizations of forest understory cover and soil conditions in individual stands. Together, the sources of data allowed the authors to estimate the number of colonizations by each herb species in contemporary forest stands, and the distance to the nearest population in the ancient stands, which was presumed to be a possible source for colonization. A total of 180 forest stands were in the final data set, with ages from 1 to 195 years old. All species that were included in the analyses are obligate forest understory perennials.

The authors' initial model of construct relations is shown in Figure 6.3. As represented here, the authors were interested in differentiating between the effects of two exogenous influences, landscape properties and soil conditions, on competitor abundance and ultimately colonization success. The authors used a two-stage analysis to evaluate the model in Figure 6.3, first deriving composite indices for the conceptual variables, and then using composite scores in a path analysis of relations among constructed composites. Here I provide a more formal illustration of how constructs and indicators can be evaluated, and discuss issues related to the solution of structural equation models containing composites. A selective subset of the data analyzed by Verheyen *et al.* (2003) is examined here, and it is important to point out that the purpose is not to confirm or contradict the biological conclusions of the original analysis, but rather, to illustrate the use of composite variables. Data characteristics were considered in this analysis and corrective actions (e.g., transformations) were taken where needed; the particulars are not discussed further here.

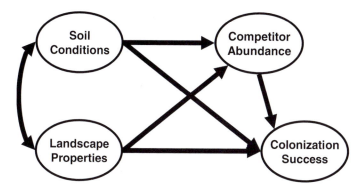

Figure 6.3. Construct model reflecting the presumed mechanisms causing herb colonization success to relate to the characteristics of forest stands.

In this case, our starting point is the initial construct model summarizing the core theoretical questions posed (Figure 6.3). We can start by considering the question, what are the various ways we might model the relationships shown in Figure 6.3? To address this question, the available indicators must be considered and then the linkages between indicators and concepts. The authors measured eight variables in the process of developing indicators for the four constructs of interest. Two indicators of landscape conditions were measured, the estimated age of each forest stand and the distance from each reforested target stand to the nearest source patch. Three indicators of soil conditions were measured, including soil texture, soil moisture, and soil pH. Two indicators of competitor abundance were measured, the cover of herbaceous competitors and the abundance of understory shrubs. For the herb species whose colonization will be considered in this example application (*Lamium galeobdolon*), shrub abundance was not significantly related to colonization success (although herbaceous cover was). So, to simplify the example, I only use a single indicator for competitor abundance, which will be herbaceous cover. The proportion of sampling points where a species was found in a forest stand serves as the single indicator of colonization success.

Figure 6.4 shows the presumed linkages between measured indicators and conceptual variables based on the theoretical reasoning of the authors. In this initial representation, no attempt is made to express the structure of the blocks, therefore, concepts are related to observed indicators with nondirectional lines rather than directional arrows. Disturbance terms are specified for Competitors and Colonization, while the diagram is ambiguous as to whether Soil and Landscape possess disturbances or not, because the directions of influences are not given.

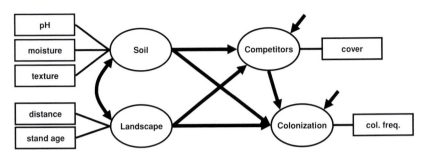

Figure 6.4. Associations between indicator and conceptual variables in Example 1.

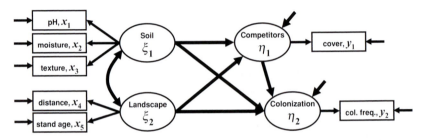

Figure 6.5. Model A, all observed (manifest) variables (in boxes) are represented as "effect indicators" associated with latent variables (in circles). Thus, all blocks are of the L→M type.

Possible model structures

There are several possibilities for how the relations in Figure 6.4 might be modeled. The primary determining factor for deciding which of the possibilities might be most appropriate is the nature of the causal relations. There are, in fact, a great many possibilities, although here I will only consider a few key contrasting types. One of these possibilities is that the most appropriate model is a classic hybrid model of the sort introduced in Chapter 4. Its specific structure is shown in Figure 6.5. In this figure we see that the block structure used to represent relations between indicators and individual latent variables is of the L→M type. In this model, which will be referred to as model A, two of the latent variables, Competitors and Colonization, are associated with one effect indicator each. As appropriate for such relationships, arrows are directed from the causes (the latent variables) to the indicators. The two other latent variables in this model, Soil and Landscape, are associated with multiple effect indicators. Causal interactions among constructs are presumed to be best represented by interactions among latent variables in this representation, and direct interactions among manifest variables are not specified.

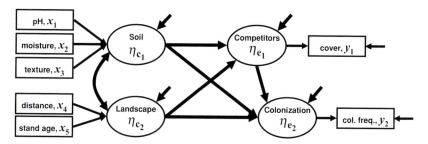

Figure 6.6. Model B, soil conditions and landscape properties are represented as components of M→L blocks, with the associated manifest variables (x_1–x_5) representing cause indicators.

A second possibility is that the multiple indicators associated with Soil and Landscape are causal indicators. This type of structure is illustrated in model B (Figure 6.6). Here, the arrows pointing from pH, moisture, and texture to Soil represent the presumption that the measured soil properties jointly determine the soil influences, rather than vice versa. A similar logic applies to distance and stand age, which are presumed to contribute to Landscape in this model. In this case, the multi-indicator blocks are of the M→L type.

If we assume that the causal indicators in Model B are themselves imperfect measures, which is very reasonable in this case, then we might represent the situation as shown in Figure 6.7 (model C). Here, Soil represents a multidimensional construct related at least in part to True pH, True Moisture, and True Texture (the use of the term "True" here does not mean that we have estimated the true value of variables using our model, instead, it means that we recognize that the true value of pH is latent or unmeasured). Similarly, Landscape is a multidimensional construct related to True Distance and True Age. As the names of these latent variables indicate, this model explicitly recognizes that our manifest variables are not perfect measures of the "true" parameter values.

Discussion of the range of possible ways to represent the relations in Figure 6.4 would be incomplete without considering another alternative, which is referred to as model D (Figure 6.8). In this model, the two multidimensional constructs, soil conditions and landscape properties, are represented simply as groups of variables. In this case, the only two block types are L→M and L→L.

Formal representations

To discuss the relationships embodied in our models more formally, we can begin with the three characteristic equations of the LISREL model (the reader

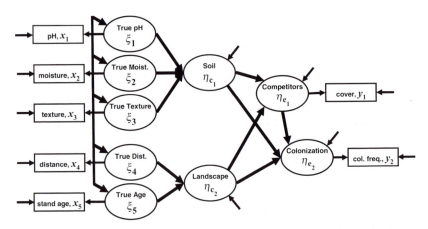

Figure 6.7. Model C, which represents Soil and Landscape and their associated causes as multidimensional constructs, allowing for measurement error in all manifest variables. In this case, Soil and Landscape are components of L→L (no M) blocks. The line with arrows connecting the latent variables represents all possible intercorrelations.

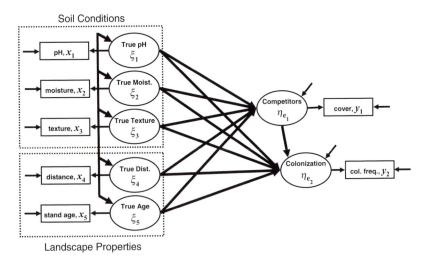

Figure 6.8. Model D, partially reduced form of model C omitting explicit consideration of collective soil and landscape effects.

may wish to refer to Appendix 5.1, where the LISREL notation is summarized, to better appreciate the following presentation). This notation, which applies to hybrid models such as model A in Figure 6.5 is

$$\mathbf{x} = \mathbf{\Lambda}_x \boldsymbol{\xi} + \boldsymbol{\delta} \qquad (6.1)$$

$$\mathbf{y} = \mathbf{\Lambda}_y \boldsymbol{\eta} + \boldsymbol{\varepsilon} \qquad (6.2)$$

and

$$\eta = \mathbf{B}\eta + \mathbf{\Gamma}\xi + \zeta \tag{6.3}$$

where $\mathbf{x}$ and $\mathbf{y}$ are vectors of observed indicators of the exogenous and endogenous latent variables, ξ and η are vectors containing the individual exogenous and endogenous latent variables, $\mathbf{\Lambda}_x$ and $\mathbf{\Lambda}_y$ are vectors of coefficients relating indicators to latent variables, $\mathbf{B}$ and $\mathbf{\Gamma}$ are coefficient matrices for effects of endogenous and exogenous latent variables on endogenous latent variables, δ and ε are vectors of measurement errors for $\mathbf{x}$ and $\mathbf{y}$, and ζ is a vector of disturbances for the η variables. For exogenous latent variables, ξ, their variances are represented by the diagonal elements of the matrix $\mathbf{\Phi}$, while the off-diagonal elements of the matrix are the covariances. The disturbance terms for the endogenous latent variables (ζ) are contained within the diagonal elements of the $\mathbf{\Psi}$ matrix, while the off-diagonal elements of that matrix represent any covariances among disturbances (normally assumed to be zero). Error variables (in δ and ε) are expected to be uncorrelated with ξ and η. However, it is possible to model correlations among errors, typically represented by nonzero off-diagonal elements in the matrices representing cross products among measurement errors, $\mathbf{\theta}_\delta$ and $\mathbf{\theta}_\varepsilon$.

In the case of a model such as model B, which contains causal indicators, we recognize the need for an additional equation to represent the M→L block

$$\eta_c = \mathbf{\Lambda}_c\mathbf{x} + \zeta_c \tag{6.4}$$

Further, for η_e variables in general,

$$\eta_e = \mathbf{B}_c\eta_c + \mathbf{B}_e\eta_e + \mathbf{\Gamma}\xi + \zeta_e \tag{6.5}$$

Here, for clarity, we distinguish two different types of endogenous latent variable. Those with causal indicators, either directly as in the M→L block, or indirectly as in the L→L (no M) block, are represented by the vector η_c, while those with effect indicators are designated by η_e. We also distinguish two different matrices of structural coefficients, $\mathbf{B}_c$ and $\mathbf{B}_e$, as well as separate vectors of disturbance terms, ζ_c and ζ_e, for the two types of eta variable. In the particular case of model B, there are no variables in the ξ vector. For model C, Eqs. (6.1) and (6.2) apply as they did for model A. However, we now have the case where we need to expand Eq. (6.4) to be more general, so that

$$\eta_c = \mathbf{\Lambda}_c\mathbf{x} + \mathbf{\Gamma}\xi + \zeta_c \tag{6.6}$$

In the herb colonization example, Soil and Landscape (collectively represented by the vector η_c) are affected by the exogenous latent variables in the ξ vector.

A summary of the equations that would apply to models A–D is presented in Table 6.1. As we can see, models A and D can be described unambiguously using

Table 6.1. *Summary of equations relevant for models A–D*

Properties and expectations	Model A	Model B	Model C	Model D
Equation 1 applies	yes	no	yes	yes
Equation 2 applies	yes	yes	yes	yes
Equation 3 applies	yes	no	yes	yes
Equation 4 applies	no	yes	no	no
Equation 5 applies	no	yes	yes	no
Equation 6 applies	no	no	yes	no

the conventional LISREL notation (Eqs. (6.1)–(6.3)). However, for models containing blocks of the M→L and L→L (no M) type, the additional equations introduced help us to distinguish among groups of variables with differing properties.

Composites

So far in our discussion of formal notation I have treated all conceptual variables as true latent variables – unmeasured variables that exist independent from our model and data, though we have no direct measures of them. We must now consider the very practical matter that, for blocks such as M→L and L→L (no M), there is usually insufficient information to estimate the true variance for latent variables that do not have at least one effect indicator. In the absence of an ability to estimate the true variance, latent variables without effect indicators can only represent composites of their causes. For this reason, in the practical case of estimating models that have latent variables without effect indicators, and where there are no means to estimate their variances, we can replace M→L with M→C and L→L (no M) with L→C. Here, C refers to a composite variable. In the case of M→C, the letter C describes a "composite of manifest variables", while in the case of L→C, the letter C describes a "composite of latent variables".

Composites are, in all cases that I describe in this chapter, considered to be endogenous (η) variables. However, since they are, in effect, perfect representations of their cause, they are variables with zero value error variances. While composites are imperfect representations of any construct they might represent, they can still be useful approximations of those constructs. Regarding the example of forest herb colonization, if stand age and distance from source constitute the predominant landscape features of importance for the model, then a composite formed from their effects will have a very general meaning. If stand age and distance from source are just two of many unique landscape properties of importance to herb colonization, our composite will simply represent their joint effects, and will be a poor representation of a general landscape effect. Typically, unless an effort has been made to obtain an exhaustive sampling of the dimensions of a construct, any composite derived from the measures of that construct should be understood to represent the collective effects of its components, regardless of the label placed on that construct. This issue notwithstanding, composites can be eminently useful as a means of representing certain types of construct, facilitating general conclusions, and managing model complexity.

Evaluating the different model possibilities – theoretical considerations

Both theoretical and empirical information contribute to an evaluation of the suitability of model architecture for a given situation. As stated earlier, there are a great number of possibilities for how a set of manifest variables may be connected. In the example under consideration here, involving herb colonization of forest stands, initial guidance comes from the theory specified in Figure 6.3, and the associations in Figure 6.4. I begin our evaluation of the applicability of models A–D in this case by considering the causal relations between constructs and indicators.

Borrowing, with modification, from Jarvis *et al.* (2003), certain conceptual criteria can help in deciding whether a block should be modeled in the traditional $L{\rightarrow}M$ format (e.g., model A), or whether $M{\rightarrow}C$ or $L{\rightarrow}C$ blocks are more appropriate (e.g., models B or C). Four kinds of questions can be considered to gauge the theoretical basis for forming models such as model A versus models B or C:

(1) What is the direction of causality?
(2) Are the indicators in a single block interchangeable?
(3) Is there an expectation that indicators in a block should covary (e.g., because of joint causality)?
(4) Do the indicators in a block have a consistent set of causal influences?

For the sake of this discussion, it is recognized that model B is a special case of model C where the *x* variables are considered to be without measurement error. For this reason, in the immediate discussion I will contrast models A and B, with the understanding that models B and C are equivalent with regard to this evaluation.

For the first question, we must begin by asking whether the construct "Soil" has causal influence on pH, moisture, and texture. Stated in a different way, we are asking whether the variation among stands in soil conditions is such that it causes common responses in pH, moisture, and texture; in which case causation flows from the general construct to the indicators. Alternatively, if it is the case that pH, moisture, and texture have some substantial degree of independent effects on Soil, then causation flows from the indicators to the construct (i.e., the construct comprises its parts). In this study, the authors felt that causation flows from the indicators to the construct, and argued that an M→C block representation was appropriate. A similar determination was made for the construct "Landscape" which is envisioned by the authors to be the product of largely independent influences by certain landscape properties.

The second question to be considered is whether the indicators in a block are interchangeable, if so, they then constitute redundant measures and are likely to represent effect indicators consistent with an L→M block. Stated in another way, we might ask if dropping one of the indicators in a block alters the conceptual breadth of the construct. For both Soil and Landscape, the indicators in the separate blocks would seem to be nonredundant based on the authors' model specification. For the construct Landscape, an M→C block specification would appear to be clearly indicated. The age of a patch is conceptually quite distinct from its distance from a source population. If data for the distance to source populations were to be absent, the construct would reduce solely to an age dimension. For Soil, there is precedent for common soil factors of the L→M type (Grace 2003b, Weiher *et al.* 2004). However, in this case, the authors felt that the individual indicators, pH, texture, and moisture, reflect somewhat separate dimensions of Soil and are best represented by an M→C block structure.

A third question is whether the indicators are expected to covary. This serves as an additional way of evaluating the flow of causation in a block. If indicators are under common causal control by a latent factor, then when that latent factor varies, the indicators should all vary likewise. Such a situation would imply that an L→M block would be an appropriate means of modeling the situation. On the other hand, if causation flows from the indicators to the latent variable, there is no basis for having an expectation for correlations among indicators, since their causes are not specified. We should, therefore, recognize that a correlation among indicators does not inform us about the direction of causal flow, although a lack of correlation among indicators would contraindicate the prospect that a block should be of the L→M form. For the herb colonization example, the authors' presentation did not produce any expectations of whether indicators in multi-indicator blocks would correlate or not. So, again, by these criteria, it would seem that Soil and Landscape are constructs best represented as M→C blocks given the available indicators.

The fourth question we might consider relates to the first, and asks whether the indicators have common antecedents. If they do, then causation flows from that common antecedent, which can be modeled as a latent variable (of course, if that latent factor is not the cause affecting other parts of the model, then a completely different model structure would be implied). On the other hand, in a model with an M→C block structure, the indicators do not have common antecedents, but rather, unique ones. In this example, it does not seem likely that patch age and distance from source have a determined common antecedent. The case is less clear for soil properties. Soil formation processes are such that general soil conditions are capable of having common antecedents, such as hydrologic and mineral influences. Thus, a potential basis for modeling Soil as an L→M block does exist based on this criterion.

Collectively, it would seem that the expectations of the authors, as reflected by the four questions, would lean towards a specification of the multi-indicator blocks as M→C for both Soil and Landscape. This does not guarantee that this is the correct causal structure, nor does it override the possibility that empirical characteristics of the data might imply a different block structure. What is most important to realize is that there are logical tests for developing, justifying, and interpreting block structure, and that automatically presuming a conventional hybrid model structure (L→M) is not justified. Neither is it advisable to rely simply on data properties to make the determination as to whether a construct is best represented by a particular structure.

Evaluating the different model possibilities – empirical evaluations of blocks

The truth is that often it is not known with absolute confidence what the causal flow is for a set of manifest variables. This is especially true for applications in the natural sciences, where the concept of latent variables is only beginning to receive widespread attention. A strength of SEM is that various means of evaluating model expectations exist (see numerous illustrations in Bollen 1989). I will address overall model fit later. For now, our considerations relate to the empirical characteristics of individual blocks. Ultimately these are of great importance, for no matter what logic one brings to a model, if the indicators in a block do not behave like effect indicators, then it will be unprofitable to model them as such. Reviews of SEM studies in certain disciplines (e.g., Jarvis *et al.* 2003) suggest that researchers commonly misjudge the empirical support for the causal direction specified in their models. The greatest error is to assume that blocks are of the L→M form, without seriously considering the use of M→L and L→L (no M) blocks (or their applied counterparts, M→C and L→C). In the example discussed here, the authors assumed the opposite form (M→C) for their multi-indicator blocks. However, it seems that the logical justification for

Table 6.2. *Correlations among variables and the standard deviations*

	Col. freq.	Distance	Age	Texture	Moisture	pH	Cover
Col. freq.	1.0						
Distance	−0.5785	1.0					
Age	0.6424	−0.5934	1.0				
Texture	−0.2553	0.1844	−0.3146	1.0			
Moisture	−0.3369	0.4604	−0.3462	0.5767	1.0		
pH	−0.0073	−0.0465	−0.0976	0.1324	0.0265	1.0	
Cover	−0.3423	0.2070	−0.4062	0.3189	0.2952	0.2394	1.0
Std. dev.	0.1867	0.8207	0.3390	0.4588	1.1359	0.7507	0.3017

this assumption is stronger for the Landscape construct and less definitive for the Soil construct. In this section, I consider some of the empirical properties to see if either block has properties consistent with the L→M form.

Table 6.2 presents covariance relations for colonization frequency and other manifest variables (represented by the correlations and standard deviations) for the species *Lamium galeobdolon*. While SEM is based on an analysis of covariance relations (as discussed in Chapter 3), an inspection of correlations can be instructive. As Bollen and Ting (2000) have described, there is an expectation that a set of effect indicators associated with a single latent variable in an L→M block will be intercorrelated, as implied by Eq. (6.1). For such a set of indicators, their degree of intercorrelation will depend on the strength of the common influence of the latent cause, relative to their total variances. So, for model A, we would expect conspicuous correlations among soil pH, moisture, and texture, because of the joint influence of Soil on those specific factors. We would have similar expectations for a strong correlation between distance and patch age. Again, the degree of correlation expected would depend on the relative importance of the errors, although for a reliable set of indicators, correlations should at least be moderately high. In contrast, for a set of causal indicators associated with a single latent variable in a single M→C block, there is no basis for expecting any particular correlation pattern. None of the equations that apply to model B imply common causal influence on sets of causal indicators. So, a set of causal indicators may or may not intercorrelate in such a case, since our equations do not describe their interrelationships, except that they are classified as being of common interest.

Inspection of Table 6.2 reveals a correlation between age and distance of −0.5934. Thus, a correlation of moderate magnitude is observed for this pair of indicators. In addition, the correlations between these variables and the other variables in the model are, very approximately, of the same magnitude. Thus, based on a crude inspection of correlations in the matrix, we are unable to rule out the possibility that either an L→M or M→C block structure would be consistent with the empirical characteristics of the indicators related to Landscape.

The correlations between pH, moisture, and texture are 0.0265, 0.1324, and 0.5767. The low magnitude of correlations between pH and the other indicators in the block suggests that these three soil properties would not be likely to represent redundant measures of the sort normally found in L→M blocks. A method for formally evaluating this has been proposed by Bollen and Ting (2000) based on vanishing tetrads. Correlations/covariances among a set of truly redundant indicators in an L→M block should possess the mathematical property of vanishing tetrads, with a tetrad being the difference between the products of pairs of covariances among four random variables. It can be said in this case that the pattern of correlations among pH, moisture, and texture do not appear to be consistent with such a block structure.

Comparing results for different models

Results for model A The data presented in Table 6.2 are sufficient to provide for an evaluation of all models discussed in this paper. The analysis results presented were obtained using the program Mplus (Muthén and Muthén 2004). An illustration of a model containing a composite programmed in Mplus can be found in Appendix I. For the purposes of this illustration involving model A, we assume a modest, nonzero degree of measurement error for the single-indicator measures (cover and colonization frequency) of 10%. Fitting of the data to model A resulted in poor fit based on model chi-square statistics, error variances for indicators, and examination of the residual covariance matrix. A chi-square of 45.20 was obtained for the model, with 10 degrees of freedom. The associated probability of good fit between data and model was found to be less than 0.00005. Note that since model A is saturated with regard to the structural model (i.e., all paths between latent variables are estimated), the inflated chi-square does not result from unspecified relations among latent variables, but instead, resides in the measurement model. In other words, in this example the lack of model fit can be attributed to inappropriate relations between latent and manifest variables. Standardized parameter estimates for model A are shown in Figure 6.9. Here it can be seen that the standardized error variance for pH is 0.99, indicating that the model provides no explanation of the variance of this variable. Finally, residuals indicate that, in general, the model does a poor job of resolving the covariances among indicators.

A modification of model A was evaluated to determine the degree to which the lack of fit for pH contributed to poor fit for the whole model. In the modified model, only moisture and texture were used as indicators for Soil, while pH was

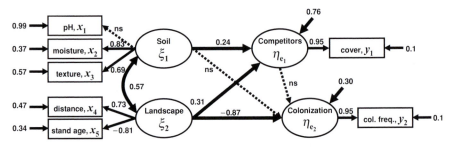

Figure 6.9. Standardized parameter estimates for model A. Chi-squared for model fit was 45.20 with 10 degrees of freedom (sample size = 180) and a p-value < 0.00005, indicating very poor fit of data to model expectations.

specified to be a single indicator for an additional exogenous latent variable, True pH. Again, 10% of the variance of observed pH was specified as measurement error. A chi-square of 34.57 with 7 degrees of freedom was obtained for this model. The associated probability of good fit remained less than 0.00005. Thus, this result indicates that the observed lack of fit between model and data is spread throughout the measurement model, and is not solely due to a lack of correlation between pH and the other soil variables.

As stated earlier, it is not likely that the observed variables measured in this study were obtained without some degree of measurement error. For this reason, model B would seem to be a less than ideal representation for our purposes here, as it assumes the causal indicators associated with soil conditions and landscape properties are error free. For this reason, we can now ignore model B and focus our attention on model C, which recognizes that soil and landscape variables are imperfect measures of the true values. As above, for single indicator latent variables in this study, an arbitrary measurement error of 10% of the variance for single indicator blocks is assumed. Before discussing model C, however, I wish to consider a general issue that relates to models of its type (those that contain composites). This issue deals with parameter identification, which can prevent the researcher from obtaining unique and valid estimates.

A digression on the issue of parameter identification in models containing composites

Model C, because it includes composite variables, has a somewhat different set of parameters that must be estimated, compared to a similar model without composites (e.g., model D). As mentioned earlier, since I define composites as having zero error variances (not all authors do), I can set these parameters to zero, thus, their identification is not an issue. However, for model C, the

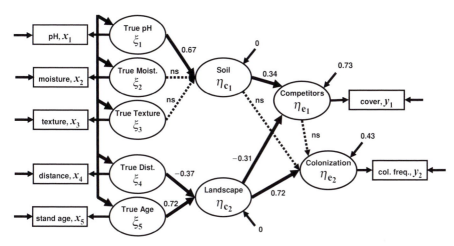

Figure 6.10. Select standardized parameter estimates for model C. Here Soil and Landscape are composites with zero disturbance terms. Model chi-square was 6.005 with 3 degrees of freedom (p = 0.1107).

composite variables introduce four new paths that represent the effects of the composites (the η_cs) on the η_e variables. In this particular case, the relationships between the exogenous latent variables (ξs) and the η_c variables are reduced to single effects from each ξ. So, for our example, the ten potential paths from the individual ξ variables to the η_e variables (e.g., in model D) are replaced with five paths from the ξ to the η_c variables, plus four paths from the η_c variables to the η_e variables. In spite of the net gain of a degree of freedom from this substitution, problems remain with parameter identification. Ultimately, there is a general problem that arises when attempting to identify all paths leading to, as well as flowing out from, a composite. This problem is similar to the routinely encountered problem associated with latent variables with effect indicators, where the scale of the latent needs to be established. Both of these problems can be solved in the same fashion by specifying a single incoming relationship, which establishes the scale of measurement.

In spite of the fact that parameter identification issues can be resolved by specification of select parameters, an issue still remains as to the significance of the specified parameters. In model C (Figure 6.10), we set the unstandardized coefficients for the paths from True pH to Soil and from True Distance to Landscape to 1.0, to establish the scale of measurement for the composites (note, this is not shown in Figure 6.10 because only the standardized parameters are presented). This procedure ignores the question of whether there are significant relationships associated with these paths. More specifically, does True pH have a significant (nonzero) contribution to Soil, and similarly, does True Distance have a nonzero contribution to Landscape? One approach to evaluating fixed paths from ξs to η_cs is to use a reduced form model such as model D, in which the composites are omitted and the direct effects of ξs on η_cs are tested. For our example, the reduced form equations are

$$\eta_{e_1} = \gamma_{e_1\xi_1}\xi_1 + \gamma_{e_1\xi_2}\xi_2 + \gamma_{e_1\xi_3}\xi_3 + \zeta_{e_1} \tag{6.7}$$

and

$$\eta_{e_2} = \gamma_{e_2\xi_1}\xi_1 + \gamma_{e_2\xi_2}\xi_2 + \gamma_{e_2\xi_3}\xi_3 + \beta_{e_2e_1}\eta_{e_1} + \zeta_{e_2} \tag{6.8}$$

For models with more than a single path flowing out from the composites, such as is the case in model C, an evaluation of model D only provides an approximate answer to the question of whether the parameters in model C are significant. The reason for this is that a single estimate for each gamma must apply to both Eqs. (6.7) and (6.8) in order to represent the situation in model C. Stated more succinctly, for model C it is assumed that

$$\eta_{e_i} = \gamma_{e\xi_1}\xi_1 + \gamma_{e\xi_2}\xi_2 + \gamma_{e\xi_3}\xi_3 + \zeta_{ei} \tag{6.9}$$

holds for all i (i.e., that the condition $\gamma_{e_1\xi_1} = \gamma_{e_2\xi_1}$ and so forth holds for all ξ). As we show below, it is possible and even desirable to evaluate Eq. (6.9) as part of the assessment process.

Results for model C   Maximum likelihood estimation yields a chi-square of 6.005 with 3 degrees of freedom and an associated probability of 0.1107. Examination of residuals and the chi-square results indicate adequate fit of the data to model C. Again, to better allow for comparisons among models, for most comparisons standardized parameter estimates are presented, and it is assumed that significance tests for unstandardized parameter values apply to the standardized values as well. In the presentation of results in Figure 6.10, all numerical estimates shown are associated with significant p-values for the relevant unstandardized parameters, except for the paths from True pH to Soil and True Dist. to Landscape, which were set to fixed values to establish the scales for the composites.

Conspicuous in the results for model C (Figure 6.10) is that neither True Moisture nor True Texture contributed significantly to the composite variable Soil. Also, Soil had a significant effect on Competitors, but not on Colonization. In contrast, the freely estimated relationship between True Age and Landscape was significant; as well as both paths from Landscape to Competitors and Colonization. Examination of the residual variances for Competitors and Colonization shows that 27% and 57% of the variance in these response variables were explained.

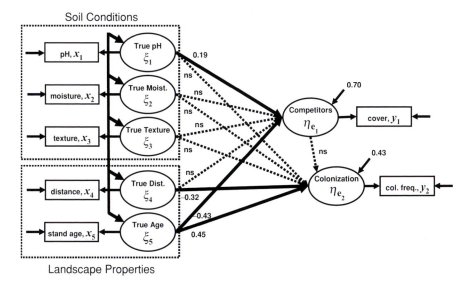

Figure 6.11. Standardized parameter estimates for model D. Model D lacks composites and represents a partially reduced form of model C.

Results for model D It is instructive to evaluate model D, which effectively represents a partially reduced form of model C in which composites are omitted. In this model, separate effects of the ξ variables on Competitors and Colonization are estimated, and the individual ξ variables are associated with constructs nominally. Since this model is saturated, maximum likelihood estimation yields a chi-square of 0 due to the fact that there are no degrees of freedom. In a side analysis, the stability of results was tested by deleting nonsignificant paths, yielding a chi-square of 9.773 with 6 degrees of freedom (p = 0.1344). This side analysis indicated that the results for model D are stable.

Results for model D (Figure 6.11) show that only four of the paths from ξ variables to η_e variables were significant. Variance explained for Competitors and Colonization in the saturated model was 30% and 57%. Again, for the purposes of comparing among models, the saturated model results are used even though nonsignificant paths are included. Aside from providing a comparison to model C, model D also provides a representation of the constructs from Figure 6.3; except that in this case, the dimensions of soil conditions and landscape properties are represented separately. It is possible in such a model to provide some degree of representation of the effects of the soil and landscape constructs, even without the use of composites. For example, selective elimination of categories of variables can be used to derive estimates of their unique and

Table 6.3. *Estimation of unique and shared variance explanation in Competitors and Colonization for soil conditions and landscape properties in model D*

	Variance explanation contribution for response variables (percent of total variance)	
Construct(s)	Competitors	Colonization
Soil only	19.5	22.1
Landscape only	21.1	57.0
Soil and Landscape combined	30.1	57.4
Soil unique contribution (combined – landscape only)	9.0	0.4
Landscape unique contribution (combined – soil only)	10.6	35.3
Soil shared contribution (soil only – soil unique)	10.5	21.7
Landscape shared contribution (landscape only – landscape unique)	10.5	21.7

shared variance explanation (described in Chapter 3). In this case, if we drop the variables associated with landscape properties (True Distance and True Age, as well as their indicators) from the model, the variance explained in Competitors and Colonization is reduced to 19.5% and 22.1% respectively. Also, if we keep the variables associated with landscape properties in the model, but drop those associated with soil conditions, the variance explained in Competitors and Colonization is found to be 21.1% and 57.0% respectively. A summary of these results can be seen in Table 6.3, along with derivations of unique and shared variance explanation. Here we can see that soil conditions and landscape properties had roughly equal unique variance explanation contributions for Competitors (9.0% and 10.6%) with 10% shared between them. For Colonization, unique variance explanation was very dissimilar (0.4% and 35.3%) for soil conditions and landscape properties, while 21.7% was shared between the two groups of predictors. In this case, the path from Competitors to Colonization was nonsignificant, therefore, all effects from predictors are direct and no indirect effects on Colonization are described.

A further model to consider – model E

Above it was mentioned that model C presumes that Eq. (6.9) holds. This equation presumes that a single set of gammas associated with the L→C blocks can successfully represent the effects of ξ variables on η_e variables. This is akin to saying that the slopes of the regression relations of ξs on η_{e1} would be the same as for the effects of ξs on η_{e2}. If this condition holds, then model C is

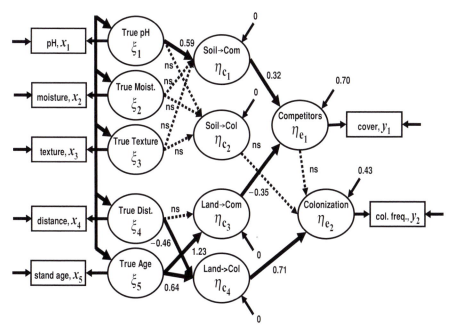

Figure 6.12. Select standardized parameter estimates for model E. Here four composites are included, one for each response variable.

our best model for the situation. On the other hand, if Eq. (6.9) does not hold because regression relations are not similar, our model will underestimate the variance explanation for Competitors and Colonization. It can easily be seen that when gammas are very different in Eqs. (6.7) and (6.8), then the gammas in Eq. (6.9) will be insufficiently relevant to accurately predict the η_es. To evaluate this possibility, we consider one additional model, which we refer to as model E. In this model, separate composites are derived to estimate effects on Competitors and Colonization.

Results for model E are shown in Figure 6.12. As with model D, when all paths are included there are no degrees of freedom for testing model fit. However, deletion of nonsignificant paths allows for model testing and, again, no unspecified paths are indicated. As before, results presented in the figure are the standardized parameter estimates for the model, with all paths included.

Comparisons among models

The exercise of comparing different models as contrasting representations of the construct relations in Figure 6.3 is meant not only to illustrate some of the variety of modeling possibilities, but also to introduce a number of important concepts and procedures. Most of the presentations of SEM in introductory textbooks are likely to lead new users to consider model A to be the appropriate representation of the construct relations in Figure 6.3. As we saw, model fit was found to be completely unacceptable for model A and the resulting parameters, therefore, unreliable. Several review papers have suggested that researchers frequently fail to consider the full range of possibilities for model development. Models that contain causal indicators and composites are rather rare compared to those in which constructs are exclusively represented by effect indicators in L→M blocks. In this example, the bulk of the theoretical information and the great majority of the empirical analyses indicate that model A is not an appropriate representation of the situation. Conceptually, the constructs were not envisioned as unidimensional underlying causes, but rather, collections of influencing factors. Furthermore, the available indicators do not represent a suite of effect indicators as would be appropriate for an L→M block. The inadequacy of fit of data to model A is clearly indicated by the very low probability associated with the chi-square test. Thus, we can reject this model as inadequate. Consideration of modifications such as splitting out pH from the Soil block, as well as other attempts at small modifications, also did not lead to the discovery of an adequate model akin to model A.

Model B was omitted from our analyses because of the strong likelihood of measurement error existing in the indicators. However, if we had presented an analysis of model B, it would be found to possess many of the same properties as were found for model C; although without the modest correction for measurement error that was built into model C.

The remaining comparisons of most interest are between model C and models D and E. All three of these models had adequate fit to the data, and the differences among them can be viewed as tradeoffs between model generality and model accuracy (Levins 1968). Model C is the most general of the three, representing the collective effects of soil conditions and landscape properties, with a single composite for each. As described in the above discussion of Eqs. (6.7)–(6.9), for model C to be appropriate, the estimated composites would need to be near optimal for representing effects on both Competitors and Colonization simultaneously. At the other end of the spectrum, model D is the most accurate and least general of the three models. No attempt is made to summarize the collective effects of the two multidimensional constructs through the use of composites in model D. While a general assessment of unique and shared variance can be used in this case (as demonstrated in Table 6.3), such calculations are also applicable to models C and E. Calculations of unique and shared variance explanation can be applied to any model, including those with composites; and to any collection of variables. Therefore, this way of dealing with the partitioning of variance explanation is not a replacement for the use of composites, but instead, a complementary procedure.

Compared to model D, which contains no composites, model E represents an advance in generality, having an individual composite for each effect of the multidimensional constructs. As would be expected for such a case, the error variances for Competitors and Colonization are virtually identical for models D and E. Thus, both models D and E are equally accurate with regard to variance explanation, but they differ in the way in which effects are represented. Overall, model D provides a more succinct representation of the individual effects of ξ variables on Competitors and Colonization. All paths are tested for significance and coefficients are readily interpretable as individual effects. In comparison, model E provides a superior representation of collective effects, with single path coefficients representing the effects of suites of variables, although at some cost in terms of the interpretation of individual influences (the paths from ξ variables to η_c variables).

An important comparison to make between models C and E has to do with the magnitude of the error variances for the η_e variables. It has been recognized previously that when composites with multiple effects on other variables are not appropriate, there is a conspicuous loss of variance explanation for the affected variables. In this case, error variances are 0.73 and 0.43 for Competitors and Colonization respectively in model C. In contrast, in model E, the values are 0.70 and 0.43. A test of the adequacy of model C is whether its error variances are significantly greater than those for the less general case where composites have single effects. For such a test, the t-value for a test of difference between the error variances for Competitors must be conducted and based on the unstandardized parameters. For model C, the unstandardized residual variance for Competitors is 0.059 ± 0.007 (std. error), while for model E the values are 0.057 ± 0.007, yielding a t-value of 0.14, and an associated probability of no difference approaching 0.9. For Colonization, residual error variances were virtually identical (0.013 ± 0.002) for models C and E. Thus, there is no indication that model E is superior to model C in variance explanation for the η_e variables. Furthermore, the paths from composites to the η_e variables are also very similar between models. Collectively, this evidence supports the conclusion that model C is superior to model E overall, because of its greater generality, and it is our best model (of those examined) for this example and these data.

Example 2: an examination of habitat associations for anurans

Background

Anurans are a group of amphibians, comprising frogs and toads, that are of high conservation concern due to worldwide population declines. This example,

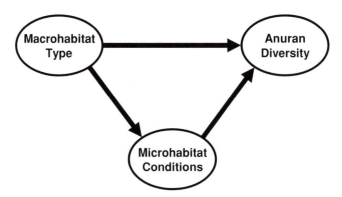

Figure 6.13. Construct model relating macrohabitat type and microhabitat conditions to anuran diversity.

developed from data taken from a study by Lichtenberg *et al.* (unpublished) in which 25 wetlands in the lower Mississippi River alluvial valley were examined for chorusing anuran species and associated habitat characteristics. One major goal of this study was to understand the habitat characteristics associated with diversity "hotspots" where a variety of species are abundant. Figure 6.13 provides an illustration of the construct relations of interest in this example. Stated in general terms, the goal of their analysis of anuran diversity was to understand the degree to which it depends on the type of habitat (lake, impoundment, etc.) versus the particular conditions (vegetation, litter, etc.) within that habitat. Specifically, they were interested in the question of whether correlations between high diversity and particular wetland types can be explained by the microhabitat conditions within the wetlands. Such information could prove useful in making decisions about types of habitat to protect and the conditions to maintain.

In this study, several types of wetlands were examined. These could be classified as being of one of four types – lakes, impoundments, swales, and riverine areas. Specific microhabitat conditions were assessed at each site, and these included a number of vegetation and topographic features. Anuran diversity was assessed using nighttime surveys of chorusing individuals during several seasons of the year. Chorus surveys during the year were used to arrive at an estimate of the species using a site.

While macrohabitat types were clearly defined a priori, microhabitat conditions were sampled in a more exploratory fashion. A wide range of characteristics of the vegetation were studied, including herbaceous cover, vegetation density at different vertical positions, woody cover, tree height, canopy cover, as well as litter cover and depth (by type). Also measured were hydrologic features at the site, including the area of open water and the mean and maximum water depths.

In conjunction with our presentation of Example 1, we provided a detailed consideration of how constructs may be represented and both theoretical and empirical criteria for arriving at decisions about block structure. In this second example, our emphasis is more on the question of how to model a situation where an endogenous variable (microhabitat conditions) has multiple indicators and may involve composites. This question was not addressed in Example 1, where multiple indicators existed only for the exogenous constructs.

In the current example, we begin our analysis with the construct labeled Macrohabitat Type. Since our measure is nominal and multi-level (whether a site is classified as lake, impoundment, swale, or riverine), it immediately suggests the need to model this construct using a set of dummy variables representing the possible macrohabitat types. We can assume for the sake of simplicity that the classification of individual sites as to habitat type was correct. Therefore, the presumption is that the construct Macrohabitat Type can be modeled using either an M→L or M→C block type. The deciding factors for choosing between these two block types are whether we believe we have a complete sampling of all possible macrohabitat types, and whether we can derive an estimate of the error of prediction for Macrohabitat Type. Since neither of these criteria hold in this case, the M→C block structure seems more appropriate.

The construct labeled Microhabitat Conditions is one where the specific details of how the measured variables would interrelate was not known a priori. For this reason, Lichtenberg *et al.* performed an exploratory factor analysis to see if the correlations among the many measured variables might suggest the operation of a smaller number of latent factors. I will not go into the details of that analysis here, but only say that the result was the recognition by the authors of two factors of importance to anuran diversity, the abundance of herbaceous vegetation and the abundance of leaf litter. Based on the conceptualization of Microhabitat Conditions by Lichtenberg *et al.*, it is clear that the indicators could represent a collection of factors that affect anurans, based on theoretical grounds. Thus, we begin with the expectation of a block structure of L→C, with two latent variables, Herbaceous Vegetation and Litter, contributing to the construct. A total of seven indicators of the two latent variables were included in their final model (see below).

Lichtenberg *et al.* discuss certain issues of measurement regarding the construct Anuran Diversity. It is widely held that there are several causes of measurement error for wildlife populations and communities. In addition to the usual matter of sampling, varying detectability can contribute to error. Lichtenberg *et al.* addressed the issue of detectability to some degree by using

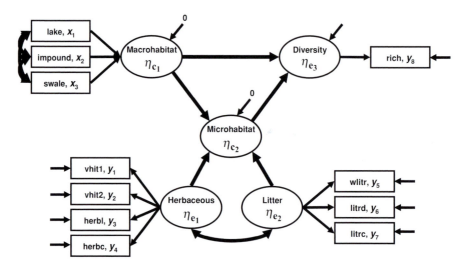

Figure 6.14. Model F, which shows one of the possible ways that indicators could be related to the construct model shown in Figure 6.13. Refer to Table 6.3 for definitions of the observed variables. Note that by omission, the riverine macrohabitat condition represents the baseline against which other macrohabitats are compared.

the total number of species recorded across samplings, instead of the mean. Nevertheless, error in assessing the true number of species at each site is likely to be significant and, while no estimate of this error exists, we again use an arbitrary estimate of 10% of the total variance.

Possible model structures

In the first example we spent some time discussing and illustrating criteria for evaluating the cause and effect relations among variables and how these influence model structure. In this second example, we forego a detailed discussion of such considerations and, instead, focus on the possible ways to model a case where composites have directional effects on other composites.

A model that logically follows from the construct relations in Figure 6.13 is shown in Figure 6.14. I refer to this model as model F to avoid confusion with the models discussed in conjunction with the first example. Based on the information presented above, we can represent Macrohabitat using the block structure M→C. The Microhabitat construct is represented in this case as an L→C block containing two latent variables, both with multiple indicators. Diversity is represented by an L→M block with a single indicator. Consistent

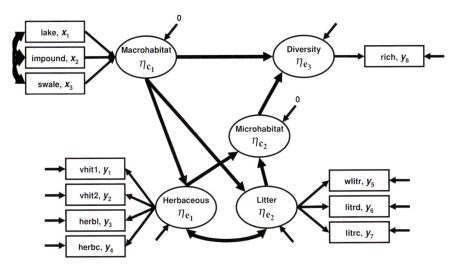

Figure 6.15. Model G, which differs from model F by allowing separate coefficients (represented by separate paths) to convey the effects of Macrohabitat on the Herbaceous and Litter dimensions of Microhabitat.

with their declarations as composites, the error variances for Macrohabitat and Microhabitat are set to zero.

Of the models we consider here, model F is the most abstract. At the same time, model F is based on the greatest number of assumptions. It is presumed in this model that the influences of Macrohabitat (η_{c_1}) on Microhabitat (η_{c_2}) can be summarized by a single coefficient, $\beta_{c_2 c_1}$, despite the fact that η_{c_2} is actually a predictor of Herbaceous and Litter effects on Diversity, rather than the microhabitat conditions themselves. Stated in other terms, in model F the covariances between x_1–x_3 and y_1–y_7 must be resolved by their joint relations to a linear predictor that depends on η_{e_3}. These are fairly critical assumptions in that their failure is likely to mean an underestimate of Macrohabitat effects on Microhabitat, and possibly unresolved covariances among manifest variables.

An alternative formulation that is perhaps more biologically meaningful, model G (Figure 6.15), represents the modeling implications of relaxing the assumptions just discussed for model F. Here we are allowed to consider effects of Macrohabitat on the two dimensions of Microhabitat, Herbaceous and Litter. Since these two dimensions are independently estimated in L→M blocks, the interpretative meaning of the paths from Macrohabitat to each dimension is clear, and also independent of other relationships in the model. In contrast, since the composite Microhabitat is defined as a linear predictor of Diversity, it depends on the covariances between three latent variables, η_{e_1}, η_{e_2}, and η_{e_3}.

If any of the covariances among these variables changes, the meaning of η_{c_2} changes, and thus, the meaning of a direct path from Macrohabitat to Micro-habitat (as in model F). In model G, the effect of Macrohabitat on Microhabitat can be summarized by calculating the total effect of η_{c_1} on η_{c_2}, which can be summarized by the equation

$$\beta_{c_2c_1} = \beta_{e_1c_1} \times \beta_{c_2e_1} + \beta_{e_2c_1} \times \beta_{c_2e_2} \tag{6.10}$$

where $\beta_{c_2c_1}$ now refers to a calculated total effect.

Certain restrictive assumptions that warrant discussion remain in model G. In particular, the assumption is implied that a single combination of coefficients from macrohabitat types (x_1–x_3) to the Macrohabitat composite (η_{c1}) simultaneously summarizes the individual effects of x_1–x_3 on η_{e_1}, η_{e_2}, and η_{e_3}. We feel that it is always wise to check such an assumption (as was done in Example 1). Here, this assumption is explicitly removed in model H (Figure 6.16), where one composite representing Macrohabitat effects is replaced by three (Macro→Herb, Macro→Lit, Macro→Div).

Also as was done in Example 1, we offer for comparison a partially reduced form model, model I (Figure 6.17), in which composites are omitted and constructs are represented nominally. While model I offers a less complete modeling of the construct relations (e.g., there are no path coefficients derived for interactions among the major constructs), it permits a complete evaluation of the significance of all individual effects, thus complementing the other models.

Comparisons among models

Sample correlations and standard deviations are presented in Table 6.4 for the manifest variables considered in this example. As stated earlier, we forego an empirical evaluation of the relations between manifest variables and either composites or latent variables, as these were addressed by Lichtenberg *et al.* We also bypass any discussion of the bivariate relations in Table 6.4 and move directly into a consideration of model results.

As was brought out in our discussion of Example 1, the solution and evaluation of general models containing composite variables often depend on information from more specific models. For this reason, we will begin with the model containing the least number of assumptions (and thereby, our least general model), model I. We will then proceed progressively through models H, G, and F to determine whether more general models result in a substantial loss of information.

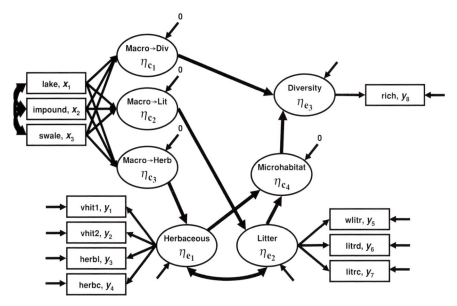

Figure 6.16. Model H, which differs from model G by using separate composites (η_{c_1}–η_{c_3}) to convey the effects of individual Macrohabitat types on η_{e_1}, η_{e_2}, and η_{e_3}.

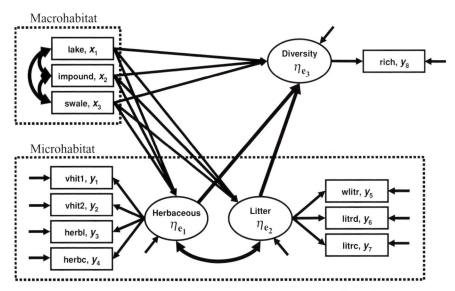

Figure 6.17. Model I. Partially reduced form model representing effects of Macrohabitat and Microhabitat nominally through grouping variables.

Table 6.4. *Correlations among variables related to anuran richness and their standard deviations. "rich" refers to the number of anurans at a site, "imp" refers to impoundments, "vhit2" and "vhit1" are measures of vegetation density, "herbl" and "herbc" are measures of dead and live herbaceous vegetation, "wlitr" is woody litter, "litrd" is litter depth, and "litrc" is litter cover*

	rich	lake	imp	swale	vhit2	vhit1	herbl	herbc	wlitr	litrd	litrc
rich	1.0										
lake	0.696	1.0									
imp	−0.167	−0.355	1.0								
swale	−0.431	−0.659	−0.253	1.0							
vhit2	0.372	0.167	0.111	−0.099	1.0						
vhit1	0.222	−0.156	0.552	−0.118	0.653	1.0					
herbl	0.060	−0.252	0.562	−0.009	0.581	0.825	1.0				
herbc	0.091	−0.087	0.419	−0.132	0.437	0.745	0.756	1.0			
wlitr	0.509	0.430	−0.284	−0.099	−0.051	−0.290	−0.395	−0.396	1.0		
litrd	0.238	0.146	−0.433	0.383	0.027	−0.097	−0.180	−0.281	0.419	1.0	
litrc	0.219	0.194	−0.442	0.273	−0.118	−0.414	−0.509	−0.580	0.568	0.762	1.0
sd	2.170	0.510	0.332	0.476	0.512	1.482	0.173	0.122	0.100	0.122	0.148

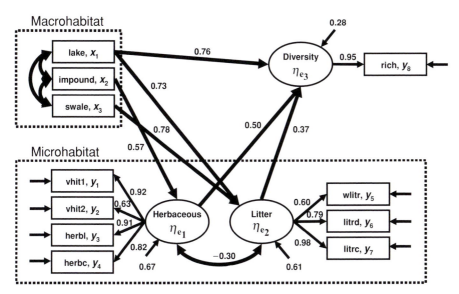

Figure 6.18. Results obtained for model I, showing standardized values for path coefficients and the error variances of latent endogenous variables. Correlations among *x*s and errors for *y*s are not shown, for simplicity. Nonsignificant effects of macrohabitat types were dropped from the final model, which possessed a chi-square of 50.42 with 39 degrees of freedom and a p of 0.104.

Results for model I   The results for model I are given in Figure 6.18. For the purposes of this evaluation (and in contrast to our practice in Example 1), nonsignificant effects of macrohabitat types on endogenous variables were dropped from the final model. In spite of the small sample size, results were stable and the fit between model expectations and data was acceptable. As these results show, impoundments had significantly higher levels of herbaceous vegetation than did other macrohabitat types. Litter accumulation, in contrast, was substantially higher in lakes and swales than in impoundments and riverine habitats (recall, the riverine variable was omitted and, therefore, serves as the baseline condition). Anuran diversity was found to be higher in lakes than in all other habitat types.

Results for model H   Model H provides for a single path from each composite to replace the multiple paths that would otherwise connect one construct with another. Aside from that, the models are very similar. Results from the estimation of model H are presented in Figure 6.19. A comparison of results from models I and H shows numerous similarities, and a few differences. Model fit parameters are identical for the two models. Also, variance explanation for

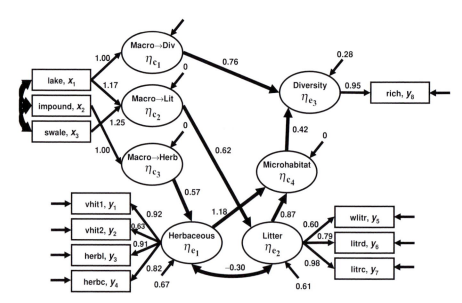

Figure 6.19. Results obtained for model H, showing standardized values for path coefficients and the error variances of latent endogenous variables. Correlations among xs and errors for ys are not shown, for simplicity. Nonsignificant effects of macrohabitat types were dropped from the final model, which possessed a chi-square of 50.42 with 39 degrees of freedom and a p of 0.104; precisely as for model I.

endogenous latent variables is the same, with R^2s of 0.33, 0.39, and 0.78 for η_{e_1}–η_{e_3} respectively. Loadings in L→M blocks are the same for both models, as are outward paths from composites possessing single causes (η_{c_1} to η_{e_3} and η_{c_3} to η_{e_1}), in comparison to the equivalent effects in model I (x_1 to η_{e_3} and x_2 to η_{e_1}). Composites with multiple causes in model H yielded parameters not found in model I, such as those associated with η_{c_4} to η_{e_3} (Microhabitat to Diversity) and η_{c_2} to η_{e_2} (Macro→Lit to Litter). The path coefficients associated with these paths represent standardized collective effects of the composites' causes on the response variables involved. Heise (1972) referred to these coefficients as "sheath" coefficients to designate the fact that they represent a collection of causes.

The most conspicuous differences between models I and H reside with the paths from causes to composites. For example, in model I, the effects of Herbaceous and Litter on Diversity are represented by two path coefficients (0.50 and 0.37), while in model H, the same effects are represented by three paths, two from Herbaceous and Litter to Microhabitat (1.18 and 0.87), and one from Microhabitat to Diversity (0.42). Upon first examination, the paths from Herbaceous and Litter to Microhabitat appear unusually inflated (contrary to popular notions, standardized coefficients can be greater than 1.0 when offsetting paths are present), particularly since Herbaceous and Litter are only modestly correlated (-0.30). However, the equivalency of relationships in models I and H can be made clear by realizing that the total effects of Herbaceous and Litter on Diversity are simply compound paths in model H (e.g., the effect of η_{e_1} on η_{e_3} = 1.18 times 0.42 = 0.50). The same holds true for all effects involving composites (e.g., the effect of x_1 and x_3 on η_{e_2}).

Results for model G   Model G, as described above, is a more general statement than model H, and presumes that a single composite is sufficient to represent the effects of Macrohabitat types on η_{e_1}, η_{e_2}, and η_{e_3}. Results from maximum likelihood estimation of model G included a chi-squared of model fit of 66.12 with 38 degrees of freedom, and an associated p-value of 0.0031, indicating poor fit. It was found that when estimated using a single composite for Macrohabitat effects, substantial residual correlations between individual macrohabitat types and the indicators for η_{e_1}, η_{e_2}, and η_{e_3}, were not resolved. These results suggested that a single composite representing the effects of macrohabitat types on Herbaceous, Litter, and Diversity was inconsistent with the data. However, neither impoundment or swale indicators contributed significantly to the composite in this case, therefore, it was possible to simplify the model by dropping these indicators from the model. With these indicators deleted, model fit improved to 30.03 with 24 degrees of freedom and a p-value of 0.1837, indicating acceptable fit. The results presented in Figure 6.20 are based on these results.

The version of model G presented in Figure 6.20, while representing a model that fits the data, fails to explain significant variation in either η_{e_1} or η_{e_2}. Lichtenberg *et al.* (unpublished) chose to select this model to represent the direct and indirect effects of Macrohabitat, because it addressed the central question of interest in their study. While it succeeds at that more narrow objective, model G fails to provide an explanation for macrohabitat effects on both diversity and microhabitat. The clear reason for that failure is that macrohabitat effects on microhabitat conditions are quite different from those on diversity, and a single composite cannot adequately represent both.

A consideration of model F   The most abstract model, model F, represents direct effects of Macrohabitat on Microhabitat rather than on the dimensions of Microhabitat (Herbaceous and Litter). Unfortunately, a proper estimation of this model using a simultaneous solution procedure cannot be achieved. The fundamental difficulty is that a zero error variance is specified for

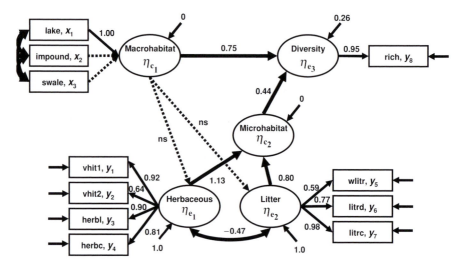

Figure 6.20. Results obtained for model G, showing standardized values for path coefficients and the error variances of latent endogenous variables. Correlations among *x*s and errors for *y*s are not shown, for simplicity. Chi-square for this model was 30.03 with 24 degrees of freedom and a p of 0.1837.

Microhabitat in order to permit it to represent the effects of Herbaceous and Litter on Diversity. However, with a zero error variance specified, it is not possible to estimate a nonzero error variance for Microhabitat based on the effects of Macrohabitat. Thus, with Microhabitat represented as a composite with zero error variance, model F is irresolvable. This serves as an additional argument in favor of modeling approaches in which exogenous influences are measured against the individual dimensions of endogenous multidimensional constructs (e.g., models H and G), rather than the composite of their combined effects (in this case, on Diversity). Using such an approach, effects on the endogenous composite can be estimated using compound paths. An alternative approach that could be used is a two-stage solution procedure in which factor scores for η_{c_2} are first derived and then used in a simpler model involving only η_{c_1}, η_{c_2}, and η_{e_3}. Such a model would, however, fail to provide a broad evaluation of the relationships embodied in model F, and is not addressed further here.

Conclusions and recommendations

It should be clear from the examples considered in this review that the standard hybrid model commonly used to describe SEM is an inadequate representation of the possibilities. A consideration of composite variables contributes balance to the modeling process by providing options and encouraging a thorough evaluation of constructs and the measures at hand. While this problem has been pointed out by some at various times, the inclusion of composites in structural equation models remains rare, while the misspecification of models using only L→M blocks is common.

At present, much of the literature on composite variables is based on the premise that composites should have two or more effects on other variables (outward-directed paths), and that composites with single effects should not be included in models (MacCallum and Browne 1993, Edwards 2001, Jarvis *et al.* 2003, Williams *et al.* 2003). This recommendation has been offered as a necessary, though not sufficient, requirement for the identification of composite error variances. In Example 1, such a model (model C) was indeed found to be appropriate and satisfactory. However, in many cases models of this sort will not be adequate, and those with single effects (e.g., model E) will be required. It can be argued that (1) error variance estimates for latent variables possessing only causal indicators will seldom be meaningful and, thus, they should not drive decisions about the appropriate form of composites to include in a model, (2) including composites having only single outward directed paths can be quite valuable even though the covariances for a set of data can be represented without them, and (3) confining the use of composites to cases where there are multiple outward directed pathways is ill-advised, because it can lead the researcher into developing and testing models that fail to match the relations in the data.

A key factor that has limited the use of composites has been the aforementioned problem of parameter identification for models with single effects (as well as some models with multiple effects). In this example we show that this can be resolved by reference to a partially reduced form model (of the type represented by model D), in which specific effects can be evaluated, in conjunction with the specification of a scale for the composite. Furthermore, we recommend that for models that incorporate composites, reduced form models such as model D and single-effect models such as model E should be routinely examined as part of the evaluation process. When this approach is taken, a more complete consideration of construct representation is possible for structural equation models.

As illustrated in Example 2, representing endogenous constructs using composites poses additional theoretical and practical issues. Models of the most general type, which posit direct effects of exogenous variables on endogenous composites, while of interest, may be difficult to solve and also to interpret. Models in which effects on endogenous constructs are modeled through influences on their dimensions prove to be more tractable, as well as more generally interpretable. Again, as a general strategy, comparing results with those from models with fewer restrictions contributes to the evaluation process.

Modern SEM using latent variables has largely developed through applications to the social and economic sciences, although it is now widely used in a broad range of disciplines. Part of the emphasis on common factor-type models (e.g., the hybrid model) in certain fields is where there is an availability of redundant measures, such as batteries of questionnaire items or exam questions, that can be used to estimate underlying causes. Even in these disciplines, it seems that data and constructs are such that composites could be widely used. In the natural sciences, redundant measures are much less common, which has contributed to an emphasis on path analysis using only observed variables, and little use of latent or composite variables. Certainly multi-indicator latent variables of the $L \rightarrow M$ block type will find wide usage in the natural sciences. However, we can anticipate that a significant need will develop for considerations of composite variables to represent collections of effects. In the study of natural systems, it is often the case that the concepts of greatest interest are quite abstract and heterogeneous. Thus, composites, when used with care, provide a useful way of summarizing groups of effects that match our theories about construct relations, and they belong in our SEM tool box.

7

Additional techniques for complex situations

As mentioned earlier, the array of techniques associated with structural equation modeling has grown continuously since the LISREL synthesis. Some of this growth has been associated with refinements and some from new inventions. It is important for the reader to realize that the development of SEM methodology is still a work in progress. As described in Chapter 6, the ability to formulate and solve models containing composite variables, though long discussed, is only now being achieved. Refinements continue to be made in our ability to create models that are appropriate for the questions of interest and the data at hand. Structural equation modeling attempts to do something quite ambitious, to develop and evaluate multivariate models appropriate to almost any situation. Not surprisingly, the development of methods to accomplish this goal takes time and certain statistical limitations must be overcome.

For the most part, the material covered in Chapters 3, 4, and 5 represents basic principles relating to SEM. Many additional capabilities exist beyond those covered thus far, and many new developments are emerging. Some of these additional techniques and new developments are described in this chapter, although because this is such a vast subject, the treatments presented are only brief introductions to a select set of topics.

While the material in this chapter is in a section called Advanced topics, in my experience, the models that are most appropriate to understanding natural systems often require advanced elements or procedures. Nonlinearities are commonplace, categorical response variables are often involved, reciprocal interactions frequently encountered, and data are typically hierarchical in some fashion. Furthermore, we may wish to create multi-level models that recognize different processes at different scales, or we may be interested in time-course models. Thus, creating the most appropriate model for a situation will often require the use of some advanced techniques beyond the basics covered in the first section of chapters. This is not to encourage researchers to use models that are any more complex than necessary. When a simple modeling approach will suffice, it is to be preferred. Also, when one is starting out with SEM, it is advisable to begin with simple models to understand the fundamentals involved. As alluded to in Chapters 4 and 6, there is a long history of misuse of latent variables and although they are presented in most basic presentations relating to SEM, to use them properly is an advanced skill.

In this chapter, I will attempt to present in brief and concise form a little about a number of more advanced topics. Nearly all of these topics have one or more books, or many articles written about them. I will not be able to cover any of them in the depth they deserve in this introductory text. Some beginning users of SEM may wish to skim this chapter and save the mastery of these topics for another day. Others may find that their applications require them to confront some of the topics covered in this chapter from the beginning. In addition to providing a brief introduction and a limited number of examples, I will provide references to in-depth treatments of the topics. It can be argued that SEM is akin to a construction process. As with modern building construction, tools, techniques, and materials can be used in a variety of creative ways to solve problems. Here I illustrate a few more of the tools that are available.

Multigroup analyses

One of the early elaborations of standard SEM practice was the development of the multigroup analysis. It is not uncommon that one wishes to address questions about groups. For example, samples may include male and female members of a population and one may wish to ask whether the multivariate relations of interest are the same for both groups. Or, we may be interested in complex interactions involving the responses of different groups. Multigroup analyses can range from simple (e.g., comparing regressions between groups) to complex (e.g., evaluating the effects of treatment applications on models containing conceptual variables). As a fundamental tool in the SEM toolbox, the multigroup analysis is quite a powerful capability.

The essence of the multigroup analysis is that elements in a data set can be assigned to one or another group membership, and comparative models that apply to each group can be developed. Of course, separate models for each group of samples can always be developed and evaluated separately. However, such an approach misses the opportunity to arrive at a general answer. What differs in multigroup analysis is that it is possible to evaluate for all model parameters whether they differ between groups and, therefore, whether the groups

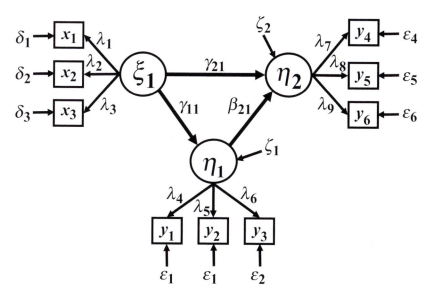

Figure 7.1. Example model used to discuss multigroup analysis.

fit a common model. With a multigroup analysis we can determine exactly what parameters are the same or different across groups, using the data from all groups simultaneously. As we will see, this framework also permits us to evaluate differences between groups in mean values, in addition to the correlations/covariances that are the standard stuff of SEM analyses. A slightly more technical presentation of multigroup analysis, along with ecological examples, can be found in Grace (2003a) and Pugesek (2003). Example applications can be found in Grace and Pugesek (1998) and Grace and Jutila (1999). A more general, nontechnical introduction to the subject can be found in Kline (2005). Here I give a brief illustration of some of the inferences that can be made by comparing groups.

Procedures

In multigroup analysis, there are quite a few parameters to compare between groups (all path coefficients, variances, error terms, and means). Figure 7.1 provides us with an example model to aid in the description of the process. Additionally, the reader can refer to Appendix 5.1 where a representation of the LISREL model is given, which may be helpful if one wishes to better understand the mathematical notation. Essentially, the lambdas (λ) describe the loadings between latent and observed variables, deltas (δ) are errors for indicators of exogenous latent variables, while epsilons (ε) are errors for indicators of endogenous latent variables. Gammas (γ) describe path coefficients relating endogenous to exogenous latents, while betas (β) describe path coefficients relating endogenous to other endogenous latent variables. Zetas (ζ) are disturbance terms for endogenous latents.

Because of the large number of comparisons being made, care must be taken to arrive at a stable solution. Two general strategies have been proposed for comparing parameters in multigroup analysis. In the first of these, one begins by performing separate analyses for each group allowing all parameters to differ between groups. Equality constraints are progressively added and the appropriateness of such constraints evaluated. Bollen (1989, pages 355–365) has suggested the following progression as a reasonable way to proceed:

H_{form}	same form
H_{λ}	loadings from latent variables to effect indicators equal
$H_{\lambda\Theta}$	loadings and correlated errors equal
$H_{\lambda\Theta B\Gamma}$	loadings, correlated errors, and structural path coefficients equal
$H_{\lambda\Theta B\Gamma\Psi}$	loadings, correlated errors, structural path coefficients, plus variances and covariances for endogenous latent variables equal
$H_{\lambda\Theta B\Gamma\Psi\Phi}$	loadings, correlated errors, structural path coefficients, plus variances and covariances for both endogenous and exogenous latent variables equal

where Θ is a matrix containing the variances and covariances for observed variables, $\mathbf{B}$ is a matrix giving the covariances among endogenous latent variables, Γ is a matrix giving the covariances between exogenous and endogenous latent variables, Ψ specifies the covariances among errors of exogenous latent variables, and Φ specifies covariances among errors of endogenous latent variables. It is always recommended that the first step in a multigroup analysis should be to consider whether the appropriate model for both groups is of the same form, for if that analysis fails, it makes little sense to evaluate all the individual parameters. The addition of constraints can deviate from the above sequence, however, depending on the comparisons of greatest theoretical importance. In this sequence, parameters associated with the measurement model are considered first, followed by an assessment of similarity in the structural model. Correlations among errors and disturbances are often of least interest, and considered last. In cases where the questions of most interest have to do with differences between groups in the structural model (the betas and gammas), they may be evaluated first. Model evaluation typically employs single-degree-of-freedom χ^2 tests as well as the use of comparative indices such as AIC.

A second approach to multigroup analysis relies on Lagrange multipliers (Lee and Bentler 1980). This approach differs from the above-described methods because the Lagrange multiplier (LM) approach evaluates the validity of equality constraints multivariately, instead of univariately. In this case, all equality constraints are evaluated simultaneously, and it is unnecessary to evaluate a series of increasingly restrictive models in order to find the best final model. In general, the LM method is both easier to implement and more reliable with regard to the final solution and is recommended (though not available in all software packages at the present time).

The reader should be reminded here of the discussion in Chapter 3 relating to standardized versus unstandardized parameters. As was stated there, when comparing populations (or groups), unstandardized parameters are often to be preferred. A key aspect behind this recommendation is the influence that variances have on standardized parameters. When variances differ between groups for variables, the basis for standardization of coefficients also differs. Thus, it is possible for unstandardized coefficients to be the same across groups while the standardized coefficients appear to differ. The reverse is also possible. Since the significance tests are based on unstandardized parameters, they are viewed as a poor basis for comparing groups when variances differ. When variances do not differ between groups, however, standardized coefficients may be suitable (as long as they meet the interpretational objectives of the researcher).

In addition to being able to compare all parameters derived from the analysis of covariances between groups, it is possible to evaluate differences in means as well. The analysis of means within SEM is based on a regression approach, where the intercept is used to relate regression results to mean responses. Typically, the evaluation of means tests to see if the differences between groups is zero, although interest is often in the magnitude of differences. The analysis of means within SEM differs from that associated with ANOVA in that it permits an assessment of the means of latent variables, and it is much more realistic with regard to the control of covariates, correlated errors, and other types of nonindependencies.

An illustration

In 1993 and 1994, Heli Jutila conducted a study of vegetation in coastal areas of Finland. Samples were taken from paired grazed and ungrazed meadows across several geographic areas. The emphasis in the SEM analysis of these data (Grace and Jutila 1999) was to understand patterns of species richness and how they might be influenced by grazing. The effects of geographic region, soil conditions, and elevation/flooding on community biomass and richness were

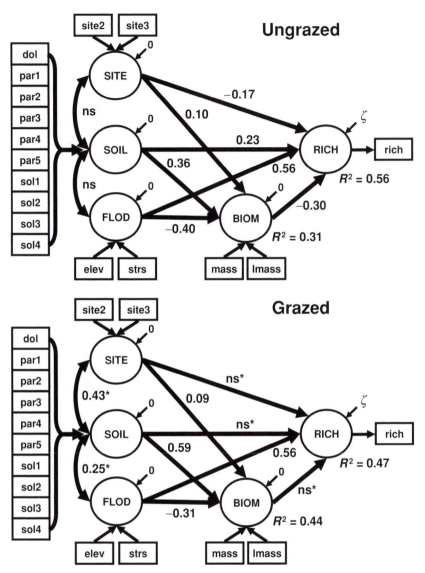

Figure 7.2. Multigroup results for study of grazing effects. Paths marked with asterisks in the lower figure are statistically different among groups. From Grace and Jutila (1999), by permission of Oikos.

believed to apply to both grazed and ungrazed sites, forming the basis for a multigroup analysis. The form of the model and results for the two groups are shown in Figure 7.2. The effects of geographic region were modeled as categorical effects using dummy (yes or no) variables. It is necessary when modeling with dummy variables to omit at least one variable (in the case of SITE, sites 1 and 4 were equivalent and were omitted). The interpretation of the SITE effect is the influence of being at sites 2 and 3 relative to 1 and 4. The overall influence of sites was modeled as a composite, as described in Chapter 5. SOIL was likewise a composite of the effects of different parent materials (par 1–6), soil types (sol 1–5), and the depth of the litter layer (dol), with all but dol being dummy variables. Both flooding (FLOD) and community biomass (BIOM) had nonlinear relationships with richness, and this was also modeled using composite effects (this procedure is discussed in more detail later in the chapter). One set of parameters evaluated in the multigroup analysis but not shown in Figure 7.2 is the variances, which in this case were not found to differ significantly. Means were not evaluated in this case as part of the multigroup analysis.

We can see from the multigroup results (Figure 7.2) that relationships between SOIL and SITE, as well as SOIL and FLOD, differed between groups. These differences support the case for suspecting that the soil differences between grazed and ungrazed meadows might have resulted from grazing itself. The results further indicate that in the grazed meadows, species richness was unrelated to site or soil effects, while these relationships were both modestly important in ungrazed meadows. There is a suggestion from these differences between groups that grazing effects on richness may be overwhelming site and soil influences. The other main difference between groups in this study is the relationship between biomass and richness. We can see that there is evidence for a strong, predominantly negative effect of biomass on richness in ungrazed meadows (path coefficient = −0.30). However, in grazed meadows there is no significant relationship between biomass and richness.

As illustrated in this presentation, multigroup analyses allow for a detailed inspection of how groups differ. One of the greatest strengths of this type of analysis is the ability to explicitly consider interactions between the group variable and all within-group relationships. The ability to consider differences in variances and means between groups also allows for an analysis framework that is superior to traditional analysis of variance approaches in many regards. As SEM becomes used more in manipulative experiments, we can expect that multigroup analyses will become very popular because of the power and flexibility they provide.

Models containing categorical variables

I should start out by making sure that the reader understands that when categorical variables are exogenous, they pose no real problems for either regression or structural equation models, as distributional assumptions do not apply. In fact, categorical exogenous variables are frequently used as alternatives to several of the procedures discussed in this chapter. Instead of performing multigroup analyses, such as described in the previous section, ofter analysts will use categorical variables to represent groups in a single model. Several examples of this will be presented in Chapter 10, dealing with the analysis of experimental data. Categorical exogenous variables can also be used to deal with heterogeneous samples, such as those that involve multi-level sampling (discussed later in the chapter). In such situations, nominal influences can be modeled as a series of dummy variables, again relying on categorical exogenous variables.

When categorical variables are endogenous, however, a number of important issues arise. Some of these issues are sufficiently challenging that many SEM software programs do not have options for analyzing such models. Both statistical and interpretational issues arise when modeling categorical outcomes. As we shall see in the next chapter, one of the strengths of Bayesian approaches to SEM is their inherent fit for modeling categorical responses. For now, however, we will stay within the framework of conventional SEM and consider both the difficulties categorical responses pose, and some remedies.

It is quite common for variables to be categorical rather than continuous. When we count species in a plot or sample, an infinite number of values are not attainable. Instead, where a maximum of 20 species are obtained in a sample, that variable has a maximum of 20 levels, and thus, is not a truly continuous variable. Even when a variable has a central tendency, the very fact that there are a limited number of levels can result in some deviations from normality. When the number of levels is high, such deviations are fairly unimportant. The question we must ask, though, is at what point are the number of levels of a categorical variable sufficiently low to result in misleading findings? Some effort has been spent considering this question (Bollen 1989, pages 433–447). Typical answers fall between 5 and 7 levels as "safe" for treating ordered categorical variables as if they were continuous. It is also safe to say that when a response variable possesses only two to three levels, special accommodations should be employed. The simplest and most extreme case is where only two outcomes are observed, such as in a dichotomous ordinal variable of the "yes or no" variety.

There are two kinds of problem that arise when dealing with categorical responses, attenuated correlations and nonnormality. First, correlations involving ordinal variables, have some undesirable properties. Such correlations are truncated in comparison to correlations with the underlying continuous response factor. Imagine that we have two continuous variables, an x and a y, that have a correlation of 0.5. Further imagine that we score the values of y as being a 0 or 1 if they fall either below or above the mean. If we derive the correlation between x and the categorical response y_c, the correlation will now be substantially less than 0.5. The reason for this drop is a loss of information. When the underlying continuous response is reduced to a classification, the loss of information truncates the correlations with other variables. The exact value of the truncated correlation will depend on the number of responses that fall into the two categories (0 or 1). Simulation studies show that as the number of categories in y_c goes up, the observed correlation between x and y_c will approach the "true" correlation between x and y. The second issue relating to categorical responses deals with the nonnormality of residuals. For a dichotomous categorical variable, the precise degree of nonnormality depends on the relative frequency of 0s and 1s. Generally speaking, however, standard errors are biased downward, leading to inaccurate estimates of probabilities.

In regression models, the approach often taken for dealing with categorical responses is the logistic model. Oversimplifying a little, the logistic model is one that treats the responses as approximating an S-shaped response curve, with the logit transformation being used to linearize that curve. In SEM, the approach most often taken is based on the probit model work by Muthén (1984). In the probit model, we assume that underlying the categorical outcomes is a continuous variable. Stated formally, we assume that behind the observed response distribution of y is a continuous underlying probability function y^*. Our goal is to understand y^* based on our observations of y.

The probit approach is one that involves three steps. In the first step, there is an estimation of the thresholds. In the case of a dichotomous response, the assumption is made that if the value of the underlying continuous response is below the threshold, we will observe a 0. On the other hand, if the value of the underlying continuous variable is above the threshold, we will observe a 1. Our estimate of the threshold value depends on the number of 0s and 1s. When we observe an equal number of 0s and 1s, we would usually assume that the threshold of y^* would be its mean value.

The second step in the probit approach involves the use of polychoric correlations. Stated simply, the polychoric correlation is the correlation between an x and a y^* that would yield the observed correlation between x and y given the estimated threshold. It is easy to demonstrate the validity of this approach. If you take some correlated pair of x and y variables and choose a threshold to use to categorize y into y_c, regression using the probit method will allow you to recover the original correlation between x and y.

The third step in the probit method involves analysis of the polychoric correlation matrix in place of the observed correlation matrix. We should be aware that since y is categorical, the mean and variance are not identified parameters. Therefore, the mean is set to 0 and the variance to 1. As a result, this is one of the few cases in SEM where we must evaluate the correlation matrix instead of the covariance matrix.

The remaining problem to address when dealing with categorical response variables is nonnormality. The earliest approach to addressing this problem was the asymptotic distribution-free method. Studies have subsequently shown that extremely large sample sizes are required for this method to yield reliable results. As an alternative approach, Muthén (1984) has proposed a weighted least squares method that has been found to behave reasonably well in providing approximately correct standard errors.

An illustration

When making observations of wildlife species, it is often the case that individuals are observed only occasionally. This alludes to the fact that animal count data often contain lots of 0s. In a study of the responses of grassland birds to fire history, Baldwin (2005) found that individual species were encountered infrequently such that it was best to simply represent the data as either observed or unobserved. Given the data in this form, the questions posed were about how different habitat factors relate to the probability of observing a bird species. In this case, the categorical observations represent y, while the probability of seeing a bird represents y^*. Thus, we envisage the problem as one in which the probability of seeing a bird varies continuously with habitat conditions, while some threshold determines whether a bird will be observed or not.

In this study, the primary driving variable of interest was the number of years since a grassland unit was burned (typically by prescribed burning). Fifteen management units were selected for sampling, with five having been burned within one year, five within one to two years, and five within two to three years. Sampling along transects within the management units produced 173 observations at a scale where bird occurrence could be related to vegetation characteristics. The vegetation characteristics of presumed importance included vegetation type, density of herbaceous vegetation, and the density and types of shrubs. The hierarchical nature of the data was accommodated using cluster techniques, which are discussed later in the chapter.

Figure 7.3 illustrates the hypothesis evaluated for each of the four most common species. The two primary questions of interest were (1) whether the probability of finding a bird in a habitat was affected by the time since burning,

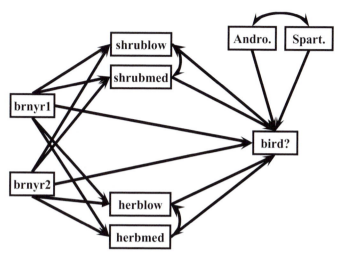

Figure 7.3. Model relating categorical observations of birds of a species to four types of influence, (1) year since burn (brnyr), (2) density of shrubs (shrublow, shrubmed, or shrubhigh), (3) density of herbaceous vegetation (herblow, herbmed, or herbhigh), and (4) vegetation type (*Andropogon, Spartina,* or mixed).

and (2) whether any relationship between time of fire and the probability of birds could be explained by associated vegetation characteristics. One may ask why shrub density and herbaceous density are represented as categorical variables? In theory, these variables could be represented as continuous influences. However, examination of the data revealed that the relationships between birds and vegetation density were nonlinear. The use of ordered categories of vegetation density proved effective in this case as a means of dealing with those nonlinearities.

The results from this analysis for one of the bird species, LaConte's sparrow, are given in Figure 7.4. For this species, the probability of observing birds was least in fields burned three years previously, thus, there was a positive association between this species and year 1 fields and year 2 fields. These associations could be explained as indirect effects, since the associated vegetation conditions (particularly low shrub density) provide an adequate explanation for the association with burn year. It can be seen that there was an additional influence of medium levels of herbaceous vegetation on LaConte's, as well as a preference for vegetation types that include *Andropogon* (upland prairie dominated by little bluestem). Altogether, these results indicate that this species is most highly associated with habitat that has been burned between 1 and 2 years previously, that has a medium level of herbaceous cover, and that is upland prairie. Not

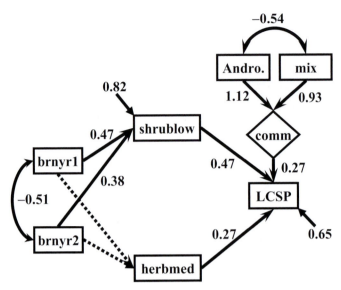

Figure 7.4. Results for LaConte's sparrows (from Baldwin 2005). A composite variable, comm, was included to represent the collective effect of vegetation type.

only does the use of categorical modeling accommodate the nature of the data in this case, the nature of the results would seem to be in a form quite usable for making decisions about habitat management.

Nonlinear relationships

It has been my experience that nonlinear relationships are very common in ecological problems. There are actually several different ways nonlinear relations can be addressed, some quite simple, and some more involved. The simplest means of addressing nonlinear relations is through transformations. In many cases, transformed variables can be used in place of explicitly modeled nonlinear relations. For monotonic nonlinear relations, simple transformations can often be quite effective. For transforming unimodal or more complex relations, however, it must be that the linearization of one relationship does not create a new nonlinear relation with some other variable. When this can be avoided, transformations can be effective. An additional way to deal with nonlinear relations was demonstrated in the previous section dealing with bird populations. By converting vegetation density into an ordered categorical variable, any assumption of a linear relationship involving vegetation was removed. Multigroup analysis, as discussed in the first section of this chapter, can be used to address a certain type of nonlinear relation, the interaction. In the example shown in Figure 7.2, by separating grazed and ungrazed meadows into contrasting groups, it was possible to allow the slopes of all relationships to differ between groups. When a slope does differ between groups, that constitutes a multiplicative nonlinearity, which we can think of as a significant interaction between group and relationship.

Continuous nonlinear relationships create some special challenges for structural equation models, both for observed variable models and especially for latent variable models having multiple indicators. Challenges posed by nonlinear interactions face both studies of ecological relations and evolutionary biology (Scheiner *et al.* 2000). Kline (2005, chapter 13) provides a useful introduction to the topic. Here I will show one example to illustrate how a simple nonlinearity can be dealt with, and the role that composites can play in summarizing nonlinear effects.

An illustration

Here I give some results from Grace and Keeley (2006) who examined the response of vegetation to wildfire in California chaparral. Some nonlinearities could be addressed using transformations. However, the relationship between species richness and plant cover was one where an explicit modeling of the nonlinearity was of interest. The results of this analysis can be seen in Figure 7.5, and afford us a means of seeing how this problem was addressed. First, visual inspection of the relationship between cover and richness revealed a simple unimodal curve. For this reason, we felt that a polynomial regression approach could be taken using cover and cover squared. This type of approach to modeling nonlinearities can often be effective, and is particularly appropriate where some optimum condition for a response exists. In this case, it appears that 100% cover is optimal for richness, and that at higher levels, richness declines.

The introduction of a higher order term, such as Plant Cover Squared, creates some potential problems. First, variables and their squares are highly correlated and this must be modeled. In Figure 7.5, the magnitude of the correlation between Plant Cover and Plant Cover Squared is not shown, as it is not of substantive interest. Instead, we followed the recommendation of Bollen (1998) and represented the relationship using a zigzag arrow that depicts that Plant Cover Squared is derived from Plant Cover. In some cases, the introduction of a higher order term results in a host of additional covariances in the model that must be included, but which are not of substantive interest because the higher order term is merely included for the purpose of representing the nonlinearity.

To solve some of the potential problems associated with the inclusion of polynomial terms, the higher order terms should be derived by first zero-centering

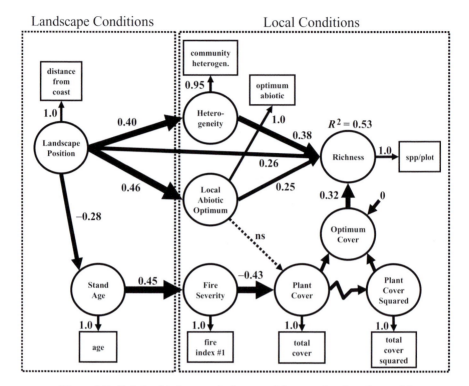

Figure 7.5. Relationship between herbaceous richness and various factors following fire in southern California chaparral (from Grace and Keeley 2006). This model includes an explicit nonlinearity between Plant Cover and Richness, along with a composite variable summarizing the relationship called Optimum Cover.

the original variable before raising to a higher power. This reduces the correlation between first and second order terms. Second, one should always specify a correlation between polynomial terms to represent their intercorrelations. High correlations between terms may still exist. However, the use of maximum likelihood estimation reduces problems potentially created by high multicollinearity, such as variance inflation, nonpositive definite matrices (ones that contain apparent contradictions), and empirical underidentification.

One further problem associated with polynomial regression is the interpretation of path coefficients. Typically, we would interpret a path coefficient, say from Plant Cover to Richness, as the expected change in Richness if we were to vary Plant Cover while holding the other variables in the model constant. However, it is not reasonable to expect to be able to hold Plant Cover Squared constant, since it is directly calculated from Plant Cover. Thus, the independent coefficients from Plant Cover and Plant Cover Squared do not have meaning, but instead, it is their collective effects that are of interest. To address this, we included a composite of latent effects, which is designated Optimum Cover. As discussed in Chapter 5, composites have their own set of issues to address, thus, this approach to modeling a nonlinear relationship involves several steps. That said, the resulting model would seem to effectively represent the relations of interest.

Latent growth models

A relatively recent innovation in SEM is the development of latent growth models. These are growth models in the sense that they deal with progressive temporal dynamics. Some, though not all, formulations of latent growth models require the analysis of the raw data, because they are based on a repeated measures concept. Latent variables are used in such models to represent population parameters, such as means, intercepts, and slopes, as well as to represent the influences of covariates. Covariates here refer to treatment variables, nonlinear terms, and both time-varying and time-invariant factors. To use such models, the researcher needs to be working with longitudinal data measured on at least three different occasions. Here I will introduce a simple example that illustrates a few of the many capabilities of latent growth modeling. Additional information about latent growth models can be found in Duncan *et al.* (1999) and Kline (2005, chapter 10).

An illustration

In the previous section, the illustration involved a study of vegetation responses following wildfire (Grace and Keeley 2006). Nonlinear relations were illustrated as part of a static model representing spatial variations in diversity across a heterogeneous landscape. In the same study, the authors were also interested in certain hypotheses regarding changes in diversity over time. Previous studies suggested that following fire in these systems, there is an initial flush in herbaceous plant diversity associated with fire-induced germination. Over time, it is expected that diversity will decline as time since disturbance increases. Examination of the temporal dynamics of richness (Figure 7.6A) shows that there was only a hint of a declining trend. The authors were aware, however, of substantial year to year variations in rainfall. Furthermore, there is strong evidence that rainfall in this system is a substantial limiting factor for plant richness. Patterns of year to year rainfall (Figure 7.6B) suggest the high levels of richness observed in 1995 and 1998 can be explained by the very high amounts of rainfall in those years. To evaluate this hypothesis, a latent growth model was constructed, with annual rainfall included as a time-varying covariate. The results are shown in Figure 7.7.

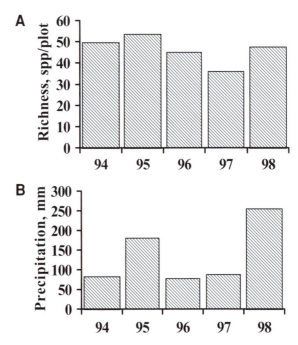

Figure 7.6. A. Changes in herbaceous richness over a five-year period following fire (from Grace and Keeley 2006). B. Variations in annual precipitation accompanying changes in richness.

The results from the latent growth analysis of richness showed that the data are consistent with the hypothesis of a general decline over time. When the influence of rainfall was controlled for in the model, an average decline of 4.35 species per year was estimated for the five-year period, although the decline function was not strictly linear. For the overall model, a robust chi-square of 14.2 was found with 9 degrees of freedom and an associated p-value of 0.115. The variance in richness explained by the model for the five years were 34, 62, 68, 76, and 60%. Overall, these results support the contention that behind the somewhat noisy observed dynamics are two major influences, post-disturbance decline and responsiveness to precipitation.

Hierarchical data and models

It is very common that data are hierarchically structured. Samples may be associated with sample units that are located within larger units or clusters. This is almost universally the case in studies of sessile organisms, and also

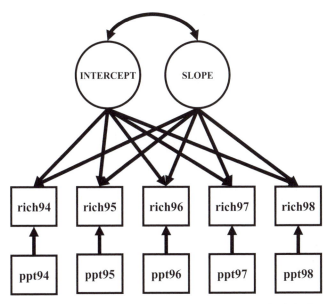

Figure 7.7. Latent growth model representing temporal dynamics in herbaceous richness based on the influence of a common intercept and a common (though complex) slope, as well as the influence of year to year variations in precipitation.

typically true for sampling efforts involving mobile animals. When the hierarchical structure of data is ignored, it can lead to downward biased standard errors; when hierarchical structure is incorporated into the analysis, it can lead to an increased understanding of the system.

There are several different ways that hierarchical structure can be modeled, ranging from the simplistic to the sophisticated. We have examined a couple of the possibilities in previous sections. Multigroup analysis is an explicit means of dealing with hierarchical structure. This approach is most useful when there are primary hypotheses of interest about the highest level of structure. If one is interested in comparing survival of males and females in a population, a multigroup analysis is a good way to look at main effects and interactions. Sampling structure can also be dealt with using exogenous categorical variables representing that structure. In Figure 7.2, we can see that the influences of three geographic areas (sites 1–3) along the Finnish coast were accommodated using two dummy variables. Such an approach permits the hierarchical structure to be included in the model, and also allows for general evaluation of the differences attributable to each site. Using variables to represent sites, as with certain other approaches, does not, however, allow for interactions between the site and the other processes to be considered.

When the units of hierarchical structure are not of interest, for example, one uses cluster sampling and is not particularly interested in the differences among clusters; the data can be adjusted to make the clustering transparent. This kind of correction can be done by hand or is implemented in some software packages. The basic approach is to estimate standard errors and chi-square tests of model fit, taking into account nonindependence of the observations.

A somewhat recent development in the field of SEM are software packages that permit multi-level modeling (also known as hierarchical linear modeling). Multi-level modeling recognizes that there are relationships of interest within and between sample levels. For example, if one samples a large number of populations collecting data on individuals in each population, it is of interest to ask questions about the processing operating within and between populations. Multi-level modeling permits the development and evaluation of population and individual models simultaneously. Given the interest in the effects of spatial scale in many ecological problems, multi-level models would seem to hold promise for addressing a new set of analyses. The interested reader is referred to Little *et al.* (2000) and Hox (2002) for a detailed discussion of this topic and to Shipley (2000, chapter 7) for an illustration of its application to natural systems.

Feedback loops: nonrecursive models

While recursive models, which we have examined throughout the book, represent only unidirectional flow of effects, there are many cases where interactions can be reciprocal, or nonrecursive. In general, nonrecursive models represent some sort of feedback between system components. Thus, there is an implicit temporal element in these models. The inclusion of reciprocal interactions can be viewed as an act of time compression, where the temporal dynamics are simplified to a static representation of feedback. Often there is more than one way to model feedback relations. The simplest form of nonrecursive model involves reciprocal effects (e.g., Figure 7.8A). Feedback can also involve more than two variables, such as in a case where $y_1 \rightarrow y_2 \rightarrow y_3 \rightarrow y_1$.

Figure 7.8A provides a representation of a nonrecursive feedback model. In this model we posit that correlations between two variables, y_1 and y_2 can be explained, in part, through their interactions. In Chapter 2, we looked at the interactions between a plant, leafy spurge, and two species of insects that feed on it. In that case, since timecourse data were available, the reciprocal interactions between species were represented in a modified panel design. A simple panel

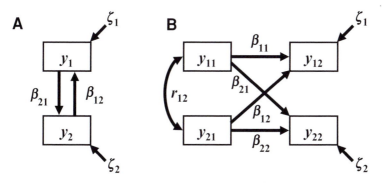

Figure 7.8. A. A simple, nonrecursive model with reciprocal influences. B. A panel model in which reciprocal interaction is played out over time; y_{ij} is entity i at time j.

model is shown in Figure 7.8B for comparison. Here it is represented that variables y_1 and y_2 influence each other over time (from time 1 to time 2). An influence of each variable on itself over time is also represented in the model (by the paths from y_{i_1} to y_{i_2}).

As was shown in Chapter 2, a temporal or dynamic approach to studying reciprocal interactions can partition out many different elements of the interaction. This might lead one to think that reciprocal interactions should always be represented using timecourse data. The detailed nature of panel models can become limiting when representing entities changing over time along with many factors that influence those entities. One other complication is the need for the precise timecourse data that captures the various steps in the interaction. Collectively, these challenges mean that in some cases we may wish to use nonrecursive models to represent reciprocal feedback relations. In such a case, we are focusing on the equilibrium net effects of the interaction instead of the dynamics and components.

If we stop to think about it, we can anticipate that nonrecursive models may pose some special challenges. Feedback loops imply an infinite series of back and forth effects between variables. This means the errors of the variables possessing reciprocal interactions can be expected to be correlated. So, nonrecursive models will typically possess (1) extra arrows (e.g., two arrows between two variables), and (2) correlated errors. With so many parameters to estimate, such models can be expected to have special problems with model identification. Below I provide an illustration of how limiting this problem can be for the inclusion of feedback in structural equation models.

There are a couple of other aspects of nonrecursive models worth mentioning. The first is the basis issue of estimation. As mentioned in Chapter 5, recursive path models with observed variables can be estimated with either OLS (ordinary least squares) techniques or using ML (maximum likelihood estimation) methods. However, nonrecursive models cannot be correctly estimated using OLS. The nonindependence of errors of the sort found in nonrecursive models leads to improper solutions. For this reason, typically maximum likelihood estimation is used. It is worth pointing out that there is actually a type of least squares approach called two-stage least squares (2SLS) that is not only suitable for estimating nonrecursive models, but has some advantages in dealing with the fact that in these models there are correlations between residuals and causes, which violates the assumptions of other estimation methods. The reader interested in this topic should refer to Bollen (1996).

Nonrecursive models have special issues regarding interpretation. Referring back to Figure 7.8, not only does y_1 have an effect on y_2, it also has an indirect effect on itself. In the simple case where $\beta_{12} = \beta_{21} = 0.5$, the indirect effect on itself through one feedback loop is $0.5 \times 0.5 = 0.25$. Also, y_1 has an indirect effect on y_2. The magnitude of that effect is 0.125. Such indirect effects diminish asymptotically, nevertheless, they must be accounted for in calculations of indirect effects and R^2s. Fortunately for the researcher, many of the modern SEM software programs perform these calculations for us. What is of greater importance is that these results depend on an assumption of equilibrium for the temporal dynamic that is being represented. As has been shown by Kaplan *et al.* (2001), violations of equilibrium cause significant bias in estimated effects. This places a burden on the researcher to argue convincingly that the interaction being modeled can be interpreted as an equilibrium result.

Illustration

There have been very few applications of nonrecursive models to ecological problems. One exception is the analysis of limnological interactions by Johnson *et al.* (1991), who examined interactions between various components of aquatic foodwebs, including reciprocal interactions between phytoplankton and zooplankton. Their work is discussed further in Chapter 9, as an example of the use of SEM with experimental studies. To illustrate the potential utility of nonrecursive models in the current, brief discussion, I will rely on a hypothetical example. In this example, we imagine two potentially competing species that occur together across some range of environmental conditions. Let us further

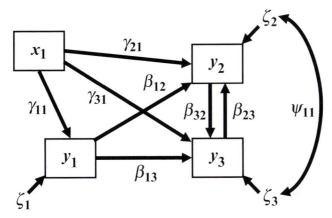

Figure 7.9. Nonrecursive model with two reciprocally interacting entities (y_2 and y_3) and two variables having joint control over them (x_1 and y_1).

imagine that we have an estimate of the degree of correlation between these species sampled across some area of interest, along with estimates of their standard errors, which permits us to examine their covariance. By simply referring to these as species 1 and species 2, we can use Figure 7.8A as a representation of their association. The first question we might ask is, can we solve for their individual effects on one another (β_{12}, β_{12}) given the available information? If we take the variances for y_1 and y_2 as known from their sample variances, we have a model with two unknown parameters (the path coefficients), but with only one known piece of information (the covariance between species). We know from our discussion in Chapter 5 that this model is underidentified and cannot be solved for unique values of the parameters. Stated in a different way, we can derive any number of values for the two path coefficients that will yield any given covariance or correlation between the two species. So, our model is inestimable.

Based on earlier discussions, we should expect that any association between species 1 and species 2 might be spurious unless there are no common factors that influence their abundances (other than their competitive interaction). Consider again the two flea beetle species that feed on leafy spurge, from our example in Chapter 2. Any association between these two could be influenced by a joint dependence on spurge for their food. Their association might also be affected by some habitat quality variable that influences their survival or reproduction. Based on this thinking, we might have a model such as the one in Figure 7.9. The question is, can we solve such a model?

A consideration of model identification in nonrecursive models

The first question we must ask for any model, but particularly for nonrecursive ones, is whether the model is identified. The basic requirements for identification were discussed in Chapter 5. Those basic requirements include the t-rule, which states that there must be as many unique pieces of information available as there are parameters to estimate. Other requirements include an adequate sample size and sufficient independence for each variable such that it constitutes unique information (i.e., empirical identification). For a recursive path model, this will usually be achievable as long as the model does not possess the simultaneous properties of being saturated plus having correlated errors. For nonrecursive models, there are additional challenges.

Examination of the model in Figure 7.9 shows that there are 8 path coefficients to be estimated. As there are 4 variables, the total number of knowns is 6. This is a case of a saturated model that also contains a reciprocal interaction and a correlated error. Typically, such a model cannot be identified unless two of the paths can be omitted. So, what alternatives are there?

One approach to satisfying the t-rule would be to obtain multiple indicators for the variables in the model and to construct a latent variable model. Having even a few multiple indicators would allow one to have more knowns than unknowns. However, while the t-rule is a necessary condition for identification, it is not sufficient. Kline (2005, pages 242–247) summarizes two additional rules that must apply for model identification. It is beyond the scope of this overview chapter to describe this somewhat intricate set of rules in detail. In essence, these rules state that one cannot achieve identification of a nonrecursive model that has correlated errors, unless there are particular patterns of effects omitted from the model. For our example in Figure 7.9, we cannot estimate both γ_{21} and γ_{31}, nor can we estimate both β_{12} and β_{13}. So, only a model with independent effects from x_1 and y_1 on each of the species (represented by y_2 and y_3 in this model) can be estimated.

Summary

Reciprocal effects and feedback loops can be important components of systems. Representing these temporal dynamics in static models using nonrecursive relationships has its limitations. There are a number of things that can be done to arrive at estimable models. However, the restrictions are rather severe and many models will not be estimable. For this reason, it is perhaps more important in this case than in any other for the researcher to consider carefully potential identification problems when developing their initial models, and when selecting parameters to measure. It is also very important to consider whether the assumption of equilibrium is approximated for the system, otherwise, estimates of reciprocal effects will not be unbiased. For all these reasons, one should be careful when incorporating feedback in structural equation models, and should treat such models as complex cases requiring advanced techniques.

PART IV

Applications and illustrations

8

Model evaluation in practice

The contribution of model evaluation
to scientific advancement

In Chapter 5 I described how the estimation process allows for evaluations of
model fit. Such evaluations form the core of SEM. In the last section of this
book I will go on to discuss how this contributes to the importance of SEM
as a research tool. Briefly, I believe that because attention has been focused
on univariate models, our theories have remained simplistic, emphasizing individual mechanisms rather than an understanding of systems. The evaluation of
general ecological theories has also suffered from being very informal, with
few rules agreed upon for deciding how evidence should be weighed in favor
of one theory or another. This informality has often resulted in prolonged and
unresolved debates (e.g., Grace 1991, Grimm 1994, Stamp 2003); signs of an
immature scientific process in operation.

In this chapter I will present a few examples of the evaluation of structural equation models that have been applied to natural systems, relying on the
methods presented in Chapter 5. As mentioned in the earlier discussion of SEM
principles, we must always be cognizant of the fact that results and conclusions
from SEM are dependent on the appropriateness of the model specified. As
was illustrated earlier and as will be shown in some of the chapters that follow,
inappropriate models can produce results that are quite misleading.

The current chapter is important because it describes some of the procedural
steps involved in arriving at our best approximation of the correct model. What
is often (though not always) omitted from papers dealing with SEM applications
in the natural sciences is a description of the degree to which investigators gain
a new level of understanding of their system through the model evaluation
process. Our first empirical example, which is presented a few pages below, is a
unique illustration of this learning process. Here we will see laid out before us

the process whereby multivariate models are evaluated and conclusions drawn, including (1) the evaluation of adequacy for individual models, (2) comparisons among alternative models, and (3) model selection.

Types of model evaluations and comparisons

We should start by recognizing that there are several categories of model evaluation types. A simple scheme is to describe them as (1) strictly confirmatory, (2) involving a nested series of models, or (3) purely exploratory. This classification recognizes the importance of the strength of a-priori support for a causal structure. It is always valuable to keep in mind the words of Sewall Wright (1968) who stated, "The method itself depends on the combination of knowledge of degrees of correlation among the variables in a system with such knowledge as may be possessed of the causal relations. In cases in which the causal relations are uncertain, the method can be used to find the logical consequences of any particular hypothesis in regard to them." What is clearly implied here is that the researcher must judge the strength of support for any causal structure and mechanistic interpretation, and involve this degree of support in the analysis process. The data set currently in hand may or may not represent our strongest source of information about the system being studied. As with the Bayesian philosophy, the relative strengths of prior and current information are situational and influenced by many things. This cannot be ignored when evaluating models and attempting to draw conclusions that have general validity.

There are many other types of model comparisons that can be recognized besides the ones just mentioned. For example, an alternative approach to model evaluation involves the use of sequential examinations, where we determine if additional variables contribute explanatory or predictive power to a base model. Such model evaluations represent somewhat different questions that are, themselves, sequential. Another kind of evaluation involves non-nested model comparisons, where models have different structures, either different numbers or types of variables, or different causal relations. Non-nested model comparisons such as these have not been a traditional part of SEM practice. As described in Chapter 5, there is currently considerable interest in information theoretic approaches to model selection in regression models (e.g., Burnham and Anderson 2002). While information theoretic approaches to model evaluation are directly applicable to SEM, their use to select among non-nested models without strong guidance from theoretical considerations is not to be recommended. The exception to this is when one is performing exploratory analyses designed to narrow the range of causal possibilities. Even here, some knowledge of causal

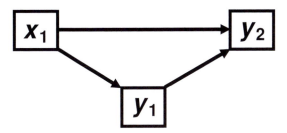

Figure 8.1. Illustration of a simple model that might be subjected to a strictly confirmatory analysis.

mechanisms is required in order to make very much progress, if the goal is to arrive at interpretable results.

Strictly confirmatory evaluations

On one end of the spectrum of possibilities is the strictly confirmatory evaluation. In a strictly confirmatory evaluation, data are compared to only a single model. Such a case might occur when a researcher has little doubt about the causal structure in a model. Thus, the focus of the study is usually on the specific values of the parameters, rather than the choice among models or different structures. In the case of a strictly confirmatory study, if an evaluation of overall model fit shows major discrepancies, the model fails and any subsequent analysis must be viewed as exploratory.

On first examination, strictly confirmatory evaluations may seem to be rather dull; this is not the case at all. Often we are primarily interested in the absolute and relative strengths of various pathways in the model. This kind of interest was clearly articulated by Sewall Wright in his early development of path analysis, who stated that path analysis gives quantitative meaning to a qualitative hypothesis. In a strictly confirmatory evaluation, even if a particular pathway turns out to have a nonsignificant path coefficient, we may not wish to interpret that result as an indication that our model is incorrect. Remember, our support for a causal structure should be supported by alternative sources of information (e.g., previous experience or known mechanisms), and what is in question in the analysis is the magnitude of the path coefficients. We can use Figure 8.1 to illustrate this point. Let us assume that we are interested in three parameters with causal order as shown. Let us further assume that we have good reason to believe, based on prior knowledge, that all three pathways among variables can be important in the system we are studying. The model shown in Figure 8.1 is a saturated model, thus, the fit of data to model will be assessed as being perfect, and no degrees of freedom exist to provide a chi-square test of model fit. In this case, even if the results show that one of the path coefficients cannot be distinguished from a value of zero, we should still retain all paths in the model. It would be a mistake in such a situation to constrain the nonsignificant path to be zero and re-estimate the model. Rather, we conclude that all pathways are valid, though in this particular sample, one of the paths cannot be distinguished from a zero value (perhaps a larger or more extensive sample would have led to a path coefficient deemed to be statistically significant at $p = 0.05$, for example). It is anticipated, thus, that future studies of this system will, at times, find all the paths in Figure 8.1 to be of significant importance. Commonly in such a case, we will be interested in the strength of the paths to inform us about the influence of different processes controlling the behavior of y_2 (assuming we continue to feel we have justification for a causal interpretation).

Nested comparisons among models

We generally recognize two types of model comparisons, *nested* and *non-nested*. Nested model comparisons involve models that are similar in causal structure (in that they possess the same variables in the same causal order), and differ only in terms of which paths are deemed significant. For any given model, there is typically a suite of nested models that differ only through the addition or subtraction of paths. Figure 8.2 illustrates the nested set of models that exists for three variables with sequential dependence as in Figure 8.1. We can see from this figure that for a simple, three-variable model, there are eight models in the nested series.

We might imagine a couple of diametrically opposed approaches to selecting a model from a nested set. The strategy of *model trimming* starts from a model that includes all the paths that could theoretically occur, and eliminates paths that are not supported by the data. Assuming some paths are eliminated through this process, there will be created some degrees of freedom that permit an estimate of the degree of model fit. Most experts in SEM advise against model trimming as a routine approach to model evaluation. When there is doubt about the inclusion of paths in a model, it is more often recommended that the researcher take a *model building* approach in which pathways with weak theoretical support are omitted from the initial model. In such a strategy, only when the model fails are other pathways considered for inclusion.

A *competing models* strategy is often possible, and when a limited set of nested models can be identified as being of prime interest, strength of inference associated with model comparisons can be protected. The reasons we may prefer

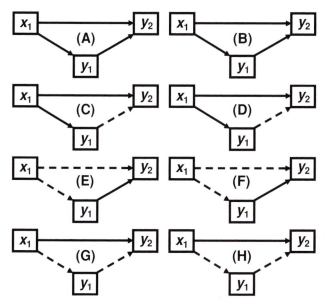

Figure 8.2. Nested set of models (A–H) with common causal structure. Solid arrows represent significant paths and dashed arrows indicate nonsignificant paths. In this case, models with correlated errors are omitted for simplicity.

a competing models approach are because (1) a more specific evaluation is being performed, and (2) our comparison-wise error rate is substantially reduced. For unlimited model comparisons, we should be aware that even simple models have a substantial number of alternatives (as suggested in Figure 8.2). Models of moderate complexity can have hundreds of alternatives (especially if we consider the possibility of correlations among errors).

In the evaluation of any given model, we can simultaneously evaluate (1) overall model fit, (2) the significance level of included pathways, (3) the consequences for model fit of including additional paths, and (4) comparative model fit. Such evaluations are accomplished both by assessments of model fit (e.g., the chi-square test), through the examination of residuals or modification indices, and by using information theoretic measures such as AIC or BIC (see Chapter 5). Residuals between predicted and observed covariances and any associated modification indices can indicate that a missing path would significantly improve model fit. If such a path is subsequently added, further evaluation can confirm that the path coefficient is indeed significant. Thus, model evaluation typically involves a comparison among nested models as an inherent part of the assessment.

It is important to keep in mind that each data set only permits a single untainted assessment of a model or limited set of competing models. Frequently, analyses will suggest either the addition or deletion of paths based on the fit to data. The fundamental principle of hypothesis evaluation in SEM is that only the minimum number of changes to a model should be made, and the results based on a modified model must be considered provisional. Thus, it is not proper to present results of an analysis based on a modified model and claim that the resulting model has been adequately evaluated. When a single data set is utilized, only the initial model is subjected to a confirmatory assessment, the modified model is actually "fitted" to the data. Where sufficient samples are available, multiple evaluations can be conducted by splitting a data set, with each half being examined separately. Even greater confidence can be achieved if there exist independent data sets for model evaluation.

Every sample is likely to have some chance properties due to random sampling events. Adding excess paths to a model in order to achieve perfect fit is referred to as *overfitting*. Overfitting can be thought of as fitting a model exactly to a set of data, representing both the general features of the data and its idiosyncrasies. When overfitting takes place, the model no longer represents an approximation to the underlying population parameters.

As stated above, additional power and interest can be achieved through the use of a limited set of a-priori competing models. When this is possible based on theoretical grounds, there is generally a greater opportunity for substantively based decisions about the appropriate model and a reduced likelihood of lapsing into empirically driven changes. We should not, of course, be unwilling to use empirical findings to suggest a modified model. This kind of empirical feedback to our models is precisely what we hope to gain from SEM. However, it is very important to always remember that any change to a model, including the addition of correlated errors, must be theoretically justified and interpreted. This sort of explicit process has not been the norm in the natural sciences up to this point. Next I present an illustration that is an exception to that pattern.

Example of nested model evaluation: hummingbird pollination

A nice ecological example of hierarchical model evaluation deals with hummingbird pollination of flowers. In 1992, Randy Mitchell (Mitchell 1992) used data from a study by Campbell *et al.* (1991) dealing with plant traits and pollinator behavior to illustrate certain principles of SEM. Table 8.1 presents the correlations among floral traits and hummingbird pollination behavior, as well as the variable means and standard deviations from that analysis.

Table 8.1. *Correlation matrix and standard deviations for plant traits and pol-*
linator behavior from Mitchell (1992) based on data from Campbell (1991).
Minimum sample size was 82

	Corolla length	Corolla width	Nectar production	No. of flowers	Approaches per hour	Probes per flower	Fruit set
Corolla length	1.0						
Corolla width	0.420	1.0					
Nectar production	0.367	0.297	1.0				
No. of flowers	0.149	0.117	0.024	1.0			
Approaches per hour	0.390	0.144	0.378	0.231	1.0		
Probes per flower	0.284	0.079	0.326	0.074	0.743	1.0	
Fruit set	0.414	0.338	0.294	−0.140	0.230	0.233	1.0
std. dev.	3.01	0.44	0.26	0.71	0.12	0.11	0.43

Background

In this example, the plant involved was *Ipomopsis aggregata*, scarlet gilia, which was pollinated primarily by two species of hummingbird, broad-tailed and rufous (*Selasphorus platycercus* and *Selasphorus rufus*). The goal of this study was to estimate the effects of plant floral traits on hummingbird visitation (both in the form of approaches and probes), and the combined effects of plant traits and hummingbird visitation on fruit set, measured as the proportion of marked flowers that developed fruits. The plant floral traits examined included the average length and width of the corolla for flowers open at that time, estimated floral nectar production, and the number of open flowers. Hummingbird approaches were measured as the number per hour, as were the number of probes by a hummingbird per flower. Some of the variables were transformed prior to analysis, including nectar production (as the square root), number of flowers (as the natural log), and fruit set (as the arcsine square root of the proportion).

The goal of the analysis by Mitchell was to evaluate the two competing models shown in Figure 8.3. For model A, it is presumed that the floral traits (corolla length, corolla width, nectar production, and number of flowers) can affect both approaches to plants and the number of probes per flower. This is the more general hypothesis of the two as it allows for more biological processes, such as repeated probing of flowers possessing high nectar content. This more liberal hypothesis was compared to a more restrictive one, model B. In the second model, it was reasoned a-priori that hummingbirds might base their choice of plants primarily on visual cues. This second model also presumed that fruit set would be affected by probes, not simply by approaches.

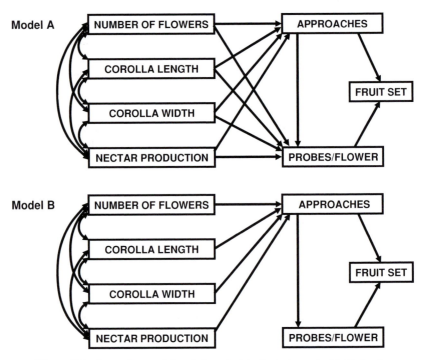

Figure 8.3. Competing models relating plant traits to hummingbird behavior (approaches to flowers and probes per flower), and ultimately to fruit set (1992, by permission of Blackwell Publishers).

Results

Mitchell found that both models failed to fit the data adequately. For model A, a chi-square of 23.49 was obtained with 4 degrees of freedom (p < 0.001). For model B, a chi-square of 26.46 with 9 degrees of freedom (p = 0.003) was found. Perhaps of equal or even greater importance in this case was that only 6% of the variance in fruit set was explained by both models.

To make a strong statement about the proper procedures for using SEM, Mitchell concluded that his two models were not adequate and he did not continue to explore further configurations that had no theoretical support.

Overview

If one performs an analysis of model A, one finds that substantial residuals exist for relationships between plant traits and fruit set. If paths from corolla length and number of flowers to fruit set are allowed, the chi-square drops to 6.08 with 2 degrees of freedom (p = 0.05), and the R^2 for fruit set increases from 6% to 23%. Mitchell was aware of this possibility, but chose not to take the analysis in this direction. Instead, he reasoned, "Although these paths [from floral traits to fruit set] have no clear biological meaning themselves, this may indicate a common factor (such as energy reserves or photosynthetic rate) that influences both fruit set and the floral characters." I applaud Mitchell for taking this opportunity to make an important point about SEM methodology – that sometimes the results indicate that key system properties were not measured and an adequate model cannot be constructed. I also applaud the reviewers and editor of his manuscript for allowing this "nonresult" to be published, providing us with a clear demonstration of this kind of SEM application.

Hummingbird pollination revisited

In 1994, Mitchell returned to the question of how plant traits relate to pollinator behavior and fruit set (Mitchell 1994), this time armed with data to estimate a more complete model. These data were collected from two, somewhat con-trasting areas in central Colorado, referred to as the Almont and Avery sites. Five distinct subpopulations of scarlet gilia plants were examined at each site, with 24–30 plants assessed in each subpopulation (yielding a total of 139 plants at Almont and 145 at Avery). Hummingbird approaches and probes per flower were again assessed for each plant, along with number of flowers per plant, corolla length, corolla width, and nectar production. Additionally, total flower production over the season was measured. Nectar production was estimated using flowers that were covered to prevent consumption and then sampled using a micropipette. Fruit set was again measured, this time by dividing the num-ber of developed fruits by the total number of flowers. Additional plant traits measured in this study (that were not measured in the previous study, Mitchell 1992) included height of the tallest inflorescence, the number of flowers open at time of observation, and the total dry mass (above and below ground) of each plant collected approximately 1 month after the period of observation. Plants for which all measures were not taken were deleted from the data to ensure a complete data set, yielding 130 plants for Almont and 127 for Avery. The corre-lations, means, and standard deviations for both Almont and Avery populations are reproduced in Table 8.2.

Mitchell devised a set of theoretically supported models to evaluate using this more complete data set. Figure 8.4 presents a graphical summary of most of these models. The figure shows, using letters B–E, the paths that were either added (for model B) or subtracted (models C–E) in comparison to model A (the model specified by all solid arrows). Two additional models not represented in Figure 8.4, F and G, were also evaluated. Since all models had the same

Table 8.2. *Correlations, means, and standard deviations for plant traits, hummingbird behavior, and fruit production (from Mitchell 1994, Table 1)*

	Open flowers (ln#)	Corolla length (mm)	Corolla width (mm)	Nectar prod. $(\mu L)^{-2}$	Height (ln cm)	Dry mass (ln g)	Total flowers (ln#)	Approaches (#/hr)	Probes (#/fl/hr)	Fruit set (prop.)	Total fruits (ln#)
Almont											
Open flowers	1.0										
Corolla length	0.084	1.0									
Corolla width	0.190	0.093	1.0								
Nectar	0.156	0.350	0.441	1.0							
Height	0.368	0.091	0.093	0.107	1.0						
Biomass	0.809	0.148	0.206	0.164	0.523	1.0					
Total flowers	0.855	0.096	0.195	0.167	0.477	0.935	1.0				
Approaches	0.248	0.174	0.157	0.271	0.155	0.226	0.277	1.0			
Probes/flower	-0.145	0.099	-0.028	0.141	-0.008	-0.115	-0.073	0.676	1.0		
Fruit set	-0.102	0.127	-0.037	0.213	0.308	-0.012	-0.072	0.182	0.247	1.0	
Total fruits	0.748	0.069	0.156	0.152	0.501	0.833	0.871	0.236	-0.050	0.296	1.0
Mean	2.56	27.8	3.22	1.80	3.73	1.12	4.88	0.151	0.056	0.99	4.32
Std. dev.	0.755	2.473	0.399	0.492	0.251	0.717	0.718	0.171	0.069	0.177	0.859
Avery											
Open flowers	1.0										
Corolla length	0.166	1.0									
Corolla width	0.002	0.248	1.0								
Nectar	0.154	0.062	0.149	1.0							
Height	0.325	0.305	0.291	0.015	1.0						
Biomass	0.650	0.340	0.261	0.001	0.402	1.0					
Total flowers	0.754	0.178	0.093	-0.036	0.390	0.748	1.0				
Approaches	0.233	-0.093	-0.003	0.203	0.080	0.240	0.220	1.0			
Probes/flower	0.060	-0.199	-0.063	0.199	0.019	0.167	0.123	0.841	1.0		
Fruit set	-0.006	-0.106	0.114	0.068	0.254	0.002	-0.108	0.180	0.166	1.0	
Total fruits	0.683	0.110	0.027	-0.073	0.417	0.637	0.881	0.197	0.119	0.165	1.0
Mean	2.18	26.8	3.92	1.85	3.62	0.92	4.35	0.156	0.081	0.94	3.52
Std. dev.	0.550	2.483	0.325	0.365	0.285	0.558	0.572	0.208	0.114	0.142	0.643

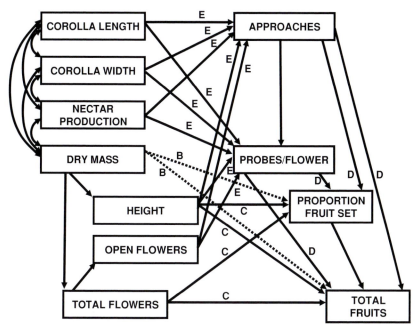

Figure 8.4. Representation of the competing models evaluated by Mitchell (1994). Model A is represented by all solid arrows. Model B involved the addition of two paths, indicated by the letter B. All other models depicted here (C–E) involved the removal of paths. By permission of Blackwell Publishers.

structure, in terms of the causal order, this evaluation is considered to be a nested model comparison.

In brief terms, the models examined in this analysis are as follows:

Model A – This model proposes that fruit set is influenced by both pollinator behavior and plant internal resources, and that pollinator behavior is influenced by certain plant traits. It is specifically hypothesized that any correlations between floral traits (corolla length, corolla width, nectar production, or number of open flowers) and fruit set will be mediated through their effects on pollinator behavior (i.e., there will be no direct paths from floral traits to fruit set or production). In model A, the effects of dry mass on fruit set and total fruits produced is completely predicted by plant height and the total number of flowers produced, which themselves depend on dry mass.

Model B – This model proposes that plant height and total flowers will not adequately represent the effects of dry mass on fruit set and total fruits.

Because of this, there will be additional effects of dry mass on fruit set and total fruits, indicated by the paths labeled B.

Model C – This model evaluates the possibility that fruit set and production are not limited by plant resources; thus, all paths from height and total flowers to fruit set and total fruits are omitted.

Model D – This model evaluates the possibility that pollinator behavior has no effect on fruit set and total fruit production.

Model E – This model evaluates the possibility that nectar production and visible plant characters have no effect on pollinator behavior.

Model F – This model evaluates the possibility that plant mass is the underlying cause of any correlations among corolla length, corolla width, and nectar production. This model is not causally nested within the general framework shown in Figure 8.4, because it involves directional arrows from dry mass to corolla length, corolla width, and nectar production.

Model G – This model considers the possibility that dry mass is merely correlated with plant height and total flower production, instead of their causal determinant. This model also involves a change in the basic causal order.

The statistical fit of these 7 models was evaluated in two ways. First, chi-squares permitted a consideration of the degree to which the data deviated from the models. This considers the absolute fit of the model. Second, chi-square difference tests were used to evaluate whether some models possessed better fit when paths were either added or removed. As described in Chapter 5, this latter analysis is based on the fact that differences between chi-squares, themselves, follow a chi-square distribution.

The results of the evaluation of competing models are given in Table 8.3. For the Almont site, model A had an adequate absolute fit to the data based on a chi-square of 28.9 with 26 degrees of freedom (p = 0.315). Adding the paths from dry mass to fruit set and total fruits (model B) resulted in a decrease in chi-square of 1.59 with two degrees of freedom. A single degree of freedom chi-square test requires a change in value of 3.841, and a two-degree-of-freedom value of 5.991 is required before a significant difference between models is achieved. Thus, model B was not found to be a significantly better fitting model than model A. Given the logical priority given to model A in this study, its greater parsimony, and the fact that paths from dry mass to fruit set and total fruits are not significant at the 0.05 level, model B was rejected in favor of model A. Deletion of paths associated with models C–E led to significant increases in chi-square, also indicating that these models were inferior to model A. Since model A fitted the data well for the Almont site and because models F and G

Table 8.3. *Measures of fit for the models evaluated in Mitchell (1994)*

	Goodness of fit			Nested comparison with model A		
	X^2	df	p	X^2	df	p
Almont						
Model A	28.91	26	0.315	—	—	—
Model B	27.32	24	0.290	1.59	2	0.45
Model C	313.1	30	0.000	284.2	4	0.0001
Model D	47.80	30	0.021	18.89	4	0.0008
Model E	75.99	36	0.000	47.08	10	0.0001
Model F	70.41	29	0.000	—	—	—
Model G	23.46	14	0.053	—	—	—
Avery						
Model A	59.01	26	0.000	—	—	—
Model B	55.33	24	0.000	3.68	2	0.16
Model C	306.5	30	0.000	247.5	4	0.00001
Model D	68.11	30	0.000	9.10	4	0.059
Model E	90.88	36	0.000	31.87	10	0.0004
Model F	67.16	29	0.000	—	—	—
Model G	25.78	14	0.028	—	—	—

Note – Model A is the baseline model

both fitted the data less well than model A, Mitchell deemed model A to be the best representation of the data of any of the models.

For the Avery site, model A did not have an adequate absolute fit to the data based on a chi-square of 59.01 with 26 degrees of freedom (p < 0.001). While not reported by Mitchell, other indices of model fit agree with this assessment. The root mean square error of approximation (RMSEA) gives a value of 0.090 and a 90% confidence interval for the RMSEA from 0.054 to 0.125. In order for the RMSEA to indicate a nonsignificant difference between model and data, the minimum RMSEA would need to include a value of 0.0 within its range, which in this case, it did not. Models B–F did not have adequate absolute fits to the data either. Only model G, which represents the case where all plant traits freely intercorrelate, showed a model fit that was close to adequate. Based on this information, Mitchell concluded that the model fitting data at the two sites was not constant and that the best model for the Avery site was not fully determined.

There are a fair number of interpretations to be drawn from the results from this study. For brevity, I will focus only on the results for the Almont site (Figure 8.5). Mitchell's original model, which he deemed most biologically

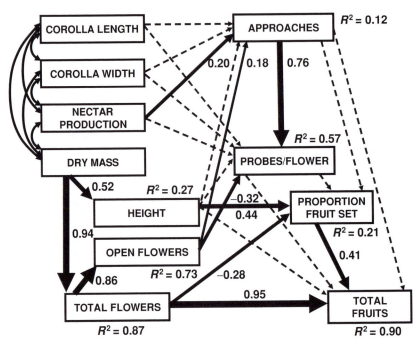

Figure 8.5. Results of analysis for Almont site. Directional paths with dashed lines were nonsignificant. From Mitchell (1994) by permission of Blackwell Publishers.

reasonable from the beginning, matched the covariance structure of the data. This does not prove that the model represents the true forces controlling the system. Instead, the adequacy of model fit serves to "fail to disprove" the model structure. This is no small achievement for a model of this complexity.

There was substantial variation in the degree to which variation in endogenous variables was explained in the model. Looking first at plant traits, plant height was only modestly related to dry mass. However, both total flowers and open flowers were related quite strongly to dry mass. Considering pollinator behavior, approaches by hummingbirds to plants were significantly related to both nectar production and the number of open flowers. However, only 12% of the variation in approaches between plants was explained by these two factors. Probes per flower were strongly determined by the number of approaches and the number of open flowers ($R^2 = 0.57$). As for reproductive success, the proportion of fruit set was significantly related to height, which is a function of dry mass. Proportion of fruit set was also found to be negatively related to the total number of flowers, suggesting that the plant was indeed resource limited in filling fruits. Variation among plants in total fruits per plant was well predicted by the total number of flowers ($R^2 = 0.90$).

Looking at overall path relations, we see that total fruit set was largely determined by the total number of flowers produced, and thus, ultimately determined by dry mass of the plant. Hummingbird behavior did not explain any of the observed variation in total fruits in this model, even though approaches to plants and fruit set were significantly correlated ($r = 0.236$). Based on this result, we must conclude that the correlation between approaches and total fruits was spurious and not causal. This does NOT mean that approaches do not affect fruit production in some broader range of circumstances. Rather, it simply means that the variation in fruit production observed in this data set was related almost entirely to plant size and not to variation in pollination.

This example does an excellent job of illustrating how critical the model is to interpretation. Mitchell was painstaking in his evaluation of model adequacy. This gives substantially more credence to the interpretations that derive from the results than if he had simply searched for the model that best fitted the data with little regard to a-priori theoretical justification. It is easy to see from the results of this analysis, that Mitchell was justified in being cautious about interpreting the results from the earlier study (Mitchell 1992), where plant size was not measured.

Example of a step-wise hierarchical analysis

Sometimes the questions we wish to ask about a system are a little different from the ones illustrated thus far. This can lead to alternative approaches to the evaluation of multivariate models. An example comes from a study I conducted, in collaboration with Glenn Guntenspergen (Grace and Guntenspergen 1999), that sought to use SEM to evaluate whether residual spatial variation in species richness might be explained by past storm events. In this case, model fit was only one of the criteria used to compare two competing models.

Background

A number of previous studies, including SEM studies using both experimental and nonexperimental data (Grace and Pugesek 1997, Gough and Grace 1999), provided a significant amount of experience upon which to base our initial models and their interpretations. The question addressed in this study was whether landscape position could explain unique variation in species richness, that could not be explained by contemporary environmental conditions. Thus, our question was of the step-wise sort. To achieve this objective we compared the two models shown in Figure 8.6. These models differ in that model B includes two

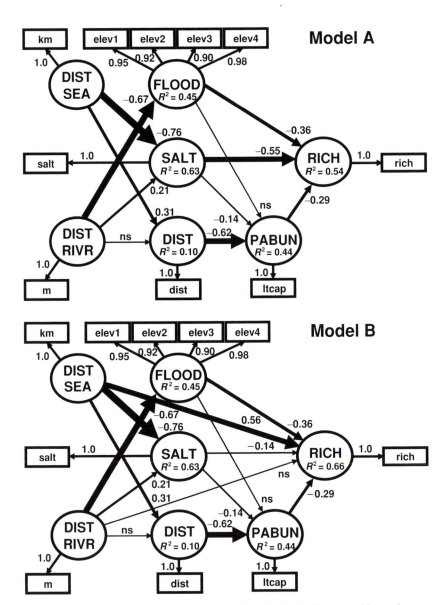

Figure 8.6. Competing models used to evaluate whether landscape position variables, distance from the sea (DIST SEA) and distance from the river's edge (DIST RIVR) contributed to the explanation of unique variation in species richness (RICH). From Grace and Guntenspergen (1999) by permission of Ecoscience.

paths not found in model A, from DIST SEA (distance from the sea) to RICH (plant species richness), and from DIST RIVR (distance from river's edge) to RICH. The results from this analysis are mentioned again in Chapter 10, where they are put into the context of a systematic use of SEM to understand plant diversity patterns.

Results and Conclusions

The process of model selection was based on two criteria. The first criterion was whether including direct effects of position variables on richness would lead to a better fit between model and data. The chi-square for model A was 87.69, with 32 degrees of freedom, a p-value less than 0.0001, and a fit index of 0.937. In contrast, the chi-square for model B was 43.54 with 31 degrees of freedom, with a p-value = 0.068. Thus, tests of overall model fit indicated that the data did not fit model A, but they did fit model B.

A second, and in this case critical, criterion was whether more variance in species richness would be explained by the second model. Just because model B is a better model than model A, it does not necessarily mean that variance explanation for species richness is higher. It is entirely possible that model B could essentially explain the same total amount of variance in richness, but through different relationships. For this reason, a t-test was used to determine whether there was a significant reduction in error variance for richness in model B compared to model A. Results showed that distance from the mouth of the river did explain an additional 12% of the observed variance in richness, while distance from the river's edge did not contribute new information. Based on these findings, we concluded that some of the spatial variation in species richness in this system can only be explained by past events, such as previous tropical storms.

An example of model selection based on chi-square evaluations

Meziane and Shipley (2001) conducted a comparative study of morphological and physiological traits for 22 plant species. Among their objectives was to determine the best model to describe the causal relationships among the set of intercorrelated traits. In addition to considering how their own data fit various models, they also evaluated two other previous data sets collected for other species, including one data set that was from an extensive field study. The traits that were included in their study are given in Table 8.4. Figure 8.7 shows the five alternative models considered in the study.

Table 8.4. *Traits examined in the study by Meziane and Shipley*

Trait	Definition
Specific leaf area (SLA)	Leaf surface area per gram leaf tissue mass
Leaf nitrogen concentration ([N])	mg nitrogen per gram tissue mass
Net leaf photosynthetic rate (A)	nmol CO_2 uptake per gram leaf tissue per second
Stomatal conductance (G)	mmol water loss per gram leaf tissue per second

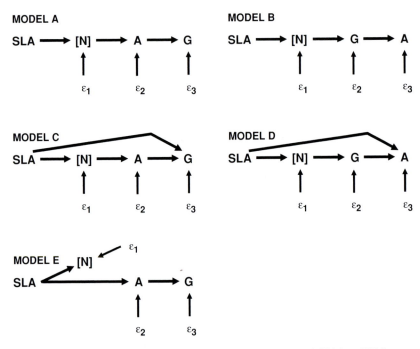

Figure 8.7. Alternative models considered in Meziane and Shipley (2001). Reprinted by permission of Oxford University Press.

In this study, the authors performed experimental manipulations of light levels and nutrient supply, so as to generate a broad range of responses and to gain insights into causal relationships. Mean responses to experimental manipulations were examined using ANOVA. Samples were combined across all treatment combinations to evaluate the path models shown in Figure 8.7. Because

Table 8.5. *Chi-squares and probabilities (in parentheses) comparing data on plant traits to the five models shown in Figure 8.7 (modified from Meziane and Shipley 2001).* ** *indicates probabilities* < 0.05

Data set	Model A	Model B	Model C	Model D	Model E
Model df	6	6	4	4	6
trt 1	3.7 (0.72)	12.6 (**)	2.8 (0.60)	7.0 (0.13)	6.4 (0.38)
trt 2	7.4 (0.29)	7.0 (0.32)	5.0 (0.28)	4.3 (0.37)	7.4 (0.28)
trt 3	12.0 (0.06)	10.2 (0.12)	9.9 (**)	4.6 (0.33)	12.9 (**)
trt 4	11.8 (0.07)	13.7 (**)	0.5 (0.97)	3.2 (0.52)	2.6 (0.86)
all trts (df = 8)	14.1 (0.08)	19.4 (**)	10.0 (0.27)	9.5 (0.30)	11.0 (0.20)
data set 2	29.8 (**)	10.7 (0.10)	22.8 (**)	1.4 (0.85)	29.6 (**)
data set 3	18.9 (**)	13.2 (**)	11.7 (**)	2.1 (0.72)	27.0 (**)
data set 4	74.5 (88)	133.0 (**)	13.0 (**)	93.3 (**)	54.3 (**)

Note that treatments 1–4 were modifications of light and nutrient supply conducted in this study. Data set 2 was from all plants studied in Shipley and Lechowicz (2000). Data set 3 was for only the C3-type plants in Shipley and Lechowicz (2000). Data set 4 was from Reich *et al.* (1999).

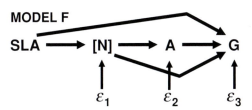

Figure 8.8. Final, general model accepted by Meziane and Shipley (2001). Reprinted by permission of Oxford University Press.

the sample size was low ($n = 22$), an alternative test statistic was employed that is exact for small samples and relatively robust to distributional violations (see Shipley 2000, chapter 3). This test statistic was evaluated using chi-square tests and results are shown in Table 8.5.

None of the models was found to fit all data sets, although model D did fit all except those from the comparative field study by Reich *et al.* (1999). Because this study sought to provide a unified solution that would hold across all data sets, the authors fitted all data to a sixth model, which is shown in Figure 8.8. Chi-square tests indicate that model F fits adequately for all data sets, and thus represents a general model for the system studied.

An example of model selection based on consistent Akaike's information criterion (CAIC)

Background

Studies of natural selection often rely on an examination of the relationships between a set of life history characteristics and a variety of environmental conditions. An example of such an analysis for intraspecific variation in fish populations comes from the work of Johnson (2002).

Brachyrhaphis rhabdophora is a fish species endemic to Costa Rica, occurring in freshwater streams. Populations can be found living under a wide range of conditions that vary in fish density, stream productivity, physical habitat characteristics, and predation risk. Substantial life history variation among populations of *B. rhabdophora* has previously been documented. Traits of importance to fitness known to vary include offspring size, fecundity, reproductive allocation, size at maturity for males, and size at maturity for females.

In this study, populations of *B. rhabdophora* were sampled in four successive years from a set of 27 different sites throughout northwestern Costa Rica, with 12 of the sites represented in all samplings. Approximately 200 fish were collected from each site during each sampling.

Johnson established a general model, shown in Figure 8.9, that represented a comprehensive hypothesis of the habitat factors that might affect life history variation in this species. Model solution was accomplished in two stages. First, principal components analysis was used to calculate estimates of life history scores. Those scores were then used in an analysis using the SEM software AMOS. Johnson developed a set of 17 a-priori candidate models based on the global model in Figure 8.9. These models were evaluated for each of the four years of data collection using the CAIC index. Only values of CAIC differing by more than 2 were considered to be substantially different.

Results and Conclusions

Model selection results showed that CAIC values were lowest for single-selection factor models for all years (Table 8.6). Furthermore, CAIC values were unable to distinguish among alternative hypotheses which selective factor was most important. These findings led the author to suggest that the selective environment may not be easily decomposed into individual components. It is important to keep in mind, however, that the sample size in this study was sufficiently low that these conclusions may not be consistent with tests of absolute fit. Typically, I would always recommend that models selected be further examined for adequate fit using measures of absolute fit, such as the chi-square test.

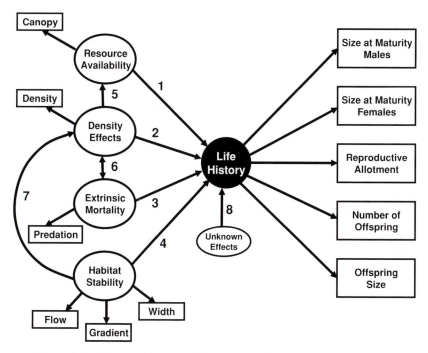

Figure 8.9. Global model evaluated by Johnson 2002 for the effects of environmental conditions on life history characteristics of the fish *B. rhabdophora*. Hypotheses tested relative to this diagram and their results are given in Table 8.6. Reproduced by permission of Oikos.

Equivalent models

A careful consideration of alternative models often demonstrates that there are multiple models existing that are indistinguishable (Figure 8.10). This may be the result of statistical equivalency (because there is insufficient power to discriminate among alternatives) or because of pure equivalency (the existence of alternative causal structures with identical statistical expectations). Furthermore, for saturated models (those specifying all possible interactions among variables), all variations of the causal order of the model are also saturated and, therefore, equivalent. There has been a significant discussion of this issue for over a decade among SEM practitioners (Glymour *et al.* 1987; Hayduk 1996, chapters 3 and 4; Raykov and Penev 1999; Spirtes *et al.* 2000). Recently, Shipley (2000) has discussed this important topic in detail using ecologically relevant examples.

A variety of rules for identifying equivalent models have been developed, the historically most important being the development of the TETRAD

Table 8.6. *A-priori set of 17 candidate models evaluated by Johnson (2002) using CAIC. For the structure of the model, see Figure 8.9. Selective agents are as follows: R = resource availability, D = density effects, M = extrinsic mortality, and H = habitat stability. Sample sizes show the number of populations sampled each year (n)*

Selective agents	Paths in model	CAIC 1996 n = 21	CAIC 1997 n = 14	CAIC 1998 n = 16	CAIC 1999 n = 19
R	1,8	20.2	18.5	18.9	19.9
D	2,8	20.4	18.4	19.1	19.7
M	3,8	20.9	18.3	18.9	22.0
H	4,8	20.7	18.2	19.6	20.2
R+D	1,2,8	33.1	29.6	31.5	32.5
R+D	1,5,8	32.6	32.6	32.3	29.8
R+D	1,2,5,8	36.5	32.8	34.2	35.6
D+M	2,3,8	36.1	32.8	30.8	34.4
D+M	2,6,8	38.7	32.4	34.0	46.6
D+M	2,3,6,8	37.4	32.8	34.3	38.4
D+H	2,4,8	34.1	31.3	42.2	32.7
D+H	2,7,8	39.0	29.0	29.6	38.4
D+H	2,4,7,8	37.7	32.9	34.4	35.6
R+D+M	1,2,3,8	48.6	53.3	43.3	50.0
R+D+M	1,2,3,6,8	50.0	53.4	46.9	53.9
R+D+M	1,2,3,5,6,8	53.3	56.5	49.6	57.0
R+D+M+H	all (1–8)	78.0	84.1	71.8	84.3

software program (Glymour *et al.* 1987), which automates the identification of equivalent models for a given set of data. Shipley (2000) reduces much of the elaborate discussion of this issue to some simple rules for recognizing which model structures indicate the presence of equivalent models that lead to identical covariance expectations. I will not go into detail on this important topic here, but instead refer the reader to recent treatments of this subject cited above. I will, however, comment on the importance of examining alternative models as a means of checking one's causal logic.

Hayduk (1996) makes a compelling case for the value of considering equivalent models as a way of advancing one's thinking about their system. For systems where the directionality of causal effect is clear, equivalent models can

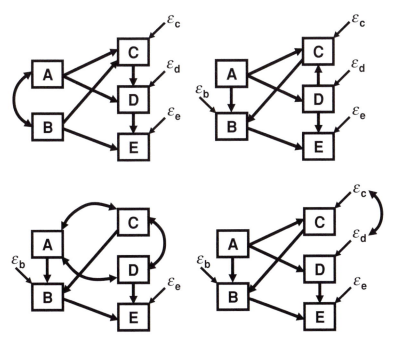

Figure 8.10. Example of a few equivalent models that possess identical covariance expectations.

easily be dismissed and robustness established. For systems with a high degree of integration or feedback, equivalent models can challenge one's assumptions and interpretations. To some degree, considering equivalent models provides one with a test of where our understanding lies relative to this problem.

Discovery triggered by lack of model fit

An important contention of this chapter and even of this book is that the process of model evaluation can lead to new discoveries about the system under study. Here, one can make an analogy to celestial mechanics, emphasizing the numerous discoveries about our solar system and universe that have resulted from the discovery of discrepancies between the predicted and observed planetary orbits. Examples of discoveries resulting from findings of inadequate model fit and residual relationships are accumulating for ecological studies as well. Here I present one brief example from Grace and Pugesek (1997) to illustrate the point.

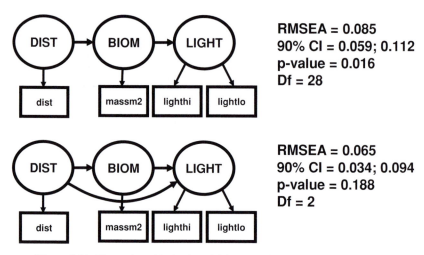

RMSEA = 0.085
90% CI = 0.059; 0.112
p-value = 0.016
Df = 28

RMSEA = 0.065
90% CI = 0.034; 0.094
p-value = 0.188
Df = 2

Figure 8.11. Illustration of lack of model fit (upper figure) resolved by addition of a pathway (lower figure). This figure only shows part of the full model (refer to Chapter 10, Figure 10.10, for the full model). DIST refers to disturbance, BIOM refers to above-ground biomass (living and dead), LIGHT refers to percent of full sunlight reaching the ground surface. RMSEA is the root mean square error of approximation (refer to Chapter 5). Results indicate that data deviated significantly from the upper model (p = 0.016), but fit to the lower model was substantially better (p = 0.188).

In the study by Grace and Pugesek (1997), we proposed initially that disturbance affects plant biomass, which in turn affects light penetration (Figure 8.11). For simplicity, only part of the whole model is shown here, although it is important to realize that the results are only valid for the full model (Chapter 10, Figure 10.10).

The finding that there was unexplained residual variance between DIST and LIGHT was initially a surprise. How is it that disturbance, which in this system was caused by grazers (nutria, rabbits, wild hogs) and by wrack deposits or scouring by water, could affect light, independent of effects on biomass? More detailed examination of the data suggested an interpretation. It seems that vegetation that has recently been disturbed has a more upright architecture than less disturbed vegetation. The result is that disturbed vegetation allows more light to penetrate through the canopy per gram biomass than undisturbed vegetation (Figure 8.12).

This finding turns out to have led to a line of thought which, I believe, may be of quite general importance. These and other subsequent results suggest that (1) light penetration is a key predictor of the dynamics of diversity in plant

Figure 8.12. Illustration of variations in plant architecture, the importance of which was discovered through an examination of residual effects. Plants on the left and right are presumed to have equal above-ground biomass values. Those on the left represent the architecture associated with recently disturbed sites, while those on the right represent the undisturbed vegetation. Through effects on architecture, disturbance leads to a greater penetration of light through the canopy, which allows other species to establish and persist in disturbed sites.

communities (Grace 1999), and (2) plant morphology and litter dynamics should be far more important than total biomass in explaining community diversity dynamics (Grace 2001). Empirical studies to evaluate this proposition are leading to a much more mechanistic understanding of richness regulation that may permit us to predict, among other things, the effects of dominant (including invasive) species on native diversity patterns (Jutila and Grace 2002).

Summary

A serious analysis of model fit is important both for the evaluation of scientific hypotheses, as well as the results and their interpretation being dependent on the model. When theory is well understood, samples are adequately large and representative, and measurements are reliable, then evaluations of model fit provide clear indications of the match between hypotheses and interpretations. One finds that most evaluations of model fit in those fields with a substantial history of using SEM (e.g., social and economic sciences) are of the nested type, where it is generally recognized that there is a limit to the ability of statistical testing to resolve issues of causal structure. The lesson for ecologists is that care must be exercised in drawing conclusions too firmly based on a single data set, regardless of how well the data fit a model.

Biologists and other scientists in many different fields are just beginning to explore the utility of SEM. This means that modeling efforts are often quite exploratory, with many more unknowns than knowns. The example by Mitchell presented early in the chapter represents an outstanding illustration of how exploratory analyses can proceed with care, and lead to convincing conclusions when the conventions of SEM model evaluation are applied. Some questions, of course, are more difficult to address than others. This is notably the case for interacting components of individuals or populations, where the high degree of integration and feedback makes causation sometimes difficult to disentangle. Here, we will require both persistence and patience to make progress, since the observations we require are often novel and without precedence in ecological study.

I believe the process of evaluating multivariate models can be a pivotal step forward in the maturation of the ecological sciences. This process can be unambiguously strong in its rejection of pre-existing theory. However, through the examination of residual effects, one can often discover new relationships that are of importance, which motivates one to modify one's theory so that a better match with nature is obtained. The net results of such model evaluations will be a reduction in entrenched theory, a higher empirical content to new theories, and will allow us to have a greater capacity to understand and predict system behavior.

9

Multivariate experiments

Basic issues

The gold standard for studying causal relations is experimentation. As Fisher (1956) labored so hard to demonstrate, experimental manipulations have the ability to disentangle factors in a way that is usually not possible with non-experimental data. By creating independence among causes, experimentation can lead to a great reduction in ambiguity about effects. There is little doubt for most scientists that well designed and properly analyzed experiments provide the most powerful way of assessing the importance of processes, when appropriate and relevant experiments are possible.

In this chapter I address a topic that generally receives little attention in discussions of SEM, its applicability to experimental studies. I hope to deal with two common misconceptions in this chapter, (1) that multivariate analysis is only for use on nonexperimental data, and (2) that when experiments are possible, there is no need for SEM. In fact, I would go one step further and say that the value of studying systems using SEM applies equally well to experimental and nonexperimental investigations.

There are several reasons why one might want to combine the techniques of SEM with experimentation. First, using experiments to evaluate multivariate relationships provides inherently more information about the responses of a system to manipulation. It is often difficult and sometimes impossible to exert independent control over all the variables of interest in a system. Examination of how the various pathways among variables respond to experimental treatment can yield important insights into system function and regulation. It can also isolate effects of interest in the presence of covarying factors.

A second reason to combine SEM with experimental studies is the fact that "replicates" are often quite dissimilar in important ways. One clear case of such a situation is with manipulations of ecosystems. Often experiments involve units of some size in order to incorporate all the processes of interest, and to achieve some degree of realism. The various "replicates" being studied may differ amongst themselves in characteristics that cause their individual responses to vary widely. The use of SEM automatically leads the researcher to consider the broader suite of variables that may influence results. These covariate variables can often be of overwhelming importance, and understanding their role in the operation of the system can greatly improve a researcher's chances of obtaining general and coherent findings.

Yet a third reason to use SEM when designing and analyzing an experiment is a desire to accommodate cases where ecosystem manipulations are not simple or precise. For example, in the case of prescribed burning in grasslands, a fire started in the morning may have quite different characteristics from a fire ignited the afternoon of that same day. Even within an individual fire, spatial variations in vegetation, topography, and fire behavior may cause substantial variation in fire temperatures, residency times, and soil heating. Recognizing that treatments such as burning may not be precise, automatically encourages the researcher to measure covariates that might impact the responses and to incorporate these covariates into the model to be evaluated.

As a fourth motivation, experimental multivariate studies can help evaluate assumptions and predictions that arise from nonexperimental manipulations. By combining intensive multivariate experiments with extensive nonexperimental studies, the strengths of both approaches can be integrated into a broader understanding of system behavior.

At present, SEM is less commonly combined with experimental studies than it might be. At the risk of being repetitive, it is difficult to study systems effectively using methods that are designed for the study of individual factors and effects. Methods such as ANOVA, MANOVA, and ANCOVA are not really designed to look at system behavior, but instead, to summarize net effects. As the following examples illustrate, such net effects usually hide a rich complement of individual processes that are only revealed when multiple pathways are considered. Furthermore, a multivariate mindset automatically motivates the researcher to incorporate a broader range of variables that control system behavior, allowing for the effects of manipulated variables to be put into system context.

I should emphasize here that I do not mean that we should abandon the use of conventional univariate analysis when performing experiments. Rather, what I recommend is that we include both kinds of analyses as complementary sources of information. Most of the examples that follow are selected from studies in which conventional analysis of variance methods were also applied, and it is important to keep this in mind.

Table 9.1. *Illustration of a response-surface design for an exper-iment that involves different levels of fertilizer additions and different frequencies of clipping. The code F0C0 refers to the unfertilized and unclipped treatment, etc.*

	Fert0	Fert1	Fert2	Fert3	Fert4
Clipped0	F0C0	F1C0	F2C0	F3C0	F4C0
Clipped1	F0C1	F1C1	F2C1	F3C1	F4C1
Clipped2	F0C2	F1C2	F2C2	F3C2	F4C2
Clipped3	F0C3	F1C3	F2C3	F3C3	F4C3
Clipped4	F0C4	F1C4	F2C4	F3C4	F4C4
Clipped5	F0C5	F1C5	F2C5	F3C5	F4C5

Dealing with treatment variables in multivariate experiments

Experiments frequently involve subjecting a system to some limited set of treat-ments. Our experiments may also involve treatments being applied to different groupings, such as vegetation types. Thus, we can expect to encounter categor-ical variables in many experimental analyses.

One way to deal with this issue is to avoid using categorical levels of the manipulated variables, but instead, to use a *response-surface design* (see Cottingham *et al.* 2005 for some of the rationale). In response-surface designs, experimental units are subjected to a large number of treatment combinations, often with only one replicate per combination. Such a design relies on a regres-sion approach to analysis, and is most informative when many levels of the experimental factors are used. An example of this approach is given in Table 9.1, for a hypothetical experiment involving different levels of fertilization and clipping in a plant community.

In Chapter 7 we addressed a number of different ways categorical variables can be handled. Here, some of that discussion is revisited in the context of treat-ment variables in experimental studies. When nominal variables are encoun-tered in an analysis, there is little choice but to treat them using dummy variable modeling. However, when dealing with ordinal variables where the levels can be ranked, there are more options as to how they can be viewed. Overall, the options are (1) reliance on standard correlations/covariances, (2) adjustment using polychoric or tetrachoric correlations/covariances, (3) performance of a multigroup analysis, and (4) use of latent class modeling. If the reader has not read about these topics in Chapter 7, they should now do so, to better follow the discussion that follows.

Reliance on standard correlations/covariances

In so-called "fixed-effect" studies, the universe of interest is defined by the treatment levels applied in the study. We might compare male and female individuals in a population, and treat sex as a fixed-effect exogenous variable in the model. Alternatively, we might compare two burning treatments and wish only to draw inferences for those two specific treatments. In this case, standard Pearson correlations or covariances are sufficient to define the relationship between treatment and continuous response variables. Furthermore, because distributional assumptions in the analysis only relate to the residuals, the statistical distribution of a categorical predictor variable does not necessarily lead to a violation of parametric assumptions. Thus, one approach to dealing with a categorical treatment variable is to treat it as you would any other variable. This has been the most common approach used in ecological studies.

It should be added here that the fixed-effect approach can be applied not only to manipulated variables, but also to hierarchical levels in the sampling scheme. In recent years, so called *hierarchical linear modeling* (Hox 2002) has evolved to allow structural equation models to be analyzed in a multi-level sampling framework. We might, thus, consider both within-population and between-population multivariate effects. In cases where the investigator wishes to account for sampling level in a single model, the choices are data adjustment (Shipley 2000, chapter 7) or incorporation of a sampling level variable in the model. Examples of this latter approach will be shown below.

Adjustment of correlations/covariances

In "random-effect" studies, inference is drawn to a larger universe of possibilities using a limited subset of treatment levels. For example, one may wish to consider the effect of nutrient loading on a lake ecosystem. The experimental treatment levels are thus viewed as finite samples from an underlying continuum. As discussed in Chapter 7, when standard correlations are used to represent an underlying continuous variable, correlations are attenuated. In practice, this means that values of the correlation fall in a narrower range of values than the true values. Through a somewhat involved set of procedures that define thresholds and make assumptions about the relationship between categories and the underlying continuum, it is possible to adjust correlations involving categorical variables. In the case of a categorical treatment variable and continuous response variable, a polyserial correlation can be substituted for the Pearson product-moment correlation and we can obtain an estimate of the correlation between the response variable and the underlying continuous treatment variable. The discrepancy between Pearson and polyserial correlations is greatest when a continuous variable is measured as a dichotomous one.

As the number of categories in an ordinal categorical variable increase, the Pearson and polychoric correlations converge. As a general rule, if an ordinal variable is measured with 5–7 levels, practitioners often perform analyses without adjustment.

As mentioned above, sometimes investigators wish only to consider the effects of the particular treatments applied in their study. For example, an experiment with two levels of fertilization may rely on unadjusted correlations/covariances, and draw inferences only to their particular study. On the other hand, it is common in the social sciences to treat many categorical variables as expressions of underlying continuous variables. Thus, there is some latitude afforded to the investigator as to the use of adjustments, depending on how one wishes to define the underlying latent variable, and the sphere of inferences they wish to draw from the analysis.

Multigroup analyses

It is always possible to subdivide data into groups (say, treatment types) and perform separate analyses on each group. Within SEM, this can be performed in a comprehensive way using multigroup analysis as described in Chapter 7. Multigroup analysis allows the investigator to determine whether parameters in a group are constant across groups, or whether they vary. This applies not only to path coefficients, but to all model parameters (e.g., factor loadings, latent variable variances), and can be extended to a comparison of parameter means across groups.

Among the many advantages of multigroup analysis is the investigation of interactions among variables. When one wishes to study the interaction between a treatment variable and a covariate, for example, one approach would be to create an interaction variable and include it in the model. This can be cumbersome and sometimes difficult to implement. Within a multigroup analysis, slopes of relationships are allowed to vary across groups, permitting a detailed examination of interactions. An example of a multigroup analysis can be found in Chapter 7.

Examples of multivariate experiments

The effects of contaminants on pond ecosystems

Background

In 1991, Johnson *et al.* published the results of a study in which SEM was used to examine the effects of atrazine additions on pond mesocosms. A primary motivation in this analysis was to determine the indirect as well as direct consequences of adding this potential toxicant to freshwater ecosystems. This study involved a 3-year investigation of 450 000-liter mesocosms (experimental ponds). Mesocosms were exposed to 0, 20, 100, or 500 µg/L of atrazine, a widely used herbicide. Mesocosms were periodically dosed to maintain the intended concentration level, with ecosystem data collected periodically. The data used in this analysis were from the third year of the study, during which variables were measured eight times from May through October. Data from the eight mesocosms were combined across the eight time periods to provide 64 measurements. These data were treated as independent estimates, which may not be justified. Nevertheless, this example provides an interesting illustration of the kind of insight that can be gained using SEM to analyze experimental data on ecosystems.

A variety of ecosystem properties were measured in this study, in addition to the atrazine levels, including phytoplankton concentration, zooplankton abundance, aquatic vegetation, and the presence or absence of grass carp in the mesocosm. Sampling of the planktonic components of the system, which were the response variables of primary interest, was performed at a variety of depths in each mesocosm, and the variable "pond depth" was included as an additional factor that might affect other parts of the system.

Results

The analyses of these data using SEM were accompanied by a detailed discussion of the process of model development and refinement. The reader is encouraged to read the original paper (Johnson *et al.* 1991) to see the steps the authors took in reaching the final model. Here I present a figure showing the final results (Figure 9.1). One major focus of this study was to determine the effects of atrazine on aquatic vegetation, phytoplankton and zooplankton. As can be seen by the number of significant relationships among the variables examined in this system, there was a complex interplay of parts that influenced how response variables were affected by atrazine. These interactions included the following:

(1) Grass carp played an important role in these mesocosms by reducing the amount of aquatic vegetation. Through this mechanism, grass carp had an indirect positive effect on both phytoplankton and zooplankton by reducing aquatic vegetation; which had a very strong negative effect on phytoplankton.

(2) The depth of the pond also had important effects, both on aquatic vegetation and on phytoplankton. In general, aquatic vegetation and phytoplankton were reduced in deeper ponds. Since aquatic vegetation had a negative effect on phytoplankton, we can see that the effect of pond depth on phytoplankton

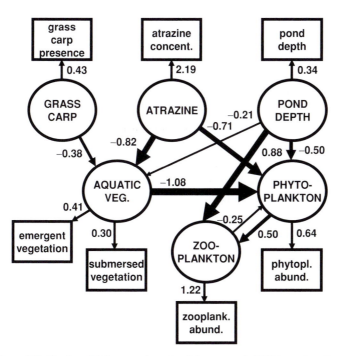

Figure 9.1. Final model from analyses by Johnson *et al.* (1991) on the effects of atrazine on aquatic mesocosms. Loadings from latent variables (in circles) to measured variables (in boxes) are influenced by the effects of standardization on units using a prior version of LISREL software which did not scale latent and indicator variables equally. Thus, loadings cannot be interpreted as if they are standardized values, although path coefficients (directional arrows) can be. Reproduced by permission of the Ecological Society of America.

consisted of a direct negative effect (likely to be caused by reduced light penetration at greater depths) and a positive indirect effect (through the adverse effects of depth on macrophyte growth). The total effect of depth can be seen to be $-0.50 + (-0.21 \times -1.08) = -0.27$.

(3) Atrazine had strong negative effects on both aquatic vegetation and phytoplankton (being a herbicide, this is to be expected). However, the net effect on phytoplankton in this system was $(-0.82 \times -1.08) - 0.71 = 0.18$, which is a positive relationship that is nonsignificant at the sample size of this study. This offsetting pair of direct and indirect effects means that the net effects of atrazine on phytoplankton will vary widely depending on the abundance of aquatic vegetation in the system studied.

(4) In order to understand the responses of zooplankton and phytoplankton in this system it was necessary to model their relationship as a reciprocal

one, with arrows going in both directions. This is basically a predator–prey system in which phytoplankton enhance zooplankton and zooplankton reduce phytoplankton. Zooplankton also responded to pond depth, perhaps because there was a greater refuge from predation from other predators, including other fish species not modeled here, in deeper ponds. The total correlation between phytoplankton and zooplankton is partitioned in quite a complex way in this model and consists of several pathways.

(a) phytoplankton → zooplankton
(b) zooplankton → phytoplankton
(c) phytoplankton → zooplankton → phytoplankton
(d) zooplankton → phytoplankton → zooplankton
(e) phytoplankton ← pond depth → zooplankton.

As Johnson *et al.* (1991) point out, the reciprocal (nonrecursive in the language of SEM) relationship means that phytoplankton affect themselves indirectly and zooplankton do likewise. As Hayduk (1987) illustrates in detail, this "effect on self" involves a loop in which a unit change, e.g., in phytoplankton, causes a change in zooplankton, which in turn causes an additional change in phytoplankton, and so on. The total effect of these loop interactions on the relationship between phytoplankton and zooplankton is composed of the *basic effect* (which is the usual direct effect) and the *loop-enhanced effect*, the effect through the loop. The indirect effect through the loop is $1/(1 - L)$, where $L = \beta_{pz} \times \beta_{zp}$. The total effect through a loop is the *product* of the direct and indirect effects (as opposed to the *sum*, which applies for non-loop relationships).

Conclusions

This example illustrates that there is substantial value in studying a system response to manipulation, in order to get a more realistic and predictive understanding of the potential effects of contaminants. Imagine, for a moment, that the web of relationships studied in this case was ignored and that only the response of phytoplankton to atrazine was examined. Depending on the sample size and statistical power, we would find for a case like the one studied by Johnson *et al.* either a nonsignificant or weak positive effect (despite the fact that the herbicide atrazine is known to have a negative effect on algae in isolation!). How would we interpret such a result? We might also imagine that when the effects of atrazine are studied in ponds, mesocosms, or whole lakes, the responses of phytoplankton vary from strong negative effects to clear positive effects, depending on the abundance and role of macrophytes in these studies. How would our chances of publication and convincing interpretation be affected by a widely varying response, as might be expected for this case? The example by Johnson *et al.* (1991) clearly illustrates many of the advantages of using SEM in the study of ecosystem responses.

Response of a prairie plant community to burning and fertilization

Background

The "coastal prairie" ecosystem in North America is the southern-most lobe of the tallgrass prairie biome, and stretches along the western Gulf of Mexico coastal plain from central Louisiana to south Texas. Approximately 99% of this endangered ecosystem has been radically altered or badly degraded by agriculture, industry, or urban development. For conservationists, a high priority is currently placed on the protection and proper management of the remaining native fragments. Our next example deals with data from a study of the effects of prescribed burning and soil fertility on the vegetative community on one such native fragment (Grace *et al.*, unpublished). In order to keep things simple, this presentation will focus on the joint responses of plant species richness and community biomass to experimental treatments. In this case, the multivariate model for analysis was expanded because of effects of spatial gradients, temporal variation, and experimental manipulations that were not anticipated when the study was designed.

The site involved in this study has been managed by annual mowing for the past few decades. In this experiment, 10×10 m plots were established and randomly subjected to combinations of burning and fertilization treatments using a random block design (note block effect was not found to be important and was removed from the analyses). Burning treatments included being (1) unburned, (2) annually burned, and (3) once burned. Fertilization treatments were (1) with, or (2) without annual applications of NPK fertilizer. A pretreatment examination of vegetation was conducted in early spring of 2000, prior to treatment applications. Vegetation, including species richness and above-ground biomass (live and dead), was measured at the end of the growing season in 2000, 2001, and 2002.

Results

Repeated measures analysis of covariance was used to examine mean responses of richness and biomass to experimental treatments (Figure 9.2). For richness, results showed significant effects of time, row (as a spatial covariate), and the fertilizer treatment. For biomass, significant effects of time and its interactions with burning and fertilizer treatments were found.

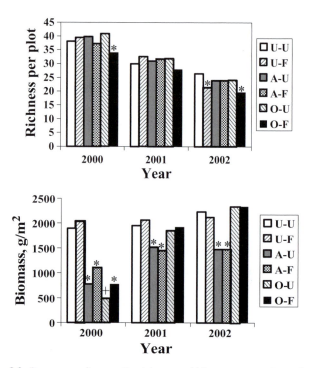

Figure 9.2. Responses of means for richness and biomass to experimental treatments over three years of study. U–U = unburned + unfertilized, U–F = unburned + fertilized, A–U = annually burned + unfertilized, A–F = annually burned and fertilized, O–U = once burned + unfertilized, O–F = once burned + fertilized. Asterisks represent means that differ significantly from the U–U treatment at $p < 0.05$, while the "+" symbol indicates differences at the $p < 0.01$ level.

In order to better understand how richness and biomass are jointly regulated in this system, a multivariate analysis was conducted to evaluate the general model shown in Figure 9.3. This model supposes that richness and biomass might influence each other, and these interactions could contribute to responses of both to treatments. Reciprocal arrows between richness and biomass were meant to include both negative effects of biomass on richness through competitive effects (which has been documented for this site by Jutila and Grace 2002), as well as postulated positive effects of richness on biomass.

The first step in evaluating the model in Figure 9.3 was to determine the shape of the relationship between biomass and richness. A positive relationship between these two variables would indicate the possibility of an effect from richness to biomass; a negative relationship would indicate the possibility of a

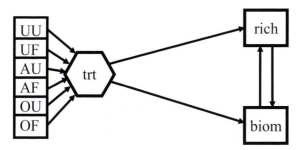

Figure 9.3. General multivariate model proposed to evaluate how interactions between richness and biomass might influence responses to treatments. Hexagon represents composite variable.

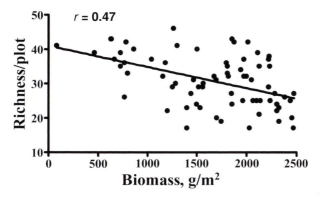

Figure 9.4. Observed relationship between biomass and richness in study of coastal prairie. Sample size in this study is 72 and includes values pooled across treatments and times.

negative effect of biomass on richness; and a hump-shaped (unimodal) relationship would indicate the possibility of both types of effect. Examination of the relationship between biomass and richness revealed a negative linear correlation (Figure 9.4). Therefore, the path from richness to biomass was eliminated for theoretical reasons, and the model shown in Figure 9.5 was used to represent the most plausible causal order of relationships. Analysis was performed using a composite variable (Chapter 6) to present a consolidated representation of treatment effects.

The effects of individual treatments are omitted from this presentation, for simplicity. The results in Figure 9.5 suggest (1) that biomass responded more strongly to treatment manipulations than did richness, and (2) treatments had

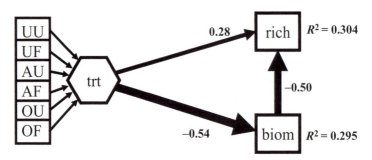

Figure 9.5. Results from analysis of initial model (Figure 9.3). Path from rich to biom was not theoretically justified in this analysis, because the observed correlation between these two variables (Figure 9.4) was negative and linear.

both direct effects on richness as well as indirect effects through impacts on biomass.

We know that the model in Figure 9.5 is an inappropriate oversimplification of the factors affecting richness. The impact of variations among years is omitted, as is the effect of spatial variation in site conditions. As to this latter point, examination of the data, as well as general field observations, indicated the presence of a subtle gradient in site wetness running along the long axis of the experimental plot array. To evaluate the role of spatial and temporal variations in wetness, indices of the known affinities of these species for wetland conditions were used to calculate a wetness index for each plot. Subsequently, the model in Figure 9.6 was evaluated, with results as shown below.

The model in Figure 9.6, with accompanying results, supports several important conclusions:

(1) The correlation between biomass and richness observed in Figure 9.4 does not represent a causal interaction between these two variables, but instead, joint control by the other variables.
(2) Row effects on richness can be explained entirely by variations in wetness across rows.
(3) Year effects were of three sorts, one being an increase in biomass over time, a second being an increase in community wetness during the experiment, and a third being a decrease in richness independent of wetness or biomass.
(4) Upon considering the year effects, the authors concluded that the path from year to rich most likely represented a system-wide decline in richness resulting from a cessation of mowing during the course of the study. This effect was further deemed to be a form of "experimental drift" that was an unintended consequence of the experiment.

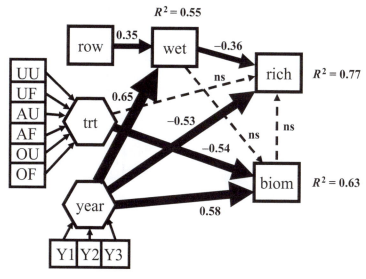

Figure 9.6. Model and results when the effects of year, spatial variation (the row variable), and vegetation wetness tolerances were incorporated.

To provide a result of more general utility (because it is not contaminated with treatment artifacts), the effects of the path from year to rich, which is presented to represent experimental drift, were removed from the data and the model rerun. By calculating the residual differences between richness and the predicted scores using the individual path coefficient, it was possible to remove this one component of the year effect. The remaining effect of year on richness mediated through wetness was retained.

The results of this modified model are shown in Figure 9.7. It can be seen that there are only two changes of significance from Figure 9.6. First, the amount of variance in richness is reduced and the percent explained drops from 77% to 43%. Secondly, the path from wet to rich increases in absolute strength from −0.36 to −0.66.

Conclusions

Conventional univariate analyses, such as the repeated measures ANCOVA are often important in a complete evaluation of experimental results. Such analyses permit a detailed examination of net treatment effects on mean responses. However, such univariate analyses are unable to evaluate the multivariate relationships among variables. Thus, a combination of univariate and multivariate techniques can be most effective.

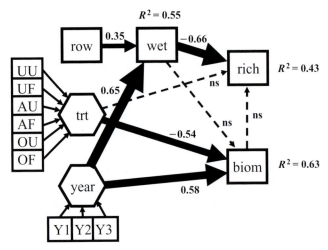

Figure 9.7. Model with effects of "experimental drift" (the path from year to rich) removed.

There has been and remains a great interest in the relationship between biomass and richness. It is instructive in this case to see how a multivariate analysis sheds light on the interpretation of this relationship. The observed correlation between richness and biomass found in this study (Figure 9.4) is suggestive of a competitive effect on richness. This correlation is supportive of an interpretation in which treatment, row, and year effects might influence richness through their impacts on biomass. However, when a multivariate analysis is performed, we can see that the correlation between richness and biomass, though it is fairly strong, results from common control rather than biological interactions. Both richness and biomass are under strong control from common causes and as emphasized in the previous chapter, relationships between variables possessing common causes cannot be accurately evaluated using a univariate or bivariate approach.

This example also illustrates another important capability of a multivariate experiment. Univariate results showed that vegetation wetness increased over time while biomass increased and richness decreased. On the face of it, it might seem that the decrease in richness over time resulted from increased rainfall and increased competitive exclusion. Multivariate analysis isolated a direct effect of year on rich that was interpreted as an undesired side effect of the experimental treatments due to the cessation of mowing during the study. It was then possible to remove this side effect (dubbed by the authors "experimental drift") from the data while retaining the other components of the year effect.

Manipulation of an intertidal marine community

Background

In 1994, Wootton published the results of an intensive analysis of a marine intertidal community using a combination of manipulative experiments and path analysis. Marine intertidal communities have been shown through previous experiments to be highly interactive, both within and between trophic levels. Wootton made several arguments in favor of multivariate experimentation. First, he argued that the possibility of indirect effects makes the analysis of species pairs an inadequate tool for predicting community responses to environmental change. Secondly, he argued that interactions were typically quite asymmetric, with some species and certain interactions being more important to overall community dynamics. Thus, he built the case for the need to determine the relative importance of pathways in the system. A third motivation he presented was that a reductionist approach that tried to understand community interactions by assembly of all the pairwise interactions was hopelessly complex for all but the most simple systems. Finally, he noted that manipulation of all the elements in a community was, at times, not possible due to logistic or other (e.g., endangered species) reasons. As Wootton clearly saw, the combination of SEM and experimentation has the potential of overcoming a variety of difficulties in studying interacting systems. These issues were reiterated in a later review of the widespread importance of indirect effects in ecological systems (Wootton 2002).

Wootton (1994) began his study with an initial experiment that excluded birds, which serve as top predators, from a middle intertidal community on an island off the coast of Washington state in North America. Five 1.5-year-old gaps in the mussel bed were selected for study and pairs of plots were established in each, with one of each pair randomly assigned to be caged or not. Snails (*Nucella*), small starfish (*Leptasterias*), mussels (*Mytilus*), goose barnacles (*Pollicipes*), and acorn barnacles (*Semibalanus*) were measured in each plot over two years. Comparisons of treatment means found that when birds were excluded (1) snails, mussels, and acorn barnacles were reduced, and (2) goose barnacles were enhanced.

Wootton recognized that at least three different mechanistic scenarios were possible given the pattern of results. To evaluate these possibilities, he pooled data across treatments and years, and performed a path analysis that compared the fit of the data to five contrasting models. Predicted and observed correlations were compared using linear regression to assess model fit. Chi-square tests were also performed. As Wootton himself noted, ". . . the conclusions [from this initial analysis] should be treated as predictions that point to the most important

Table 9.2. *Correlations and standard deviations from initial bird exclusion experiment conducted by Wootton (1994). GooseB refers to goose barnacles. AcornB refers to acorn barnacles*

	Birds	GooseB	Mussels	AcornB	Snails ln	Tide Ht.
Birds	1.0					
GooseB	−0.955	1.0				
Mussels	0.399	−0.468	1.0			
AcornB	0.802	−0.809	−0.103	1.0		
Snails ln	0.403	−0.349	−0.303	0.532	1.0	
Tide Ht.	0	0.039	−0.444	0.335	−0.210	1.0
Std. dev.	0.47	26.76	16.97	15.48	0.90	0.16

experiments to be conducted next, not as conclusions to be set in stone." This is true not only because of the exploratory (though theory-driven) nature of the analysis, but also because of the low sample size and the fact that data from the two years were pooled and thus treated as independent observations.

Results

The results from the initial bird exclusion experiment are presented in Table 9.2, and the model selected to best represent the data is shown in Figure 9.8. Examination of the correlations indicate that exposure to bird foraging leads to a strong reduction in goose barnacles and increases in acorn barnacles, snails, and mussels. These interpretations from the correlation matrix are matched with results from the analysis of mean responses as well. The correlation matrix further indicates that both goose barnacles and mussels are negatively associated with all community members, while acorn barnacles and snails are positively associated with each other.

Comparing the correlation matrix to the path model results indicates the following:

(1) The effects of birds on snails, acorn barnacles, and mussels are all indirect, being mediated by direct effects on goose barnacles. Thus, birds are primarily feeding on goose barnacles.
(2) Goose barnacles have strong negative effects on acorn barnacles that are only partially offset by indirect beneficial effects caused by reductions in mussels.

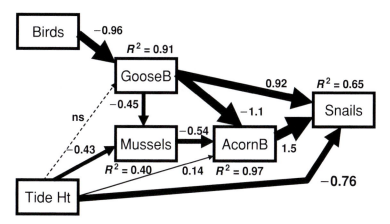

Figure 9.8. Model selected to represent initial bird exclusion experiment in Wootton (1994). Path coefficients presented are standardized. GooseB refers to goose barnacles. AcornB refers to acorn barnacles. Reproduced by permission of the Ecological Society of America.

(3) Acorn barnacles have a strong positive effect on snails, and there is no indication that there is a reciprocal effect of snails on acorn barnacles.

(4) Goose barnacles have a complex effect on snails. This effect has positive direct and indirect components that are offset by a negative effect on acorn barnacles, which stimulate snails.

(5) Tide height plays an important part in this system. Its actual influence is poorly represented by the correlation results because of the importance of the indirect effects that tide height has on acorn barnacles and snails.

Conclusions

It can be seen from this example, as with previous examples, that a multivariate examination of the data yields a very different interpretation of the underlying mechanisms. In this case, the author possessed several plausible alternative interpretations about underlying causal mechanisms. However, two of the three models evaluated were found not to fit the covariance patterns in the data. Thus, SEM has the ability to provide guidance as to which proposed mechanisms do not appear consistent with the results. In this study, Wootton went on to make predictions from this initial experiment that were subsequently tested with further experiments. Such experimental tests are considered in the final chapter relating SEM to ecological forecasting.

The effects of fire on an exotic tree that invades coastal tallgrass prairie

Background

Ecosystem manipulations, such as those involving prescribed fire, often pose special challenges for experimental study. This example comes from a study of the potential for prescribed burning to control an invading exotic tree, Chinese tallow (*Triadeca sebifera*) (Grace *et al.*, unpublished). The system being invaded is coastal tallgrass prairie, one of the most endangered ecosystems in North America. Chinese tallow poses a special threat because of its ability to turn a diverse and fire-dependent native grassland into a nonflammable monoculture thicket in only a few years. Because the coastal prairie is typically managed using prescribed fire to mimic the natural fire regime, the question of interest is whether fire can control this exotic tree in the same way that fire naturally keeps the prairie from succeeding to woodland.

A few characteristics of the biological interactions in this system are of prime importance. First, as with most native grasslands, the coastal tallgrass prairie is a fire-dependent ecosystem. Secondly, Chinese tallow is a fire suppressing species. It both suppresses fuel species and itself rarely carries a fire. Thirdly, it is known that once Chinese tallow establishes to a certain point, it becomes immune to fire management. The objective of this study was to determine whether there exists some minimum tree size below which fire control is effective. If such a critical minimum size exists and can be identified, it can be used to develop protective habitat management plans that are effective and efficient. Thus, of prime interest was the relationship of tree size to its response to burning.

This study was conducted at the Brazoria National Wildlife Refuge in coastal Texas which is one of the most important pieces of coastal prairie under federal protection. Approximately 5000 hectares of virgin prairie remain at this site. In addition, thousands of acres of abandoned agricultural lands are in the process of recovering prairie vegetation. As with many habitats of conservation importance, conditions were not favorable at this site for generating a large number of replicate habitat units for experimental manipulation. Several factors had to be considered. First, it was important that the destructive process of creating fire breaks in this system be kept to a minimum. Secondly, numerous gradients and historical differences contribute to a mosaic landscape in which pre-existing management units (which can be burned independently) each have unique properties. Thirdly, the trees themselves contribute to the development of a mosaic in fuel and other conditions, creating a heterogeneous fire that can burn one tree and completely miss the tree next to it. Finally, stands of tallow contain a

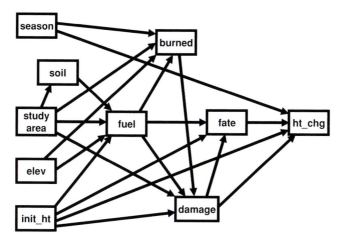

Figure 9.9. Initial model of how height and other factors might influence the effects of burning on the Chinese tallow tree.

continuum of sizes from seedling to reproducing adult. While seedlings often establish beneath adult trees, they are dispersed by birds and also establish in the open or in gaps in the vegetation caused by animal activities.

In this experiment, 20 trees in each of five size classes (0–0.1 m, 0.1–1 m, 1–2 m, 2–3 m, and >3 m) were randomly selected in each of four habitat management units, for a total of 400 trees. Some seedlings did not survive to the time of initial burning and tags were lost from a few other trees, resulting in a total sample size of 378. For each tree, a 1 meter diameter plot was established with the tree in the center. Variables measured before burning included tree height, basal diameter, estimated fuel load, elevation, and soil texture. One management unit at each of the two areas was selected for summer burning and the other selected for winter burning. Following each burn, the percentage of the plot that burned was recorded, along with the degree of damage the tree incurred (specifically, how high the tree was scorched and what fraction of the tree was damaged), and whether it ultimately died, retained its original height, or was topkilled. The heights of all trees were tracked over a two-year period, with the end of the second growing season designated for the final comparative measurements.

The model proposed initially, shown in Figure 9.9, incorporates both controlled variables, such as (1) initial tree height, (2) area, and (3) season of burn, along with uncontrolled variables, such as (4) location along elevation gradients, (5) soil conditions, and (6) fuel under or around each tree. The response variables measured included (7) the percentage of a plot that burned, (8) the

Table 9.3. *Correlations among variables remaining in model of fire effects on Chinese tallow. Htchg refers to tree height change during the study. Initht refers to the initial height of the tree prior to burning. Numbers in bold are significant at p < 0.05*

	Fuel	Burn	Damage	Fate	Htchg	Season	Area	Initht
Fuel	1.0							
Burn	**0.21**	1.0						
Damage	**0.20**	**0.88**	1.0					
Fate	−0.07	**−0.42**	**−0.57**	1.0				
Htchg	**−0.18**	**−0.32**	**−0.45**	**0.60**	1.0			
Season	−0.12	**−0.39**	**−0.27**	0.01	**−0.25**	1.0		
Area	**0.16**	**0.59**	**0.54**	**−0.39**	**−0.26**	0.0	1.0	
Initht	**−0.26**	−0.03	**−0.21**	**0.48**	**0.38**	0.0	0.0	1.0

percentage of a tree damaged, (9) its fate (whether it died, was topkilled, or survived intact), and (10) the height change of the tree during the study. Height change basically quantified the degree to which resprouting might have allowed the tree to recover from the burn. The logic of this initial model was that some factors of importance, such as soil conditions and fuel would potentially depend on study area and elevation gradients within sites. It was also hypothesized that the amount of fuel beneath trees would be affected by tree size.

The amount of fuel was expected to influence both the completeness of burn, as well as the amount of damage that would be done to trees. However, fires are also affected by immediate weather and other influences, such as soil moisture, that vary from site to site and time to time. In this model, such generalized effects were confounded with study area, which was postulated to include such effects.

Finally, the fate of a tree and ultimately its change in height during the study were expected to depend on how complete the burn was around a tree, and how much damage it sustained. In woodland burns, heterogeneity in fire behavior can be substantial at the level of the individual tree, and obviously only trees that actually sustained significant fire damage are expected to respond to burning.

Results

Initial model results found that both soil conditions and elevation influenced fuel, but did not affect plant responses in any major way. For this reason, it was possible to simplify the model by removing these two factors. Correlations among the remaining factors are shown in Table 9.3 and the final model is shown in Figure 9.10.

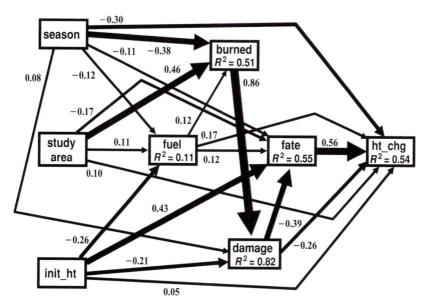

Figure 9.10. Final model for fire effects on Chinese tallow tree.

Figure 9.10 reveals 20 significant direct relationships among variables, suggesting that the factors affecting tree responses to fire are quite complex. To a certain degree, this complexity of outcome results from the large sample size associated with this study. We can see that paths whose standardized coefficients were as low as 0.05 were deemed statistically significant in this analysis. Eight paths had coefficients less than 0.15. The actual complexity of this model was even greater than apparent in Figure 9.10, because the relationships between initial tree height and fuel, fate, and height change were nonlinear, each having a unique shape. Appendix I at the end of this book presents the program statements for the full model, as well as an explanation for the procedures for estimating the strength of the nonlinear paths.

Several main points can be drawn from the results of this study.

(1) Initial tree height was well correlated with the responses of trees to burning. While a number of processes appear to be involved, the biggest fraction of this relationship was through a direct effect on the fate of the tree that was unrelated to fuel suppression, or to the fact that larger trees suffered proportionally less damage.

(2) The study areas also had a substantial impact on the results. This effect could result from a number of factors relating to the nature of the fires, the overall fuel conditions, or the conditions affecting tree growth. The authors concluded that the study area effect was most likely to be related

to differences in fuel conditions (both general and at the time of the burn), which had strong effects on the completeness and intensity of the burns. It would seem that in this study, the fuel load immediately around the tree did not represent the general effects of fuel on fire effects, although there were some modest effects detected.

(3) The season of burn was related to several pathways in the model. Some of these appear to result from a confoundment of factors caused by the small number of burn units. Effects of season on initial fuel conditions and the percentage of plots that burned were deemed coincidental. The main effect of season that was important in this study was the direct effect on height change. This effect represents the growth responses of resprouts to season. It was apparent that trees burned during the dormant season produced resprouts that fared much better than those produced by trees burned in summer. There was a similar but weaker effect of season on tree fate.

Conclusions

This example represents a case where an analysis of multivariate relationships among trees seeks to overcome the limits of field experimentation. Since the ultimate objective of the research was to develop a predictive model that can be tested against repeated trials, the limits of the results will ultimately be judged by the success of prediction over a range of conditions. Because of the goal of predicting effects in other locations, this experiment contributes to a program of study that seeks to be generally consistent over space and time, rather than intensively precise for a particular space and time.

Linking experimental and nonexperimental studies of coastal plant diversity

While this chapter emphasizes the value of an experimental approach, ecologists, perhaps more than many other natural scientists, are keenly aware of the limits imposed by experimentation. Typically, we do not strive simply to understand the pieces of natural systems that fit within the confines of aquaria, incubators, test tubes, greenhouses, mesocosms, or even individual study sites. Rather, we wish to know how whole ecological systems function, and how they will respond to perturbations and environmental changes. Nonexperimental hypothesis testing, a strong suit of the SEM tradition, can play an invaluable role in allowing the researcher a more extensive view of how a system works. Our interpretations from nonexperimentally evaluated models are nevertheless limited in the strength of their inference in many cases (see Chapter 4). Experimentation plays a vital role in evaluating our assumptions and

Table 9.4. *Correlations. Those in bold are significantly different from zero at the p < 0.05 level for a sample size of 254*

	Richness	Fenced	Fertilized	Abiotic	Disturb.	Biomass
Richness	1.0					
Fenced	0.1076	1.0				
Fertilized	**−0.2683**	0.0041	1.0			
Abiotic	0.0249	−0.0180	0.0014	1.0		
Disturb.	**−0.4400**	**−0.3114**	**−0.1341**	**0.1730**	1.0	
Biomass	**0.5343**	**0.2119**	**0.3172**	**−0.2401**	**−0.5525**	1.0

hypotheses, as well as in determining the limits of our causal interpretations. For this next example, we return to an experimental study conducted by Gough and Grace (1999). In this study, several variables were experimentally manipulated in order to test the assumptions of prior nonexperimental SEM.

Background

In part because of a desire to test experimentally assumptions about the relationships among environmental and community properties, a study was undertaken to manipulate as many of the factors thought to be important in controlling species richness as feasible. This study was conducted at the Pearl River (see Chapter 10 for a more complete description of this system) in oligohaline and mesohaline marshes. The manipulations included (1) the addition of NPK fertilizer to alter community biomass, (2) changing the levels of flooding stress by raising or lowering sods of plants, (3) exposing sods to different salinity regimes by transplanting them between oligohaline and mesohaline locations, and (4) the use of fences to exclude herbivores and thereby reduce disturbance levels. Treatments were applied in a full factorial study. While species composition was measured in this study, the focus of the model was on species richness as the primary response variable of interest. Eight replicates of each of the 32 treatment combinations were used in this study, which included a total of 256 experimental units. Problems resulted in the loss of data for two experimental units, leaving 254 samples in the analysis.

Results

Table 9.4 gives correlations for the variables analyzed by Gough and Grace (1999). Prior to analysis using LISREL, compositing techniques were used to provide estimates of total abiotic effects, disturbance, and biomass for subsequent analysis. In the preanalysis, first- and second-order polynomial effects

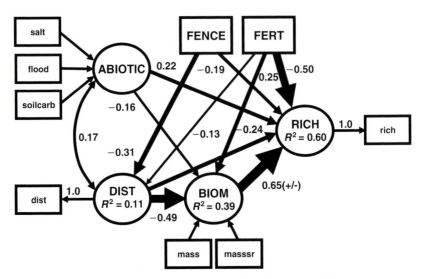

Figure 9.11. SEM results for experimental studies of the factors affecting species richness in coastal wetland plant communities (from Gough and Grace 1999). Reproduced by permission of the Ecological Society of America.

of salinity, flooding, and soil organic variations were formative indicators for the statistical composite variable "abiotic". First- and second-order polynomial terms were also incorporated into both "disturbance" and "biomass" in order to achieve linear relations among variables. In the process of performing the preanalysis, all variables were z-transformed to means of zero and variances of 1.0.

Comparison of the SEM results to those apparent from only the raw correlations is revealing. To reduce complexity, only the effects of fencing and fertilization on richness will be emphasized here. Additional interpretations can be found in Gough and Grace (1999).

Variations in species richness in this study were unrelated to whether or not the plots were fenced ($r = 0.108$), even though fencing reduced disturbance levels and disturbance, in turn, was related to richness. As the SEM results show (Figure 9.11), the experimental manipulation of fencing actually had three significant effects.

(1) One effect of fencing was an indirect enhancement of richness caused by a reduction in direct disturbance effects. This is represented by the path from Fence to Disturbance to Richness. We interpreted this indirect effect as a suppression of the direct loss of disturbance-sensitive species.

(2) The other indirect enhancement was through a reduction in disturbance, subsequently leading to a recovery in biomass and an associated recovery in richness (the path from Fence to Disturbance to Biomass to Richness).
(3) The third significant effect of fencing observed was a direct negative effect of fencing on richness. This path appears to represent increased competitive exclusion as litter built up within the fenced areas. The reason the loss of species through this path was not related to biomass accumulation appears to be because the accumulation of litter suppressed both richness and biomass accumulation.

Conclusions

The value of this multivariate experimental approach and analysis should be clear. A univariate experiment would only have revealed that fencing had no net effect on richness. What would have been hidden from view were the effects of three significant processes, two positive and one negative, which offset one another.

As for the effects of fertilization, behind the net negative effect on richness there appear to lie four significant processes.

(1) Two rather weak effects operated through a reduction in disturbance associated with fertilization. We hypothesize that, in this case, the more rapid growth rate of plants in fertilized plots showed a more rapid recovery from disturbance and, thus, evidence of disturbance was slightly lowered by fertilization. As described above for the effects of fencing, reducing disturbance can promote richness through two somewhat different paths.
(2) The third indirect effect of fertilization was through an enhancement of biomass and an associated enhancement of richness, presumably primarily in plots recovering from disturbance.
(3) The fourth process, implied by Figure 9.11, is a direct negative effect of fertilization on richness. This strong negative effect occurred independent of increases in biomass, as was also seen for the fencing treatment. Analysis of the timecourse of events in this study would indicate that fertilization led to an early increase in biomass that ultimately inhibited later plant growth. Ultimately, much of the loss of species associated with fertilization was not accompanied by an increased biomass at the end of the study.

The story for fertilization would seem to be similar to that for fencing in that the net effect only tells a small part of the total story. The actual direct negative effect, independent of the other variables, is actually quite a bit stronger (path coefficient $= -0.50$) than the net negative effect ($r = -0.27$) representing all the processes. It is possible that our interpretations of all the paths are not complete. However, the multivariate analysis clearly indicates that fertilization is influencing richness through a variety of different processes, and it gives an estimate of the relative importance of direct and indirect influences. It is worth pointing out that the rather large number of total experimental units in this study was important in revealing many of the indirect effects that were observed.

Conclusions

It is hopefully clear through the examples presented in this chapter that experimental studies of systems can and often should be conducted using SEM. The basic test an investigator can apply to determine their needs is to ask themselves the following question: am I interested in how the various parts of the system interact to produce the results? If the answer is yes, conventional univariate methods will not be adequate, although they can complement the analyses. Once an investigator decides that they wish to use SEM in an experimental situation, they are automatically encouraged to include the important unmanipulated factors into their models. This moves the experiment from being simply an investigation of a single process, to the study of how their system is regulated. I expect that often ecologists will find that the process of initial interest to them is not really the one most important in regulating their system, at least that has been my experience.

Society asks us to provide answers that are relevant to real world concerns and that can be applied to conservation solutions. Understanding the effects of individual processes will not, in my opinion, generate the information we need. The conduct of multivariate experiments is a largely neglected topic that I believe will become the standard for understanding ecological systems. There exist great opportunities for developing methods and applications for experimentally evaluating multivariate hypotheses using SEM.

10

The systematic use of SEM: an example

This chapter illustrates the systematic application of a multivariate perspective using SEM to explore a topic. In this presentation, the statistical details of the analyses will be ignored; these have been presented in earlier chapters, or can be found in the various publications referenced throughout. Here, the emphasis is on illustrating the broad enterprise of developing, evaluating, refining, and expanding multivariate models in order to understand system behavior and regulation. Throughout, the focus will be on the research enterprise rather than the analytical details. Thus, the philosophy and practice of SEM will be in the forefront, while the analysis of covariances, maximum likelihood, and mathematical details will be de-emphasized.

Background studies and findings

In 1992, Laura Gough and I conducted a study designed to examine the relationship between plant community biomass and species richness. This work was conducted in coastal marsh communities. The purpose of this study was to first characterize the relationship between biomass and richness. Then we planned to determine the role of competition in controlling the relationship. We expected that we would find a unimodal relationship between biomass and richness, primarily because of several key papers that had been published previously (Al-Mufti *et al.* 1977, Huston 1980, Wheeler and Giller 1982, Moore and Keddy 1989, Wisheu and Keddy 1989, Shipley *et al.* 1991, Wheeler and Shaw 1991). We also expected this relationship because there were several competing theories attempting to explain this phenomenon (Grime 1979, Huston 1979, Tilman 1982, Taylor *et al.* 1990, Keddy 1990). Figure 10.1 presents one of the early examples that inspired much of the subsequent work on this topic. A further influence on us at that time was work by Paul Keddy and his

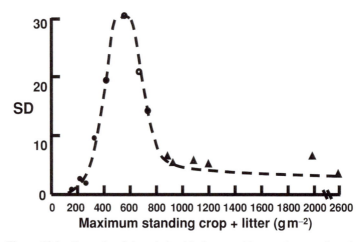

Figure 10.1. Example of the relationship between biomass (measured as the maximum standing crop including litter), and species richness (SD, or species density), presented by Al-Mufti *et al.* in 1977. Solid circles represent woodland herbs, open circles represent grasslands, and triangles represent tall herbs of open areas. Reproduced by permission of Blackwell Publishers.

colleagues (see above references), who were attempting to establish general, quantitative, predictive relationships between community biomass and richness.

Combining our data from two coastal riverine systems with the data of one of our colleagues, Kathy Taylor, we found a pattern rather unlike the one we expected (Figure 10.2). Instead of a unimodal curve, we found a unimodal envelope (see additional discussion of this relationship in Marrs *et al.* 1996). Also, we found biomass to be rather unimportant as a predictor, but found that species richness was strongly correlated with microelevation and sediment salinity and, to a lesser degree with soil organic matter. Table 10.1 shows the results of the multiple regression that we performed using all of the measured predictor variables. The fit of this multiple regression model to the data is shown in Figure 10.3.

Based on the results we obtained and our familiarity with wetland systems, we formulated a multivariate conceptual model (Figure 10.4). We further supported this model with additional data about the existing species pools (we used the term "potential richness") and how they varied with salinity. To quote Gough *et al.* (1994),

> In conclusion, in this study we found that biomass was not an adequate predictor of species richness. One reason for this inadequacy appears to be that while stresses such as flooding and salinity may greatly reduce the pool of potential species that

Table 10.1. *Multiple regression results for species richness as a function of environmental variables (modified from Gough* et al. *1994)*

Predictor variables	Coefficient	Std error	Cumulative R-square	p <
Constant	−3.90	1.084		0.001
Biomass	−0.0011	0.0003	0.02	0.001
Elevation	3.10	0.377	0.57	0.001
Salinity	0.51	0.137	0.69	0.001
Soil organic	0.052	0.011	0.82	0.001

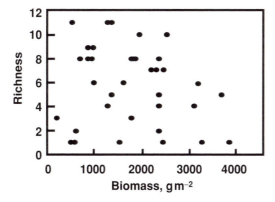

Figure 10.2. Relationship between total above-ground community biomass (live + dead) per m² and number of species per m², found by Gough *et al.* (1994) in coastal marsh systems. Reproduced by permission of Oikos.

can occur at a site, those species that have evolved adaptations to these factors may not have substantially reduced biomass. Thus, we recommend that models developed to predict species richness should incorporate direct measurements of environmental factors as well as community attributes such as biomass in order to increase their applicability.

Multivariate hypothesis formulation and evaluation

Initial evaluations of a multivariate model at the Pearl River

In 1993, Bruce Pugesek and I initiated a more extensive study designed to evaluate the ideas presented in Figure 10.4 using SEM. The system to which we wished to apply this model was a coastal riverine marsh landscape located

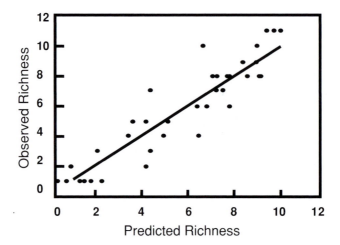

Figure 10.3. Fit of data to the multiple regression model in Table 10.1 (from Gough *et al.* 1994). Reproduced by permission of Oikos.

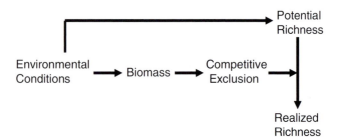

Figure 10.4. Hypothesized conceptual model of factors controlling species richness in plant communities.

on the shore of the Gulf of Mexico (Figure 10.5). This landscape contains a number of conspicuous environmental gradients, including gradients in salinity (salt marsh to fresh marsh), microelevation (from plants in deep water to those growing on raised levees), and soil organic content (from sandy soil deposits to organic muck sediments). We also knew from previous studies that natural disturbances were common and resulted from the activities of wild mammal populations, as well as from flooding and storm effects. Thus, this system contained a variety of stresses and disturbances of the sort commonly invoked in theories about diversity regulation.

Figure 10.5. Aerial photograph of the Pearl River marsh complex, which was the site of these investigations.

The next step in the process was to convert the conceptual model (Figure 10.4) into a construct model, as represented in Figure 10.6. The process of specifying a construct model is an important step forward in theory maturation. The conceptual model presents important ideas, however, it is very general and the meanings of the terms are somewhat vague. This is not to say that the construct model in Figure 10.6 is without ambiguity. Models always have a context, some set of physical circumstances under which the model makes sense. I have argued previously (Grace 1991) that the context for models is often not clearly specified in ecological theories, leading to irresolvable debate. The application of SEM seeks to make concepts and context tangible in stages, which preserves both general and specific perspectives on the problem. This topic will be discussed in more detail in Chapter 12 as it relates to the concept of theory maturation.

One thing that happens when we specify our construct model is that there is an immediate expectation that the concepts represented will have to be made operational. This means that it is soon going to be necessary to specify the meaning of the concepts by describing exactly how they will be measured. This reality suggested to us a distinction that we wanted to make that was not specified in the conceptual model; that there are two distinctly different kinds

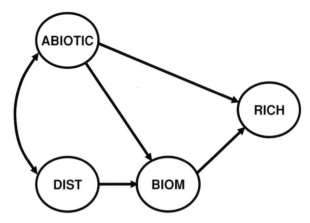

Figure 10.6. Construct model showing major factors presumed to be controlling species richness (taken from Figure 1 in Grace and Pugesek 1997). ABIOTIC refers to abiotic environmental variables, DIST refers to disturbances of vegetation by animals and flooding, BIOM refers to community biomass, and RICH refers to species richness. Reproduced by permission of The University of Chicago Press.

of environmental variables, abiotic conditions and disturbances. Making this distinction was actually not a mandatory requirement, as the use of composites (Chapter 6) does allow us a method for dealing with highly heterogeneous concepts. However, since much attention has been paid to the effects of disturbance versus the effects of stress on richness, the distinction between abiotic factors and disturbance was one we thought would be valuable.

The next step in the process was to develop the structural equation model (Figure 10.7). As indicated by the model structure, we specified that abiotic conditions would be measured by combining specific abiotic measurements into indices. We also proposed to characterize the disturbance regime by quantifying the observable signs of disturbance in the vegetation. To measure community biomass, we decided to measure the standing crop of plant material, which was the parameter measured by Al-Mufti *et al.* (1977), and also to measure the amount of light passing through the vegetation, as an additional measure of the quantity of vegetation. Richness was specified as being measured simply by the number of species we found in one m^2 plots.

An important concept associated with SEM is that the observed variables are only required to be indicators of the processes and parameters of interest rather than perfect measures. In order for a measured variable to serve as an adequate indicator, it is only necessary for the relative values of that variable to be correlated with the underlying process of mechanistic importance. For example, when we specify that the conceptual variable DIST would have an effect on

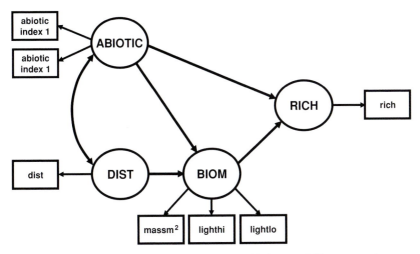

Figure 10.7. Initial structural equation model with latent variables representing concepts and observed variables representing indicators. Reproduced by permission of The University of Chicago Press.

BIOM, what is meant is that the disturbance regime has an effect on community biomass. When a measure of recent disturbance is used as an indicator of DIST, we are proposing that recent indications of disturbance correlate with the disturbance regime over a period of time, reflected by the vegetation.

Once the initial structural equation model shown in Figure 10.7 was formulated, we designed a sampling scheme and schedule. Data were then collected over a two-year period to test this model. Only the results from the first year were used in Grace and Pugesek (1997), with the second year's data saved for a subsequent test of whether the model results would hold up over time, and how the system changes between years. Data collected included sediment salinity, site microelevation, soil organic and mineral content (components of the abiotic indices), recent disturbance (dist), measured as percentage of the plot disturbed, above-ground biomass per m^2 (massm^2), percentage of full sunlight reaching the ground surface in the densest part of the plot (lightlo), percentage of full sunlight reaching the ground surface in the sparsest part of the plot (lighthi), and the number of species in a plot (rich).

As is often the case when evaluating multivariate models, the fit between our data and the initial model indicated that it was not adequate. Simply put, our data were not consistent with the expectations implied by the initial model. The part of the hypothesis in Figure 10.7 that failed was the proposition that biomass and light readings can both be used to represent a single conceptual variable. The symptoms of this failure were that lighthi and lightlo were highly correlated,

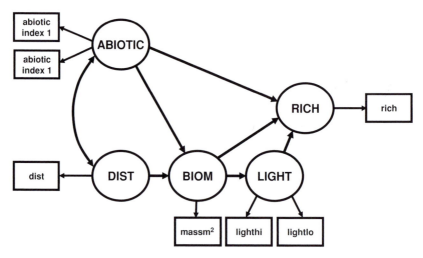

Figure 10.8. Modified full model defining BIOM and LIGHT as separate conceptual variables.

but that massm^2 was not well correlated with either light variable. Because of this, we reformulated our model, as shown in Figure 10.8. An important lesson was learned here, regardless of your conceptualization of the problem, if two variables are not consistently and equally well correlated, they will not function as multiple indicators of a single conceptual variable. Of course, we could have used the heterogeneous indicators to represent a composite. However, that did not fit with our objectives in this analysis.

Once the model was reformulated and reanalyzed, another inconsistency between model and data emerged. A large residual correlation between DIST and LIGHT was found to exist. As was discussed in Chapter 8 (see Figure 8.12), this particular residual represents an effect of disturbance on plant morphology that moderates the effect of disturbance on light. In order to proceed further, it was necessary to include a pathway from DIST to LIGHT. Only then was there a consistent match between the relationships in the model and those in the data.

The results shown in Figure 10.9 represent the partitioning of covariances in the data as specified by the relationships in the model. Since these results were obtained using a maximum likelihood statistical procedure, they satisfy the criterion of being a simultaneous solution for all relationships. It is not my purpose here to describe all the ecological interpretations of these results. The interested reader can consult the paper by Grace and Pugesek (1997). What I would like to point out, however, is that while this model fits the data, we must conclude that our original formulated model (Figure 10.7) did not. Thus, further

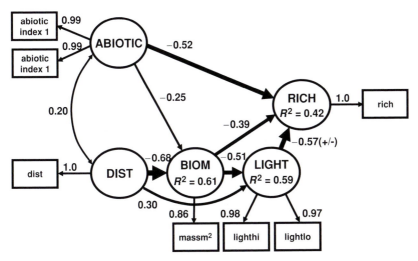

Figure 10.9. Results for accepted model. Standardized partial regression coefficients are given. The (+/−) next to the path from LIGHT to RICH signifies that this path was unimodal. Reproduced by permission of The University of Chicago Press.

evaluation is still needed using an independent data set, before we can conclude that our accepted model is valid for the system sampled. As this rather weak conclusion reveals, the demands that SEM places on empirical validation are quite stringent. Stated in another way, the model evaluation philosophy pushes the scientist rather hard to demonstrate that their results have consistent validity (i.e., consistent applicability in different places and over time), not just local application.

A more detailed examination of the data

As mentioned earlier, the construct model presented in Figure 10.6 actually represents a family of models that can be represented using a single data set. To illustrate this point, Figure 10.10 shows the results of a more specific and detailed model in which the abiotic factors were represented individually. The results are based on the exact same data set used to arrive at the more general results in Figure 10.9, except for the fact that the more general model combined the individual abiotic data into indices. Again, no discussion of the ecological interpretations will be presented here. Later in the chapter, I will present an example that used a derivative of this model for the purpose of exploring the role of historical factors in controlling species richness.

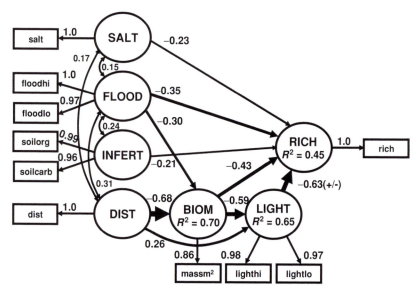

Figure 10.10. Results for a more specific version of the model. Reproduced by permission of The University of Chicago Press.

An experimental test of the multivariate model

A certain amount of experimental evidence exists that supports the dependency assumptions in the above models (for a review of some of this literature, see Grace 1999). This is not to say that there are no feedback processes that have been omitted; for example, a reciprocal effect of species richness on community biomass. What has been assumed is that the relationship between biomass and richness is asymmetric, with the predominant influence being in the direction specified. Regardless of this, the principle of theory maturation pushes us to ask whether the results from the nonexperimental studies so far described have any predictive power. Testing predictions based on our accepted models (Figures 10.9 and 10.10) not only addresses the question of whether there is consistent validity, but also represents an opportunity to further refine our model and to determine the limits of its applicability.

Between 1993 and 1995, Laura Gough devised and conducted an extensive experimental study designed to manipulate a number of key variables believed to control species richness in the Pearl River system. The results from these experiments were then used in two ways to evaluate multivariate hypotheses (Gough and Grace 1999). First, her results were compared with predictions from a model like the one in Figure 10.10, except that it was based on the second year's

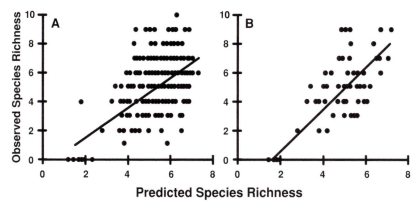

Figure 10.11. Comparisons between predicted and observed species richness taken from Gough and Grace (1999). A. All plots. B. Excluding fertilized and fenced plots. Reproduced by permission of the Ecological Society of America.

data collected by Grace and Pugesek. Secondly, the results were represented as a structural equation model of their own. This model was presented in Chapter 9 and can be seen in Figure 9.11.

Figure 10.11 presents two graphs showing how observed values of species richness in Gough's experiments compared to those predicted from non-experimental data in the broader landscape. When all plots were included (Figure 10.11A), there was considerable scatter and only 35% of the variance was explained. Further analyses showed that this was due to the fact that fencing and fertilizing caused effects that were not quantitatively predicted. With plots subjected to either of these treatments removed (Figure 10.11B), the remaining treatments, which included those subjected to changes in salinity and flooding as well as the controls, demonstrated a stronger correlation between predicted and observed ($R^2 = 0.63$).

Details of the interpretations of the experimental study can be found in Gough and Grace (1999). What should be pointed out here, however, is that many aspects of the model of this system based on nonexperimental data were supported by the results of the experimental treatments. It was our interpretation that where the model based on nonexperimental data failed to predict accurately was for conditions that were experimentally created, but that did not exist naturally in the field. In other words, it appears that the nonexperimental data can be used to reveal how factors relate in the unmanipulated community, while experimental treatments permit one to ask the question, what will happen if we change the conditions in the system? Thus, when it comes to comparing the strengths and limitations of experimental versus nonexperimental studies, each has a role to contribute.

A search for evidence of historical effects on species richness in the Pearl River system

In 1994, Glenn Guntenspergen and I set out to see if we could discover the existence of additional factors that might explain variation in plant species richness at the Pearl River study area. Of particular interest to us were factors that could be related to landscape position and that might reflect past events. Prior work (Brewer and Grace 1990) had suggested that periodic tropical storms, which are common in this region, leave a long-lasting effect on plant community zonations. To examine the possibility that this might be important in understanding diversity patterns at the Pearl River, we established a sampling scheme that placed plots relative to the mouth of the Middle Pearl River (downstream to upstream), and relative to the river channel (streamside to interior). The assumptions that we wished to test were (1) that distance from the river's mouth would reflect the effects of past saltwater intrusions from tropical storm events, and (2) that distance from the stream channel would reflect past overbank flooding events. It is important to point out that the specific question we were asking was not if these events happened, but whether they had lingering effects of richness that were not reflected in current environmental conditions.

To address this question, we first developed a multivariate model that included a minimum set of the best predictors of richness (based on the previous experience of Grace and Pugesek 1997). This model included soil salinity, microelevation, disturbance, and light readings (as a measure of plant abundance). Then we asked, if the inclusion of landscape position variables might explain additional variance in richness. This model and its results were presented in Chapter 8 as an illustration of sequential hypothesis testing (see Figure 8.6) and will not be reproduced here. What is important to the current discussion is that we found that distance from the mouth of the river did explain an additional 12% of the observed variance in richness, while distance from the river's edge did not contribute new information. Based on these findings, we concluded that landscape position could reveal effects of past events that influence current diversity patterns.

A further examination of spatial effects

At a later time, Glenn Guntenspergen and I returned to the question of whether there were hidden controls of richness that could be detected from landscape position. This time, we were joined in the search by an eager group of graduate students at the University of Louisiana, who were involved in a multicampus course in Biocomplexity offered by the National Center for Ecological Analysis and Synthesis. Together, we re-examined the earlier data Guntenspergen and I collected to see if the grids of plots at each site along the river held additional clues. This time, the question we wished to address was whether small-scale historical effects might show up as positive correlations in richness among adjacent plots that were not related to known environmental gradients (Mancera *et al.* 2005).

Starting with an examination of the data, we determined that there was spatial autocorrelation among plots. In other words, we found that plots that were spatially close were similar to one another in richness, more often than would be expected by chance. Such spatial autocorrelation has been reported before (Legendre 1993) and is probably very common. It is entirely possible, of course, that such spatial autocorrelation in richness simply reflects spatial autocorrelation in controlling environmental conditions. As seen in Figure 10.12, the relationship between spatial patterns in richness and spatial patterns in environmental variables represents an important problem for interpretation. Do the spatial patterns represent a tight mapping to spatial variations in environmental conditions, or do they represent historic effects such as dispersal? To address this problem we first factored out the variation in species richness that could be ascribed to known environmental factors, and then tested for whether residual richness still showed spatial autocorrelation. This sequential hypothesis testing is represented in Figure 10.13, with the test of neighbor richness represented by a "ghost" variable, indicating that its effect was determined after the effects of the other variables had been considered.

The analyses showed that once environmental factors were considered, spatial autocorrelation in species richness disappeared. This means that we were unable to find any evidence of small-scale historical effects, or other unmeasured causes of spatially controlled variations in richness in this system.

Applicability of findings to other systems

More recently, the questions that have interested me are (1) how plant diversity is regulated in a wide array of systems, and (2) whether there are general features that apply broadly across systems. In a study of meadows in Finland, Grace and Jutila (1999) examined the relationships of plant richness to both grazing and environmental gradients (see Figure 7.2). These results generally indicate support for a common construct model such as shown in Figure 10.6.

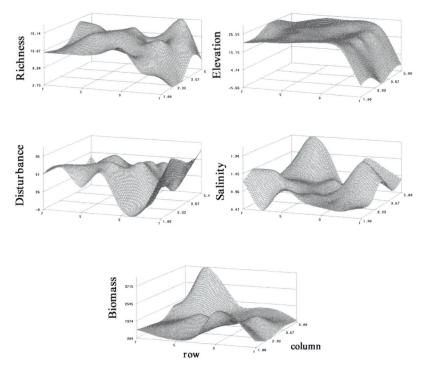

Figure 10.12. Topographic plots of spatial variation in species richness and other variables at one of the five sample sites along the Pearl River, based on sampling in a 5×7 grid of 1 m^2 plots. In these figures, rows are at different distances from the river's edge (in meters) and columns are at different locations along the river at a site (also in meters). From Mancera *et al.* 2005. Reproduced by permission of Springer Publishers.

General support for such a construct model was also found by Grace *et al.* (2000) in coastal tallgrass prairie, although the influence of recent disturbances was minor in this system. In a study of woodlands in Mississippi, Weiher *et al.* (2004) found that the presence of trees in a prairie grassland moderates soil and biomass effects on herbaceous richness; requiring an alteration of the general construct model for such situations. Investigations of diversity regulation in California chaparral (Grace and Keeley 2006) revealed both similar construct relations, along with the importance of landscape features, and the increasing importance of spatial heterogeneity with increasing plot sizes. In other studies, the overwhelming importance of abiotic constraints on diversity patterns of serpentine endemics (Harrison *et al.* 2006) suggests a different balance of forces at play for plants occupying extreme environmental

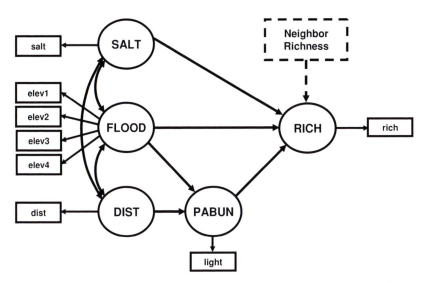

Figure 10.13. Model used to evaluate relationship between species richness and contemporary variables at each of the five grid sample sites at the Pearl River. PABUN represents plant abundance. The "ghost" variable, Neighbor Richness, was evaluated for a relationship to RICH after the effects of all other variables were removed; representing a sequential variance explanation test.

conditions. Altogether, these studies suggest support for certain general features across systems, and numerous specific factors of importance in particular situations or contexts. We will return to the question of generality in our final chapter, where we consider how SEM methods may evolve to permit the evaluation of very general models that can apply across systems diverging in specific properties.

Summary

This chapter has sought to give the reader an insight into an example of the ecological perspective that can be created through a committed approach to multivariate model development, evaluation, and refinement. The point of presenting such an extensive example is not to imply that all of these steps are required. Instead, what I hope to have accomplished is to show the reader how the adoption of a multivariate perspective opens up a new way of learning about ecological systems. It has been my personal experience that the pursuit of a multivariate understanding has greatly enhanced the ecological insights

I have gained. I am eager to extend these studies to include additional variables and pathways, such as reciprocal interactions between biomass and richness, exploration of the role of habitat variability, and interactions with other trophic levels. In Chapter 12, I follow up on this extended example with a more philosophical discussion of how multivariate theories can contribute to the maturation of ecological science.

11

Cautions and recommendations

In this chapter I consider some of the pitfalls that can be encountered, and present a few recommendations that may help to avoid problems in implementing and interpreting results from SEM. Once the reader is finished with this chapter, they may wish to visit Appendix I to see how some of the recommendations from this chapter are applied to example SEM applications.

General limits of statistical analysis

Robert Abelson, a statistics professor at Yale for many years, published a book a few years ago entitled, *Statistics as Principled Argument* (1995). The thesis of this book is that the proper use for statistical analyses and results is as an aid to interpretation rather than as a set of rigid protocols for establishing facts. A related principle is that statistical analysis of data is a matter of approximation. We seek to use models that are approximately correct for our systems. We rely on samples of data that are hoped to approximate some larger population. We rely on distributional assumptions that are approximately correct. And, we hope that our next effort will be an even better approximation.

Those of us in fields that are just beginning to use SEM are in the luxurious position of being able to benefit from decades of intense work that has gone on in other disciplines. Structural equation modeling developed to its current state through the combined efforts of practitioners working in a variety of fields, but especially the humanities. There now exists a vast body of literature on SEM. Importantly, several software packages are available for SEM analyses, and many have gone through numerous improvements over the years. There exist dozens of books summarizing both basic and advanced issues related to SEM. Finally, there are thousands of trained practitioners and many opportunities for training for the student wishing to get started. Thus, the beginner can take some comfort that this "new" method has substantial theoretical and practical backing.

It would be a mistake, however, to think that the proper application of SEM methods is straightforward, or that all the major issues with multivariate modeling have been worked out. Many of the models we might wish to solve are currently not solvable. Sometimes the solutions offered by authors are not appropriate. A few of these issues have been discussed in previous chapters. Aside from these important technical issues, there is a significant need to rely on fundamental SEM principles rather than prepackaged protocols, if we are to apply the methodologies to environmental problems where the context of data, theory, and research objectives may be different. There are many opportunities for misapplication of SEM methods, some with minor consequences and some with major. In the first two sections of this book, I tried to be rather careful to emphasize proper applications and interpretations. In the third section (Chapters 8, 9, and 10), however, I have been quite liberal in my use of published applications of path analysis and SEM in the ecological sciences. This was done deliberately so that I could emphasize the merits of using multivariate models. It must be disclosed, however, that many of the examples presented do not provide good illustrations of the best way to conduct analyses. Therefore, in this chapter I provide a brief description of some of the problems faced in the application of SEM. This is followed by a brief set of recommendations to provide additional guidance for the newly beginning SEM practitioner.

Cautions

Kline (2005) offers a list of 44 common errors made using SEM. Here I borrow heavily from his description of such problems, with the caveat that I qualify some of his comments. These problems fall under the four headings of errors of model specification, problematic data, errors of analysis, and errors of interpretation. Table 11.1 contains a paraphrased list of the problems as he presents them, and I provide some limited discussion of them by group afterwards. In this discussion I do not address all of the listed issues, some are not discussed because they are self-evident, and some because they are explicitly covered elsewhere in the book and cannot be encapsulated briefly.

Specification errors

Specification errors can indeed cause some of the greatest problems with SEM results. Basing analyses on an inappropriate model can lead to results that are not close to the true values, because the model structure does not match the

Table 11.1. *List of commonly made errors (adapted from Kline 2005)*

Errors of specification
1. Failure to specify model(s) prior to data collection.
2. Omission of important factors from model.
3. Failure to have sufficient number of indicators for latent variables.
4. Using unsound indicators for latent variables.
5. Failure to carefully consider directionality of arrows.
6. Specification of feedback effects to mask uncertainty about relations.
7. Overfitting of model.
8. Including error correlations without sufficient theoretical reasons.
9. Cross-loading indicators on multiple factors without justification.

Improper treatment of data
10. Failure to root out errors in the data.
11. Ignoring whether pattern of missing data is systematic (versus random).
12. Failure to examine data distributional characteristics.
13. Failure to screen for outliers.
14. Assuming relations are linear without checking.
15. Ignoring lack of independence among observations.

Errors of analysis
16. Failure to rely on theory to guide decisions of model acceptance.
17. Failure to check accuracy of computer syntax.
18. Failure to check for admissibility of solutions.
19. Reporting only the standardized parameter estimates.
20. Analyzing a correlation matrix when inappropriate.
21. Improperly performing covariance analysis using correlation matrix.
22. Failure to check for constraint interactions.
23. Failure to properly address collinear relations.
24. Estimation of complex model using small sample size.
25. Setting inappropriate scales for latent variables.
26. Ignoring problems resulting from improper starting values.
27. Failure to check model identification when solving models.
28. Failure to recognize empirical underidentification.
29. Failure to separately analyze measurement and structural models.
30. Failure in multigroup analyses to establish common measurement model.
31. Analysis of categorical items as continuous indicators.

Errors of interpretation
32. Relying solely on indices of overall model fit.
33. Interpreting good model fit as proving validity of model.
34. Interpreting good fit as suggesting model is good at explaining variance.
35. Relying solely on statistical criteria for model evaluation.
36. Relying too heavily on p-values.
37. Inappropriate interpretation of standardized parameters.
38. Failure to consider equivalent models.
39. Failure to consider alternative nonequivalent models.
40. Reification of latent variables.
41. Equating a latent variable with its label.
42. Believing SEM can compensate for either poor data or weak theory.
43. Failure to report sufficient information to permit proper scrutiny.
44. Interpreting significant results as proof of causality.

situation. Kline begins this set of errors by stating that the failure to specify your model prior to collecting data is an error to avoid. While it is certainly true that it is desirable to have your model prior to collecting your data, I do not believe (1) it is reasonable to expect beginning practitioners to be sufficiently experienced to always specify a correct or near-correct model prior to data collection, (2) forming a model based on pre-existing data always leads to problems, or (3) forming a model prior to collecting data necessarily leads to a correct model. We must first recognize that initial applications of SEM to a problem take place in the face of insufficient information. Often we do not have sufficient experience to anticipate the appropriateness of the data and models used. While I do recommend specification of models before data collection, this still does not solve the problem of insufficient experience. With experience in modeling a system, initial specification of models provides important opportunities.

Omitting important factors from models can be a major limitation to our success. When omitted factors are uncorrelated with other predictors, their omission leads to reduced predictive power. When omitted factors are correlated strongly with included factors, their omission can bias coefficients. Only the relentless pursuit of a problem can uncover either the adequacy of a model, or the missing factors and their degree of correlation with included factors.

In the social sciences general recommendations exist for the number of indicators to include when using a latent variable model. The "magic number" often recommended is 3 indicators per latent. Such prescriptions must be understood within context, however. In Chapter 4, I describe the fundamental principles associated with latent variables and their measurement. I show that the specification of single-indicator latents can be quite valuable. I also argue that the criterion of indicator replaceability should guide decisions about the adequacy of a set of indicators. Furthermore, whether the objective of an analysis is inward- or outward-focused strongly influences questions about the number of indicators per latent. Finally, the nature of the data relative to the concept embodied by the latent variable is particularly important. Keep in mind that a latent variable is simply an unmeasured variable. It may represent a narrow concept, such as an individual's body weight, or it may represent something more abstract, such as the concept of body size. When latents represent narrow concepts, it may be that only one or two indicators are needed to assess that concept adequately. The more general the concept, the more important it will be to assess a wide array of properties that relate indicators to its meaning.

Errors 4–6 in Table 11.1 all relate to the general problem of having an inappropriate model. Sometimes this results from insufficient experience with the subject being modeled, and sometimes it results from carelessness by the researcher or analyst. The point here is to urge the practitioner to avoid being careless by developing an appreciation of the possibilities of alternative model structures, and the consequences of making a poor choice of model. It is usually when an author makes incautious claims from a weakly justified model that harsh criticism is due. Again, the solution (hopefully) is the sustained testing and further application of a model to ascertain its ability to withstand repeated examination and analysis.

Errors 7–9 in Table 11.1 all relate to questionable decisions about details of modeling. We have previously discussed the pitfalls of overfitting (Chapters 5 and 8). In the process of evaluating models, we will find that modification indices produced when programs judge the fit to be poor, often indicate that incorporation of error correlations will improve model fit. Careful scrutiny of output will also reveal that often the same problem can be "solved" by including directed paths. A correlation, whether between errors or not, represents either an unanalyzed relation or the influences of an unmeasured factor. Either way, we should avoid the temptation of inserting error correlations in models as a convenient way of getting them to fit. Rather, they should be indications for a careful search for the cause of the offending discrepancy between data and model. Finally, the existence of cross loadings of indicators on multiple factors can *sometimes* represent a poorly formed model. Again, reference to theory is required to provide an assessment of whether cross loadings make theoretical sense or not.

Improper treatment of data

There are generally two types of error that relate to our data. The first set relates to things that can only be found by looking at the data, such as entry errors, distributional characteristics, outliers, or nonlinearities. The obvious solution to these problems is to inspect the data carefully and be aware of the consequences of such errors. The second set of errors relate to not thinking enough about the data. Are data missing by design? For example, if values are missing when organisms die in a study, the data are not randomly missing from the sample. Fortunately there exist solutions for such problems, but only if one thinks deeply enough about the issue to correctly diagnose the situation. Also, are the observations independent or are there obvious dependencies (e.g., repeated measures or nested sampling)? Remedies for these issues are discussed in Chapter 7, although again, the problem must be recognized.

Errors of analysis

Most of the errors of analysis listed in Table 11.1 are technical problems. Basically, we find that the results achieved from SEM analyses are dependent on properly coded models that achieve admissible solutions providing unique estimates based on the proper algorithms for the data used and model specified.

There are also certain requirements for proper results that involve recognizing when certain conditions are not met (e.g., common measurement model across groups), or being aware that the test of overall model fit integrates lack of fit in both the measurement model and structural (inner) model.

Only a few of the errors listed require additional, specific mention. It is a mistake to rely exclusively on statistical criteria when judging model acceptance. The good news is that for observed variable models, judging adequacy of fit is usually fairly clear cut. Latent variable models with lots of indicators, on the other hand, pose the greatest difficulties. As we discussed in Chapters 4 and 6, such models tend to accumulate a lack of fit load, and when combined with large sample sizes, discrepancies between model and data become very noticeable. The point is, even well-fitting models can be way off the mark if theory is either insufficient or ignored. At the same time, lack of fit may represent an isolated misspecification in a model that does not apply to the model generally, although it must still be addressed.

The problem of sample size adequacy is one that has no easy answers. It is true that certain sample sizes are so low that they do not provide much opportunity to detect relationships. Bootstrapping methods, as well as other approaches (Bayesian estimation), can allow us to avoid the large-sample assumptions of maximum likelihood. On the other hand, some models are not easily resolvable even with large samples, and others can provide stable, reasonable solutions even with very small samples. It is true that model complexity plays a role. However, the clarity of patterns in the data also plays an overwhelming role in sample size adequacy. Thus, it is not possible to make reliable pronouncements in the absence of knowing something about the data. More discussion of this topic can be found in Shipley (2000, chapter 6).

The management of collinear relations in models is indeed one that requires care. When two predictors are very highly correlated ($r > 0.85$), they begin to become somewhat redundant. If appropriate, modeling them as multiple indicators of a common latent factor is an effective solution that removes problems of variance inflation and parameter bias. When it is not appropriate to model them as multiple indicators, some other means of reducing the model to something equivalent to a single predictor may be needed. Options range from dropping a variable, to the use of composites, as is needed in the challenging case of nonlinear polynomial relations, where first- and second-order terms are highly correlated (Chapter 7).

Errors of interpretation

A few of the errors of interpretation listed in Table 11.1 result from a failure to understand technical issues. If one relies solely on indices of overall model fit, they fail to recognize that lack of fit can either be spread uniformly throughout a model, or be concentrated in one spot. When all but a few expected covariances match observed ones exactly, the average discrepancy may not be too high, even though one or more of the specific discrepancies may indicate a problem. Also, interpreting measures of fit as indicating a model is "adequate" for all purposes is a mistake. While we judge a model first by adequacy of fit, poor predictive power (indicated by low explained variances) can indicate that the utility of the model may be low. This could be an inherent limitation of the phenomenon being studied, or it could be a data or model problem. Further, equating the magnitude of p-values with effect sizes represents a major mis-understanding of what p-values mean. It is the parameter value that is ultimately important. Finally, inappropriate use of results, such as an incorrect usage of standardized path coefficients, usually results from a misunderstanding of subtle technical issues influencing these parameters. This issue is discussed in detail at the end of Chapter 3. The improper use of standardized parameters is a very common problem that needs attention, so care does need to be paid to this issue.

Most problems in this category, however, represent a misunderstanding or misuse of statistical analysis. The most egregious error is to assume or imply that adequacy of fit equates to a demonstration of causation. Many pieces of evidence are needed, including both an absence of equivalent models with equal theoretical support, and the existence of independent information supporting a causal interpretation. The consideration of alternative (either equivalent or nonequivalent) models (Chapter 8) is a very good way to take a reality check. If you can convince a skeptic that the other possibilities are not supportable, you will have achieved a strong "fail to reject" result for your model. Similarly, even the most sophisticated SEM application cannot change the underlying data and availability of theory. More likely, SEM will uncover the inadequacies. It is my experience that adding an SEM analysis to a manuscript does not change the journal for which it is appropriate. That is determined by the data. Structural equation modeling can, however, greatly improve our extraction of information from that data, assuming analyses are correct and meaningful.

Summary recommendations

Given that there are so many particulars that need to be considered in an SEM application, as implied from the above list of possible errors, my advice to the beginning practitioner is rather general. In many ways, the following account is redundant with previous advice, though I believe it may be appreciated by some readers that it should be presented in one place in simple form.

Getting started

The transition to SEM is often a bit of a bumpy ride for a number of reasons. It is hoped that the other chapters of this book will be of some help to the beginning SEM user by providing a basic understanding of concepts and procedures. The examples presented (as well as the analyses presented in Appendix I) also provide opportunities for the reader to become familiar with some of the variety of possible applications. The suggestions presented here are not meant to be a rigid protocol, but instead, suggest one approach to take so as to proceed in an orderly fashion.

The starting point for an SEM analysis will often be the selection of a system property, or set of system properties, whose variations one wishes to understand. Note that this is a different emphasis from univariate analyses, which typically place the focus on a relationship between two variables (e.g., the effect of fertilizer addition on plant growth), or perhaps a pair of relationships (e.g., the interactive effects of fertilizer and herbivore exclusion on plant growth). Certainly a key relationship between two variables can be central to a multivariate model. However, for a multivariate analysis to be successful, we need to include the main variables that control the variations in our focal system properties. Since our objective is to understand some response variable within a system context, we need to approach the problem with a system perspective.

It is often useful to select or develop a conceptual or other model before developing the structural equation model. A conceptual model used as a starting point should include the processes and properties that are known or suspected to control the focal system properties, regardless of whether they will all be measured in this study or not. This can help with both model development and the interpretation of results.

Translation of a conceptual or other nonstatistical model into either a construct model or directly into a structural equation model is the next step. Developing the initial structural equation model can begin either with a consideration of the inner model among concepts, or with a measurement model that seeks to understand factor structure. Regardless of where model development begins, a model that considers the conceptual variables to be studied as well as the way they will be measured is the objective at this stage. Sometimes, the development of the structural equation model will occur without the development of an associated conceptual or other model. Ultimately, this depends on the amount of prior knowledge.

What is often unappreciated is the variety of ways an analysis can be formulated. The flexibility of SEM permits an array of possibilities for how to formulate a hypothesis. For example, tests of categorical variable effects on a system can be evaluated using either the inclusion of·a dummy variable in a general model, or the use of multigroup analysis. Also, longitudinal data can be analyzed using either growth or time series modeling. Multi-stage analyses, such as the evaluation of covariates on residuals, can accomplish things not generally achieved in conventional analysis. Being aware of this flexibility may permit a researcher to recognize how models different from the examples they have seen can be formulated to answer the questions that interest them.

Sampling considerations

Once an initial model has been developed, sampling proceeds and the decisions made at this step can have a substantial influence on subsequent analyses, results, and interpretations. It should be clear that the degree to which results can be said to represent something beyond the sample itself depend on how well the sample represents the sphere of generalization.

Sample size

A first point of consideration is sample size. Again, earlier chapters showed that even very small samples can be analyzed by resorting to small-sample methods. However, we are rarely able to have a great deal of confidence in the generality of studies based on small samples. In many cases in ecological studies, the ecological units of interest may be large and replication may be challenging. It is realistic to realize that not all ecological units will make ideal study subjects for multivariate models, where many parameters are to be estimated. This is not to say that multivariate models cannot be evaluated for, say, replicate large ecosystems; only that it cannot be done very precisely using a limited number of such systems.

Some guidelines are available regarding sample size requirements. Monte Carlo simulation studies can be implemented in several of the current SEM software packages, and this is the most efficient way to determine the sample size needed to obtain particular levels of power. In the absence of such information, many authors make recommendations as to the number of samples needed to be estimated per parameter, a common number being 10. Other authors have more general recommendations such as, 200 samples is a satisfactory number, 100 samples as minimal, and 50 samples as a bare minimum. When working with smaller sample sizes, bootstrapping procedures are especially recommended because they do not rely on large-sample assumptions. Additional discussion of this subject can be found in Hoyle (1999).

Sample distribution

Multigroup analysis has long permitted analysis of samples that fall into distinct categories of interest. However, problems arise when data are clustered or subsampled, and that subsampling is ignored in the analysis. Typically, ignoring subsampling leads to an increase in the chi-square of the model, because there is a source of variation in the data that is not reflected in the model. Also, R-squares and standard errors are overestimated when data structuring is ignored.

A simple and common procedure for handling data hierarchy is the use of so-called background variables. Several approaches to this problem have been discussed in both Chapters 7 and 9. However, until fairly recently, more sophisticated methods explicitly designed for handling data structure in multivariate modeling were not available in SEM software packages. Now, both LISREL and Mplus, as well as a program called HLM (Hierarchical Linear Modeling, www.ssisoftware.com) have capabilities for handling hierarchical data. These more complete methods for hierarchical data handling are based on analysis of raw data and cannot be accomplished through the analysis of covariances. As a consequence, results akin to those obtained by repeated measures ANOVA can be obtained, allowing individuals in the population to possess different response patterns. Recent advances in Mplus permit an amazing array of analyses to be performed at different levels in hierarchical data.

One other issue related to sample distribution has to do with distribution in parameter space. The span of variation in variables captured by sampling, as well as the distribution of those samples, can have a substantial effect on results and interpretations. If the goal of a study is to obtain a representative random sample, random or stratified random sampling is required. Often, however, sampling is stratified or restricted, for example, sampling across gradients. While various sampling approaches should arrive at similar estimates for the unstandardized coefficients (slope of relationship), they will differ in the standardized coefficients, as well as the R-squares. This is basically a signal to noise problem. Sampling at two ends of a gradient will be expected to generate a strong regression relationship. This can actually be helpful if the goal is to estimate a linear slope and to ensure that endpoints are well measured. Samples spread evenly along a gradient will provide an even better representation of a gradient, although there will be more unexplained variance. Systematic sampling, regardless of its merits for efficiency, does not provide an accurate measure of variance explained for the population at large. Traditionally, most hypothesis testing enterprises are based on a presumption of random sampling. Sequential methodologies, such as SEM or Bayesian learning, seek repeatability and can thus be less restrictive about sampling so as to adequately estimate population variances.

Analysis

Initial evaluation

When working with pre-existing data, one should be aware that the strength of inference that can be achieved is dependent on the degree to which analyses are exploratory versus confirmatory. Beginning users often have the impression that confirmatory evaluation of models requires that they should not look at the data prior to fitting the proposed model. This is both a practical and a theoretical mistake. The appropriate criterion for a confirmatory analysis is that the researcher should not have used exploratory SEM analyses of the data to arrive at the final model, unless it is to be acknowledged that the results are exploratory and provisional. This applies to both the analysis of pre-existing data as well as cases where initial models were developed prior to data collection.

The place to start with an analysis is a thorough screening and examination of the data, point by point in most cases. Paying inadequate attention to this step is a common mistake made by new analysts. Results of all sorts, particularly regression results (and therefore, SEM results as well) are extremely sensitive to outliers. These outliers cannot always be detected in univariate space or even in bivariate space (an outlier in bivariate space is a combination of x and y that is very different from any other combination). The researcher needs to know that all the points are representative. Often, apparent outliers can be found in random samples because random samples do not capture the edges of parameter space easily unless there is a very large sample. In that case, such samples are not true outliers. Nevertheless, a decision must be made whether to remove an outlying sample value that is useful in defining a slope in order to avoid overestimating variance explained by a relationship. Again, the choice may depend on whether the goal of the study is to estimate population values, or to develop general equations.

Preparing for model evaluation

It is important to provide summaries of the data that describe overall characteristics, in addition to those that relate to model evaluation. It is also useful to perform more conventional analyses such as ANOVA to provide overall assessments of mean differences, although means can also be evaluated in SEM (Pugesek 2003).

Statistical assumptions play a major role in all statistical analyses. Therefore, it is necessary to examine the characteristics of variables and their residuals to determine what kind of data are being analyzed. When it does not appear that residuals will meet the assumption of multivariate normality (which is admittedly difficult to evaluate), options that do not require this assumption should be used. Fortunately for the modern user of SEM, such methods are available. For large samples, the Satorra–Bentler Robust method provides standard errors that are accurate for a variety of residual distributions. For small or large samples, bootstrapping methods can accomplish this. It is important to point out that parameter estimates, such as path coefficients, are unaffected by residual distributions, because their estimation does not depend on the normality assumption.

While normality problems are easily addressed, extreme skew can affect covariance, and therefore, path coefficients. For this reason, transformations of the individual variables may be required. Categorical variable modeling options in programs like Mplus provide a variety of ways to address the analysis of extremely skewed or otherwise nonnormal variables.

Nonlinearities can lead to serious problems in analyses. Generally it is possible to detect nonlinearities through the examination of bivariate plots. The simplest approach to correcting for nonlinear relations is through transformations of the raw variables. As illustrated in Chapter 7, nonlinear modeling for cases where multi-indicator latent variables are not involved can be accomplished. Nonlinear relationships (including interactions) among latent variables have generally been quite difficult to implement due to the complexity of specification. This is no longer true for the latest version (version 3) of Mplus, which now automates the process.

A number of strategies can be used for missing data. While listwise deletion (deletion of any cases where values for a variable are missing) is often the simplest approach, there are other options. Imputation of missing values has received considerable attention and can often be used successfully if there are not very many missing values for a variable, and they are considered to be missing at random. Some programs have rather elaborate and quite clever ways of dealing with missing values, particularly if values are missing for a reason (for example, through mortality of individuals). In such situations, deletion of cases with missing values can lead to bias in the sample, and is to be avoided.

Evaluation of models

Once data have been prepared for analysis, it may be necessary to modify the initially hypothesized model(s). The processes of data collection, data examination, and data screening can often lead to the conclusion that the resulting data set differs in important ways from what was initially intended. One should make as few changes as possible to theoretically based models. However, it should be clear that in the initial stages of evaluating models relating to a system, there will be substantial learning associated with all parts of the process.

The formulation of competing models is highly useful as a means of bringing focus to an analysis. When causal structure of a model is clear, alternative models will usually represent evaluations of various processes. When causal structure is not clear, alternative models may be used to eliminate some of the logical possibilities.

Analyses of models can often proceed in parts. It is typical for models with multi-indicator latent variables for analysis of the measurement model to proceed prior to evaluation of the full model. At all stages in this process, evaluation of model fit will need to be made. As discussed in Chapter 5, the current convention for covariance modeling is to use a variety of fit indices in making decisions about models. In spite of their present popularity, indices of relative model fit, such as the AIC, are not sufficient to determine model adequacy, although they can support model comparisons. Absolute measures, such as the model chi-square are very informative, and if the chi-square indicates data fit to the model, that is usually a reliable indicator of model adequacy. Unfortunately, chi-square values are sensitive to sample size and for large samples, chi-squares usually indicates significant deviations from the model, though these may be trivial differences in parameter values. For this reason, a number of other indices have been developed that are adjusted for sample size. An examination of the residuals should also be standard practice. The analyst is referred to Fan *et al.* (1999) and Marsh *et al.* (2004) for recent discussions of this topic.

Interpretation of findings

Virtually everything we have covered so far in this book can come into play when we draw interpretations. Results are certainly highly dependent on the correctness of the model structure. They are also dependent on the way data are sampled. For these reasons, in manuscripts it is best to describe SEM results in terms that make the fewest assumptions, saving causal inferences for the discussion section of the paper. Few things raise reviewers' concerns as readily as what sounds like pre-interpreted results. Structural equation modeling lingo contains plenty of terms that can encourage us to state results as if their interpretations are pre-judged, such as discussions of direct and indirect *effects*. Sensitivity to this issue can save the author from harsh reactions.

Often, results and associated modification indices will indicate that models should be changed. When deciding on both model modification and the interpretation of results the first priority should be given to reliance on substantive (theoretical) logic. An additional caveat is to avoid overfitting to the data and thereby capitalizing on chance characteristics of the data set. It is important to always report how the analysis was conducted and never present a final result that was formulated through a very exploratory process, as if it was the initial model and the study was confirmatory. When data sets are large, consider splitting the data set into an exploratory sample and a confirmatory sample. Finally, plan to do followup studies in which modified models receive further testing with new data sets. Ultimately, the two ingredients for success are a sustained, multifaceted approach to a problem (Chapter 10 may provide the reader with some ideas on this subject) combined with a strong reliance on theory. It is unlikely that we will determine the general validity of our solutions from a single study, but with repeated efforts conducted using comparable methods, strong inference can develop.

Conclusions

While the evaluation of multivariate models holds great promise for ecological studies, the current level of rigor for ecological applications is less than it needs to be. Proper application of methods such as SEM, requires an appreciation of the need to collect appropriate samples, handle data properly, formulate models correctly for the sample being analyzed, perform analyses carefully, and interpret results appropriately. Because of the complexity of the issues involved, a commitment of some time and effort is required, compared with many of the univariate procedures ecologists are accustomed to learning. I believe the effort is well worth it and hope that the material in this book will make the process easier for others.

PART V

The implications of structural equation modeling for the study of natural systems

12

How can SEM contribute to scientific advancement?

Motivation for studying complexity

Ecological science has changed in character over the past few decades. Of course it changed before that time, but the past 30 years is the part to which I have been a direct witness. I like to say that during that period, ecologists have gone from being the harbingers of doom to the advisors of the future. Increasingly, we are asked, what will happen if . . . ? While general opinions abound, it is rare that we have solid answers.

A rising awareness that the ecological science of the past will not meet tomorrow's needs can be seen in several recent major science initiatives from many of the world's leading science agencies. Among these initiatives are ones that promote greater focus on long-term studies, those that enhance efforts to promote ecological synthesis, those that foster interdisciplinary studies, and those that encourage a broader range of scientists to apply their knowledge to applied problems.

Recently, the call for studies designed to address "biocomplexity" has been taken up in several parts of the world. One of the leading proponents for the study of biocomplexity has been Rita Colwell, of the US National Science Foundation, who states, "The fundamental and underlying principle [behind the NSF Biocomplexity Initiative] is that we must move from strictly reductionist research to research that synthesizes information and work toward a holistic approach to understanding and wisely managing the environment." She goes on to say, "After investing in biocomplexity research, we'll be able to make [better] predictions concerning environmental phenomena as a consequence of human actions taken." Similar research initiatives in other nations are also under way at this time.

Implied by the recent emphasis on biocomplexity is that many of our past efforts have emphasized what I will call "biosimplicity", which I define as the search for simple general explanations for complex ecological problems. Simple generalizations will continue to fascinate ecologists. They will not, I contend, provide adequate answers to environmental problems. We have been doing the best we can with the resources and tools available to us. This book presents new tools and approaches for the biologist to consider, ones that are specifically designed to confront complexity. There is a special emphasis in this book on ways to analyze complex data and achieve answers that are specific to a particular system, and yet have generality across systems as well.

Methodologies that have been developed for the study of multivariate relations provide us with a means to advance ecological understanding in a number of new ways. Their capacity to sort out simultaneous effects can allow us to move beyond dichotomous debates of this factor versus that factor. They can also provide us with the means to accommodate both the specific and general features of data. Perhaps of greatest importance, they push us to collect data in a different way, one that will, I believe, clarify our ideas and refine our understanding. Ultimately, the premise of this book is that the study of multivariate relationships using methods like SEM can advance our understanding of natural systems in ways not achieved through other methods.

A critical look at the current state of ecological theory

When Peters (1991) published his book, *A Critique for Ecology*, I must admit that I agreed with many of his criticisms, although not with his solution. What is most relevant here, though, is that sometimes we gain an appreciation for the value of a new approach through the eyes of a critical discussion of existing practice. It has been my experience that the merits of studying multivariate models are often not fully appreciated unless we first consider some of the limitations of more familiar approaches. This chapter will discuss a number of examples of existing ecological models and hypotheses that, I believe, can be advanced using a multivariate approach. These criticisms must be tempered by the recognition that virtually all current ecological models will presumably be replaced by more mature and refined models as further work proceeds. The switch from univariate to multivariate theory, however, represents a change from looking at individual effects to system responses. Thus, it can potentially transform the scientific process. The criticisms offered in this chapter may offend some. It is not my intent to be demeaning. Instead, what I do wish to do is to challenge the reader to think of how we may take ecological models and hypotheses to a different level of refinement. If the reader is moved to consider how we might progress our understanding, even if it is not along the lines suggested in this book, a valuable purpose will have been served.

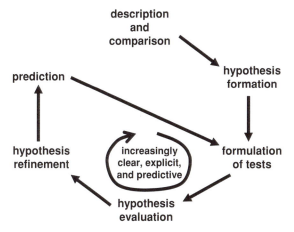

Figure 12.1. Representation of the progress of the scientific method.

In this chapter, I will set the stage for a critical look at current ecological theory by first discussing concepts relating to the development and maturation of scientific theories. I contend that a univariate mindset has caused ecologists and others studying natural systems to develop and cling to simplistic theories that fail to mature. There are many conspicuous properties of immature theories, and it is readily apparent that such properties are commonly associated with the most discussed ecological theories of the day. I go on to discuss properties of SEM that can contribute to theory maturation, and within that discussion point out topics in our field where current limitations are apparent. In the last part of the section, I discuss and illustrate an associated set of scientific behaviors, such as theory tenacity, that contribute to the accumulation of a large set of immature theories that contradict each other but that do not evolve over time and for which there is no resolution of merit. My thesis is that the ability to develop and evaluate multivariate theories has the capacity to greatly enhance the maturation of theory and lead to scientific progress.

The concept of theory maturation

The study of multivariate hypotheses can be viewed as following the same logic as the study of any other hypothesis, going from formulation to testing and refinement. Figure 12.1 provides a very simplistic representation of the scientific method. One reason I review the steps in the scientific method here is because I believe that, for the most part, studies of ecological systems have often not gone beyond the initial stages of the process. Furthermore, I believe this is primarily because the mindset created by conventional univariate hypothesis testing has

Figure 12.2. The starting and ending points in theory maturation.

limited the completeness of the theories we have developed. Considering where we are in the process of theory maturation and the contribution that multivariate models can make, may contribute to our understanding of what is gained by using SEM to study natural systems.

The concept of theory maturation parallels our advancement through the scientific process. An excellent introduction to this important subject was presented by Loehle (1987), who discussed where the study of hypotheses should lead us. Figure 12.2 provides the dominant characteristics of the end points of the process. Theory development often begins with an exciting idea that suggests a new perspective. Some scientists prefer to emphasize this stage of the process, offering a continuous progression of novel or bold propositions. Usually controversy surrounds these ideas specifically because the theories are in need of clarification and evaluation. Other scientists can spend a career trying to verify and support a new theory they have proposed. Such a tendency is described by Loehle (1987) as theory tenacity, which can be important in the early stage of theory assessment, although it eventually becomes an impediment to progress.

The process of theory maturation is one that continues to refine predictions and evaluate hypothesized models to the point where our models possess what can be called the "traits of mature theory". Such traits include clarity, operational meaning, high empirical content, quantitative expression, and predictive power.

According to the concept of theory maturation, the study of many scientific problems is initially characterized by a crudeness of understanding that complicates the process of evaluation. This has been a factor contributing to many disputes in ecology. Often new hypotheses are presented in terms that are not clearly defined, and such hypotheses must go through a period of refinement before it is even clear how to develop appropriate tests (see, for example, the treatment of such a debate in Grace 1991). Furthermore, it is often the case that the meanings of key terms in models are ambiguous and "unbounded", lacking a description of the realm of space, time, and system components to which they best apply. Analysis of many of the most visible debates in ecology over the past 30 years shows that theories possessing immature characteristics are often associated with these discussions.

In general, it is helpful for the researcher to assess the maturity level of a theory before deciding how to study it. To some degree, such assessments are usually made, although often not in an explicit fashion. An awareness of the processes involved in theory maturation can facilitate the scientist's approach to a problem. Scientists may, of course, differ from one another in their own objectives – some wishing to focus on developing new ideas, and others more interested in working on a problem until its associated theory is mature enough to allow for predictive applications to ecological management. What is important is to be aware of the elements in the progress of theory maturation, and to conduct studies that will advance the development of our understanding.

The properties of structural equation modeling that can contribute to theory maturation

Here I think it may be useful to describe in greater detail how a multivariate perspective on scientific theory, as exemplified by the procedures associated with SEM, can contribute to theory maturation. To accomplish this, we need to consider some of the general properties that are associated with SEM. The reader should be aware that these properties are not always incorporated into each SEM use. As with the concept of theory maturation, there is a process of methodological maturation that can be expected when new methods are introduced. Thus, the discussion that follows really represents the mature use of SEM in a sustained application.

Property 1: encourages a careful consideration of theory and measurement

It is to be expected that in the initial stages of exploring a topic, models and ideas will be vague, unbounded, and frequently nonoperational. It can also be argued that some ecological ideas appear to have remained in such a state for decades, without resolution of exactly what mechanisms are being evaluated, how they are to be measured appropriately, and where the associated models apply. One factor that can help keep theories in an abstract state is the desire by some to emphasize the generality of a principle over its applicability. Often generality is emphasized by making terms more general and, in the process, even less well defined. There can be merit to such an approach, for a time. Eventually, I will contend, there comes a time when the merits of a theory must be demonstrated in unambiguous terms. For this to happen, a clear system for evaluation is needed.

Structural equation modeling begins with a consideration of the construct model, a general statement about the kinds of processes contributing to relationships and ultimately to observed patterns. Not all applications of SEM may begin in this way, however. Rather, one may start with an abstract theory or an empirical result from an exploratory study. Both these starting points can lead to the formulation of an explicit structural equation model.

The researcher interested in developing a multivariate theory about a problem might begin with a path model involving only relations among observed variables. This represents the stage of development of the great majority of applications of SEM/path analysis to ecological problems. Often when a model is in this form, we may be unclear as to whether the researcher has considered the distinctions between the underlying concepts and the observed indicators, or the issue of measurement error.

A more explicit way to express a multivariate model is as a latent variable model. This may be a model that has only single indicators for each conceptual variable. The value in showing the full form, even though the statistical meaning of the conceptual variables is exactly represented by the indicator variables, is clarity. Expressed in the form of a full structural equation model, a clearer distinction is made between the variables of conceptual interest and the data at hand, which can often be a rather poor substitute for perfect measures of the factors that are interacting. Stated in a different way, a path model with unspecified variable type incorporates one level of theory, one that considers how components interrelate. However, it ignores another level of theory, measurement theory, the science of considering how observations relate to underlying causes. A full structural equation model with single indicators may or may not resolve how concepts are to be measured, but at least it recognizes that these issues exist and deserve future consideration. Sometimes there is existing information about the reliability of a given indicator variable as a measure of a conceptual variable that can be used to remove bias from parameters.

A full structural equation model with multiple indicators typically represents a multivariate model in which issues of measurement have received substantial thought. An example of such a model can be found in Pugesek and Tomer (1996). As indicated in Chapter 4, models with multi-indicator latent variables can become quite complex. The main point is that SEM encourages a careful consideration of how conceptual variables are measured and how they interrelate, contributing to theory refinement and maturation.

Property 2: models are open to inclusion of additional factors

Multivariate models are well suited to inclusion of additional factors. In the case of the Pearl River example in Chapter 10, results suggested that plant biomass and light penetration were not adequate indicators of a single latent conceptual variable. Inclusion of two latent variables not only resulted in a greater consistency between theory and data, but also led to a greater explanation of variance, and an isolation of two different kinds of effects of biomass on richness. A further example was the work by Grace and Guntenspergen (1999) in which two spatial variables were tested to see if they provided additional insight into patterns of richness; one variable did and the other did not. If we had relied only on logic, as we might have in a purely theoretical modeling effort, we certainly would have included both terms. Model evaluation usually provides clear guidance as to when variables contribute new information and when they do not.

Examination of some ecological topics shows a preponderance of "closed" models. By closed models, I refer to those that emphasize some small number of factors and that are not able to incorporate additional factors, even if they are known to be important. One topic that has historically shown a tendency towards closed models is life history theory. In the early 1970s there was substantial interest in the theory of r- and K-selection (MacArthur and Wilson 1967, Pianka 1970, Gadgil and Solbrig 1972), which emphasizes the importance of the tradeoff between reproduction and survival (Figure 12.3). Once sufficient examples had been examined, it became clear that other factors also influenced reproductive effort and survival, and also that many different mechanisms could play a role (Stearns 1977). Shortly after this discovery, confidence in the empirical utility of distinguishing between r- and K-selected species waned, and the importance of this theory in explaining life histories received little additional discussion.

Another example of a one-dimensional model is the R* model of Tilman (1982), which emphasizes the effects of a tradeoff between tolerance of low resource levels and the ability to grow under high resource levels. Tilman has subsequently incorporated a number of other assumptions into his models (e.g., Tilman 1988). However, these models remain set with a fixed and limited number of processes, unable to easily detect or accommodate additional factors based on deviations between predictions and observations.

Following criticisms of the theory of r- and K-selection, Grime (1977) proposed a two-dimensional model of plant life histories, involving tradeoffs among growth rate, tolerance, and reproduction (Figure 12.3). There has been

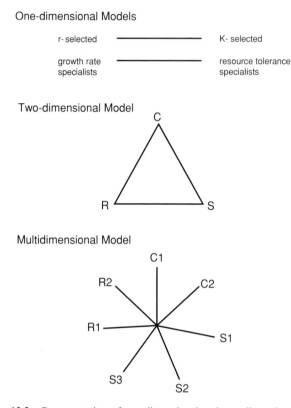

Figure 12.3. Representation of one-dimensional and two-dimensional closed models, in comparison with a multidimensional model that can accommodate as many dimensions as the data indicate are important.

a long history of resistance to the acceptance of this model by many (Tilman 1987, Loehle 1988, Grubb 1998, Wilson and Lee 2000) in spite of the fact that it makes some important and previously ignored distinctions. I believe that the reason for this resistance is the inherently closed nature of the model. Is there a reason why the theory cannot become refined to accommodate additional dimensions, as Grubb (1998) has proposed? Perhaps the very structure of the model, as well as the nonstatistical nature of the theoretical modeling process contribute to this inflexibility. The lowermost model in Figure 12.3 shows the form that a more complete, multidimensional model might take. Here, the model shows how multiple components of competitive ability and stress tolerance could be incorporated into a multidimensional model of open architecture. Through the use of SEM, it would be possible to allow the data to tell us how many dimensions are important, and also exactly how important each dimension is under different circumstances. I believe that the adoption of such a model would represent an increase in theory maturation for a topic that has remained in gridlock for 25 years.

Property 3: allows for strong and constructive feedback from empirical results

In the years of Sir Francis Bacon (circa 1561–1626), there existed in European university education and scholarly circles a kind of scientific orthodoxy in which ideas were deemed to reign supreme over observations. Theories, both about nature and mankind, were hotly debated and resolutions were obtained through logic and reasoning. Whenever nature failed to behave as expected, based on the carefully crafted conclusions of philosophers, most notably followers of the Aristotelean tradition, it was concluded that observations were "messy", not a clear reflection of truth. It was Bacon's contribution that he advocated an empiricist's philosophy that sought to liberate us from logical orthodoxy. At the same time, Bacon was also skeptical about an overreliance on pure description. Rather, he espoused an approach to the development of theory that relied heavily on empiricism and experiment. Bacon represented his philosophy using several classic drawings that served as frontispieces for his books. Figure 12.4 shows one such drawing from his book *Novum Organum*, which represents the ship of scientific exploration passing beyond the pillars of established ideas.

I think that to a significant degree, the empirically directed theory building nature of the SEM process is in line with the scientific philosophy espoused by Sir Francis Bacon. Users of SEM will attest to the fact that these techniques place strong demands on their models. Theory, no matter how logical in the mind of the scientist, must be able to reconcile deviations that are found between model and data. At the same time, empirical findings typically result in model evolution and thereby cause our models to grow. The process of rigorous model evaluation ultimately leads to a high degree of empirical content of the resulting model, encouraging the scientist to sail beyond his or her established notions about what is important, and incorporate those factors demonstrated to have importance.

Property 4: flexible and useful under a wide range of conditions

One of the attributes of SEM is that it imposes a certain logical procedure in which ideas about systems are compared with observable properties. As we have seen throughout this book, metricians have worked very hard to find creative

Figure 12.4. Engraved title page in Sir Francis Bacon's book, *Novum Organum*, published in 1620 (engraving by Simon Pass). The latin motto written beneath the ship translates into, "Many shall pass through and learning shall be increased". Image reproduced by permission of Richard Fadem.

ways to devise appropriate representations for a variety of multivariate models. Examples of this creativity can be seen in the selection of ecological topics covered in Pugesek *et al.* (2003), as well as in examples shown in Marcoulides and Schumacker (1996), Schumacker and Marcoulides (1998), and Cudeck *et al.* (2001). In spite of all these efforts, structural equation models still have a limit to their flexibility. Much of my efforts in working with SEM have been aimed at adapting and combining techniques in order to evaluate models that fall outside of the mainstream of application. Often this process involves tradeoffs and compromises that give up one model attribute (e.g., estimation of measurement error) for another (e.g., across-system generality). Examples of these efforts are found throughout this book, though particularly in Chapters 6, 7, 10, and 13. Two of my several objectives in this work have been to demonstrate the ability of SEM to be flexible, and also to strive for continued developments that will permit us to address a broader range of models. There remain, at the present time, a number of important difficulties in dealing with certain kinds of problems. Given the methodological advances that are being made, I am hopeful that further progress can permit SEM to achieve the degree of flexibility needed for use by researchers studying ecological systems.

Property 5: contributes to development of a predictive level of understanding

From a strictly statistical perspective, SEM is not always an optimal vehicle for prediction. The philosophy of covariance-based SEM is geared towards general theoretical explanation, instead of variance explanation. In particular, latent variables seek generality over precision. Nevertheless, when the goal is prediction, structural equation models can be formulated in a way that is well suited to the task. I believe that the simplest way this will be accomplished will be by linking structural equation models to forecast and system dynamic models (Grace 2001), combining the strengths of each. Illustrations of this will be given in the next chapter.

Examples of how multivariate theory might contribute to theory maturation

Consideration of the progress of theory maturation in the case of the intermediate stress hypothesis

It may be useful to consider the progress of theory maturation for a particular ecological topic, to illustrate some of the preceding points. Here I will focus on clarity of theoretical concepts and their measurement as it relates to the *intermediate stress hypothesis*, also known as the hump-backed model of diversity and productivity.

In 1973, Grime (1973) found a number of interesting patterns in a comparative study of plant species richness in central England. Initially, he emphasized two primary and separate hypotheses about the factors controlling these

Table 12.1. *Concepts and variables associated with the Intermediate Stress Hypothesis*

Author	Name of theoretical structure	Scope of application	Causal or (predictor) variables
Grime 1973a	Intermediate stress hypothesis	Plants	Intensity of environmental stress
Grime 1979	Hump-backed model	Plants	(1) dominance, (2) stress, (3) disturbance, (4) niche differentiation, (5) ingress of suitable species, (6) species pool (standing crop and litter)
Huston 1979	Dynamic equilibrium model	All organisms, latitudinal gradients, regional variations	Rate of competitive displacement, population growth rates (soil resource availability, productivity, population densities, environmental fluctuations)
Tilman 1982	Resource ratio model	All organisms	Resource supply rates, environmental heterogeneity (productivity)
Taylor *et al.* 1990	Species pool hypothesis	Plants	Pool size of adapted species (soil fertility)
Rosenzweig & Abramsky 1993	Unimodal model	All organisms	Productivity (rainfall, ocean depth, evapotranspiration, soil fertility)
Grace 1999	Multivariate model	Herbaceous plants	Environmental conditions, species pool, total biomass, (environmental indicators, above-ground biomass + litter, light reaching ground surface)

patterns, the intermediate stress hypothesis and the intermediate disturbance hypothesis. The intermediate stress hypothesis stated that species density (= species richness) is highest at intermediate levels of environmental stress, because of offsetting effects of abiotic limitation and competitive exclusion. In 1979, Grime presented the humped-back model, which proposed that low above-ground standing crop could serve as an indicator of high environmental stress. A number of authors have since proposed that there exists a general relationship between species diversity and environmental stress or habitat productivity. Most commonly they have proposed that diversity is highest at intermediate levels of stress or productivity.

Table 12.1 summarizes information on some of the conceptual and predictor variables that have been proposed to control diversity in conjunction with the intermediate stress hypothesis. It can be safely stated that, at the present time, despite a great deal of theoretical and empirical work on this topic, there is little consensus about the mechanisms that are most important, and even whether there is a consistent humped-back relationship that applies generally. A major effort to evaluate and synthesize our understanding of this relationship and its empirical support has taken place in the past few years (Palmer 1994, Abrams 1995, Grace 1999, Waide *et al.* 1999, Gross *et al.* 2000, Mittelbach *et al.* 2001). Overall, this literature suggests:

(1) A weak but discernible unimodal (= humped-back) relationship is common, but not consistent.
(2) Empirical supporting evidence is strongest for herbaceous plants, and generally weak for consumer species.
(3) Even in the best cases, measures of productivity explain only a modest portion of the observed variance in species richness.
(4) Control of species richness in natural systems is strongly multivariate and, where data are sufficient, multivariate models do quite well in explaining richness variations (average R^2 for herbaceous communities is 57%).
(5) The theoretical basis whereby environmental stress may affect animal diversity is strongly disputed, with a large number of competing hypotheses.
(6) The mechanisms whereby herbaceous plant richness is regulated are more generally agreed upon.
(7) It is argued by most who have reviewed this topic that more theoretical and empirical work is needed to clarify the issues.

My own assessment is that this topic exhibits a low degree of theory maturation. Most models are based on vague and even nonoperational theoretical constructs. Also, most deal with only one or two of the many processes that control diversity. A few, such as Grime's humped-back model have a high degree of empirical content and a well-bounded realm of applicability. However, most have no clearly defined relationship between constructs and indicators, and have made little effort to provide rigorous empirical evaluations. What is perhaps most distressing is that there is little indication of theory maturation for most models. The model presented by Grime in 1979 is identical to the one presented in his recent update of that book (Grime 2001). The model presented by Huston in 1979 is unchanged in his 1994 assessment of diversity, although he does discuss species pools in his 1999 paper (Huston 1999). Tilman's model has likewise remained unchanged between its first appearance in 1982 and in its most recent treatment (1997). The same can be said for the species pool model, which is unchanged from Taylor *et al.* (1990) to Aarssen and Schamp (2002).

Examining the body of work dealing with this topic, it would appear that, following the initial publication of their ideas, most authors have focused on a tenacious defense of their original formulation. When changes are presented they are usually one of two types, (1) extending the generality of their ideas by using even more abstract terms, or (2) providing a broader range of supporting examples that rely on a greater array of indicators. The result is that, generally speaking, there is little movement towards a consensus on even the most basic points of concept and measurement. Typifying this situation is the fact that virtually the same handful of various and poorly defined examples are presented in support of the three contrasting models of Grime (1979), Tilman (1986 – see his Figure 2.4) and Huston (1994 – see his Figure 5.4). Rosenzweig and Abramsky (1993) noted that, of all the studies they examined linking productivity to diversity, none actually measured productivity, but instead, used indicators ranging from annual precipitation to depth below the ocean surface. As Palmer (1994) has noted, individuals continue to propose more and more competing explanations for diversity patterns (there are now over 100) without any resolution. Abrams (1995) arrived at a similar conclusion.

Consideration of the progress of theory maturation in the case of the effects of species diversity on community productivity

Current disagreement about the relationship between species diversity and community productivity (Tilman *et al.* 1996, Huston 1997, Wardle 1999, Hodson *et al.* 1998, Lawton *et al.* 1998, Loreau *et al.* 2002) reminds us that controversy is a common part of our science. In order to put this debate in its proper perspective, we can view it in terms of theory maturation. I believe it is accurate to say that the hypothesis that species diversity enhances habitat productivity has remained in a fairly immature state until very recently. I would further argue that this debate has been complicated by ambiguous definitions, unclear predictions, equivocal tests, and considerable controversy – all signs that the hypothesis being addressed needs clarification and refinement. I believe that adoption of a multivariate approach to theory construction would faciliate the theory maturation process in this case as well.

We have already seen that certain refinements in both definitions and experimental methods have had to be made in order to facilitate progress. First, the consequences of drawing a limited number of species from a larger pool of species are not really so simple (Huston 1997, Wardle 1999, Mikola *et al.* 2002). Separating the number of species selected from the productivities of the particular species that wind up in a sample has turned out to be more difficult than most investigators initially expected. The recognition of this "sampling effect" has forced researchers to make a distinction between the effects of having a variety of species in a sample, and the effects of winding up with a particularly productive species in a sample just because many were selected. As the importance of this distinction has started to sink in, it has been necessary to recognize that a key process that should be isolated is "overyielding", the capacity for a mixture of species to be more productive than any of the individual species in the mixture. Thus, we now see that evaluating the hypothesis that diversity enhances productivity requires us to partition at least two processes: the sampling effect and the overyielding effect.

A second area in which definitions have had to be refined deals with the term diversity. Initially it was assumed that species diversity automatically led to functional diversity. However, it has now been found quite useful to estimate the effect of growth form or functional group diversity on productivity because, on average, species of different functional groups are more reliably different than species of the same functional group. Again, here it seems that separating the effects of the diversity of specific plant attributes, such as the ability to fix nitrogen, from other types of plant variety may help us to further refine our hypotheses and experiments.

Many of the experiments that have been conducted to address the potential effects of diversity on productivity have been extremely impressive from the standpoint of the effort involved. In spite of this, there has been much controversy about the interpretation of the results. Some problems have resulted from the fact that the above-described distinctions had not been made at the time the experiments were initiated. Other problems arose because of the difficulties associated with developing an operational test of an abstract hypothesis. The particular set of species considered, the growing conditions, and the duration of the study can all have specific effects that might confound any attempt to understand the general effect of diversity on productivity from an individual study. The process of theory maturation requires that we use the lessons learned from trying to implement experimental tests in order to further refine hypotheses. One such refinement that is often valuable is to "bound" the hypothesis by describing the conditions under which it is more or less likely to occur.

Failure to reconcile the hypothesis that diversity enhances productivity with other ideas about how these two variables relate represents another area in which refinements need to be made. Some of the initial resistance to the hypothesis that diversity enhances productivity comes from evidence that high productivity inhibits diversity for herbaceous plants. So, in experiments involving herbaceous plants that have examined the effect of diversity on productivity (the majority of studies thus far), how is it that the negative feedback from enhanced productivity on diversity is ignored? Reconciliation of the opposing processes relating diversity and productivity will ultimately need to be considered if we are to draw conclusions about the effects of diversity on productivity that are meaningful in the real world.

Another area where further refinement is needed deals with the spatial scale at which the relationship between diversity and productivity is examined. We may imagine (and even predict) that for a natural landscape, having a large pool of species in that landscape will enhance the ability of plants to colonize disturbed sites rapidly, occupy stressful areas more completely, and respond to environmental changes more quickly. However, this is not the question that has been addressed up to this point, at least not at the scale of experimental evaluation (Symstad *et al.* 2003). Whenever there is a disconnect between the idea being tested, that the number of species existing in a small plot affects the productivity of that plot, and the broad appeal of the idea that diversity is important in maintaining a productive landscape, further theory maturation is needed.

Finally, another factor that is playing a role in the debate over the relationship between diversity and ecosystem function is the relevance of this idea to conservation efforts (Grime 2002). There has been a great deal of emphasis placed by some ecologists on the prospect that an enhancement of productivity by diversity represents a justification for the preservation of diversity (Naeem 2002). Many ecologists, myself included, think we should be careful in this arena. Does this mean that if a species is rare and has no measurable effect on ecosystem function, as certainly will be true for many rare species, that it has no value? Traditionally ecologists have argued that diversity is important because it represents successful evolutionary experiments, and the loss of diversity is a loss not only of variety itself, but also of genetic information. It is important that we should not allow a desire to justify the importance of diversity to society to be the supporting basis for keeping a scientific hypothesis in an immature form.

Overall, the current controversy about how species diversity influences habitat productivity represents one stage in the development of an important question. Compared to most previous ecological debates, I am encouraged by the degree to which ideas, definitions, and experimental tests have been refined. Much of this has been caused by the intense scrutiny the work on this topic has faced. However, there is much to do. Ecological questions of this magnitude require a long-term sustained effort to evaluate. Furthermore, I believe that an explicitly multivariate approach could help in a number of ways. There is still little effort aimed at integrating any positive effects of diversity on productivity with models that explain how productivity and other factors can control diversity.

Multivariate models offer opportunities for maturing our ideas and predictions

It should be pointed out that SEM by itself is not an ultimate solution for understanding the regulation of species diversity, or for arriving at some general synthesis of the topic. However, I believe that the methods and philosophy associated with SEM can greatly add to theory maturation on this subject. Admittedly, this conclusion is based on my perceptions of what I have learned studying herbaceous plant diversity using a multivariate approach. As Kaplan (2000) has recently emphasized, the interface between SEM and more complete theoretical understanding is in need of further work; a theme expanded upon in the chapter that follows.

Generally, what are needed are approaches that facilitate a progressive refinement of ideas and explanatory power, while permitting broad general comparisons. This is a tall order and will not be achieved easily. Nevertheless, I believe the organizational framework of SEM, its capacity for representing multifactor explanations, its openness to modification, and its uncompromising feedback from empirical tests will help. I further believe that this framework will allow a continued refinement of models and tests that will lead to the inclusion of more factors of importance and the explanation of a greater array of field conditions.

What will not be accomplished by using a multivariate framework alone is a resolution of the exact mechanisms behind all the relationships. A combination of approaches will be required to achieve this lofty goal. It is also unclear at present whether the widespread usage of a multivariate approach will contribute to consensus, or simply a proliferation of various multivariate models. I believe that regardless of what happens, the new models that will evolve will be more explicit, more realistic and more predictive, all of which will contribute to theory maturation. Towards the end of the next chapter, I present an example of a multivariate theory developed from the sustained use of SEM.

13

Frontiers in the application of SEM

The "symphonic" nature of natural systems

A system can be defined as an interacting set of parts. There are, of course, many kinds of system. I sometimes like to draw a parallel between natural systems and symphonic music (another kind of system), as a means of conveying certain ideas about what we gain from a multivariate approach to ecology. In symphonic music, a composition relies on the participation and interplay of many instruments. As we listen to an orchestra (preferably live for greatest effect) we gain an entirely different experience compared with the effects of listening to the instruments individually. The same is true with the study of natural systems. The preceding chapters have sought to convey through examples what can be gained from achieving a multivariate perspective. While descriptive multivariate methods have been increasingly employed by natural scientists, the study of hypotheses has largely relied on univariate methods. The result has been an emphasis on individual processes, with little opportunity to consider their role in the system. My own earlier experience with the study of competitive interactions convinced me of the value of building and evaluating multivariate hypotheses, where the importance and impact of individual processes can be seen in some context. It is, of course, true that the simultaneous study of all parts of a system is not feasible. However, it would seem that our understanding of the observed variation in a system property of key interest can often be improved without resorting to extremely complex models.

Frontiers in statistical methodology

Recent and future advances in statistical methodology have the potential to add in important ways to the questions that can be posed and addressed. Already we have seen how the introduction of a statistical concept such as a latent variable can imply new elements of our research paradigm, leading to new lines of inquiry. A significant number of statistical inventions have been described in this book and their role in permitting different types of models to be estimated has been illustrated. In Chapter 7, a number of more advanced statistical techniques were referenced, including multigroup analysis, categorical variable modeling, the treatment of nonlinear relationships, latent growth models, hierarchical methods such as multi-level modeling, and the modeling of reciprocal interactions. All of these open up new questions that can be addressed by the researcher.

Currently, progress is being made on many fronts related to conventional SEM. Recent compilations of advancements can be found in Cudeck *et al.* (2001), Marcoulides and Schumacker (2001), and Pugesek *et al.* (2003). These address a wide range of topics from nonlinear modeling to alternative estimation techniques, to categorical variable modeling. The reader should be aware, however, of parallel methodological advances taking place outside of the traditional domain of SEM that have the potential to greatly alter the way we work with multivariate hypotheses. The broad enterprise of modeling multivariate relations is currently undergoing a staggering rate of growth, with a wide variety of approaches being developed and promoted under the umbrella concept of "graphical models" (e.g., Borgelt and Kruse 2002). These efforts have been driven by a wide variety of objectives, from the desire to develop artificial intelligence to the wish to mine vast quantities of data. These methods are also highly dependent upon the capacity for high-speed computers as well as new algorithms for solving multiequational systems and searching iteratively for solutions. Borgelt and Kruse (2002) provide the following list of approaches to the search for relationships in multivariate data:

- classical statistics
- decision/classification and regression trees
- naive Bayes classifiers
- probabilistic networks (including Bayesian and Markov networks)
- artificial neural networks
- neuro-fuzzy rule induction
- k-nearest neighbor/case-based reasoning
- inductive logic programming
- association rules
- hierarchical and probabilistic cluster analysis
- fuzzy cluster analysis
- conceptual clustering

Consideration of many of these approaches is beyond the scope of this book. The reader can find out more about these and other methods in Dasarathy (1990), Bezdek and Pal (1992), Langley *et al.* (1992), Muggleton (1992), Pearl (1992), Agrawal *et al.* (1993), and Anderson (1995). Shipley (2000) also provides an overview of some of these methods in chapter 8 of his book.

It would seem that one important external influence impinging on classical, maximum likelihood SEM is Bayesian reasoning. Bayesian thinking is leading to distinctively different methods for estimating and interpreting statistical models. It is also leading to novel approaches to evaluating networks of relationships. Emerging from the growth in interest in, and applications of Bayesian statistics is the recognition of a new future for SEM, Bayesian structural equation modeling (Jedidi and Ansari 2001). Thus, it is valuable, I think, to describe briefly what these new ideas might mean for SEM.

Bayesian inference and structural equation modeling

Bayesian ideas

There has long been debate and dissatisfaction within the field of statistics on how to express probabilities in a meaningful way. While there have been a number of different systems proposed for describing probabilities (Oakes 1990), the two dominant approaches today are frequentist (von Mises 1919) and Bayesian (Bayes 1763). While conventional SEM practice shares some characteristics with the Bayesian philosophy, such as an emphasis on sequential learning, a disregard for null hypotheses, and a less rigid approach to hypothesis testing, likelihood methods, as emphasized in Chapter 5, are frequentist in nature. At the heart of the frequentist view, there is an assumption of the existence of population parameters and general probabilities, as well as a belief that the long run frequency of repeatable events provides an estimate of those population probabilities. In this system, inferences are drawn concerning populations, and the p-value refers to the probability that if a study were conducted 100 times, the true value would fall within the 95% confidence intervals 95% of the time. Characteristic of the implementation of the Neyman–Pearson protocol (Chapter 1), either–or conclusions are typically drawn about the truth of some proposition relative to an alternative hypothesis.

Long before the frequentist view became the backbone of modern statistics, the alternative ideas known as Bayesian inference were elaborated, first by Bayes himself, and then shortly after that by Laplace (1774). There are many different ways we could describe the Bayesian view and, in fact, a great many "flavors" of Bayesian inference have been proposed (Good 1983). I think it is most helpful to define Bayesian inference as the *quantification of uncertainty*. This definition makes clear from the outset that the emphasis is on what is known (our current knowledge) about the probability of observing some event, and the associated range of uncertainty. *This is quite a contrasting emphasis from the frequentist goal*, which is estimating the value of a population parameter, which is presumed to exist, but is unknown to us.

What is of great practical importance at the present time, is that the ways of solving a wide range of models using Bayesian methods has very recently become possible, thanks to the development of efficient ways of sampling data and very fast computing speeds. This means that a discussion of the merits of Bayesian methods is suddenly much more relevant. This is particularly true for structural equation models, which are typically much more complex than the average univariate model, and therefore, even more challenging for Bayesian estimation.

Because the Bayesian view emphasizes uncertainty, it is inherently referenced to the person's perspective. In other words, uncertainty is a property of the quality of a person's knowledge, rather than a statement about a population. This has profound implications for the way that inference is drawn, the nature of the conclusions, and the reactions that different individuals have to its validity. From an abstract perspective, it would seem that how uncertain we are about something is more of a psychological issue than a scientific matter. However, from a practical perspective, we interface the world and make decisions based on our estimated certainty about observable events. Applied science is typically driven by uncertain information (as well as perceived importance). For this reason, a Bayesian approach has, at the very least, a substantial niche in the conduct of statistical inference.

Among the many differences between frequentist and Bayesian views is that Bayesian's are not simply interested in estimating the first and second moments of the distribution (mean and variance), they are interested in describing the entire probability distribution. Once we know the probability distribution of some occurrence or co-occurrence, we can estimate directly and precisely the likelihood of any particular range of events of interest. This preoccupation with the probability distribution is precisely why Bayesian inference gives more detailed and potentially more accurate estimates, and also why it is more computationally difficult. Frequentists can invoke many different assumed probability distributions. Typically, however, the normal distribution is assumed for continuous functions, and a few different distributions such as binomial or poisson are assumed for discrete events. A presumption that one's variables approximate the normal or multinormal distribution provides frequentists with a "quick and dirty" calculation of confidence intervals for the population parameters. This has been (and continues to be) an enormously valuable compromise in drawing statistical inference.

Because Bayesian inference is focused on uncertainty, it is inherently linked to sequential learning. Here I define sequential learning as the progressive refinement of one's knowledge based on accumulated experience. Sequential learning implies that our estimate of the probability of observing some outcome is updated based on additional data. This concept is embodied in the *Bayes Theorem*, which stated in words is, *our estimated odds of observing some outcome are equal to the observed frequency of outcomes from data plus our prior estimate of the odds before we had the data.*

Now, when one hears this definition, I expect we may have two, nearly simultaneous reactions (I certainly do). First, it seems unreasonable on the face of it to combine one's uninformed prior estimate of odds with those informed by data. At the same time, if one possessed really good prior information about the odds of an event, then combining the odds derived from pre-existing experience (and potentially a lot of previously obtained data) with those derived from the current sample would seem like a superior idea (if one's purpose is prediction). I think this pair of reactions summarizes nicely the view that Bayesian estimates can either be worse than or better than those derived from frequentist estimation methods, depending on the quality of prior information. Furthermore, the relevance of combining prior information with current data to derive an averaged estimate will depend on both (1) the quality and magnitude of the data, and (2) the relevance of prior information to the current case. In the study of natural systems, it is not always clear that we are sampling repeatable phenomena. Natural systems, particularly communities and ecosystems, can possess a great deal of spatial and temporal heterogeneity. This fact of life adversely impacts both frequentist and Bayesian inference, the latter because it affects the relevance of prior information.

Now, some claim that the issue of combining prior odds with results from a data set may not pose as large a problem for Bayesian estimation as it might seem. The use of uninformative priors (vague initial estimates) presumably reduces their influence on the estimated posterior odds. Of course, there is a tendency for uninformative priors to contribute to a broad probability distribution, even if it does not have a strong influence on the estimation of the mean response. Thus, uninformative priors may adversely impact parameter estimates.

To some degree, the use of priors in Bayesian estimation can initially distract us from a number of potential advantages that arise from the mechanics of the estimation procedure. Those mechanics now involve various resampling methods, such as the Metropolis–Hasting method (Hastings 1970) or the Gibbs method (Casella 1992) which are used to estimate the precise shape of the probability (or joint probability) distributions. Having the precise shape of the probability distribution yields inherently superior information, at least in theory. In practice, there are a number of things that can interfere with reaping the potential benefits of Bayesian estimation, especially problems in estimation. Nevertheless, available information based on comparisons and considerations of Bayesian versus frequentist (typically maximum likelihood) estimates yield the following points (all of which should be considered preliminary at the present time).

(1) With large samples that conform well to distributional assumptions and in the absence of informative priors, Bayesian and frequentist (maximum likelihood) estimates produce similar results (Scheines *et al.* 1999).

(2) Bayesian estimates of centrality and precision measures are substantially superior when maximum likelihood is used on data that deviate a great deal from the associated distributional assumptions.

(3) Bayesian estimation is more suited to small sample data because maximum likelihood depends on asymptotic behavior.

(4) The choice of priors has a greater impact on small samples in Bayesian estimation.

(5) Bayesian methods provide more intuitively useful statements about probabilities, particularly in the context of decision making.

(6) Bayesian estimation, when good priors exist, can overcome some problems of model underidentification, enhancing the range of models that can be solved.

(7) Bayesian modeling holds promise for facilitating the modeling of non-linear and complex model structures.

(8) Bayesian estimation may be inherently better suited for modeling categorical outcomes, because it is based on conditional probabilities.

(9) Bayesian estimation for structural equation models with multi-indicator latent variables is potentially problematic, because the lack of a simultaneous solution procedure can yield inconsistent estimates (Congdon 2003, chapter 8).

(10) It is unclear whether methods for evaluating model fit under Bayesian estimation are as reliable as, or superior to, those achieved under maximum likelihood.

Overall, it would seem that Bayesian approaches hold promise for general application to SEM (Rupp *et al.* 2004). That said, maximum likelihood may be comparable for a significant range of applications. Current SEM software has now automated a very wide range of model types, including latent class analysis, mixture growth modeling, incorporation of interactions in latent variable models, and hierarchical models. Finally, the potential pitfalls for Bayesian estimation in complex models have not been adequately researched as of yet. Initial indications are that particular problems arise in latent variable models involving multiple indicators per latent, when using Bayesian estimation. Since this is a particular strength of ML SEM procedures and represent a very common model type, further work is needed to ascertain whether Bayesian methods will be applicable to the full range of model types.

Bayesian networks

What we might refer to as "Bayesian SEM" goes beyond considerations of estimation and can be viewed as falling under the umbrella of "Bayesian networks" (Pearl 2000, Jensen 2001, Neapolitan 2004). This is a topic currently experiencing explosive growth and interest. Thus, any attempt to generalize about it is subject to significant misrepresentation. That said, it would seem that the field of Bayesian networks includes interest in both causal as well as descriptive and predictive modeling, and is thus not synonymous with Bayesian SEM. Nevertheless, there is a great deal of applicability of Bayesian network (BN) methods to SEM problems. This applicability relates not just to Bayesian estimation, as described above, but also to a Bayesian perspective on conditional probability that can be used to evaluate network structure. I am reluctant to delve too deeply into the specifics of BN methods in this book, because the terminology associated with networks is both completely different from that used in conventional SEM, and somewhat involved. Bayesian network methods make reference to "directed acyclic graphs" (DAGs) instead of "recursive models", "nodes" instead of "observed variables", "edges" instead of "paths", and so on. Therefore, I refer the reader to Pearl (2000), Shipley (2000), and Neapolitan (2004) for a description of this terminology, as well as the topic of "d-separation" which deals with how models can be evaluated for conditional independence.

Conclusions about Bayesian methods and SEM

In this discussion of Bayesian inference and its relation to SEM, I have tried to give a very general description of a highly complex topic. A thorough treatment of Bayesian SEM would require a book of its own, if for no other reason than the fact that it involves completely different solution procedures, software, and terminology. In spite of all that, the scientific goal of developing and testing multivariate hypotheses so as to understand systems goes beyond whether we use frequentist or Bayesian methods. The questions addressed by SEM, many of the interpretations, and the insights produced also apply regardless of the method of estimation and inference. Whether maximum likelihood methods remain widely used, or whether Bayesian procedures and ideas come to predominate in SEM applications, I believe the study of multivariate models will lead us to a better understanding of natural systems and a greater maturation of our theories. Ultimately, Bayesian methods are focused on providing the best prediction of the next event, while ML emphasizes an evaluation of the data.

Frontiers in research applications

While advances in analytical methods can allow us to address new questions, new ways of applying methods can also advance the scientific enterprise. Up to the present, structural equation modeling has been largely confined to playing a strict role as a means of statistical modeling. While the inclusion of latent variables can allow us to more directly represent concepts in our models, in most cases, the latent variable effects in our models must represent single effects. This limitation is discussed in the chapter on latent variables (Chapter 4) and in Chapter 5, composite variables are introduced as an aid to modeling multi-dimensional constructs. I believe that composite variables have the potential to be applied in ways that will permit some entirely new kinds of research applications. In particular, the use of composites allow us to begin to formulate more general statistical models that better match our theories. In this book, the use of composite variables, either to represent general constructs, or to represent non-linear effects, has been prominent. I have included this material despite the fact that many of the statistical procedures for analyzing models containing composites have not been established in the literature. Thus their inclusion is one of necessity rather than because they represent an accepted element of SEM.

There are other necessities that drive our application of SEM. One is that we need to have greater flexibility in relating general theoretical models to structural equation models. We also need to be able to better link mechanistic theory to statistical implications. This implies a desirability of linking SEM with statistical forecast models and with system simulation models. Such linkages between model types are limited only by example applications. Thus, much of the potential for multi-modeling approaches can be revealed simply by discussing ways different techniques can be combined. Let us begin by considering some of the strengths of each major model type.

Conceptual models have long served as the primary means of summarizing general features of ecological systems. In the past few decades, mathematical modeling, either of particular processes (commonly accomplished using analytical mathematics), or of system dynamics (commonly accomplished using system simulations) has played a major role in ecological investigations. To some degree, each type of modeling has a particular kind of utility. Conceptual models are capable of great generality and flexibility. They can, in some cases, imply a great deal of content without requiring specification of explicit details. They may also serve as logical starting points for exploring topics or organizing our knowledge. Analytical mathematical models, in contrast, seek to make mechanistic assumptions and their consequences explicit. They are often used to explore the interactions between a small number of variables. Such models can have very general implications, although the business of determining their relevance to real ecosystems is often left to the field biologist. System simulation models have come to be the most common type of mechanistic model. Motives for their development and usage range from organizational to exploratory to predictive. Their size and complexity also vary greatly. System simulations can grade from those exploring the dynamics of a single process to those involving hundreds of equations. Traditional statistical models also have a long history of application in ecology. Experimental designs and analyses, sampling programs, and hypothesis evaluations of all sorts rely on statistical models. Such models can, and often are, used for static or dynamic predictive modeling.

Relating conceptual models to structural equation models

The first step in multivariate hypothesis testing is to translate the important elements of an initial conceptual model into a construct model. This step represents an opportunity to evaluate our general conceptual models for tangibility. The researcher may find, for example, that the way that a concept is described or represented in a general conceptual model may not make sense in a statistical modeling context. Concepts represented may prove to be too abstract to translate in a general way, or may need to be subdivided or even renamed before their theoretical meaning becomes clear. It may also be the case that conceptual models include processes or components that are virtually impossible to measure. As described in Chapter 12, this translation process has the potential to lead to theory maturation and clarification of our general conceptual models. Thus, it is expected that the interplay between conceptual modeling and multivariate hypothesis testing will lead to refinement of conceptual models, in addition to hypothesis testing.

Because of the capacity for latent variable models to represent both linkages between conceptual variables and how concepts are to be measured, such models can play an expanded role compared to our traditional use of statistics. Certainly the construct model can be viewed as a particular type of conceptual model. Perhaps the biggest differences between structural equation models and general conceptual models are (1) there is an agreed upon convention for expressing and interpreting structural equation models, (2) structural equation

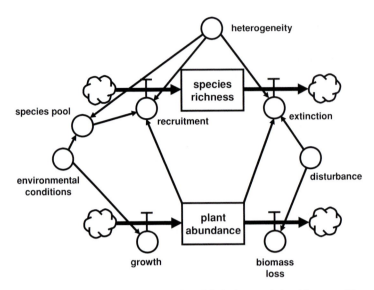

Figure 13.1. A multivariate conceptual model of primary relationships controlling species richness (from Grace 1999). The model is presented in dynamics systems format and follows the conventions of Hannon and Ruth (1997). State variables are shown in boxes. Clouds indicate unspecified sources and sinks. Circles represent control variables and those with linkages to thick arrows regulate changes in state variables. Reproduced by permission of Elsevier Publishers.

models only include system variables that can be measured or estimated from data, and (3) the measurement portion of structural equation models explicitly defines how the concepts will be quantified, and therefore, their explicit meaning. For these reasons, it is expected that structural equation models will come to play a role in the conveyance of ecological theory that extends beyond their role as a specific statistical hypothesis. The construct model, which represents the statistical expectations in a more general way, without concern for how the constructs are to be measured, can play a special role in transitioning from the general to the specific. An illustration of this transitioning was presented in Chapter 10 (compare Figures 10.4, 10.6, and 10.7).

Incorporating statistical results into conceptual models

By combining the results of our site-specific studies of species richness with a thorough review of the published literature, I have proposed a more explicit conceptual model, informed by structural equation model results (Grace 1999). This multivariate conceptual model (Figure 13.1) seeks to subsume the individual mechanisms for richness control proposed by Grime (1979), Huston (1979), Tilman (1982), and Gough *et al.* (1994) into a single multivariate framework that is consistent with field and experimental data. According to this conceptual model, species richness is controlled by the size of the species pool, species recruitment into a site, and local extinction, all of which can be affected by habitat heterogeneity. At the same time, community biomass is controlled by growth and loss processes and, in turn, can suppress recruitment and increase extinction at elevated levels. Finally, this model presumes that environmental conditions can have differential effects on species pools and plant growth. Thus, an environmental condition can be evolutionarily stressful (i.e., few species can live there) and yet not appear to be ecologically stressful (i.e., the species that can tolerate those conditions are quite productive). Collectively, this conceptual model differs from any of the pre-existing models of this subject by being both multivariate and relatable to the statistical expectations of field data. I believe it also has many of the desirable properties described in Chapter 12, such as being able to accommodate new information as it is found, operational, reasonably general, and predictive. Current work is seeking to incorporate additional processes that are now believed to be important, and to include more explicit information about the relative importance of different pathways.

Statistical forecasting

The linkage of statistical models to forecasting is simple and direct. Regression relationships have historically been used to estimate coefficients that can be applied to forecast future outcomes (Pankratz 1991). Here I use the term forecast to emphasize that projected outcomes are conditional on a number of assumptions that may or may not hold. It is reasonable to expect that estimation of predictive relationships can often be improved upon using modern multivariate methods. There are two basic characteristics of structural equation and related models that make this so. First, multivariate models partition net effects into separate pathways, allowing for greater accuracy in conditional predictions. Secondly, the use of latent variables allows for the removal of measurement error and the production of more accurate path coefficients.

The value of isolating effects using SEM can be illustrated by referring back to the example of atrazine effects on ponds by Johnson *et al.* (1991; Figure 9.1). When atrazine, a phytotoxin, was added to replicate mesocosm ponds, the responses of algal populations were variable and did not consistently differ from control ponds overall. Use of this net outcome as the basis for predicting risk would be of limited generality or utility, as it was found that other factors, including aquatic vegetation, grass carp, pond depth, and zooplankton densities all affected algal populations. Once the effects of other factors were considered using SEM, the direct negative effect of atrazine on algae was found to be quite strong. Furthermore, the dissection of effects using a model

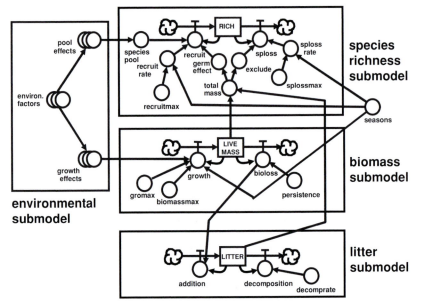

Figure 13.2. Representation of a system model used to simulate dynamics of richness, live biomass, litter, and environmental effects. Model symbolism represents the STELLA programming language (High Performance Systems®). Refer to Grace (2001) for details. Reproduced by permission of Oikos.

containing causal dependence gives more accurate prediction coefficients than would be obtained from a multiple regression approach. A direct translation of unstandardized path coefficients into a forecast model would allow forecasting under a broad range of scenarios. In general, results from multivariate models should permit more versatile and accurate forecasting in most cases.

System simulation

I believe there can be an important complementarity between system simulation and SEM. System simulation has tremendous flexibility and the capacity to incorporate a nearly unlimited amount of theoretical detail. A considerable variety of kinds of mechanism can be included, and these can readily be partitioned to incorporate spatial heterogeneity and scalability. The primary limitation with system simulation models is that they generally project or extrapolate from what is already known. Thus, like other theoretical mathematical models, the potential for informative feedback is limited. Discrepancies between predicted and observed can certainly be detected and analyzed. However, for many models, the number of estimated parameters that might be involved can mask

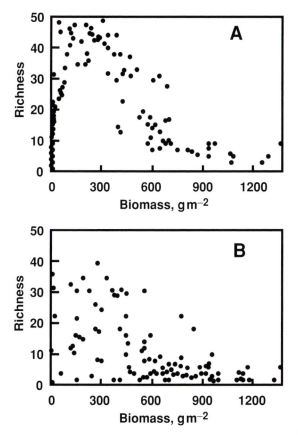

Figure 13.3. A. Relationship between total biomass and richness expected along a resource gradient based on simulation results (Grace 2001). B. Relationships expected along a nonresource gradient. Field results are generally more consistent with case B than with case A, and emphasize the importance of nonresource stresses on communities.

the reasons for observed discrepancies. Because of their capacity for directed discovery, structural equation models can not only reveal that data do not fit a model overall, but can also show precisely where discrepancies occur. Through this capability, SEM has the ability to assist in the construction and evaluation of simulation models.

On the other side of the process, it is possible to use the results of system simulations to generate multivariate theoretical expectations that can be evaluated using subsequent SEM analyses. Such an approach was used to explore in more detail the explicit interworkings of the various processes in Figure 13.1 (Grace 2001). To accomplish this, I created a system simulation model (shown in Figure 13.2) designed to capture some of the processes implied by the

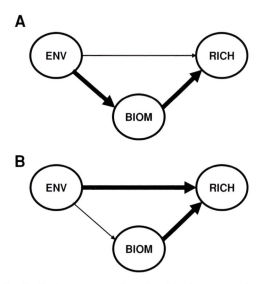

Figure 13.4. Qualitative representation of multivariate expectations based on simulations whose results are shown in Figure 13.3. A. Expected pattern for change in richness along a resource gradient where environmental effects on richness parallel those on biomass. B. Expected pattern for change in richness along a nonresource gradient where environmental effects on richness are independent of effects on biomass.

conceptual model. To provide a greater degree of realism, I separated biomass into live and dead components and confined plant growth, species recruitment, and species loss to occur during the growing season. Another distinction I made was to distinguish two kinds of environmental gradient, resource gradients (such as a soil fertility gradient) and nonresource gradients (such as a salinity or flooding stress gradient).

Among the explorations made using the dynamic system model was the consideration of how biomass and richness would respond to resource gradients versus nonresource gradients. The presumption made was that resource gradients would affect both community biomass and species pools, while nonresource gradients would also affect species pools, but not necessarily impact biomass. As shown in Figure 13.3A, a unimodal curve between biomass and richness would be expected along a purely resource gradient. Along a nonresource gradient, however, the most likely pattern would be a unimodal envelope of values (Figure 13.3B). Within a multivariate statistical context, Figure 13.4A shows the expected pattern of relationships associated with a resource gradient and Figure 13.4B shows that expected for a nonresource gradient. If these theoretical explorations are valid, based on a review of the field data, it appears that environmental gradients in the field typically behave as nonresource gradients in that environmental effects on richness are often unrelated to environmental effects on biomass.

Conclusions

Structural equation modeling will not always be appropriate or useful in every study. Furthermore, it will not solve all our problems and can yield results no better than the data upon which analyses are performed. Yet, it would seem that it has the ability to allow us to tune in to nature's symphony to a greater degree than ever before. Only time and experience will tell whether these methods will revolutionize science. It would seem from the current vantage point in history that they have great potential. It is my hope that biologists will be open to the process of exploring their utility in helping us to understand natural systems and their dynamics.

Appendix I
Example analyses

Purpose

The purpose of this appendix is to give the reader a little experience with the process of structural equation modeling. I should make the disclaimer that my treatment of the illustrations in this appendix is admittedly superficial. I expect that most readers will forgive this transgression, although some methodological experts may wish that I went into far more detail here rather than assuming that the reader understood all the more subtle nuances from the main chapters of the book. It is beyond the scope of an appendix such as this to give a complete exposition on model evaluation. It is also beyond our scope to give even a superficial overview of the variety of models that can be analyzed using SEM. Our task is further complicated by the significant number of competing software packages, their various features, and the significant issue of how they arrive at the results they yield. Somehow, in spite of all this, it seems useful to provide some illustrations of example analyses, allowing the reader to see some of the steps in the process, some sample output, some of the pitfalls and how they may be avoided or resolved.

It seems that the wisest thing to do in this appendix is to first give an overview of some of the various resources that are available to help the reader towards becoming a competent SEM analyst. I will assume, rightly or wrongly, that the material and advice given in the text will be sufficient for the individual to understand at least the basic analyses. Chapter 11 provides a brief summary of some of the main things to avoid and to attempt to accomplish when performing SEM. So, if we assume that one knows what one wants to do, this appendix serves to provide some examples of analyses, including how to translate questions into models and how to interpret output and create revised models. Additional supporting material can be found at www.jbgrace.com.

About SEM software

In this appendix I emphasize model construction and interpretation. It is not my intent to train the user in the use of particular software packages. Each software program comes with its own user manual, and all have a great number of features that go far beyond what can be covered here. That said, it is useful to at least comment on the various software programs designed to perform SEM analyses.

There are a number of commercial software programs currently available for performing SEM. The first widely used program of this sort was LISREL, which as of this writing is in its eighth generation. Over the years, the authors (Karl Jöreskog and Dag Sörbom) have added a number of modules and features to LISREL, as they continue to do. The original programming language for LISREL involved a rather cumbersome specification of matrix elements. Since that time, a more intuitive programming language, SIMPLIS, has been added and most recently, a graphical programming capability has been introduced. A number of other programs are also available for covariance analyses, including EQS, AMOS, CALIS (a module of SAS), SEPATH (a module of Statistica), and Mplus. New users of SEM inevitably wish to know which of these programs is best. One point in this regard is that most of these programs are updated fairly frequently, making any description I might give of the limitations of a program potentially out of date by the time this material is read. For this reason, I suggest readers perform internet searches for the programs that interest them and go to the software developer's web site to find out the latest features and associated costs. Also, free student editions of the software are available for download for many of these programs and many of the examples that follow can be run using the free versions of the software. Finally, published reviews can often be found in the journal *Structural Equation Modeling*, as well as in other outlets.

Given the above caveats, I will go on to say that as of this writing, AMOS, EQS, and LISREL all possess graphical programming capabilities. It is generally true that most new users would prefer to begin with a graphical programming environment, so these all make good choices. On the other hand, I think when one is aware of how simple the command-based programming is for programs such as Mplus, CALIS, and the SIMPLIS module of LISREL, there is no need to automatically pick a graphical-based package. More important to the selection process in my opinion is the availability of features. When it comes to features, most of the main programs being used today possess some unique features, which frustrates our ability to choose one program that is "the best" at all things. Again, this can change at any time, so the reader may wish to compare features at the time they read this. At the moment, I will note my enthusiasm for Mplus, which is the program I use most often, for having the most features. Other programs such as LISREL and EQS are also feature rich, while the program AMOS has some very friendly bootstrap features. Again, let the buyer be aware that all these comments will soon be out of date. Also, some programs are considerably more expensive than others, which can influence choices.

Example applications

In this appendix I offer just a few simple examples to illustrate some of the kinds of models that can be run and the type of output produced. First I set the stage and then present a graphical representation of the model or models of interest. One or more hypothetical data sets are presented for the purpose of seeing if the data fit the expectations of any of the models. Note that the data will typically be summarized as the correlations plus the standard deviations. This information is sufficient for calculating the covariances, which will be the raw material for our analyses in most cases. Next, output from analyses are presented, along with a brief discussion. Those interested can download the student version of Mplus from their web site to run these and other models

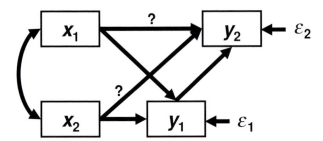

Figure A.1. Simple path model representing a set of possible relations between exogenous and response variables.

if they like. The Mplus program code that accompanies the example analyses presented in this appendix can be downloaded from www.JamesBGrace.com.

One additional comment about the examples to follow is warranted. In these examples I tend to discuss the estimation of the "effects" of one variable on another. It is important to always keep in mind that the SEM analysis does not establish causality, but that the ability to interpret relationships as effects or influences depends on outside information. Of course, when such outside information is lacking, the whole enterprise of SEM is somewhat compromised. For that reason, I make the assumption that there is reason to justify the structure of the models presented. For those working with real examples, sometimes thought experiments can help to establish or justify model structure. For example, for an $x \rightarrow y$ relationship, we can ask, if we were to manipulate x, would we expect y to respond? We may also ask, if we were to manipulate y would x respond? If the reasonable answers to those two questions are yes and no, respectively, a basis for establishing directional influence is established, although the degree of confidence in that conclusion is influenced by many things.

Example 1: a simple path model

The situation

Imagine we are interested in the influences of some system drivers on a system response, in the presence of an intervening variable. In such a case, our system drivers might be represented as exogenous observed variables x_1 and x_2, our intervening variable as y_1, and the ultimate system response of interest as y_2 (Figure A.1). There are a number of questions we might ask about this system. It is often the case that we wish to know if the relationships between the x variables and y_2 are mediated by y_1. The model in Figure A.1, omitting the paths with question marks, might be designated the "indirect effects" model. In this model we ask if any effects of x_1 or x_2 on y_2 can be explained by y_1. Models that contain the paths with the question marks then become alternatives to the indirect effects model. The direct paths from x_1 or x_2 to y_2 presumably represent separate mechanisms whereby the exogenous variables influence y_2 (separate from those mechanisms that involve mediation by y_1).

Some possible applications

One example that would fit this situation is where x_1 and x_2 are soil conditions, y_2 is the proportion of plants in a plot that are flowering, and y_1 is the average size of the plants

Table A.1. *Hypothetical data for simple path model example. N = 100*

	x_1	x_2	y_1	y_2
x_1	1.0			
x_2	0.200	1.0		
y_1	0.387	0.576	1.0	
y_2	0.679	0.356	0.766	1.0
Std. dev.	1121.6	1.79	278.9	0.0856

Table A.2. *Variance/covariance matrix derived from Table A.1. N = 100*

	x_1	x_2	y_1	y_2
x_1	1 257 986			
x_2	401.53	3.204		
y_1	121 059	287.56	77,785	
y_2	65.19	0.054 55	18.287	0.007 327

in the plot. In a situation such as this, one might naturally ask whether variations in soil conditions relate to the frequency with which plants flower, and if so, whether this can be explained by the fact that plants are larger under certain soil conditions and larger plants are more likely to flower.

Another example that would fit this situation is where we are interested in variations in population densities of an herbivorous insect as our y_2 variable, and we wish to relate population densities to the abundance of its preferred food plant, y_1, when there are two habitat factors x_1 and x_2 thought to influence plant growing conditions. We might wonder if there is something about either of the habitat factors that might have some additional influences on insect populations, independent of influences mediated by influences on its food plant. These additional influences would show up as significant direct paths from the xs to y_2.

Data

Illustration 1.1

Here I wish to convey a simple but critical lesson about running models. To accomplish this, we will first convert the data in Table A.1 into its raw form, a variance and covariance matrix. Typically when one analyzes data using any of the SEM software packages, the raw data will be examined and for many (though not all) analyses, a variance–covariance matrix will be used to perform the analyses. Let us see what our raw data will look like. We can make the calculations directly. The variances that will go into the diagonal will simply be the squares of the standard deviations from Table A.1. The covariances can be calculated by multiplying the correlations by the product of the standard deviations of the two variables involved. The logic for this can be seen by revising Eq. (6) in Chapter 3. The results are presented in Table A.2.

Table A.3. *Recoded data from Table A.1.*
N = 100

	x_1	x_2	y_1	y_2
x_1	1.0			
x_2	0.200	1.0		
y_1	0.387	0.576	1.0	
y_2	0.679	0.356	0.766	1.0
Std. dev.	1.1216	1.79	2.789	0.856

Our goal now will be to use the data in Table A.2 to evaluate the model in Figure A.1 that omits the paths with question marks. The output from that analysis is as follows:

Results and discussion of initial analysis for Illustration 1.1

NO CONVERGENCE. SERIOUS PROBLEMS IN ITERATIONS CHECK YOUR DATA, STARTING VALUES AND MODEL

What you have just witnessed is the result of out-of-bound calculations resulting from having numbers in the variance/covariance matrix that are too large. This is a very common problem for first time analysts. Fortunately, the solution is very simple, to recode the data. I would recommend that the data be coded so that the standard deviations are all in the range between 0.1 and 10. With that in mind, we now adjust our data from Table A.1, with the resulting data presented in Table A.3.

Illustration 1.2

The goal now is to use our recoded data to evaluate the model in Figure A.1. We again start with the "indirect effects" model, which omits the paths with question marks. The results obtained from that analysis are presented below. Note that the form of the results, including the types of indices presented and the form of the output vary depending on software package. The Mplus package presents a fairly abbreviated form of output compared with some others, such as LISREL.

Results for Illustration 1.2

THE MODEL ESTIMATION TERMINATED NORMALLY
TESTS OF MODEL FIT

```
Chi-Square Test of Model Fit
    Value                      57.425
    Degrees of Freedom         2
    P-Value                    0.0000
RMSEA (Root Mean Square Error of Approximation)
    Estimate                   0.526
    90 Percent C.I.            0.414, 0.648
    Probability RMSEA <=0.05   0.000
```

Discussion of Illustration 1.2

So, we now have a successful run and have achieved output. If the reader has read Chapter 5, they will be able to recognize that the measures of fit given, the chi-square test and the RMSEA, both indicate some important deviations between model expectations and data. We would generally prefer the p-value associated with the chi-square to be one that gives us confidence that model and data are reasonably consistent. As was discussed earlier, chi-square increases with increasing sample size, and this measure of fit is sometimes too sensitive for practical purposes. However, a sample size of 100, which is what is used in this case, it not excessively large, and as a result, we would reasonably expect a p-value greater than something like 0.05 if data supported this model. The RMSEA adjusts for sample size, so we do not attribute its indication of significant deviations to a sample size problem, regardless of how many samples we have. Since both indices indicate we have a poorly fitting model, we reject this model.

Since our data did not match the initial model, we conclude that this is the wrong model for these data. Therefore, we do not bother to look at the parameter estimates or to see whether any of the paths appear to be nonsignificant. Since we have concluded that we ran the wrong model, we cannot trust the results. What we would do next depends on our a-priori theoretical position. Our choices are (1) to run the models of initial theoretical interest – a "competing models" strategy, (2) to look at model residuals or modification indices in order to educate our guess about which path(s) need to be added to achieve good model fit, and which path(s) should be eliminated because they are not significant, (3) to make changes until we stumble across a model that shows good fit to the data, or (4) to include all paths (which would give us perfect fit) and then eliminate those that are nonsignificant.

In this case, we started with an initial set of alternatives that we wished to compare. Our interest was equal between the possibility that effects of x_1 and x_2 on y_2 are completely mediated by y_1, and the possibility that a direct path from either x_1 or x_2 to y_2 might exist. Our most powerful move at this point is to run our next model without looking at residuals or modification indices. This means we are not letting an interim look at the data influence our testing process.

Illustration 1.3

Our next move will be to run an alternative model, one that includes a path from x_1 to y_2 (refer back to Figure A.1).

Results for Illustration 1.3 – model fit

TESTS OF MODEL FIT

```
Chi-Square Test of Model Fit
    Value                          3.548
    Degrees of Freedom             1
    P-Value                        0.0596
RMSEA (Root Mean Square Error of Approximation)
    Estimate                       0.160
    90 Percent C.I.                0.000, 0.353
    Probability RMSEA <=0.05       0.092
```

Discussion of Illustration 1.3 – model fit

The addition of the path from x_1 to y_2 resulted in a reduction in the model chi-square from 57.425 to 3.548. Thus, our single-degree-of-freedom change was 53.877. Since the change in chi-square also possesses a chi-square distribution, we can treat the difference as a test criterion. Typically we would judge a decrease in chi-square of 3.84 or more to indicate a significant improvement in fit when relaxing a single constraint on the model. Clearly, the data fit the new model substantially better that they did the original model.

Now, we have judged the second model to be better than the first, but is the fit of the data to this model adequate or do additional paths need to be added? The absolute values of the fit indices suggest a reasonably good fit between data and model. The p-value for the chi-square is 0.0596, while the p-value of the RMSEA is 0.092. We can also note that the 90% confidence interval for the RMSEA includes the value of 0.0. This means that perfect fit between data and model cannot be ruled out with these data.

Since our measures of absolute model fit are adequate based on usual criteria, we conclude that our second model *may* be acceptable. We might feel sufficiently confident to simply accept the model. However, if we were of a suspicious mind about this model, we might worry that a p-value for our chi-square of 0.0596 suggests that with a larger sample size, we would be able to detect deviations between data and model. There are other things we can and should examine to evaluate our model, particularly the model residuals.

Results for Illustration 1.3 – expected covariances, residuals, and modification indices

Observed Covariances

	Y1	Y2	X1	X2
Y1	7.779			
Y2	1.829	0.733		
X1	1.211	0.652	1.258	
X2	2.876	0.545	0.402	3.204

Model Estimated Covariances

	Y1	Y2	X1	X2
Y1	7.701			
Y2	1.810	0.725		
X1	1.198	0.645	1.245	
X2	2.847	0.654	0.398	3.172

Residuals for Covariances (observed-estimated)

	Y1	Y2	X1	X2
Y1	0.078			
Y2	0.019	0.008		
X1	0.013	0.007	0.013	
X2	0.029	−0.109	0.004	0.032

Standardized Residuals

	Y1	Y2	X1	X2
Y1	0.000			
Y2	0.000	0.000		
X1	0.000	0.000	0.000	
X2	0.000	−0.076	0.000	0.000

MODIFICATION INDEX FOR Y2 ON X2 = 3.486

Discussion of Illustration 1.3 – residuals and modification indices

An examination of the estimated variance–covariance matrix points out that an unsaturated model imposes a set of expectations on the data. These expectations guide the process of parameter estimation. However, our best estimates of parameter values typically still leave us with deviations between observed and estimated/expected values. The residuals are the deviations between observed and expected. Generally, the standardized deviations are easier to interpret as these are in correlation metric. It is possible to ask most programs to calculate the expected decrease in chi-square that should occur if we were to include a path in the model (these are the so-called *modification indices*). In this case, the chi-square change expected for adding a path from x_2 to y_2 is 3.486. This value is below the single-degree-of-freedom chi-square change value of 3.84, indicating that if this change was made the model would not be significantly improved.

The examination of residuals is informative. In this case, it is fairly easy to know where to look for possible improvements in the model, since there is only one pathway that is not included in our model. However, for more complex models, residuals and modification indices can provide valuable clues about where data are failing to match the expectations of a model. When we use these residuals and indices to find where changes need to be made for models that are clearly inadequate, we are now applying SEM in an exploratory mode. In this example, we managed to avoid lapsing into exploratory mode by focusing on models of initial interest, and basing our evaluation on indices of model fit. That said, I would rather wind up with a model that matches the data well using an exploratory process than base my interpretations on a model that obviously does not match the data. It is really only through repeated applications or very large samples that we will find out whether our model has general validity.

Results for Illustration 1.3 – parameter estimates

Now, we are finally ready to examine parameter estimates. Some output relating to path coefficients and other parameters are presented here.

MODEL RESULTS

	Estimates	S.E.	Est./S.E.	StdYX
Y1 ON				
X1	0.704	0.195	3.608	0.283
X2	0.809	0.122	6.618	0.519
Y2 ON				
Y1	0.182	0.016	11.114	0.592
X1	0.343	0.041	8.449	0.450

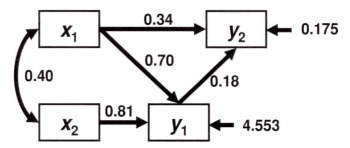

Figure A.2. Unstandardized parameter estimates for accepted model.

Residual Variances

Y1	4.553	0.644	7.071	0.591
Y2	0.175	0.025	7.071	0.241

Discussion of Illustration 1.3 – parameter estimates

The "estimates" presented in this case are the unstandardized parameters. Associated with each is the normal-theory standard error estimate. If we had reason to believe that our data failed to meet parametric assumptions, we could choose either ROBUST estimation, which corrects, at least partly, for nonnormality in the calculation of the standard errors. Alternatively we could use BOOTSTRAP procedures, which estimate standard errors using resampling methods. Determinations of whether parameters are significantly different from zero can be made using the "Est./S.E." ratios, which approximate a t-distribution. The p-values can be obtained elsewhere for deciding whether the investigator is confident that the parameter is indeed a nonzero value. For a sample size of 100, a p-value great than 0.05 is obtained when the t-value is less than 1.984 (two-tailed test). Finally, since we requested them, the standardized parameter values are presented.

We should note that the tests of parameter significance are based on the unstandardized parameters, and that the standardized parameters are simply summaries of the model results. We should also note that the R^2 values can be calculated simply as 1 minus the standardized error variances. Thus, the R^2 for y_1 is 0.409 and the R^2 for y_2 is 0.759.

It is customary and convenient to summarize our results graphically, which is done in Figure A.2. Here I present the unstandardized parameters to get the reader accustomed to their use. Since the path coefficients are in absolute units, we can relate results to the population at large. Considerable discussion in Chapter 3 deals with the interpretation of coefficients, and the interested reader should refer to that section if needed.

It is often the case that we also examine the standardized results, which are summarized in Figure A.3. Here, the path coefficients are summarized in standard deviation units. As discussed in Chapter 3, for normally distributed variables, standardized path coefficients can be approximately interpreted as representing the variation across the range expected for a response variable, as you vary a predictor across its range. We must be careful to realize, however, that coefficients standardized based on the sample standard deviations suffer from some loss of precision compared with unstandardized

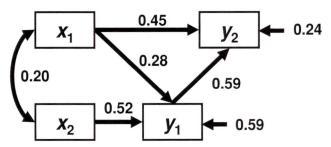

Figure A.3. Standardized parameter estimates for accepted model.

coefficients. This can be remedied by selecting relevant ranges for the variables and using those to standardize the raw parameters, providing a means of standardization that does not suffer from reliance on sample variances. Again, see the latter part of Chapter 3 for a discussion of this option.

The ultimate interpretations the researcher makes concerning the results depend on many things, including the system being studied, the associated theoretical knowledge and prior experience, the questions being asked, and characteristics of the sample. Hopefully the main chapters in this book, along with illustrative publications using these methods, provide sufficient instruction on how to draw careful and meaningful interpretations of results such as these. Basically, my advice is to rely on fundamental statistical principles rather than someone else's protocol.

Example 2: a multigroup comparison

The situation

There are many reasons to compare groups. This can be an excellent approach to use when analyzing experimental data. It can also be used to compare different samples or populations. Multigroup analyses can allow for the detection of interactions as well as main effects. For continuity, we will continue with our previous example and now assume we have a second sample we wish to compare to the original. In such a case, we wish to know whether the relationships in the two samples are the same, or whether the relationships in the two samples differ in important ways. We can represent the situation graphically with a two-group model as shown in Figure A.4.

Some possible applications

Imagine that we performed an experiment in which we randomly assigned fertilizer to half our plots, and again looked to see how soil factors and plant size relate to frequency of flowering. In this case, we might wish to ask the basic question of whether the system responded in a fundamentally different way when it was fertilized. Perhaps we might think that there should be no important differences in model parameters, although we might shift the mean plant size to a larger value and likewise shift the incidence of flowering to a higher proportion. Alternatively, we might think that direct addition of fertilizer would eliminate the importance of one of our soil factors by removing nutrient limitation. Or, perhaps we wonder whether fertilization might enhance flowering for

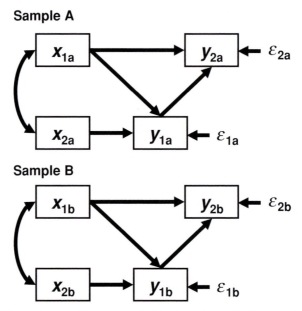

Figure A.4. Multigroup model of the form obtained in Example 1.

plants of any given size. All these questions can be addressed using the results from a multigroup analysis.

It is not necessary for our comparison to involve an experimental treatment, of course. We might again consider a case where we are interested in how herbivorous insects associate with a particular food plant in the face of covarying habitat factors. This time we ask whether the species initially studied has the same responses and relationships to habitat as a second, closely related species also found in the same sample. Here, our two groups would be independent estimates of each insect species and their relations to plant density and habitat conditions. In such a situation, our questions may have to do with differential efficiency of converting food into individuals, differential habitat preferences, or mortality rates for the two species.

Data

Let us imagine that we have two samples now, our original sample (from Table A.3) and a second sample. These are shown together in Table A.4. Keep in mind, that while I show the correlations, the models will be assessed using the covariances.

Results for Illustration 2.1 – model fit and equality constraints

The overall concept in a multigroup model is to determine whether a single model applies to all data sets. In this case, we have two data sets, each representing a separate group. We are assuming independence among samples in this example, although that assumption could be relaxed if need be. Our goal in this analysis is to determine which if any parameters differ between groups. Parameters in this case include the path coefficients,

Table A.4. *Correlations and standard deviations for the two insect species.* $N = 100$ *samples for each group*

	x_1	x_2	y_1	y_2
Group 1				
x_1	1.0			
x_2	0.200	1.0		
y_1	0.387	0.576	1.0	
y_2	0.679	0.356	0.766	1.0
Mean	6.22	0.756	100.75	10.25
Std. dev.	1.1216	1.79	2.789	0.856
Group 2				
x_1	1.0			
x_2	0.212	1.0		
y_1	0.501	0.550	1.0	
y_2	0.399	0.285	0.389	1.0
Mean	6.01	0.998	95.56	21.55
Std. dev.	1.32	1.66	2.505	1.701

the variances of the variables, and the means for the variables. There is a particular sequence of evaluations usually recommended for determining whether parameters are equal across groups. Stated briefly, our strategy is to begin by allowing all parameters to be uniquely estimated for each group. It is a basic requirement that the models be of the same form, which is something that is tested by allowing all parameters to be unique, and then determining whether model fit is adequate for each model separately. In this case, our data do fit a common model.

Discussion of Illustration 2.1 – model fit and equality constraints

Once we have determined that both data sets fit a common model, we then begin a series of single-degree-of-freedom chi-square tests by setting individual parameters to be equal across groups. Some programs (EQS) have the ability to perform one multivariate test for all equalities using Lagrange multipliers. In this case, we illustrate the method of multigroup analysis using the more commonly used univariate stepwise procedure.

Table A.5 gives the results for our series of equality tests. Our baseline model allowing all parameters to be unequal across groups had a chi-square of 4.981 with two degrees of freedom. The two degrees of freedom come from the fact that the paths from x_2 to y_2 for the two groups were not specified in the base model. When we forced path coefficients to be equal across groups one at a time, there was a slight, but nonsignificant increase in the model chi-square with each additional degree of freedom. Therefore, we conclude that all pathways have the same quantitative slopes across the two groups. When we forced variances to be equal across groups, only the variances of y_2 were found to be different among the groups. An indication of this difference can be seen in Table A.4, where the standard deviation of y_2 in group 1 can be seen to be 0.856, while the standard

Table A.5. *Summary of tests for equality of parameters across groups. The base model is one where all parameters are unique for each group. As parameters are constrained to be equal across groups, we determine whether model chi-square increases significantly, if so, the parameter is not equal across groups. If chi-square does not increase significantly, parameters are judged to be indistinguishable across groups*

		Chi-square	Model df	Equal across groups?
Base model		4.981	2	
Pathways:	$x_1 \rightarrow y_1$	5.042	3	equal
	$x_2 \rightarrow y_1$	5.413	4	equal
	$x_1 \rightarrow y_2$	5.416	5	equal
	$x_2 \rightarrow y_2$	5.433	6	equal
Variances:	x_1	8.079	7	equal
	x_2	8.752	8	equal
	y_1	10.995	9	equal
	y_2	143.606	10	not equal
Means:	x_1	12.474	10	equal
	x_2	14.076	11	equal
	y_1	211.882	12	not equal
	y_2	695.039	12	not equal

deviation of y_2 in group 2 is 1.701. Finally, two of the means were found to be equal across groups, those for x_1 and x_2. When the means for y_1 and y_2 were constrained to be equal across groups, model chi-square was greatly inflated and overall model fit was poor.

Results for Illustration 2.1 – parameter estimates

In Figure A.5, I show both the unstandardized and standardized path coefficients. Both types of results are presented here to make a very important point about interpreting multigroup analyses. First, we should note that all unstandardized path coefficients were found to be equal across the two groups (Table A.5). Thus, we may judge that the structural parameters defining the effects in this model are constant. Upon close inspection of Figure A.5, you will notice that some of the standardized path coefficients are rather different between groups, despite the fact that the unstandardized coefficients are judged identical. In particular, this can be seen for the paths from x_1 to y_2, and from y_1 to y_2. Why is this the case? The answer lies in the fact that the variances differ among groups for y_2. More specifically, the variance of y_2 in group 2 is roughly double that in group 1. Since standardized coefficients are standardized by the standard deviations, their values are "contaminated" by the unequal variances among groups. There is also an effect of unequal variances on the error variance of y_2; in this case both the unstandardized and standardized error variances are affected.

These results are designed to bring home the points mentioned earlier about the challenges to interpreting results based on standardized coefficients. This does not mean

Sample A

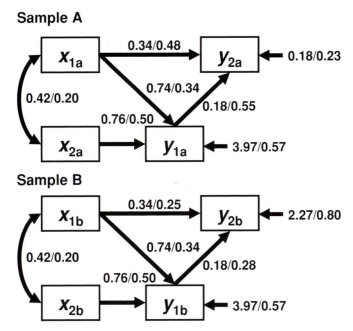

Sample B

Figure A.5. Results from multigroup analysis. Coefficients presented are the unstandardized values followed by the standardized values. The parameters that were found to be significantly different among groups are summarized in Table A.5 and only included the variance of y_2 and the means of y_1 and y_2.

that all comparisons are automatically incorrect. It is only when variances differ among groups that we will have a problem. In fact, since the declaration of significant differences among groups is based on tests of the unstandardized parameters, we know that the standardized path coefficients in Figure A.5, even those that appear to be different, do not represent significant differences. If those paths did differ significantly and there were also differences in variances among groups, then the standardized coefficients could lead to some incorrect inferences. Again, the solution mentioned at the end of Chapter 3 to standardize based on relevant ranges would solve the problem, and if applied to this example, we would see that all such standardized path coefficients would be equal across groups.

One other point that is made by this example to illustrate why statisticians are not enamored with judging a model by the R^2 values. The R^2 for y_2 in group 1 is 0.769, while the R^2 for y_2 in group 2 is only 0.204. Would we judge the model for group 2 to be inferior to the one for group 1? We should not, because the path coefficient estimates are the same for both. It may be that we actually obtained the correct path coefficients in group 2 in the face of more noise, which could be construed as a major success. There is a natural attraction for researchers to focus on explained variance in the response variables. As we see here, it is not one that should be accepted too readily, as it focuses on the wrong parameters.

Table A.6. *Data borrowed from Table A.4, with the added component that a dichotomous cluster variable is now included. N = 100*

	c	x_1	x_2	y_1	y_2
c	1.0				
x_1	0.25	1.0			
x_2	0.41	0.200	1.0		
y_1	0.33	0.387	0.576	1.0	
y_2	0.37	0.679	0.356	0.766	1.0
Mean	0.5	6.22	0.756	100.75	10.25
Std. dev.	0.20	1.1216	1.79	2.789	0.856

Example 3: hierarchical data

The situation

It is extremely common for data to be sampled in some fashion that restricts randomization. A multigroup analysis can be used when we are explicitly interested in different subgroups of our sample. However, in many cases, we are not interested in the sample clusters, but instead, simply wish to control for their effects. There are two basic approaches we can use, one is to include cluster variables and the other is to perform behind-the-scenes adjustments to the data. Both can be effective.

Some possible applications

For experimental data, use of a random block design creates a structure in the data that needs to be taken into account in the analysis. Likewise, stratified random sampling, in which coverage of a range of conditions is enhanced by defining strata and randomly sampling within those strata, is a commonly used device. Even when not used as a strategy per se, the subsampling of disjunct locations or populations creates a kind of structure in the data that needs to be accounted for. Sometimes the researcher is interested in the magnitude of this effect, and sometimes it is the across-strata results that are of greatest interest.

Data

For this example, we continue using the data from Example 1, which was utilized as the data for group 1 in Table A.4. In this case, we imagine that these data were actually taken from two disjunct sampling locations and combined, and we now wish to control for this cluster sampling in the analyses. It would be our general assumption that if the clusters differed consistently in some fashion, ignoring them should create bias in the parameter estimates observed in Figure A.2.

Results

Here we will not worry about the steps involved in the process of arriving at the final results, as the reader should now be familiar with the process. Instead, we focus on

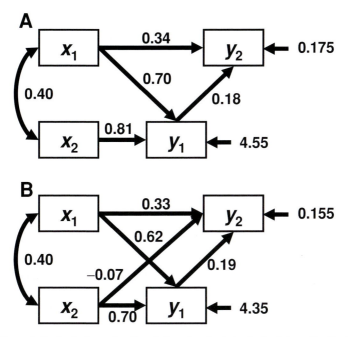

Figure A.6. Analysis results either A. ignoring clustering in the data, or B. adjusting for clustering.

the results obtained. For comparison, we will refer to the results in Figure A.2, which represent what one would obtain here if we ignored the clustering. When our model was modified to include the cluster variable, the first thing that was found was that model fit was substantially reduced. Instead of a chi-square of 3.548 with 1 degree of freedom (p = 0.0596), we now have a chi-square of 7.803 with 2 degrees of freedom (p = 0.0197). Inclusion of a path from x_2 to y_2 was indicated by these deviations, which could lead us to accept a different model from these same data once clustering is taken into account. The model with the path from x_2 to y_2 included is found to have a chi-square of 1.226 with 1 degree of freedom (p = 0.2681), indicating good fit.

Results from the analysis including a cluster variable can be seen in Figure A.6. For simplicity, the paths involving the cluster variable are omitted from the presentation. The principal change in results compared to when the effects of clustering were ignored (Figure A.2), is the inclusion of the path from x_2 to y_2. Since these are the unstandardized results, which seems like the appropriate metric to use when comparing non-nested models as we are here, it is a little more challenging to judge the magnitude of the differences in parameters. We can improve our perspective a little by expressing the differences in path coefficients as percentage changes, and they range from 0% up to a maximum of 17% (for the path from x_2 to y_1). The take home message here is that it is both possible and desirable to control for nonindependencies in the data.

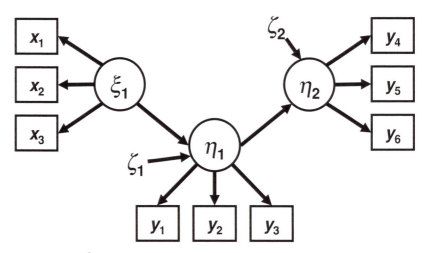

Figure A.7. Latent variable model with multiple indicators. Error terms for indicators are omitted for simplicity of presentation.

Example 4: evaluating latent variable models

The situation

Latent variables can be incorporated into models in a great many different ways. Here I will offer a single illustrative example designed to cover some of the more common issues, as well as some more specialized points. Figure A.7 shows a classic "hybrid" model that considers directed relations among latent factors possessing multiple indicators. In this model we assume that the entities of theoretical importance are the latent factors and it is these that interact (i.e., no direct interactions among indicators is specified). We also assume that we have appropriate indicators for each latent variable and that the indicators possess the properties of validity and reliability. Chapter 4 provides an extended discussion of the properties of latent variables. Additional references giving more detail on this subject include Bollen (1984) and Bollen and Ting (2000).

Some possible applications

It would seem certain subject areas, such as population biology, might be fertile ground for latent variables. Individual organisms, be they whales, mites, or macroalgae, have correlated sets of attributes that are presumably reflective of underlying traits we cannot measure directly. Perhaps the model in Figure A.7 might apply to a case where ξ_1 is body size, η_1 is a male bird's territory range, and η_2 is that bird's reproductive success. The indicators in such a case would be those that we believe adequately reflect the latent factors of interest. In truth, any situation where we believe (1) that unmeasured variables lie at the heart of the interactions of interest, and (2) we have various ways of approximating the properties of those unmeasured variables, will potentially be suitable for the use of multi-indicator latent variable models.

Table A.7. *Correlations among indicators associated with latent variable example. s.d. refers to standard deviations.* $N = 100$

	x_1	x_2	x_3	y_1	y_2	y_3	y_4	y_5	y_6
x_1	1.0								
x_2	−0.86	1.0							
x_3	−0.64	0.70	1.0						
y_1	−0.23	0.25	0.24	1.0					
y_2	−0.19	0.20	0.19	0.64	1.0				
y_3	−0.22	0.24	0.23	0.77	0.62	1.0			
y_4	−0.19	0.20	0.20	0.38	0.31	0.71	1.0		
y_5	−0.16	0.18	0.17	0.33	0.27	0.62	0.72	1.0	
y_6	−0.17	0.19	0.18	0.35	0.28	0.66	0.76	0.66	1.0
s.d.	2.9	1.1	0.06	0.9	1.0	2.3	1.6	0.8	1.9

Data

I begin by throwing another curve at the reader. One that represents an easy programming mistake to make which has fatal consequences. We will then correct the data and proceed through the model analyses.

Results – initial analyses of data in Table A.7

It is convention that the analysis of hybrid models begins with a test of the measurement model. This is accomplished by allowing the latent variables to intercorrelate freely, thereby saturating the structural model (i.e., specifying all possible paths among latents). When we do this with the data in Table A.7, we obtain the following:

NO CONVERGENCE. NUMBER OF ITERATIONS EXCEEDED.

We can get some idea why our model failed by examining the initial estimates, which tell us about the direction the iterations were heading when the program gave up. One part of the printout looks immediately suspicious. The notation here refers to the measurement of the latent variable XI-1 by the indicators X1, X2, and X3.

MODEL RESULTS

```
                Estimates
XI1    BY
   X1         1.000
   X2         ********
   X3         8697.837
```

These results describe the initial estimates of the loadings for the three indicators on the latent variable ξ_1 ("XI-one"). The loading for x_1 is set at 1.0 automatically by the program in order to set the scale for the latent variable (the scale for latent variables must always be specified in some fashion). The results presented indicate that the program was unable to estimate a loading for the path from ξ_1 to x_2, and that the loading for x_3 was very unrealistic. To see what a more normal pattern would look like, here we see the interim results for η_1.

```
ETA1    BY
  Y1    1.000
  Y2    0.894
  Y3    2.474
```

There are a number of things we might try at this point to get started. Since SEM programs use iterative algorithms, we might specify starting values. We can also increase the number of iterations attempted. None of these changes will help in this case, however. Another approach is to set the scale for the latent variable using a different indicator. When we do this, we achieve the following:

THE MODEL ESTIMATION TERMINATED NORMALLY

If we now examine the estimates for loadings for ξ_1, we find

```
XI1     BY
  X1   −2.418
  X2    1.000
  X3    0.041
```

So, we obtained seemingly reasonable estimates. However, we see that one has a negative loading (X1) and the others are positive. Programs vary in how well they are able to handle this situation where indicators are not coded to correlate positively. In general, this is to be avoided. So, to eliminate this as a potential source of problems, we recode our original data in Table A.7 so that the indicators X2, X2, and X3 are positively correlated. Our new matrix of correlations is given in Table A.8.

This may be a good time to comment on another problem that frequently arises in analyses of latent variable models, the so-called Heywood case. A Heywood case refers to a solution that is inadmissible, in that some parameter estimates have illogical values. The most common such situation is when one obtains negative error variance estimates. Sometimes this can be solved by recoding the data or by changing the indicator used to fix the scale of the latent variable. Another approach is to constrain the estimate to be greater than or equal to zero (using programming constraints). However, in recalcitrant situations where this results in unacceptable solutions, one further alternative is to specify a small, nonzero, positive value for the error variance that keeps coming up with a negative estimate. This approach invalidates our estimates of loadings and residual variances for the indicators on that latent variable. However, it at least allows us to have an admissible solution with which to proceed. It is hoped that the researcher will eventually identify the true source of the problem and resolve it through a reformulation of the model.

New data

Further results and discussion – evaluation of the measurement model

As stated above, our evaluation of a hybrid model is usually performed as a two-stage process, with the first stage being a test of the measurement model. As stated above, this is accomplished by modifying the model in Figure A.7 so that the latent variables intercorrelate freely, thus allowing us to focus on the adequacy of our measurement model in a separate analysis. When we run such a model using the data in Table A.8, we get the following message:

Table A.8. *Data were recoded from Table A.7 so that indicators for all latent variables are positively correlated. N = 100*

	x_1	x_2	x_3	y_1	y_2	y_3	y_4	y_5	y_6
x_1	1.0								
x_2	0.86	1.0							
x_3	0.64	0.70	1.0						
y_1	0.23	0.25	0.24	1.0					
y_2	0.19	0.20	0.19	0.64	1.0				
y_3	0.22	0.24	0.23	0.77	0.62	1.0			
y_4	0.19	0.20	0.20	0.38	0.31	0.71	1.0		
y_5	0.16	0.18	0.17	0.33	0.27	0.62	0.72	1.0	
y_6	0.17	0.19	0.18	0.35	0.28	0.66	0.76	0.66	1.0
s.d.	2.9	1.1	0.06	0.9	1.0	2.3	1.6	0.8	1.9

THE MODEL ESTIMATION TERMINATED NORMALLY WARNING:
THE RESIDUAL COVARIANCE MATRIX (THETA) IS NOT POSITIVE DEFINITE.
PROBLEM INVOLVING VARIABLE Y3

A nonpositive definite matrix means that something does not add up; in this case, it relates specifically to the theta matrix, which contains information about the residual covariances among indicators. This is a serious problem that means our results cannot be trusted. We can obtain more information from the printout to help us spot the source of the problem. If we examine the residuals for the indicator y_3, we find the highest values for its covariances with y_4 and y_6. In and of themselves, these do not provide us with enough of a clue as to the possible misspecification we are dealing with. It is important at this point to consider some of the reasons we might have a problem in a measurement model. Some of the possibilities might include (1) inadequacies in the data, (2) unmeasured influences affecting indicators, and (3) incorrect causal specification. We will ignore the first of these here. Our data have been selected to represent an underlying structure and we accept for the moment their adequacy.

The second of the above possibilities (unmeasured influences) would suggest a correlated error that represents the effects of some unmeasured factor on two or more of our indicators. In this case, the residuals represent linkages between indicators loading on different latent variables. It is certainly possible that some unmeasured factor is causing us to have correlations among the indicators of different latent variables. We can look further for clues to see if such error correlations could cause our lack of fit. If we request modification indices, they suggest the following as ways of improving model fit.

MODEL MODIFICATION INDICES

BY	Statements	M.I.
ETA2	BY Y1	8.887
ETA2	BY Y3	23.864

WITH	Statements	M.I.
Y2	WITH Y1	21.814
Y3	WITH Y2	8.153

Note that the lingo in which these results are expressed is such that "BY" is shorthand for "measured by" and "WITH" is shorthand for "correlated with". The modification indices suggest that if we allow the errors of Y2 and Y1 to correlate (which is indistinguishable from allowing an additional correlation between Y2 and Y1), we would reduce our chi-square by 21.814. This is an interesting possibility to consider. We see elevated residuals between Y3 and Y4 and between Y3 and Y6, which does not fit logically with the suggestion of allowing Y1 and Y2 to correlate. Furthermore, if we examine the correlations between Y1, Y2, and Y3 in Table A.8, we do not see anything imbalanced in the triad of correlations. We might still be tempted to see if we can solve our estimation problem by including a correlated error between Y1 and Y2. Our evidence does not indicate that Y1 and Y2 are unusually correlated, however, suggesting that we should look elsewhere for our clues about the problem. If, despite the warning signs, one includes a correlation between the error of Y1 and Y2, just to see if this would indeed fix our estimation problem, the answer is "no". We still have a nonpositive definite matrix indicative of unresolved relationships involving Y3.

Returning to our modification indices, these statements indicate that the largest reduction in model chi-square could be obtained by allowing Y3 to load on ETA2. We might be sufficiently frustrated at this point to simply make that change. That could be a fatal error unless theory suggests that as a reasonable way to reformulate our model. So, instead, we ask ourselves, does it make substantive sense that Y3 could be an indicator for both ETA1 and ETA2? Typically, the answer to this question will be "no". Crossloading indicators can sometimes make sense, but in a model such as this one where the indicators have been selected for the purpose of representing our separate constructs, we would hope we had a sufficiently clear rationale that we could obtain good indicators in the first place. For example, if Y3 was an indicator of territory size, like singing frequency and ETA2 is reproductive success, it would not make sense to equate singing frequency with indicators of reproductive success, such as number of eggs produced by the bird's mate.

Now, I have made this example tricky for a reason, we need to take to heart the message at the end of Chapter 4 that the causal logic in the standard hybrid model (as shown in Figure A.7) does not necessarily represent the true situation. In Figures 4.18 and 4.19 I describe some other possible types of misspecification that involve direct causal effects by individual indicators. This represents our third category of possibilities. Can we find clues as to a specific effect of an indicator in the output? Since the modification indices suggest a linkage between ETA2 and Y3 and the residuals suggest unspecified relationships between Y3 and Y4 and between Y3 and Y6, perhaps there is a specific effect of Y3 on ETA2. There are other possibilities, but what is being raised here is that perhaps the specific attribute associated with Y3 has, for example, a specific benefit on reproductive success. If that were the case, this influence should be included in the model. If we include this path, we now obtain a proper solution, as well as a good fit of data to model,

TESTS OF MODEL FIT

Chi-Square Test of Model Fit
  Value   23.315
  Degrees of Freedom   25
  P-Value   0.5592

Subsequent examination of parameter estimates and residuals reveal no signs of any problems. We have now obtained an adequate measurement model. While the results are not presented here, the form of this model is as shown in Figure A.8.

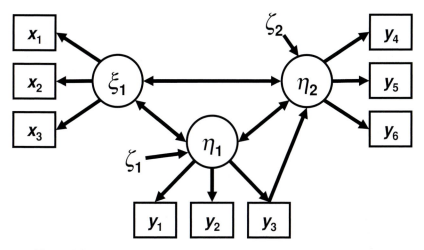

Figure A.8. Modified measurement model evaluated in stage one of the analysis. In measurement model evaluations, all latent variables are allowed to intercorrelate freely, so that the measurement relations are the focus of the analysis. The modification made was to specify an effect of y_3 on η_2.

Evaluation of the full model

We now move on to consider the full model, which includes the hypothesis of whether the data are consistent with the structural relations (directed relations among latents) specified in Figure A.7. Omitting the path from ξ_1 to η_2, we obtain a model chi-square of 3.517 with 24 degrees of freedom, which is a nearly perfect fit. We can be pretty confident now that our data fit our model. The results are shown in Figure A.9.

We will not take the time to interpret the results obtained. Hopefully the reader has sufficient grasp of the issues to realize both the subtleties involved in interpreting SEM results and the role of theory in guiding interpretations, which will depend on the particular system under study.

Example 5: models including composite variables

The situation

Chapter 6 goes into great detail discussing the considerations involved in deciding when to use composite variables. My purpose here is simply to walk through the stages of an analysis so the reader can see the mechanics of the operation. As the reader may be aware from Chapter 6, there are problems in solving models containing composites, because the composites introduce new parameters to be estimated. We generally set the error variances for composites to zero and also set the scale for the composites by fixing a path from one of the component causes. While these specifications allow the model to be solved, there is a loss of information associated with fixing the path from one of the component causes to the composite. Basically, the problem is that because the path is specified at a fixed value by the investigator, it cannot be tested. The resolution of this is

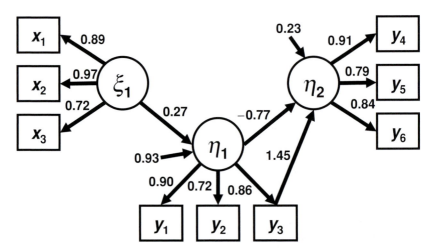

Figure A.9. Results obtained for modified latent variable model. Errors for indicators are omitted to simplify presentation. Coefficients shown are standardized values.

to use a two-stage analysis with the composite omitted from the model in the first stage. This process will be illustrated below.

Some possible applications

I find that there are a great variety of situations when I might wish to incorporate a composite variable, usually so as to achieve a more general perspective on findings. For example, in the immediately preceding illustration (Figure A.9), we find two influences of ξ_1 on η_1, one general and one specific. The path coefficients from ξ_1 to η_1 and from y_3 to η_1 are challenging to interpret because ξ_1 and y_3 are highly intercorrelated ($\lambda = 0.86$). We might wish to know the combined effects of ξ_1 and y_3 on η_1. This could be accomplished using a composite variable representing their combined influences. In an alternative situation, we might have a whole suite of specific effects that we wish to compare to some other set of effects, for example the combined influences of soil factors compared to the combined influences of disturbance factors on plant growth. Composites could be used here as well. Finally, I typically find it necessary to use composites when modeling nonlinear relationships. The individual path coefficients for first and second order terms in a polynomial regression are rather uninterpretable. How are we to examine the sensitivity of y to variations in x when holding x^2 constant? Since x^2 is a direct function of x, it is not possible to hold it constant while varying x, except in a very abstract sense. What we wish to know is the combined influences of x and x^2 on y. A composite can allow us to estimate such an effect. Here I present a simple example involving a set of exogenous predictors and a single response variable (Figure A.10) to illustrate the two-stage nature of the modeling process.

Table A.9. *Correlations among variables in composite model. N = 100*

	x_1	x_2	x_3	x_4	y_1
x_1	1.0				
x_2	0.25	1.0			
x_3	0.02	0.26	1.0		
x_4	0.12	0.31	0.25	1.0	
y_1	0.55	0.47	0.42	0.41	1.0
Std. dev.	1.23	0.66	2.30	1.56	2.09

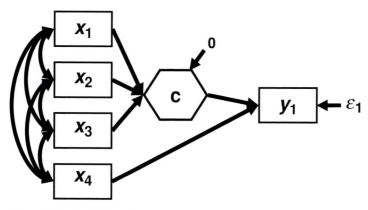

Figure A.10. Model in which a composite variable is used to represent the collective effects of x_1–x_3 on y_1.

Data

Results and discussion of first stage of analysis of composite model

As stated above, the first stage in the analysis is to omit the composite from the model and evaluate the component processes whose effects will be composited. In this particular case, we simply have a saturated model equivalent to a multiple regression (Figure A.11). Since the model is saturated, the fit is perfect, thus, our evaluation is quantitative – determining the magnitudes of the path coefficients, their significance, and the variance explained by the model.

Results and discussion from second stage of analysis

The second stage of the analysis includes a so-called "sheaf" coefficient (Heise 1972) from the composite to y_1 representing the collective effect of x_1–x_3. It is most common that we present standardized coefficients in models involving composites because of the difficulties associated with interpreting unstandardized parameters for composites (Figure A.12). We omit the coefficients from the components to the composite in this

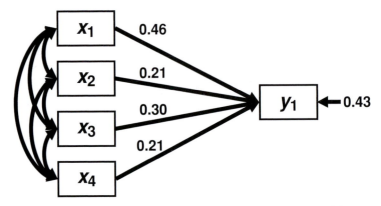

Figure A.11. Results from first stage of analysis of composite model.

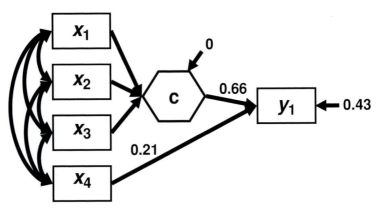

Figure A.12. Results from second stage of analysis of composite model. Coefficients shown are standardized values.

presentation because we wish to focus on the net effect. One can see that aside from compositing the effects of x_1–x_3, the other results are the same as those from stage 1 of the analysis. Now we can consider the collective effect of x_1–x_3, giving us flexibility to provide results that match with our constructs of theoretical interest.

Conclusions

A facile use of SEM comes from a reliance on fundamental statistical and scientific principles, not from blindly following conventions. One way (actually the best way) to develop confidence in one's analysis is to generate simulated data where you control what relationships are built into the data. Then you can analyze those data in various ways to see what you get out. It is extremely instructive if you use conventional univariate analyses in comparison with multivariate ones to gain a respect for how far off the mark univariate results can be. You will also find out that ignoring certain features of the situation in multivariate models (e.g., data clustering) can have either subtle or not so subtle effects. Several of the SEM programs have the capability to generate simulated data. It is also possible to simulate data sets using any number of other means. You will gain both an appreciation for the assumptions that lie behind the analyses and an appreciation for SEM. Try it, you will be glad you did.

References

Aarssen, L. W. & Schamp, B. S. (2002). Predicting distributions of species richness and species size in regional floras: Applying the species pool hypothesis to the habitat templet model. *Perspectives in Plant Ecology, Evolution and Systematics*, **5**, 3–12.

Abelson, R. P. (1995). *Statistics as Principled Argument*. Hillsdale, NJ: Lawrence Erlbaum Publishers.

Abrams, P. A. (1995). Monotonic or unimodal diversity – productivity gradients: what does competition theory predict? *Ecology*, **76**, 2019–2027.

Agrawal, R., Imielienski, T., & Swami, A. (1993). In: Mining association rules between sets of items in large databases. *Proceedings of Conference on Management of Data*. New York: ACM Press.

Akaike, H. (1974). A new look at the statistical model identification. *IEEE Transactions on Automatic Control AC*, **19**, 716–723.

Al-Mufti, M. M., Sydes, C. L., Furness, S. B., Grime, J. P., & Band, S. R. (1977). A quantitative analysis of shoot phenology and dominance in herbaceous vegetation. *Journal of Ecology*, **65**, 759–791.

Andersen, J. A. (1995). *An Introduction to Neural Networks*. Cambridge, MA: MIT Press.

Anderson, D. R., Burnham, K. P., & Thompson, W. L. (2000). Null hypothesis testing: problems, prevalence, and an alternative. *Journal of Wildlife Management*, **64**, 912–923.

Bacon, F. (1620). *Novum Organum*. London: Bonham Norton and John Bill.

Baldwin, H. Q. (2005). Effects of fire on home range size, site fidelity, and habitat associations of grassland birds overwintering in southeast Texas. M.S. thesis, Louisiana State University, Baton Rouge.

Bayes, T. (1763). An essay towards solving a problem in the doctrine of chances. *Philosophical Transactions of the Royal Society of London*, **53**, 370–418.

Bezdek, J. C. & Pal, N. (1992). *Fuzzy Models for Pattern Recognition*. New York: IEEE Press.

Blalock, H. M. (1964). *Causal Inferences in Nonexperimental Research*. Chapel Hill, NC: University of North Carolina Press.

Bollen, K. A. (1984). Multiple indicators: internal consistency or no necessary relationship. *Quality and Quantity*, **18**, 377–385.

Bollen, K. A. (1989). *Structural Equations with Latent Variables*. New York: John Wiley & Sons.

Bollen, K. A. (1996). An alternative 2SLS estimator for latent variable models. *Psychometrika*, **61**, 109–121.

Bollen, K. A. (1998). Path analysis. pp. 3280–3284. In: *Encyclopedia of Biostatistics*. P. Armitage and T. Colton (eds.). New York: John Wiley & Sons.

Bollen, K. A. (2002). Latent variables in psychology and the social sciences. *Annual Review of Psychology*, **53**, 605–634.

Bollen, K. A. & Lennox, R. (1991). Conventional wisdom on measurement: a structural equation perspective. *Psychological Bulletin*, **110**, 305–314.

Bollen, K. A. & Long, J. S. (eds.) (1993). *Testing Structural Equation Models*. Newbury Park, CA: Sage Publications.

Bollen, K. A. & Stine, R. (1992). Bootstrapping goodness of fit measures in structural equation models. *Sociological Methods and Research*, **21**, 205–229.

Bollen, K. A. & Ting, K. (2000). A tetrad test for causal indicators. *Psychological Methods*, **5**, 3–22.

Borgelt, C. & Kruse, R. (2002). *Graphical Models*. New York: John Wiley & Sons.

Bozdogan, H. (1987). Model selection and Akaike's Information Criterion (AIC). *Psychometrika*, **52**, 345–370.

Brewer, J. S. & Grace, J. B. (1990). Vegetation structure of an oligohaline tidal marsh. *Vegetatio*, **90**, 93–107.

Browne, M. W. & Cudeck, R. (1989). Single sample cross-validation indices for covariance structures. *Multivariate Behavioral Research*, **24**, 445–455.

Burnham, K. P. & Anderson, D. R. (2002). *Model Selection and Multimodel Inference*. Second Edition. New York: Springer Verlag.

Byrne, B. M. (1994). *Structural Equation Modeling EQS and EQS/Windows*. Thousand Oaks, CA: Sage Publications.

Byrne, B. M. (1998). *Structural Equation Modeling with LISREL, PRELIS, and SIMPLIS*. Mahway, NJ: Lawrence Erlbaum Associates.

Byrne, B. M. (2001). *Structural Equation Modeling with AMOS*. Mahway, NJ: Lawrence Erlbaum Associates.

Campbell, D. R., Waser, N. M., Price, M. V., Lynch, E. A., & Mitchell, R. J. (1991). A mechanistic analysis of phenotypic selection: pollen export and corolla width in *Ipomopsis aggregata*. *Evolution*, **43**, 1444–1455.

Casella, B. (1992). Explaining the Gibbs sampler. *The American Statistician*, **46**, 167–174.

Congdon, P. (2001). *Bayesian Statistical Modeling*. Chichester: Wiley Publishers.

Congdon, P. (2003). *Applied Bayesian Modeling*. Chichester: Wiley Publishers.

Cottingham, K. L., Lennon, J. T., & Brown, B. L. (2005). Knowing when to draw the line: designing more informative ecological experiments. *Frontiers in Ecology*, **3**, 145–152.

Cudeck, R., Du Toit, S. H. C., & Sörbom, D. (eds.) (2001). *Structural Equation Modeling: Present and Future*. Lincolnwood, IL: SSI Scientific Software International.

Dasarathy, B. V. (1990). *Nearest Neighbor (NN) Norms: NN Pattern Classification Techniques*. Los Alamitos, CA: IEEE Computer Science Press.

Diamantopoulous, A. & Winklhofer, H. M. (2001). Index construction with formative indicators: an alternative to scale development. *Journal of Marketing Research*, **38**, 269–277.

Duncan, T. E., Duncan, S. C., Strycker, L. A., Li, F., & Alpert, A. (1999). *An Introduction to Latent Variable Growth Curve Modeling: Concepts, Issues, and Applications*. Mahwah, NJ: Lawrence Erlbaum Associates.

Edwards, J. R. (2001). Multidimensional constructs in organizational behavior research: an integrative analytical framework. *Organizational Research Methods*, **4**, 144–192.

Fan, X., Thompson, B., & Wang, L. (1999). Effects of sample size, estimation methods and model specification on structural equation modeling fit indexes. *Structural Equation Modeling*, **6**, 56–83.

Fisher, R. A. (1956). *Statistical Methods and Scientific Inference*. Edinburgh, UK: Oliver and Boyd.

Fornell, C., ed. (1982). *A Second Generation of Multivariate Analyses: Volumes 1 and II*. New York: Praeger Publishers.

Gadgil, M. & Solbrig, O. T. (1972). The concept of r- and K-selection: evidence from wild flowers and some theoretical considerations. *American Naturalist*, **106**, 14–31.

Gelman, A., Carlin, J. B., Stern, H. S., & Rubin, D. B. (2004). *Bayesian Data Analysis*. Boca Raton: Chapman & Hall.

Glymour, B., Scheines, R., Spirtes, R., & Kelly, K. (1987). *Discovering Causal Structure: Artificial Intelligence, Philosophy of Science, and Statistical Modeling*. Orlando, FL: Academic Press.

Goldberger, A. S. & Duncan, O. D. (1973). *Structural Equation Models in the Social Sciences*. New York: Seminar Press.

Good, I. J. (1983). *Good Thinking*. Minneapolis: University of Minnesota Press.

Gough, L. & Grace, J. B. (1999). Predicting effects of environmental change on plant species density: experimental evaluations in a coastal wetland. *Ecology*, **80**, 882–890.

Gough, L., Grace, J. B., & Taylor, K. L. (1994). The relationship between species richness and community biomass: the importance of environmental variables. *Oikos*, **70**, 271–279.

Grace, J. B. (1991). A clarification of the debate between Grime and Tilman. *Functional Ecology*, **5**, 503–507.

Grace, J. B. (1999). The factors controlling species density in herbaceous plant communities: an assessment. *Perspectives in Plant Ecology, Evolution and Systematics*, **2**, 1–28.

Grace, J. B. (2001). The roles of community biomass and species pools in the regulation of plant diversity. *Oikos*, **92**, 191–207.

Grace, J. B. (2003a). Comparing groups using structural equations. chapter 11, pp. 281–296. In: B. H. Pugesek, A. Tomer, & A. von Eye (eds.). *Structural Equation Modeling*. Cambridge: Cambridge University Press.

Grace, J. B. (2003b). Examining the relationship between environmental variables and ordination axes using latent variables and structural equation modeling. chapter 7, pp. 171–193. In: B. H. Pugesek, A. Tomer, & A. von Eye (eds.). *Structural Equation Modeling*. Cambridge: Cambridge University Press.

Grace, J. B. & Bollen, K. A. (2005). Interpreting the results from multiple regression and structural equation models. *Bulletin of the Ecological Society of America*, **86**, 283–295.

Grace, J. B. & Guntenspergen, G. R. (1999). The effects of landscape position on plant species density: evidence of past environmental effects in a coastal wetland. *Ecoscience*, **6**, 381–391.

Grace, J. B. & Jutila, H. (1999). The relationship between species density and community biomass in grazed and ungrazed coastal meadows. *Oikos*, **85**, 398–408.

Grace, J. B. & Keeley, J. E. (2006). A structural equation model analysis of post-fire plant diversity in California shrublands. *Ecological Applications*, **16**, 503–514.

Grace, J. B. & Pugesek, B. (1997). A structural equation model of plant species richness and its application to a coastal wetland. *American Naturalist*, **149**, 436–460.

Grace, J. B. & Pugesek, B. H. (1998). On the use of path analysis and related procedures for the investigation of ecological problems. *American Naturalist* **152**, 151–159.

Grace, J. B., Allain, L., & Allen, C. (2000). Factors associated with plant species richness in a coastal tall-grass prairie. *Journal of Vegetation Science*, **11**, 443–452.

Grime, J. P. (1973). Competitive exclusion in herbaceous vegetation. *Nature*, **242**, 344–347.

Grime, J. P. (1977). Evidence for the existence of three primary strategies in plants and its relevance to ecological and evolutionary theory. *American Naturalist*, **111**, 1169–1194.

Grime, J. P. (1979). *Plant Strategies and Vegetation Processes*. London: John Wiley & Sons.

Grime, J. P. (2001). *Plant Strategies, Vegetation Processes, and Ecosystem Properties*. London: John Wiley & Sons.

Grime, J. P. (2002). Declining plant diversity: empty niches or functional shifts? *Journal of Vegetation Science*, **13**, 457–460.

Grimm, V. (1994). Mathematical models and understanding in ecology. *Ecological Modelling*, **74**, 641–651.

Gross, K. L., Willig, M. R., & Gough, L. (2000). Patterns of species density and productivity at different spatial scales in herbaceous plant communities. *Oikos*, **89**, 417–427.

Grubb, P. J. (1998). A reassessment of the strategies of plants which cope with shortages of resources. *Perspectives in Plant Ecology, Evolution and Systematics*, **1**, 3–31.

Hägglund, G. (2001). Milestones in the history of factor analysis. pp. 11–38. In: R. Cudeck, S. H. C. Du Toit, & D. Sörbom (eds.). *Structural Equation Modeling: Present and Future*. Lincolnwood, IL: SSI Scientific Software International.

Hair, J. F., Jr., Anderson, R. E., Tatham, R. L., & Black, W. C. (1995). *Multivariate Data Analysis*. Fourth Edition. Englewood Cliffs, NJ: Prentice Hall.

Hannon, B. & Ruth, M. (1997). *Modeling Dynamic Biological Systems*. New York: Springer.

Hargens, L. L. (1976). A note on standardized coefficients as structural parameters. *Sociological Methods & Research*, **5**, 247–256.

Harrison, S., Safford, H. D., Grace, J. B., Viers, J. H., & Davies, K. F. (2006). Regional and local species richness in an insular environment: serpentine plants in California. *Ecological Monographs*, **76**, 41–56.

Hastings, W. (1970). Monte Carlo sampling methods using Markov chains and their applications. *Biometrika*, **57**, 97–106.

Hayduk, L. A. (1987). *Structural Equation Modeling with LISREL*. Baltimore, MD: Johns Hopkins University Press.

Hayduk, L. A. (1996). *LISREL Issues, Debates, and Strategies*. Baltimore, MD: Johns Hopkins University Press.

Heise, D. R. (1972). Employing nominal variables, induced variables, and block variables in path analyses. *Sociological Methods & Research*, **1**, 147–173.

Hodson, J. G., Thompson, K., Wilson, P. J., & Bogaard, A. (1998). Does biodiversity determine ecosystem function? The ecotron experiment reconsidered. *Functional Ecology*, **12**, 843–848.

Hox, J. (2002). *Multilevel Analysis*. Mahway, NJ: Lawrence Erlbaum Associates.

Hoyle, R. H. (ed.) (1999). *Statistical Strategies for Small Sample Research*. Thousand Oaks, CA: Sage Publications.

Huston, M. A. (1979). A general hypothesis of species diversity. *American Naturalist*, **113**, 81–101.

Huston, M. A. (1980). Soil nutrients and tree species richness in Costa Rican forests. *Journal of Biogeography*, **7**, 147–157.

Huston, M. A. (1994). *Biological Diversity*. Cambridge: Cambridge University Press.

Huston, M. A. (1997). Hidden treatments in ecological experiments: Re-evaluating the ecosystem function of biodiversity. *Oecologia*, **110**, 449–460.

Huston, M. A. (1999). Local processes and regional patterns: appropriate scales for understanding variation in the diversity of plants and animals. *Oikos*, **86**, 393–401.

Jarvis, C. B., MacKenzie, S. B., & Podsakoff, P. M. (2003). A critical review of construct indicators and measurement model misspecification in marketing and consumer research. *Journal of Consumer Research*, **30**, 199–218.

Jedidi, K. & Ansari, A. (2001). Bayesian structural equation models for multilevel data. pp. 129–158. In: Marcoulides, B. A. & Schumacker, R. E. (eds.), *New Developments and Techniques in Structural Equation Modeling*. Mahway, NJ: Lawrence Erlbaum Associates.

Jensen, F. V. (2001). *Bayesian Networks and Decision Graphs*. New York: Springer Verlag.

Johnson, M. L., Huggins, D. G., & deNoyelles, F., Jr. (1991). Ecosystem modeling with LISREL: a new approach for measuring direct and indirect effects. *Ecological Applications*, **1**, 383–398.

Johnson, J. B. (2002). Divergent life histories among populations of the fish *Brachyrhaphis rhabdophora*: detecting putative agents of selection by candidate model analysis. *Oikos*, **96**, 82–91.

Jöreskog, K. G. (1973). A general method for estimating a linear structural equation system. pp. 85–112. In: A. S. Goldberger & O. D. Duncan (eds.). *Structural Equation Models in the Social Sciences*. New York: Seminar Press.

Jöreskog, K. G. & Sörbom, D. (1996). *LISREL 8: User's Reference Guide*. Chicago: Scientific Software International.

Jutila, H. & Grace, J. B. (2002). Effects of disturbance and competitive release on germination and seedling establishment in a coastal prairie grassland. *Journal of Ecology*, **90**, 291–302.

Kaplan, D. (2000). *Structural Equation Modeling: Foundations and Extensions*. Thousand Oaks, CA: Sage Publishers.

Kaplan, D., Harik, P., & Hotchkiss, L. (2001). Cross-sectional estimation of dynamic structural equation models in disequilibrium. pp. 315–339. In: R. Cudeck, S. H. C. Du Toit, & D. Sörbom (eds.). *Structural Equation Modeling: Present and Future*. Lincolnwood, IL: SSI Scientific Software International.

Keddy, P. A. (1990). Competitive hierarchies and centrifugal organization in plant communities. pp. 265–289. In: J. B. Grace & D. Tilman (eds.). *Perspectives on Plant Competition*, New York: Academic Press.

Keesling, J. W. (1972). *Maximum Likelihood Approaches to Causal Flow Analysis*. Ph.D. Dissertation, Department of Education, University of Chicago.

Kelloway, E. K. (1998). *Using LISREL for Structural Equation Modeling*. Thousand Oaks, CA: Sage Publications.

Kline, R. B. (2005). *Principles and Practice of Structural Equation Modeling*. 2nd Edition. New York: The Guilford Press.

Langley, P., Iba, W., & Thompson, K. (1992). An analysis of Bayesian classifiers. In: *Proceedings of the 10th National Conference on Artificial Intelligence*. pp. 223–228. Cambridge, MA: MIT Press.

Laplace, P. S. (1774). Mémoire sur la probabilité des causes par les événements. *Mémoires de l'Academie de Science de Paris*, **6**, 621–656.

Larson, D. L. & Grace J. B. (2004). Temporal dynamics of leafy spurge (*Euphorbia esula*) and two species of flea beetles (*Aphthona* spp.) used as biological control agents. *Biological Control*, **29**, 207–214.

Lawton, J. H., Naeem, S., Thompson, L. J., Hector, A., & Crawley, J. J. (1998). Biodiversity and ecosystem function: getting the ecotron experiment in its correct context. *Functional Ecology*, **12**, 848–852.

Lee, S. Y., & Bentler, P. M. (1980). Some asymptotic properties of constrained generalized least squares estimation in covariance structure models. *South African Statistical Journal*, **14**, 121–136.

Legendre, P. (1993). Spatial autocorrelation: Trouble or a new paradigm. *Ecology*, **74**, 659–673.

Levins, R. (1968). *Evolution in Changing Environments*. Princeton, NJ: Princeton University Press.

Li, C. C. (1975). *Path Analysis – A primer*. Pacific Grove, CA: Boxwood Press.

Little, T. D., Schnabel, K. U., & Baumert, J. (eds.) (2000). *Modeling Longitudinal and Multilevel Data*. Mahway, NJ: Lawrence Erlbaum Associates.

Loehle, C. (1987). Hypothesis testing in ecology: psychological aspects and the importance of theory maturation. *The Quarterly Review of Biology*, **62**, 397–409.

Loehle, C. (1988). Problems with the triangular model for representing plant strategies. *Ecology*, **69**, 284–286.

Loehlin, J. C. (1998). *Latent Variable Models*. Third Edition. Mahway, NJ: Lawrence Erlbaum Associates.

Loreau, M., Naeem, S., & Inchausti, P. (2002). *Biodiversity and Ecosystem Functioning*. Oxford: Oxford University Press.

MacArthur, R. H. & Wilson, E. O. (1967). *The Theory of Island Biogeography*. Princeton, NJ: Princeton University Press.

MacCallum, R. C. & Browne, M. W. (1993). The use of causal indicators in covariance structure models: some practical issues. *Psychological Bulletin*, **114**, 533–541.

Mancera, J. E., Meche, G. C., Cardona-Olarte, P. P. *et al.* (2005). Fine-scale environmental control of spatial variation in species richness in a wetland community. *Plant Ecology*, **178**, 39–50.

Marcoulides, G. A. & Schumacker, R. E. (eds.) (1996). *Advanced Structural Equation Modeling: Issues and Techniques*. Mahway, NJ: Lawrence Erlbaum Associates.

Marcoulides, G. A. & Schumacker, R. E. (eds.) (2001). *New Developments and Techniques in Structural Equation Modeling*. Mahway, NJ: Lawrence Erlbaum Associates.

Marrs, R., Grace, J. B., & Gough, L. (1996). On the relationship between plant species diversity and biomass: a comment on a paper by Gough, Grace, and Taylor. *Oikos*, **75**, 323–326.

Marsh, H. W., Balla, J. R., & Hau, K.-T. (1996). An evaluation of incremental fit indices: a clarification of mathematical and empirical properties. pp. 315–353. In: B. A. Marcoulides & R. E. Schumacker (eds.). *Advanced Structural Equation Modeling*. Mahway, NJ: Lawrence Erlbaum Associates.

Marsh, H. W., Hau, K. T., & Wen, Z. (2004). In search of golden rules: comment on hypothesis testing approaches to setting cutoff values for fit indexes and dangers in overgeneralizing Hu and Bentler's findings. *Structural Equation Modeling*, **11**, 320–341.

Maruyama, G. M. (1998). *Basics of Structural Equation Modeling*. Thousand Oaks, CA: Sage Publications.

McCune, B. & Grace, J. B. (2002). *Analysis of Ecological Communities*. Gleneden Beach, Oregon: MJM.

Meziane, D. & Shipley, B. (2001). Direct and indirect relationships between specific leaf area, leaf nitrogen and leaf gas exchange. Effects of irradiance and nutrient supply. *Annals of Botany*, **88**, 915–927.

Mikola, J., Salonen, V., & Setälä, H (2002). Studying the effects of plant species richness on ecosystem functioning: does the choice of experimental design matter? *Oecologia*, **133**, 594–598.

Mitchell, R. J. (1992). Testing evolutionary and ecological hypotheses using path analysis and structural equation modelling. *Functional Ecology*, **6**, 123–129.

Mitchell, R. J. (1994). Effects of floral traits, pollinator visitation, and plant size on *Ipomopsis aggregata* fruit production. *The American Naturalist*, **143**, 870–889.

Mittelbach, G. G., Steiner, C. F., Scheiner, S. M. *et al.* (2001). *Ecology*, **82**, 2381–2396.

Moore, D. R. J. & Keddy, P. A. (1989). The relationship between species richness and standing crop in wetlands: the importance of scale. *Vegetatio*, **79**, 99–106.

Muggleton, S. (ed.) (1992). *Inductive Logic Programming*. San Diego, CA: Academic Press.

Muthén, B. (1984). A general structural equation model with dichotomous, ordered categorical, and continuous latent variable indicators. *Psychometrika*, **49**, 115–132.

Muthén, L. K. & Muthén, B. O. (2004). *Mplus User's Guide*. Third Edition. Los Angeles, CA: Muthén and Muthén.

Naeem, S. (2002). Ecosystem consequences of biodiversity loss: the evolution of a paradigm. *Ecology*, **83**, 1537–1552.

Neapolitan, R. E. (2004). *Learning Bayesian Networks*. Upper Saddle River, NJ: Prentice Hall Publishers.

Oakes, M. (1990). *Statistical Inference*. Chestnut Hill, MA: Epidemiology Resources Inc.

Palmer, M. W. (1994). Variation in species richness: towards a unification of hypotheses. *Folia Geobot. Phytotax. Praha*, **29**, 511–530.

Pankratz, A. (1991). *Forecasting with Dynamic Regression Models*. New York: John Wiley & Sons.

Pearl, J. (1992). *Probabilistic Reasoning in Intelligent Systems: Networks of Plausible Inference*. San Mateo, CA: Morgan Kaufmann.

Pearl, J. (2000). *Causality*. Cambridge: Cambridge University Press.

Pedhazur, E. J. (1997). *Multiple Regression in Behavioral Research*, 3rd edition. Toronto: Wadsworth Press.

Peters, R. H. (1991). *A Critique for Ecology*. Cambridge: Cambridge University Press.

Pianka, E. R. (1970). On r- and K-selection. *American Naturalist*, **104**, 592–597.

Popper, K. R. (1959). *The Logic of Scientific Discovery*. London: Hutchinson.

Pugesek, B. H. (2003). Modeling means in latent variable models of natural selection. pp. 297–311. In: B. H. Pugesek, A. Tomer, & A. von Eye (eds.). *Structural Equation Modeling*. Cambridge: Cambridge University Press.

Pugesek, B. H. & Tomer, A. (1996). The Bumpus house sparrow data: a reanalysis using structural equation models. *Evolutionary Ecology*, **10**, 387–404.

Pugesek, B. H., Tomer, A., & von Eye, A. (2003). *Structural Equation Modeling*. Cambridge: Cambridge University Press.

Raftery, A. E. (1993). Bayesian model selection in structural equation models. pp. 163–180. In: K. A. Bollen & J. S. Long (eds.). *Testing Structural Equation Models*. Newbury Park, CA: Sage Publishers.

Raykov, T. & Marcoulides, G. A. (2000). *A First Course in Structural Equation Modeling*. Mahway, NJ: Lawrence Erlbaum Associates.

Raykov, T. & Penev, S. (1999). On structural equation model equivalence. *Multivariate Behavioral Research*, **34**, 199–244.

Reich, P. B., Ellsworth, D. S., Walters, M. B. *et al.* (1999). Generality of leaf trait relationships: a test across six biomes. *Ecology*, **80**, 1955–1969.

Reyment, R. A. & Jöreskog, K. G. (1996). *Applied Factor Analysis in the Natural Sciences*. Cambridge: Cambridge University Press.

Rosenzweig, M. L. & Abramsky, Z. (1993). How are diversity and productivity related? pp. 52–64. In: R. E. Ricklefs & D. Schluter (eds.). *Species Diversity in Ecological Communities*. Chicago: University of Chicago Press.

Rupp, A. A., Dey, D. K., & Zumbo, B. D. (2004). To Bayes or not to Bayes, from whether to when: Applications of Bayesian methodology to modeling. *Structural Equation Modeling*, **11**, 424–451.

Salsburg, D. (2001). *The Lady Tasting Tea*. New York: Henry Holt & Company.

Satorra, A. & Bentler, P. M. (1988). Scaling corrections for chi-square statistics in covariance structure analysis. pp. 308–313. In: *Proceedings of the American Statistical Association*.

Satorra, A. & Bentler, P. M. (1994). Corrections to test statistics and standard errors in covariance structure analysis. pp. 399–419. In: A. von Eye & C. C. Clogg (eds.).

Latent Variables Analysis: Applications for Developmental Research. Thousand Oaks, CA: Sage Publishers.

Scheiner, S. M., Mitchell, R. J., & Callahan, H. S. (2000). Using path analysis to measure natural selection. *Journal of Evolutionary Biology*, **13**, 423–433.

Scheines, R., Hoijtink, R., & Boomsma, A. (1999). Bayesian estimation and testing of structural equation models. *Psychometrika*, **64**, 37–52.

Schermelleh-Engel, K., Moosbrugger, H., & Müller, H. (2003). Evaluating the fit of structural equation models: Test of significance and descriptive goodness-of-fit measures. *Methods of Psychological Research – Online*, **8**, 23–74.

Schumacker, R. E. & Lomax, R. G. (eds.) (1996). *A Beginner's Guide to Structural Equation Modeling*. Mahwah, NJ: Lawrence Erlbaum Associates.

Schumacker, R. E. & Marcoulides, G. A. (eds.) (1998). *Interaction and Nonlinear Effects in Structural Equation Modeling*. Mahway, NJ: Lawrence Erlbaum Associates.

Shipley, B. (2000). *Cause and Correlation in Biology*. Cambridge: Cambridge University Press.

Shipley, B. & Lechowicz, M. J. (2000). The functional coordination of leaf morphology and gas exchange in 40 wetland plant species. *Ecoscience*, **7**, 183–194.

Shipley, B., Keddy, P. A., Gaudet, C., & Moore, D. R. J. (1991). A model of species density in shoreline vegetation. *Ecology*, **72**, 1658–1667.

Spirtes, P., Glymour, C., & Scheines, R. (2000). *Causation, Prediction, and Search*. Cambridge: MIT Press.

Stamp, N. (2003). Theory of plant defense level: example of process and pitfalls in development of ecological theory. *Oikos*, **102**, 672–678.

Stearns, S. C. (1977). The evolution of life history traits: a critique of the theory and a review of the data. *Annual Review of Ecology and Systematics*, **8**, 145–171.

Steiger, J. H. (1990). Structural model evaluation and modification: an interval estimation approach. *Multivariate Behavioral Research*, **25**, 173–180.

Symstad, J. J, Chapin, F. W., Wall, D. H. *et al.* (2003). Long-term and large-scale perspectives on the relationship between biodiversity and ecosystem functioning. *Bioscience*, **53**, 89–98.

Taper, M. L. & Lele, S. R. (2004). *The Nature of Scientific Evidence*. Chicago, Illinois: University of Chicago Press.

Taylor, D. R., Aarssen, L. W., & Loehle, C. (1990). On the relationship between r/K selection and environmental carry capacity: a new habitat templet for plant life history strategies. *Oikos*, **58**, 239–250.

Tilman, D. (1982). *Resource competition and community structure*. Princeton, NJ: Princeton University Press.

Tilman, D. (1986). Resources, competition and the dynamics of plant communities. pp. 51–75. In: M. J. Crawley (ed.). *Plant Ecology*. London: Blackwell Scientific Publications.

Tilman, D. (1987). On the meaning of competition and the mechanisms of competitive superiority. *Functional Ecology*, **1**, 304–315.

Tilman, D. (1988). *Plant Strategies and the Dynamics and Structure of Plant Communities*. Princeton, New Jersey: Princeton University Press.

Tilman, D. (1997). Mechanisms of plant competition. chapter 8. In: M. J. Crawley (ed.). *Plant Ecology*, 2nd edn. Malden, MA: Blackwell Scientific Publications.

Tilman, D., Wedin, D., & Knops, J. (1996). Productivity and sustainability influenced by biodiversity in grassland ecosystems. *Nature*, **379**, 718–720.

Tomer, A. (2003). A short history of structural equation models. pp. 85–124. In: B. H. Pugesek, A. Tomer, & A. von Eye (eds.). *Structural Equation Modeling.* Cambridge: Cambridge University Press.

Tukey, J. W. (1954). Causation, regression, and path analysis. pp. 35–66. In: O. Kempthorne, T. A. Bancroft, J. W. Gowen, & J. D. Lush (eds.). *Statistics and Mathematics in Biology.* Ames, IA: Iowa State College Press.

Turner, M. E. & Stevens, C. D. (1959). The regression analysis of causal paths. *Biometrics*, **15**, 236–258.

Verheyen, K., Guntenspergen, G. R., Biesbrouck, B., & Hermy, M. (2003). An integrated analysis of the effects of past land use on forest herb colonization at the landscape scale. *Journal of Ecology*, **91**, 731–742.

von Mises, R. (1919). Grundlagen der Wahrscheinlichkeitsrechnung. *Mathematische Zeitschrift*, Vol. 5. (referenced in Neapolitan (2004).)

Waide, R. B., Willig, M. R., Steiner, C. F. *et al.* (1999). The relationship between productivity and species richness. *Annual Reviews in Ecology and Systematics*, **30**, 257–300.

Wardle, D. A. (1999). Is "sampling effect" a problem for experiments investigating biodiversity–ecosystem function relationships? *Oikos*, **87**, 403–407.

Weiher, E., Forbes, S., Schauwecker, T., & Grace, J. B. (2004). Multivariate control of plant species richness in a blackland prairie. *Oikos*, **106**, 151–157.

Wheeler, B. D. & Giller, K. E. (1982). Species richness of herbaceous fen vegetation in Broadland, Norfolk in relation to the quantity of above-ground plant material. *Journal of Ecology*, **70**, 179–200.

Wheeler, B. D. & Shaw, S. C. (1991). Above-ground crop mass and species richness of the principal types of herbaceous rich-fen vegetation of lowland England and Wales. *Journal of Ecology*, **79**, 285–302.

Wiley, D. E. (1973). The identification problem for structural equation models with unmeasured variables. In: A. S. Goldberger & O. D. Duncan (eds.). *Structural Equation Models in the Social Sciences.* New York: Seminar Press A. S.

Williams, L. J., Edwards, J. R., & Vandenberg, R. J. (2003). Recent advances in causal modeling methods for organizational and management research. *Journal of Management*, **29**, 903–936.

Wilson, J. B. & Lee, W. G. (2000). C-S-R triangle theory: community-level predictions, tests, evaluation of criticisms, and relation to other theories. *Oikos*, **91**, 77–96.

Wisheu, I. C. & Keddy, P. A. (1989). Species richness-standing crop relationships along four lakeshore gradients: constraints on the general model. *Canadian Journal of Botany*, **67**, 1609–1617.

Wootton, J. T. (1994). Predicting direct and indirect effects: an integrated approach using experiments and path analysis. *Ecology*, **75**, 151–165.

Wootton, J. T. (2002). Indirect effects in complex ecosystems: recent progress and future challenges. *Journal of Sea Research*, **48**, 157–172.

Wright, S. (1918). On the nature of size factors. *Genetics*, **3**, 367–374.

Wright, S. (1920). The relative importance of heredity and environment in determining the piebald pattern of guinea pigs. *Proceedings of the National Academy of Sciences*, **6**, 320–332.

Wright, S. (1921). Correlation and causation. *Journal of Agricultural Research*, **10**, 557–585.

Wright, S. (1932). General, group, and special size factors. *Genetics*, **17**, 603–619.

Wright, S. (1934). The method of path coefficients. *Annals of Mathematical Statistics*, **5**, 161–215.

Wright, S. (1960). Path coefficients and path regressions: alternative or complementary concepts? *Biometrics*, **16**, 189–202.

Wright, S. (1968). *Evolution and the Genetics of Populations, Vol. 1: Genetic and Biometric Foundations*. Chicago: University of Chicago Press.

Wright, S. (1984). Diverse uses of path analysis. pp. 1–34. In: A. Chakravarti (ed.). *Human Population Genetics*. New York: Van Nostrand Reinhold.

Index